Unwanted Warriors

Studies in Canadian Military History
Series editor: Andrew Burtch, Canadian War Museum

The Canadian War Museum, Canada's national museum of military history, has a threefold mandate: to remember, to preserve, and to educate. Studies in Canadian Military History, published by UBC Press in association with the Museum, extends this mandate by presenting the best of contemporary scholarship to provide new insights into all aspects of Canadian military history, from earliest times to recent events. The work of a new generation of scholars is especially encouraged, and the books employ a variety of approaches – cultural, social, intellectual, economic, political, and comparative – to investigate gaps in the existing historiography. The books in the series feed immediately into future exhibitions, programs, and outreach efforts by the Canadian War Museum. A list of the titles in the series appears at the end of the book.

Unwanted Warriors
The Rejected Volunteers of the
Canadian Expeditionary Force

Nic Clarke

UBCPress · Vancouver · Toronto

© UBC Press 2015

All rights reserved. No part of this publication may be reproduced, stored in a retrieval system, or transmitted, in any form or by any means, without prior written permission of the publisher, or, in Canada, in the case of photocopying or other reprographic copying, a licence from Access Copyright, www.accesscopyright.ca.

23 22 21 20 19 18 17 16 15   5 4 3 2 1

Printed in Canada on FSC-certified ancient-forest-free paper
(100% post-consumer recycled) that is processed chlorine- and acid-free.

Library and Archives Canada Cataloguing in Publication

Clarke, Nic, author
   Unwanted warriors : the rejected volunteers of the Canadian Expeditionary Force /
Nic Clarke.

(Studies in Canadian military history)
Includes bibliographical references and index.
Issued in print and electronic formats.
ISBN 978-0-7748-2888-8 (bound). – ISBN 978-0-7748-2889-5 (pbk.). –
ISBN 978-0-7748-2890-1 (pdf). – ISBN 978-0-7748-2891-8 (epub)

   1. Canada. Canadian Army. Canadian Expeditionary Force – Recruiting, enlistment, etc. – World War, 1914–1918. 2. Canada. Canadian Army. Canadian Expeditionary Force – Recruiting, enlistment, etc. – Evaluation – History – 20th century. 3. Canada. Canadian Army. Canadian Expeditionary Force – Medical examinations – History – 20th century. 4. Canada. Canadian Army. Canadian Expeditionary Force–History–World War, 1914–1918. 5. Military service, Voluntary – Canada – History – 20th century. 6. World War, 1914–1918 – Canada. I. Title. II. Series: Studies in Canadian military history

UB325.C3C63 2015   355.2'23620971   C2015-903071-4
                                                       C2015-903072-2

Canadä

UBC Press gratefully acknowledges the financial support for our publishing program of the Government of Canada (through the Canada Book Fund), the Canada Council for the Arts, and the British Columbia Arts Council.

This book has been published with the help of a grant from the Canadian Federation for the Humanities and Social Sciences, through the Awards to Scholarly Publications Program, using funds provided by the Social Sciences and Humanities Research Council of Canada.

Publication of this book has been financially supported by the Canadian War Museum.

UBC Press
The University of British Columbia
2029 West Mall
Vancouver, BC V6T 1Z2
www.ubcpress.ca

*In memory of those who went and those who would have gone
if they had been permitted*

Contents

Acknowledgments / ix

Introduction / 3

1 Grading Blocks of Meat: The Fit and the Unfit / 13

2 No Longer Cause for Rejection / 35

3 An Imperfect System / 50

4 Clashing Concepts of Fitness / 79

5 Not Visibly Different: Describing the Rejected / 93

6 Uncounted Casualties: The Costs of Rejection / 113

7 Claiming Disability to Avoid Military Service / 133

Conclusion / 152

Appendices / 162

Notes / 182

Bibliography / 218

Index / 231

Acknowledgments

It is oft-quoted wisdom that writing a book is a lonely endeavour. I cannot agree. While writing this work, I enjoyed the support and camaraderie of many people, in Canada and abroad. The support I received was so great that these acknowledgments are likely incomplete. To those whom I missed, I offer my deepest apologies.

To start, I would like to recognize financial support from various grants: an Ontario Graduate Scholarship, a Social Sciences and Humanities Research Council of Canada Doctoral Fellowship, an Associated Medical Services Hannah Senior General Scholarship, and a number of excellence scholarships from the University of Ottawa. Furthermore, the Association of Part-Time Professors of the University of Ottawa; the Canadian Battlefields Foundation; and the Faculty of Arts, Royal Military College of Canada, gave me generous support that enabled me to share my research with colleagues outside of Canada.

I also wish to thank both the Canadian War Museum and UBC Press for including this book in their well-respected Studies in Canadian Military History series. To have my work included in a series that contains some of the most important recently published books on the military history of Canada is thrilling, not least because I hold so many of the other authors in high esteem. In addition, my editor, Emily Andrew, guided this manuscript through the publication process with a firm and steady hand, and an abundance of patience, understanding, and support. Her reputation as a first-class editor is well deserved.

The list of scholars to whom I am indebted for their support, advice, and encouragement is long and crosses the globe. Some likely have very little idea how much a fortuitous comment, observation, or, indeed, critique assisted me in researching and writing this book. In Canada, Tim Cook, Serge Durflinger, Galen Perras, Richard Connors, Chad Gaffield, Kris Inwood, and the late Vasilis Vourkoutiotis all deserve special thanks. As well as offering large amounts of their time to hear my half-baked ideas (and then gently guide me back to reality), they ungrudgingly shared with me the fruits of their own research. Desmond Morton, one of Canada's most influential military historians, also offered sound advice and support. Bill Rawling, whom I frequently cornered in the reading room of Library and Archives Canada, gave freely of his time with good humour. Outside of Canada, Jeffrey Grey's gentle ribbing about rugby and cricket were just as valuable to me as his encyclopedic knowledge of Australian and New Zealand military history. Peter Stanley was generous with his research and valuable advice. Maartje Abbenhuis always offered deep insight and a friendly word. Laura Rowe, Kerry Neale, and Bart Ziino were great conference companions and fonts of useful knowledge.

My colleagues at the Canadian War Museum must also be recognized. I am truly blessed to work with a group of individuals who not only are extremely knowledgeable but also give so generously of themselves no matter what the circumstance. Andrew Burtch, Peter Macleod, Amber Lloydlangston, Laura Brandon, and Mélanie Morin-Pelletier deserve particular acknowledgment in this regard.

I owe a great debt of gratitude to my friends John Maker, Anthony Di Mascio, Leigh Hortop-Di Mascio, Adam Gough, Angela Crawley, Stephen Sink, Antony Bellingall, Matt Pietz, Rob Dienesch, and Mark Bourrie. The insightful critiques they offered on my work – while enjoying a coffee, watching a game, building fences, or playing hockey – have greatly improved the final product. More important, they provided a place where I could escape the First World War when I needed to, and they were always willing to lend a sympathetic ear. As a result, I am sure they all know far more about this topic and me than they ever wanted to know. Angela deserves special recognition for taking time away from her valuable medical research to draw the graphs that appear in this work. John and Anthony cheerfully edited and heavily marked the multiple drafts of chapters that turned up in their e-mail inboxes with nary a complaint and only a hint of a manic grin.

My mother-in-law, Anne George, and my aunt-in-law Marcia Rioux, both talented academics in their own right, provided me with encouragement, guidance, and challenging and thought-provoking criticism. Diana Monnet opened her home to my wife, Marcia, and me when we first moved to Ottawa and has been a great support ever since. Mary George, my sister-in-law, taught me all I need to know about hockey.

My parents, Rob and Judy Clarke, have always supported me in my endeavours. Their often unrecognized advocacy work for people with disabilities has always been a great source of pride and inspiration to me. My brother and sister, Tim and Jane, also deserve special thanks for the love and support they have provided their "geeky" brother through the years. My grandmother Joan Clarke always had an encouraging word.

As this book neared completion, my son, Nelson, was born. Sadly, he died four days later. The support Marcia and I received from our families, friends, neighbours, and colleagues during this difficult time was, and continues to be, amazing. While the pain of losing Nelson will never leave us, we are both comforted by and grateful for the acts of kindness that we received. We are particularly grateful to the staff of the Neonatal Intensive Care Unit and Roger's House at the Children's Hospital of Eastern Ontario (CHEO), Ottawa. Their professionalism and compassion have helped us face a reality that no parent should have to confront. I would also like to recognize the other members of our neonatal bereavement support group. Although I would not wish membership in this "club" on anyone, these people have done much to help Marcia and me down the path towards healing. I can only hope I have done as much for them.

My final thanks go to Marcia and our daughters, Nyah and Niobe. Marcia has not only suffered my ramblings and rants about rejected volunteers with good humour but also pulled me back from the abyss that most writers face on more than one occasion. To say that I could not have completed this work without her is to make light of her encouragement, support, and sacrifices. Nyah and Niobe offered laughs, hugs, and compelling questions (not always about rejected volunteers) in equal measure. They have also motivated and helped me to improve my French. *Merci beaucoup mes belles filles!* Importantly, Marcia and the girls' incredible strength and love in the face of Nelson's death gave me the will to carry on when despair, grief, and anger threatened to overwhelm me. It is for this I am most thankful.

Any errors and omissions in this work are mine alone.

Unwanted Warriors

Introduction

MICHAEL DUNNE
Name?

DAVID MANN
David Mann.

DUNNE
What's your marital status, David?

MANN
Single.

DUNNE
And you're of legal age?

MANN
Look, I applied before.

DUNNE
Yeah, I see that and according to this file you were rejected because you have asthma. Do you now have medical clearance on that asthma?

... [Mann angrily indicates he does not, and stresses his patriotism] ...

As long as I'm sitting at this desk you will not be going to this war. Next.

– DIALOGUE FROM THE FILM *PASSCHENDAELE*[1]

LIKE THE FICTIONAL David Mann, many Canadian men who volunteered for service in the Canadian Expeditionary Force during the Great War were turned away from recruiting stations because they were considered medically unfit for service. It is impossible to know exactly how many men were rejected on these grounds between 1914 and 1918, but evidence suggests that they may have numbered well over 100,000, perhaps even 200,000. The Department of Militia and Defence estimated in early 1917 that in 1916 alone over 50,000 men – almost 25 percent of those who volunteered – had been deemed unfit to serve. Stunning as this figure may seem, this estimate was rough at best. Rejection-rate data provided by Military District 13 (Alberta) were so fragmented that they were not included in the department's final calculations. Other districts stated that they were unable to provide information regarding men who had been rejected by civilian practitioners conducting examinations outside the military's purview.

Moreover, the framers of the report were also careful to point out that the statistics related only to men who had failed the medical examination and did not include those who had been turned away by recruiting sergeants even before they crossed a recruiting station's threshold. On the other side of the ledger, it was (and still is) equally impossible to know how many of these rejections represented multiple unsuccessful enlistment attempts by a single individual.[2]

No matter what the exact figure, these numbers indicate that rejected volunteers were a significant minority within Canada's wartime population. Their numbers dwarfed those of many other wartime minorities, such as conscientious objectors.[3] In addition to (and in part because of) this, rejected volunteers also occupied a central place in the public consciousness. These men and issues relating to them were routinely featured in cartoons, private letters, diaries and memoirs, newspaper articles, military policy documents, and government debates and memoranda during the Great War. Questions relating to fitness for military service, and specifically to men who had been deemed fit when they should not have been, featured prominently in the greatest controversy that surrounded the Canadian Army Medical Service both during the war and immediately after: Colonel Herbert A. Bruce's "Report on the Canadian Army Medical Service," otherwise known as the Bruce Report, of 1916.[4]

Besides comprising a significant social and numerical minority, rejected volunteers were also some of the Dominion of Canada's first casualties of the war. Labelling them as casualties highlights the fact that the deleterious impact of the Great War reached far beyond the sharp end of the conflict. Far from being insulated from its effects, many of those on Canada's home front also suffered – albeit in different ways from those in the trenches – as a result of the war. The emotional, social, and economic injuries inflicted upon families by the loss or serious wounding (be it physical or psychological) of a loved one in battle could be both long-lasting and severe.[5] However, less visible but often equally cruel forms of wounding also existed, including the psychological, social, and, in some cases, physical injuries suffered by conscientious objectors or so-called enemy aliens as a result of persecution by both the state and private individuals.[6]

The experiences of many rejected volunteers fit within this wider rubric of wounding. Although their injuries were different from those suffered by soldiers in the trenches, they could be just as debilitating, and some were even fatal. Condemned as cowards and slackers by those who did not understand why they were not in uniform, many rejected volunteers endured ostracism or worse. As though this were not enough, the nagging guilt and often all-consuming self-doubt about their masculinity and social and biological worth experienced by many rejected men could be crippling. Faced with such external and internal assaults, some rejected volunteers chose social exile. Others chose to end their lives. Eighteen-year-old Daniel Lane, for example, took strychnine after failing the Canadian Expeditionary Force medical examination in September 1914.[7] He was by no means the only volunteer to choose death after being rejected for service.

Despite having been a highly visible and important group in Canada during the Great War, rejected volunteers, generally speaking, are virtually nonexistent in both public and academic memories of the war. With the notable exception of Paul Gross's 2008 film, *Passchendaele*, dramatic and literary works about the war have largely ignored them. Likewise, when historians have mentioned individuals who were rejected as being medically unfit, they have generally done so in passing, in the course of exploring other issues, such as recruiting or the postwar eugenics movement.[8]

There is also a paucity of material relating to *how* men were deemed fit or unfit for service. The Canadian military's minimum physical standards for service – not to mention military medical examination – have received little scrutiny from historians other than, as with rejected volunteers, through the exploration of other matters. The relative invisibility of the military medical examination as well as the minimum standards for service is reflective of period literature. Although a key experience in an individual's transformation from civilian to soldier, the examination is only infrequently mentioned, let alone described, in soldiers' wartime letters or postwar reminiscences. When discussed at all, it is portrayed as either dehumanizing and insulting, or laughably lax and easily defeated. Little is said about how it worked. Likewise, physical standards for service are generally derided as unrealistic and stupid regulations that were better ignored than followed. Much the same can be said with regard to wider public discussions of these subjects. For example, Canadian newspapers were inundated with letters to the editor criticizing the "old-womanish" regulations that prevented potential recruits from taking their place in the growing pantheon of Canadian military heroes.

That the history of rejected volunteers has received so little attention is unfortunate not only because of their numbers but also because they present an important opportunity to augment our understanding of the Canadian experience of the Great War, both civilian and military. Most obviously, their experiences and the issues surrounding them provide us with a lens through which to examine how the concept of military fitness was constructed and understood and how it evolved in early-twentieth-century Canada. More broadly, the myriad, often bitter conflicts between civilians, the medical profession, and the military authorities over what made an individual fit to fight can be a springboard for exploring the often strained state of civil-military relations in Canada during the Great War.

At the outset of the war in the summer of 1914, Canadian military authorities had, on paper at least, a black-and-white model of military fitness. An individual was either fit or unfit to serve. There was no middle ground. Moreover, the physical standards an individual had to meet to be deemed fit to serve were exceptionally high. By the end of the war, however, the military authorities' definition of military fitness had changed radically. This transformation took the form of both a lowering of the minimum physical standards for service in many units and a wider reconceptualization of what it meant to be fit for military service.

The changes in minimum height and visual acuity criteria are but two of many examples of how standards for service were lowered between 1914 and 1918. At the start of the war, recruits were required to be at least 5 feet, 3 inches tall. By the end of the war, this had been lowered to 5 feet for infantrymen, and some support units could accept men standing 4 feet, 11 inches. Visual acuity standards also became less stringent as the war progressed. Whereas recruits were expected to have perfect vision in 1914, this was certainly no longer the case by the time Canadian troops stormed Vimy Ridge in April 1917. Furthermore, by the end of the conflict recruits were permitted to use glasses to meet the Canadian Expeditionary Force's new, lower standards, an allowance that only officers could avail of at the start of the war.[9]

The lowering of physical standards for combat infantry was accompanied by a change in the way Canadian military authorities conceptualized military fitness more generally. By 1918, they had shifted from the dichotomous system (fit/unfit) it used to categorize recruits in 1914 to a complex taxonomy of military fitness that recognized multiple levels of ability. This metamorphosis came about in part because of the realization that even if a recruit might not possess the physical attributes of a successful combat soldier, he could still play an important role in uniform. For example, he could usefully fill one of many mid- and rear-echelon positions that the Canadian Expeditionary Force required in order to operate effectively. An increasingly complex organization, the force needed men for typing and carrying out other administrative and logistical tasks as much as it needed them for operating machine guns and launching trench raids. Men with physiques deemed unsuitable for combat were progressively employed in these positions as the war continued. In its waning years, recruiting staff were instructed to direct potential recruits found unfit for combat to apply for positions in support units. Importantly, employing such men in these positions would enable those soldiers deemed to have the physical attributes necessary for combat to be placed at the frontlines rather than behind a desk at the rear.

Thus, by 1917 the military authorities had begun carefully combing through the rear echelons looking for men fit for the trenches whom they could replace with those who met a lower standard of military fitness.

Such seemingly judicious use of manpower resources had its critics, however. A number of officers in command of support units complained when one or more of their men were reassigned to combat units and replaced by men deemed unfit for combat. Headquarters also received complaints from officers when they lost men who had been accepted but later judged unfit for military service. In both instances, the officers' complaints were founded on concerns that they were losing men who, because they had important skills that were rare in the general population, could not be easily replaced. For these officers at least, definitions of military fitness came second to the important skills an individual brought to the table. Such complaints highlight the fact that the multiple categories of military fitness developed during the war could *hinder* as much as support the efficient use of manpower resources. The military authorities did recognize useful skill sets, and on occasion made allowances for men based on their specialist skills and experience, but the set categories of military fitness remained the benchmarks by which men were defined and their roles in the war effort determined.

Note that the reconceptualization of military fitness did not reflect a panic-driven, pell-mell race to the bottom of the recruiting barrel in the face of manpower shortages. In 1918, as in 1914, men were still turned away at recruiting stations if they did not meet the requirements of service, while those in uniform who were found to be unfit were often discharged from the ranks regardless of their skills or experience. Moreover, the first changes to the Canadian military's minimum physical standards occurred in 1915, well before the Expeditionary Force experienced a manpower crisis. To be sure, changes to the minimum dental standards, for example, were designed to significantly broaden the recruiting pool available to the ever-growing Canadian Expeditionary Force, but they were also a direct recognition of, and reaction to, the general dental health characteristics and practices of the Canadian population as well as related civilian constructions of health. Military authorities had to change their dental standards in light of how Canadians perceived dental health, particularly the role they attributed to teeth in the general health of an individual. The same can be said of the aforementioned changes in visual acuity standards and the related move to allow troops to wear glasses.

The perceptions of health held by medical professionals and civilians sometimes collided violently with military regulations as they intersected in the bodies of recruits. Civilians and some medical professionals were often shocked by the military's rejection of men for characteristics, such as bad teeth, that they believed to be minor impairments, unlikely, in their minds, to impinge on an individual's ability to become an efficient soldier. Such disagreements with the military's definitions of fitness caused many people – recruits, recruiters, civilians, and medical professionals alike – to attempt to undermine the medical examination, and indeed to ignore military regulations. Often successful, especially at the beginning of the war, these attempts were aided by the inexperience of medical examiners, the limited resources the military had to invest in the medical examination of recruits, and pressure to fill the ranks. As a result, many unfit individuals, including men who had undergone amputations or suffered from mental illness, made it into the ranks. Twenty-four-year-old Cecil Hamilton, for example, arrived in England minus his right arm. "Weeded out" in England or, in some cases, upon arrival in France, the presence of these men in the ranks of the Expeditionary Force caused Canadian military authorities considerable consternation, especially since some units saw over 40 percent of their strength deemed unfit for service upon arrival in England.[10] As a result of these concerns, military authorities worked steadily throughout the war to improve the systems for assessing a recruit's fitness for service. By the end of the war, recruits were undergoing multiple medical examinations before leaving Canada, not to mention before being shipped from England to France. This was accompanied by better training and instruction for medical examiners as well as growth in the amount of paperwork that accompanied medical examinations. Although they never completely eliminated the problem of unfit men entering the ranks, these changes were largely successful. By the end of July 1917, Sir Edward Kemp, Minister of Militia and Defence, could inform the House of Commons, with considerable justification, that the myriad problems that had characterized the medical examination of troops in 1914–15 had been corrected.[11]

There is little doubt that the decline in unfit men arriving in England trumpeted by Kemp in 1917 was partly due to the lowering of physical standards required for service in some units. It should be noted, however, that the lowering of standards did not occur across the board. The minimum physical requirements for some specialist units *increased* as the war continued. For example, after a brief dip, the minimum height requirement for heavy artillery gunners rose; likewise, the physical standards for a Royal Flying Corps pilot were far above those for an infantryman and did not shift as the war continued. In addition, we should be careful not to attribute an overly negative connotation to the word "lowered" when discussing the changes to the Canadian Expeditionary Force's minimum physical standards. Although these standards were lowered in the sense that less was required of some recruits, the changes implemented did not impact negatively on the ability of individual recruits to successfully carry out their mission or that of the force as a whole. The victories at Vimy Ridge and Passchendaele and during the Hundred Days were achieved with many men who would have been rejected as unfit to serve in 1914.

These observations directly challenge the common belief – evident as much today as it was during the war – that Canadian Corps was composed of muscle-bound supermen who were, to paraphrase the film *Passchendaele,* the only ones capable of getting anything done. Indeed, far from being the British Empire's *übermensch,* many members of the Corps had distinctly uninspiring physiques.[12] More broadly, these observations also raise a number of compelling questions about how military fitness was defined during the Great War. In particular, how did the military authorities come to define what constituted the minimum physical standards for service? How did medical examination work? In what ways, and why, did concepts of military fitness differ between Canadian military authorities, Canadian medical professionals, and laypeople? How did such differing constructions impact on recruiting, recruits, and those rejected for service? How did civilian society view, and treat, those deemed unfit to serve? How did those turned away as unfit navigate their rejection for service?

This book is the result of my exploration of these questions. The first four chapters examine the interrelated factors that led to an individual's being deemed fit or unfit to serve and how these factors evolved over the period of the conflict. In particular, they examine the general characteristics that Canadian military authorities believed made a man fit to fight, the factors on which they founded their constructions of military fitness, and how and why these constructions evolved over the course of the war. The chapters also undertake an in-depth exploration of the mechanics of the military medical examination, its many problems, and how the military authorities moved to mitigate those problems.

The final chapters focus on rejected volunteers as a group. They offer a description of men rejected for service at Valcartier in 1914, demonstrating that the vast majority of those turned away were not visibly different from their successful colleagues. In light of this reality, these chapters also explore the impact that being rejected for service had on men, and how they navigated rejection.

Structuring the book in this manner has enabled me to provide a detailed examination of the wider bureaucratic and material means through which Canadian military authorities defined men as fit for service during the Great War, while retaining a sharp focus on the experiences of individual rejected volunteers and their families. This approach is informed by, reflects, and builds on public and academic interest in the "roots level" experience of the Great War. Over the last thirty years, historians of the Great War have increasingly turned away from the halls of power and blood-soaked frontline trenches to the streets, alleys, and hearths of the homefront in a concerted effort to discover how societies of belligerent nations were transformed by their experience of the war. This repositioning to the homefront has given rise to a cornucopia of new topics. Historians have examined the war's impact on the women's suffrage movement, concepts of citizenship and gender roles, civilian health, ethnic minorities, perceptions of disability, the environment, and the way in which the war was – and continues to be – understood and remembered.[13]

Those scholars who have remained at the firing step have also recalibrated their sights. Increasingly, researchers have included, if not focused on, the experiences and perceptions of the common soldier in their explorations of the bloody mire that was the Western Front. As a result, historians have gained not only a new vantage point from which to survey the battlefield – the soldier's-eye view – but also insight into both day-to-day life in the trenches and the ways in which the common infantryman or gunner understood and experienced the conflict in which he was embroiled. In the Canadian context, one example of this shift in battlefield focus is Tim Cook's two-volume study of Canadian soldiers in the Great War, but it is certainly not the only one.[14] His earlier study of gas warfare focused on how the use of chemical weapons in the Great War impacted on, and was perceived by, the average soldier.[15] Likewise, Bill Rawling has explored the relationship between soldiers and the technologies of industrialized warfare. In doing so, he has argued convincingly that the decisive factor on the battlefields of the Great War was not technology but rather how soldiers adapted to and employed it.[16]

In conjunction with historians' move to substitute the views and experiences of generals, diplomats, and politicians' with those of common soldiers and civilians,[17] there has been a surge in the publication or republication of soldiers' memoirs, diaries, and letters. Edited by experts and family members alike, and published by both academic presses and private individuals, these works have given further voice to those who directly experienced the war, and provide deep insight into life at the "sharp end" of the conflict. They highlight the oft-overlooked fact that life in the trenches was characterized as much by boredom and petty inconvenience as by mud, blood, and machine gun fire. They also give us some measure of access to the human relationships and emotions, both good and bad, that coloured Canadian troops' views of the battlefront, the homefront, and the war in general.[18]

Taken as a whole, this shift in focus has helped to humanize a conflict that was, and often still is, described and understood in mechanistic and dehumanizing terms, and to democratize it.[19] Soldiers as well as the populations of combatant nations are no longer portrayed as passive and hapless automatons buffeted by factors beyond their control but instead as active participants who questioned and strove to control, often successfully, the situations in which they found themselves.

This was, as we shall see, certainly the case with rejected volunteers. Many men turned away as unfit steadfastly refused to accept rejection and travelled across the country visiting recruiting station after recruiting station until they were finally accepted. Others called in favours from powerful friends, or employed all manner of skullduggery to get in. Those who were unable to pass the medical examination in spite of their best efforts actively sought to counter the potential negative impact of their rejection by creating their own pressure group, the Honourably Rejected Volunteers of Canada Association. Acting as a pseudo-veterans group, the association lobbied the provincial and Dominion governments on behalf of its members. Employing a discourse of hindered heroism, members differentiated themselves from both shirkers and conscripts while concurrently arguing for the same benefits afforded to veterans.

Importantly, other men actively sought to be rejected. Indeed, some went so far as to fabricate impairments with the aim of being turned away by medical examiners. Some family members also advanced claims of disability to keep their loved ones from serving. Far from being a reaction to the horrific realities of trench warfare or to the imposition of conscription in 1917, the use of these tactics began almost immediately after war was declared in August 1914. Thus, for some, claiming disability could be seen as a form of resistance against pressures to enlist.

The persistent invisibility of rejected volunteers in current Great War historiography – and indeed wider public memories of the war – despite the move towards highlighting roots-level experience of the war might suggest a scarcity of material pertaining to these men. The truth is quite the opposite, however. Newspapers, government debates and reports, military memoranda, and the letters and memoirs of individual Canadians contain a plethora of material directly and indirectly touching on rejected volunteers and related issues. This book utilizes all these materials, especially two collections held by Library and Archives Canada: (1) Files of CEF Volunteers Who Were Rejected, and (2) the William Babtie Fonds.[20] This is the first time that the files of rejected volunteers have been subjected to close historical examination and that the Babtie Fonds have been used in order to examine rejected volunteers. The former consist of the personnel files of 3,068 men who were rejected for service, usually on medical grounds, by the Canadian Expeditionary Force. The vast majority – 3,050 – were turned away at Valcartier mobilization camp in August and September 1914, and represent approximately 60 percent of the total number of men rejected at Valcartier during the formation of the First Contingent of the Canadian Expeditionary Force. The collection contains the rejected men's attestation papers, pay information, and, on occasion, personal letters and other documentation.[21]

The William Babtie Fonds contain documentation relating to the 1916 board of inquiry called by the Dominion government to examine the claims made in the Bruce Report. Lieutenant General Sir William Babtie, VC, director of medical services for the British Imperial Forces, presided over the inquiry. The documentation includes a list of 350 men who were rejected as unfit for service upon arrival in England.[22] These men are of interest not only because they were considered some of the best representative examples of the "unfit" individuals arriving in England as part of the Canadian Expeditionary Force but also because the entries relating to each individual contain both a description of his impairment and his regimental number. These numbers made possible the referencing of the men's attestation papers and service records.

The information contained in these sources enabled me to examine the physical and social characteristics of men rejected for service at Valcartier in 1914 and to analyze the reasons they were rejected. They also enabled me to construct detailed personal histories – some extending well beyond 1918 – for a number of the men. These histories often included multiple enlistment attempts throughout the period of the war, as well as postwar efforts to gain recognition. The physician's notes in the files provide great insight into individual medical examiners' views of certain impairments, the medical examination, and the minimum physical requirements for service.

Both the rejected-volunteer files and the Babtie Fonds present useful vantage points from which to examine how the position of rejected volunteers changed as the war continued, and how the military authorities' definitions of fitness for service evolved and expanded between 1914 and 1918. Indeed, when used in concert with other sources, the data that they provide can be extrapolated to paint a broad-brush picture of the characteristics and experiences of rejected men during the entire period. Although definitions of military fitness and the nature of the medical examination evolved in various ways as the war progressed, government memoranda, unit reports, newspaper articles, service records, and individual memoirs strongly suggest that little changed on the most basic levels with regard to many men rejected as unfit for service, regardless of when they were turned away.

1

Grading Blocks of Meat
The Fit and the Unfit

> ... [Somers] took off the jacket and was cleanly naked, and stood to be measured and weighed – being moved about like a block of meat, in the atmosphere of corrosive derision. Then he was sent to the next section for eye–tests ... Then after a time to the next section, where he was made to hop on one foot – then on the other foot – bend over – and so on: apparently to see if he had any physical deformity ... [an] elderly fellow then proceeded to listen to his heart and lungs... he [another, younger examiner] put his hand between Somers' legs and pressed it upwards, under his genitals ...
>
> "Cough," ...
> "Again," ...
> "Turn around," ...
> "Put your feet apart." ...
> "Bend forward – further – further – "
> Somers bent forward, and realised that [the examiner was] look[ing] into his anus.
> "That will do. Get your jacket and go over there."
> ... They gave him his card: C2. Fit for non-military service.
>
> – EXTRACT FROM *KANGAROO*, BY D.H. LAWRENCE[1]

THE MEDICAL EXAMINATION was the key event in an individual's transformation from recruit to enlisted man. Like sides of beef being graded, Canadian Expeditionary Force recruits were (in theory at least) subjected to an intensive examination during which their medical, physical, mental, and moral worthiness for service was judged by medical examiners against a set of standard criteria. Failure to meet these standards – which reflected the general characteristics that Canadian military authorities believed made an individual fit to shoulder a rifle – led to a recruit's being declared "unfit" for service and denied membership in the khaki brotherhood.

The relationship that medical examiners had with potential recruits was not a doctor-patient relationship in the traditional sense. Unlike civilian practitioners, medical examiners were acting not as healers but as adjudicators. Their concern was not with ensuring the long-term "well-being and full health" of the men who stood before them, but rather with the impact of their health on their ability to serve. The health needs of the individual were subsumed in, and superseded by, the needs of his unit and the military as a whole. Indeed, by passing a recruit fit to serve, a medical examiner was potentially threatening the recruit's long-term health. Battlefields were, after all, dangerous places where soldiers almost daily faced the possibility of sickness, maiming, and death. The same could be said of medical officers operating in the field. Often military necessity required them to return to the frontlines men whose fragile physical or mental health would have required close medical attention in civilian society. As we shall see in the following chapters, some medical officers struggled with this fundamental difference between military and civilian medicine, while others chafed at the many restrictions and pressures that military service placed on their professional autonomy.[2]

Despite the central role that medical examinations played in their metamorphosis from civilian to soldier, soldiers seldom spoke of them in their wartime letters or postwar memoirs. When they did, the information provided was sparse at best. Most simply offered a general description of their often negative feelings about the examination or, in some case, how they managed to pass it despite having a disqualifying impairment.[3] Much the same can be said of the histories of the Canadian Expeditionary Force, both official and scholarly. All mention the medical examination, often in connection with its problems, but few, if any, stop to engage with its mechanics or guiding principles.[4]

With these observations in mind, this chapter explores in detail the mechanics of the Canadian military medical examination and its evolution as the war dragged on, as well as the fitness classification systems used to categorize potential enlistees and serving soldiers. Far from being fixed, the medical examination continually evolved. In 1914, the relatively simple examination recognized only two categories of fitness – fit and unfit – that relied as much on medical examiners' subjective opinions as on objective analysis. By 1918, it was a highly complex process, with multiple fitness categories and a much greater empirical bent.

Although the medical examination was the final arbiter of a recruit's fitness for service, an informal weeding-out process began on the streets of Canadian towns and cities before men faced any type of formal examination. Recruiting officers did not approach men on the street that they deemed, based on visual inspection, unfit to serve, and they turned away such individuals when they attempted to enlist. The prime candidates for such filtering were the visibly different; those whom civilians would have readily recognized as "unfit"; and those afflicted with paralysis, severe deformity, debilitating sensory impairment, or obvious intellectual or psychological impairment. Ethnicity could also be a factor. Canadians of African and Asian descent were seldom, if ever, approached by recruiters, and those who offered their services were usually turned away at the recruiting station. First Nations people also faced ethnically based hurdles when attempting to enlist, although these were often much lower than those erected for African and Asian Canadians. Skin colour was, in this sense, a perceived impairment that made one unfit to serve in what was, for all intents and purposes, a "white man's war."[5]

The decisions of recruiting officers were also guided by their knowledge of recruiting requirements. Five-foot-tall Alexander Bachelor of Toronto, for example, was turned away by the recruiting sergeants of a number of different units in August 1914 because he did not meet the Canadian Expeditionary Force minimum height requirement.[6] Meanwhile, fifteen-year-old Thomas Raddall of Halifax was rejected because the recruiting sergeant knew his father – a British officer serving as an instructor in the Canadian Militia – and was therefore aware that Raddall was well below the minimum age requirement.[7] At the other end of the scale, seventy-one-year-old Torrance Glazier, a veteran of the Fenian Raids, the Northwest Campaign, and the Anglo-Boer War – was twice turned away by recruiting officers of the 21st Canadian Infantry Battalion because of his age.[8]

If a potential recruit was accepted by a recruiting officer, he was then subjected to a number of medical examinations. The number and quality of these examinations changed during the war. Recruits in the First Contingent of the Canadian Expeditionary Force generally underwent three or four medical examinations. The first, and often the most cursory one, was conducted by the medical officer of, or a civilian practitioner linked to, the unit he had joined. The second was conducted at Valcartier and the third upon arrival in England. Most soldiers would also undergo another examination before they left England for the front. By late 1916, recruits were undergoing at least six medical examinations before seeing action in France. The first, which was now recognized as simply preliminary, was carried out by a Canadian Army Medical Corps officer or civilian practitioner linked to the recruit's local recruiting station. The second was held at the nearest mobilization centre and was conducted by a medical board made up of three Medical Corps officers and an eye and ear specialist. Besides evaluating a recruit's suitability to serve, these boards played an important protective function: they acted as both a check on and a safety net for local recruiters and medical examiners, and they were designed to prevent the re-enlistment of men who had been previously rejected as unfit to serve.[9] If the recruit passed the medical board examination, he was sent to the headquarters of the overseas unit for which he had signed up, where he was subjected to a careful examination by the unit's medical officer. If the medical officer disagreed with the medical board's findings, he had to notify his commanding officer as soon as possible and request the medical board to reconsider its decision. If the medical officer found the recruit to be fit, the recruit underwent another medical examination immediately before embarking for Europe. He had a fourth medical examination upon arriving in England,[10] and another after training and before being placed in a draft for France, where he was examined yet again before being sent to a base depot for final training. After completing his training, he was examined before being allowed to proceed to the front, where he was examined again upon arrival.[11] A soldier could be declared unfit to serve at any point in this chain of examinations. The multiple examinations were intended to act as a fail-safe mechanism to catch men who had been incorrectly (for whatever reason) passed as fit to serve, or who had experienced a decline in physical condition at some point between recruitment and arrival at the battlefront. Despite the apparently watertight system for detecting unfit men before they reached the trenches (and a tacit acknowledgment that the medical examination of recruits was rife with problems), the process could and did break down, especially early in the conflict. This meant, as we shall see in Chapter 3, that recruits were often able to avoid one or more of their medical examinations.

The physicians tasked with examining the sea of volunteers that washed across Canada in August and September 1914 received guidance from a sixty-six-page booklet, the *Regulations for the Canadian Medical Service, 1910*.[12] This document contained directives covering the medical officer's responsibilities. Directives relating to the physical examination of recruits were listed in three parts of the document: Section IX (paragraphs 250 to 60) in the main text, and appendices 5 and 6, "Physical Examination of Recruits" and "Instructions for the Physical Examination of Candidates for Commissions in the Militia and Cadets, Royal Military College," respectively.

Section IX, "Physical Examination of Candidates for Commissions in the Permanent Force, for Admission to the RMC [Royal Military College], and of Recruits," was concerned with bureaucratic procedures and the medical officer's responsibilities, rather than the actual mechanics of the medical examination. There were instructions for filling out attestation papers, and information on what records relating to medical examinations needed to be kept, where they should be housed, and under what circumstances they could be removed. The section noted that medical officers were to be directly "responsible for the measurement of recruits with regards to height, chest and weight," and for the recording of information about any distinctive marks a recruit might have. It warned medical officers that by affixing their signatures to an attestation paper they were declaring that they: (1) had personally examined the recruit in question; and (2) were personally guaranteeing the information on the attestation paper.[13]

The process that medical officers were to follow and the minimum standards that recruits had to meet were contained in appendices 5 and 6. "The greatest care must be taken in the examination of a recruit. Every man presented for examination must be stripped, and the examination conducted in a thorough and systematic manner." Furthermore, there were to be no grey areas or middle ground in relation to a recruit's suitability to serve. Each man was to "be declared either unfit or fit for general service."[14] Medical officers were to ensure that a recruit:

- had normal vision
- had normal hearing[15]
- had normal speech[16]
- had full use of limbs and had no physical deformities
- had an ample chest
- had teeth that were good and was not fitted with plates
- showed no evidence of cutaneous (skin) disease, past or present
- did not suffer from a hernia
- did not have marked varicocele (an abnormal enlargement of the veins in the scrotum draining the testicles)
- did not have varicose veins
- had "the appearance of being an intelligent and sober man and likely to make an efficient soldier in the Permanent Force."[17]

What defined an intelligent and sober man was not described, but it is evident that besides being a means of preventing men with intellectual or psychiatric impairments from enlisting, this last condition was also a catchall requirement that could be invoked by military authorities to justify their rejection of men who they believed to be potential troublemakers or to have unwanted personality traits. It was also used in order to discharge men who were found, for whatever reason, to be unsuited for military life. C.E. Lamond, who later lost a leg serving in Europe, was one individual rejected at Valcartier because he was considered to be "inefficient." On what grounds this decision was made was not explained.[18]

The question of desirability was also used at Valcartier for the same general purpose. For example, F. Bennett of Chesley, Ontario, was declared unfit to serve and was discharged because he was "homesick and undesirable to his unit." Described as both "incorrigible" and "undesirable" in his discharge papers, J. Norris was rejected both times he attempted to enlist.[19] Likewise, J. McCeary was discharged for "misconduct," specifically for being "drunk and bringing liquor [into the dry] camp." Obviously considered a troublemaker with little respect for authority, McCeary was "sent to the station with an escort to ensure he gets away." He was not the only soldier to be sent home for drinking and lack of discipline. In fact, it became common knowledge that drunkenness and misbehaviour were sure ways of escaping Valcartier. As the lonely wife of one recruit wrote: "Dearest I saw in the papers that if any of you got drunk & kicked up now you got sent back Home [sic], why can't you do that Johnnie[?]"[20]

The lack of direction provided by the *Regulations for the Canadian Medical Service, 1910* as to what typified "an intelligent and sober man" also characterized the instructions it provided medical officers more generally. Indeed, its only detailed guidance on conducting the medical examination dealt with testing a recruit's visual acuity.[21] Regulation test cards were to be placed six metres in front of the recruit, who, standing with his back to the light, was to read them off as directed. This test was to be conducted in "ordinary daylight."[22] In order to pass, recruits were required to have a visual acuity of either 20/20 in both eyes, or 20/15 vision in one eye and no less than 20/30 vision in the other. Glasses could not be used in the test unless one was applying either for a commission or as a cadet to the Royal Military College.[23]

Medical officers did have other sources to fall back on. The 1904 instructions for the medical examination of Royal Military College cadets and men seeking commissions in the permanent militia contained, for example, detailed instructions on how to measure both a recruit's height and expanded chest.[24] Access to such documentation was probably limited, however, and it is evident that the 1910 regulations were the primary guide, at least at the local level, for medical examinations in 1914. In November of that year, for example, Dr. G.B. Henderson of Creston, British Columbia, wrote to Ottawa requesting that the regulations for the medical examination of volunteers for active service be sent to him so he could be sure that he was conducting such examinations correctly. He was advised to contact the Assistant Director of Medical Services, Military District 11, Victoria, BC, or to refer to the *Regulations for the Canadian Medical Service, 1910*, especially appendix 5.[25]

Appendix 5 of the 1910 regulations ended by directing medical officers to paragraph 243 of the *King's Regulations and Orders for the Canadian Militia, 1910* for the minimum height and chest measurements for enlisted men. This paragraph specified a minimum height of 5 feet, 6 inches for Garrison Artillery and 5 feet, 4 inches for all other corps. The recruit's expanded chest was to be at least 34 inches in girth. The maximum age of enlistment was set at forty-four years.[26]

As with visual acuity, the minimum physical requirements for men seeking commissions and for Royal Military College cadets also differed slightly from those for enlisted men. The minimum standards for these men and boys (cadets were accepted into the college at the age of sixteen) were calculated on a sliding scale. For example, the minimum height for a sixteen-year-old cadet was 5 feet, and the minimum chest girth was 33 inches. A sixteen-year-old standing 5 feet, 5 inches, on the other hand, was expected to have a chest that measured at least 34 inches when expanded. At the other end of the scale, men over twenty years of age were to stand a minimum of 5 feet, 2.5 inches tall and have an expanded chest of no less than 35 inches in girth.[27] The smaller minimum sizes allowed for cadets was implicit recognition of the fact that sixteen-year-olds had not yet stopped growing.

Appendices 5 and 6 in the 1914 edition of the *Regulations for the Canadian Medical Service* (published in 1915 and therefore not available to medical examiners in 1914) were identical to those found in the 1910 edition.[28] Changes to requirements were published outside of these regulatory documents. Militia Order 372 of 17 August 1914 lowered the minimum height for an infantryman from 5 feet, 4 inches to 5 feet, 3 inches, and the minimum chest measurement from 34 inches to 33.5 inches,[29] bringing the Canadian minimums in line with British standards. The order also set the minimum and maximum ages for service in the Canadian Expeditionary Force at eighteen and forty-five years, respectively. The height requirement for artillerymen was set at 5 feet, 7 inches.[30] These physical requirements were far from onerous, considering that the average height of a Canadian man in the early twentieth century was approximately 5 feet, 7 inches.[31] We have no formal information regarding the average chest girth of Canadian men in this period, but evidence suggests that most measured well over 33 inches.[32]

As one might suspect, the mechanics of the Canadian military medical examination were closely aligned with those of the British; they sprang from the same military tradition after all, and all Canadian troops were examined upon arrival in England. There were some differences between the two, however, specifically certain physical characteristics required of combat troops. These differences were to cause problems for the Canadian forces when they arrived in England. As the British (Imperial) regulations took precedence over those used in Canada, more than a few men deemed fit according to Canadian regulations were not considered so in England.

According to the *Instructions for the Physical Examination of Recruits* issued with British Army Orders on 1 August 1914, a fit recruit had the following characteristics:

- had sufficient intelligence
- met the required standards of visual acuity in each eye
- had good hearing
- could speak without impediment

- had no glandular swellings
- had a capacious and well-formed chest, with a sound heart and sound lungs
- was not ruptured in any degree or form
- had well-formed and fully developed limbs
- had free and perfect motion in all of his joints
- had well-formed feet and toes
- had no congenital malformation or defects
- bore no traces of previous acute or chronic disease that indicated he had an impaired constitution
- possessed "a sufficient number of sound teeth for efficient mastication." [33]

Almost immediately following this list of the basic physical qualities, and with obvious reference to said virtues, the instructions stated that the following conditions were grounds for immediate rejection:

- indication of tubercular disease
- constitutional syphilis
- bronchial or laryngeal disease
- palpitation or other diseases of the heart
- a generally impaired constitution
- visual acuity below required standard
- defects in voice or hearing
- pronounced stammering
- loss or decay of teeth to such an extent as to materially interfere with efficient mastication
- contraction or deformity of chest or joints
- abnormal curvature of spine
- defective intelligence
- hernia
- hemorrhoids
- severe varicose veins or varicocele
- inveterate cutaneous disease
- chronic ulcers
- fistula (abnormal connection or passageway between organs or vessels that normally do not connect)
- "any disease or physical defect ... [that the examiner believed would make a recruit unfit] ... for the duties of a soldier."[34]

Besides being free of the listed impairments, a recruit was also required to meet some basic physical standards. The instructions issued in August 1914 required recruits for line infantry to be between nineteen and thirty years of age and at least 5 feet, 3 inches tall. They also required a minimum expanded-chest girth of no less than 33.5 inches, although, unlike the Canadian requirement, this varied depending on a recruit's height and age. Minimum requirements also varied between units. The Household Cavalry and Foot Guards had higher minimum standards, as did the artillery and cavalry of the line. The British Territorial Force, on the other hand, had lower standards.[35]

The examiner was provided with detailed instructions for conducting the examination. Recruits, as the passage quoted at the beginning of this chapter indicates, were examined naked, preferably after they had washed. The examining doctor stood "about 6 feet" from his subject, with the recruit being so placed "that the light might fall upon him."[36] The recruit's height, weight, and chest measurements were taken in that order, after which his vision was tested.

A recruit's height was measured against a measuring standard (stick). He would stand erect but not rigid, with heels, calves, buttocks, and shoulders touching the standard. His weight would be on his heels, with his chin depressed so that the vertex of his head was level under the standard's horizontal measuring bar. The recruit's height was recorded to one-eighth of an inch. Chest measurements were taken with equal precision. The recruit would stand erect with his feet together, then raise his hands above his head. The examiner then placed his measuring tape around the recruit's chest, making sure that the upper edge of the tape touched the inferior angles of the shoulder blades at the back, while the lower edge touched the upper part of the nipples at the front. The recruit then lowered his arms so that they hung loosely at his side, taking care not to displace the measuring tape. Once all was ready, he would take a number of deep breaths so that the maximum expansion of his chest could be measured. The examiner would then note both the girth of the recruit's chest when fully expanded and the range of expansion. Fractions less than one-half of an inch were not recorded.

If a recruit had not brought "satisfactory proof of his age," the examiner would estimate his age based on his height, weight, general development, and appearance, and then record his judgment in the "apparent age" column of the recruit's attestation paper. This practice was intended primarily to permit detection of overage men and underage boys. If the examiner was "in doubt as to [a] recruit's age," he would return the attestation paper to the recruiting officer, who was then expected to gain proof of the individual's age.[37] Canadian medical examiners conducted similar age assessments despite the absence of such tests from the Canadian literature at the start of the war. For example, one reason for Joseph Blake's rejection at Valcartier in 1914 was the belief of his medical examiner, Lieutenant E. Wilson, that the age Blake had provided was "manifestly wrong" – he looked fifty rather than forty-four. Jules Henri Mercier, on the other hand, was rejected because Lieutenant C.R. Graham felt that the purported eighteen-year-old looked "about sixteen."[38]

British recruits underwent the same visual acuity test as Canadian recruits, but their required level was very different. In order to be considered fit for frontline service, recruits had to have visual acuity of either 20/80 in both eyes, or 20/20 and 20/270 in their right eye and left eye, respectively. Men with no less than 20/20 vision in their left eye and 20/200 in their right eye were considered fit for support positions. Like the Canadians, British recruits who wore glasses were rejected out of hand unless they were to be officers.[39]

If a recruit passed these tests and appeared otherwise eligible, a more detailed general examination was conducted. The recruit was first asked to walk across the room two or three times in front of the examiner. The procedure was then repeated with the recruit hopping on his toes. After successfully completing these tasks, the recruit was directed to halt, stand upright, and place his arms above his head. The medical examiner then walked around him slowly, "carefully inspecting the whole surface of his body."[40]

These tests were designed to enable the examiner to ascertain the recruit's general physical development, especially the formation, development, and power of limbs and joints. They also permitted the detection of extreme flatness of feet, deformed toes, skin diseases, varicose veins, cicatrices (scars) or ulcers, birthmarks, and tattoos. While conducting these tests, the examiner also had to consider whether the recruit presented the appearance of having served in the military in the past. This requirement was meant as a defence against recruits who, for whatever reason, failed to acknowledge previous military service.[41]

If no disqualifying impairments were uncovered during this visual inspection, the recruit's trunk was subjected to closer examination. Standing with his arms extended above his head and the backs of his hands touching, the recruit was inspected by the medical examiner in the following order. First, his genitalia were scrutinized for any indications that he was suffering (or had recently suffered) from venereal disease. Next, his scrotum was examined to ascertain that both of his testicles had descended and whether he was suffering from varicocele. If the recruit was found to have an undescended testicle, the examiner had to determine where the testicle was situated. If it was either within the inguinal canal or at the subcutaneous ring, the recruit was declared unfit; otherwise an undescended testicle did not disqualify a man for service.[42] The recruit was then examined for hernias by being asked to cough as the examiner inserted his finger into the subcutaneous ring on each side of the scrotum.

After a successful examination of the recruit's lower torso, the medical examiner turned his attention to his subject's chest. First, he asked the recruit to inhale deeply a number of times, in order to visually examine the man's breathing action and chest capacity. This visual inspection was followed by a stethoscopic examination of the recruit's lungs and heart in order to establish whether he suffered from any defects of these organs.

After the recruit's trunk came his arms and hands. The recruit was directed to stretch out his arms, palms upward, and bend his fingers backward and forward, then his thumbs across his palms, and then his fingers across his thumbs. Next, the examiner asked the recruit to bend his wrists backward and forward, then bend his elbows, and then turn the backs of his hands upward. Finally, he was asked to swing his arms around. The objectives of this part of the medical examination were threefold: (1) to detect whether the recruit had lost or suffered from defects in his digits, wrists, elbows, and shoulder joint; (2) to establish the forearm's power of rotation; and (3) to examine the recruit for vaccination marks.

The examination then turned to the recruit's lower extremities and back. Facing the examiner, the recruit first stood on one foot and put the other one forward, then bent his ankle and toes backward and forward. The process was repeated with the other leg. Next the recruit was asked to bend down on one knee and then the other, then to go down on both knees and spring up from this position using both legs. Finally, turning his back to the examiner, the recruit had to separate his legs and touch the ground with his hands.

The purpose of this inspection of the recruit's legs, feet, and back was to determine whether he had lost, or had suffered from defects in, his toes, ankles, knees, and spinal column. The inspection also enabled examiners to make sure that the recruit did not suffer from hemorrhoids, *prolapsus ani* (the eversion of the lower portion of the rectum, which causes it to protrude through the anus), and *fistula in perinaeo* (a congenital malformation of the anus and rectum in which the anus is imperforate and there is a fistula exiting via a tiny hole in the perineum).

The final part of the examination focused on the recruit's head and neck, from the top of the head downward. First, the examiner asked whether the recruit had ever received blows or cuts to the head, and whether he was subject to fits of any kind. The examiner then examined the recruit's scalp, followed by, in turn, the ears, eyes, eyelids, and nostrils. Next came the mouth, teeth, palate, and fauces (hind part of the mouth, which leads into the pharynx). The examiner then asked the recruit to say loudly, "Who comes there?" before examining the potential soldier's neck.

The purpose of this part of the examination was to further detect whether the recruit had suffered head injuries or manifested any of the following ailments: "deafness; disease of the ears; defect of the voice; polypus of the nose [an abnormal swelling of the mucous membrane of the nose and sinuses that can lead to breathing difficulties]; tubercular ulceration; glandular enlargement; and defects of the eyes and teeth."[43] If the recruit was found to have a squint or any morbid condition of the eyes or eyelids that might worsen or recur during service, he was rejected. Individuals suffering from hearing loss or outright deafness were also declared unfit to serve. Indeed, when conducting this part of the examination, medical officers were directed to take particular care to ascertain whether the recruit's eardrums had been perforated.

Visual and aural deficiencies were grounds for immediate rejection, but this was not necessarily the case with dental insufficiencies. Although section 16 of *Instructions for the Physical Examination of Recruits* noted that loss or decay of teeth were grounds for rejection, recruits with dental deficiencies were not to be rejected outright. Rather, acceptance or rejection of a recruit with bad teeth depended upon how his limited or corroded dental assets related to his general health. The instructions stated that "the loss of many teeth in a man of indifferent constitution would point to rejection, whilst a robust recruit who had lost an equal number might be accepted." Stressing the importance the military placed on the influence of other factors on whether or not a dentally deficient recruit was accepted or rejected, the British instructions went on to state that "too much attention cannot be paid to this latter point." Conversely, men with dentures were to be rejected even if their general physical appearance indicated robust health. Similar directives were not added to Canadian instructions for the medical examination of recruits until 1916.[44]

The only required characteristic of a recruit that did not receive a detailed discussion or explanation in the British instructions was that of sufficient intelligence. As with the Canadian regulations, medical examiners were given no guidance as to what constituted sufficient intelligence for service or how one was to ascertain – as was required – a recruit's mental capacity. As a result, medical examiners fell back on largely subjective indicators of intelligence or lack thereof. Captain S.T. Beggs, a Royal Army Medical Corps officer involved in recruiting, offered the following description of how recruits' intelligence was judged by medical examiners in his 1915 study *The Selection of the Recruit*:

> Mental capacity is determined by noting mental characteristics, such as – Powers of observation or sense perception; quickness of apprehension; scope of apprehension – that is, the capacity for apprehending complex relations and multiplicity of detail; power of concentration of attention, which may be measured by noting the readiness with which attention is drawn from task in hand; capacity for sustained application (that is, perseverance or repeated concentration of attention upon a given task; retentiveness of memory; inventiveness; power of

reasoning; confidence in oneself; conscientiousness; industriousness; energy for mental work, etc.

Defective intelligence will be carefully looked for by noting such conditions as follow: Want of expression, want of changefulness, vacancy, fixed expression, extreme slowness of cerebration, general clumsiness, malformation of the skull (cranium bossed, too large or too small, forehead defective, asymmetry in the cranium), external ear defective in size or form or parts, palate abnormal or defective (arched, V-shaped, too narrow, horseshoe shaped, cleft, etc.); evidence of unteachableness, such as gross ignorance of matters of common knowledge, illiteracy, grinning and over-smiling; features badly proportioned (thick lips, open mouth, drooped jaw); response in action defective, following a command or imitation; speech defective (stammering, or defective in articulation, or speech indistinct, or not replying to question); defective hearing.[45]

Thorough medical examinations, especially if they were to include an intelligence examination along the lines described by Beggs, took time. In fact, even without testing a recruit's intelligence, a single medical examiner would have had to spend at least twenty to thirty minutes on each recruit if the examination was to be conducted correctly. Given the sea of men lining up to fight and the limited number of medical examiners available – at Valcartier in 1914, approximately 30 medical officers and 100 administrative orderlies were responsible for testing the over 35,000 men who volunteered to serve in the First Contingent – such time expenditures were simply not feasible. Pressed to pass as many men as possible in the shortest amount of time, medical officers – often working in conditions reminiscent of a production line – gave the most perfunctory of examinations. As a result, many large British and Canadian recruiting stations quickly came to "resemble factories, moving thousands of men through their doors as quickly as possible."[46]

Neither the Canadian nor the British medical examination included a test for tuberculosis (TB). Given both the disease's debilitating nature and the fact that it was endemic in early-twentieth-century Canada, the military authorities' failure to actively test recruits for it might seem at first to be an inexcusable oversight. It was certainly portrayed as such by Ernest Scammell, the secretary of Canada's Military Hospitals Commission during the postwar period. Faced with a deluge of veterans claiming disability pensions on account of suffering from TB, and believing, but unable to prove, that most had suffered from the disease prior to enlistment and therefore should not be eligible for government support, Scammell angrily declared "that a $3 tuberculin test [on each recruit] could have saved the government an average of $5000 of pension and treatment for each sufferer [that the Military Hospitals Commission had to care for]."[47]

Scammell's comments indicated little understanding of how tuberculin testing worked and of its limitations as a selection tool. The tuberculin skin test indicates whether an individual is infected with the tubercle bacillus, not whether he has the active disease. In populations – such as Canada's during the early twentieth century – in which infection with the tubercle bacillus was almost universal, the test was useless as a means of gauging the health of an individual or as a selection tool because most adults tested were likely to give a positive result. In addition, far from being reliable, the test was well known by physicians to give both false positive and false negative results. Further undermining its usefulness as a tool for hard-pressed medical officers attempting to examine as many recruits as quickly as possible was the fact that the test took approximately forty-eight hours to produce a result.[48]

The only other means of testing for TB, X-ray screening, was equally problematic, albeit for different reasons. Limited in number and expensive to use, X-ray machines were too primitive to reliably provide the detailed images of a subject's lungs required to diagnose the disease. Moreover, those trained to operate the machines and make sense of the images they produced were also few and far between. Even if X-ray machines and trained experts had been readily available to medical examiners, their usefulness as a selection tool would have been limited by the fact that they indicated the presence of the disease only after it had become active. In other words, an X-ray would only confirm the existence of the full-blown disease (a reality likely already disclosed by other symptoms). It would not screen for infection. [49] As a result of these problems, the Canadian military began screening recruits for TB only at the outbreak of the Second World War in 1939, when X-ray technology was far more advanced.[50] X-ray screening of immigrants for TB became mandatory eight years later.[51]

Other than changes in physical requirements for recruits and a few relatively minor additions for clarification purposes or to highlight particular areas of concern, Canadian documentation relating to medical examination of recruits saw little change until 1917. The 1916 *Instructions regarding Physical Qualifications and Medical Inspection of Recruits C.E.F.* contained the same list of disqualifying impairments as in 1910, except for bad teeth because dental requirements had changed in 1915.[52] Like the earlier guidelines, the 1916 document gave medical officers little direction on how to conduct the examination. It did, however, warn them to exercise great caution when accepting men for service – an indication of the ongoing problems with those who should have been rejected but were not. The warning concluded: "In most cases ... [these men had been passed] ... as a result of carelessness and lack of attention to details on the part of the Medical Examiner."[53]

In 1917, the Canadian military adopted British documentation relating to medical examinations as the new General Officer Commanding Canadians in England, Lieutenant-General Sir R.E.W. Turner, VC, attempted to align Canadian standards of training, equipment, and fitness with those of Britain.[54] The twelve-page *Physical Standards and Instructions for the Medical Examination of Recruits for the Canadian Expeditionary Force and for the Active Militia of Canada* issued to Canadian medical officers was largely the same as the document provided to British medical examiners in 1914, but with some notable deletions and additions. Absent from the Canadian document were two-and-a-half pages of general instructions relating to the administration of the medical examination, and detailed height and weight comparison charts. Added were a page discussing the special (relaxed) standards for support units and three appendices. The first two appendices dealt with standards of vision and hearing required of recruits for both combat and support units. The third stated that men with "severe nasal obstruction" were not to be enlisted because it had been found that those suffering from such conditions found it difficult, if not impossible, to use gas masks. Although polypus of the nose had been a reason for rejection because it could limit breathing, the addition of this appendix indicates how changing battlefield realities – in this case the introduction of chemical weapons – affected who was considered fit for combat. Men who were unable to use respirators were of no use in the gas-poisoned world of the trenches.[55] A graphic description of what constituted severe (marked) varicocele was also added to the first page of the document in a paragraph outlining the general grounds for rejecting a recruit: "Varicocele will be considered severe when the mass of veins is so great that it hangs down in front of the testicle when the candidate stands up or if the cord is so elongated that the testicle hangs abnormally low."[56] The necessity for such direction had been obvious since at least mid-1915. In July that year, a letter from the Adjutant General's office stressed that while considerable care should be taken not to recruit men who suffered from "marked varicocele," medical examiners should not be too eager to reject those with the condition: "Recruits pursuing in civil life active and laborious occupations, have been pronounced 'unfit' on account of slight varicocele, which prior to medical examination was unsuspected. It is requested that a very careful examination be made in order that men who wish to serve may not be rejected on insufficient grounds."[57]

The 1918 edition of the *Physical Standards and Instructions* was even more detailed.[58] At twenty-six pages, it was fifteen pages longer than the 1917 edition and a full twenty-four pages longer than the instructions provided to medical examiners in 1916. Although reflecting some changes in recruiting requirements, much of the additional detail came in the form of guidelines for categorizing military fitness based on two alphanumeric classification systems – the *Classification of Men by Categories in Canada* and the *Classification of Men by Categories in the British Isles* – that had been adopted by Canadian authorities in 1917.

Adopted by the Canadian military on 15 May, the *Classification of Men by Categories in Canada* placed all enlisted men serving in Canada in one of five categories (A to E), which were in turn divided into a number of subcategories identified by a number. Men were no longer graded "fit" or "unfit," but rather categorized according to their perceived physical development and level of training. Category A1, the highest category, comprised recruits who were considered to be "fit for despatch overseas both with regards to [their] training in Canada and [their] physical and mental qualifications." Categories A2 through A4 covered men who were considered fit for general service but had yet to meet the A1 standard. The subdivisions within Category A were used only in Canada. All men proceeding overseas were simply classified as Category A men.

Category B men were those considered fit for service overseas, but not in direct combat positions. Included in this category were men deemed fit to serve in the Canadian Army Medical Corps, the Canadian Army Dental Corps, and in forestry, pioneer, labour, and construction units. Category C men were considered fit for service only in Canada. Category D, "Temporary unfit," was used as a holding category for men awaiting medical treatment. Quarantined men were not placed within this category but retained their original classification. The final category, E, was for men awaiting discharge or reclassification. This category was used most often to indicate a man found unfit for any form of service.[59]

Besides outlining where and in what units men in each of the categories could serve, the *Classification of Men by Categories in Canada* provided a general guide to medical examiners for placing men in the various categories:

A. Men already serving, recruits when trained or returned C.E.F. men when their physical condition warrants it. Able to march, see to shoot, hear well and absolutely well able to stand active service conditions.

B. Men already serving, recruits when trained or returned C.E.F. men when their physical condition warrants it. Free from serious organic defects, able to stand service conditions in the line of communications in France.

B.1. Able to march at least 5 miles, see to shoot with glasses and hear well[60]

B.2. Able to walk to and from work at least five miles, see and hear sufficiently for ordinary purposes and fulfilling conditions laid down in special instructions

B.3. Only suitable for sedentary work[61]

C. Free from serious organic disease, able to stand service conditions in Canada

C.1. Able to march at least 5 miles, see to shoot with glasses and to hear well
C.2. Able to walk to and from work, a distance not exceeding 5 miles
C.3. Only suitable for sedentary work[62]

These standards provide a clear indication of the Canadian military authorities' general expectations regarding the physical characteristics and abilities of men placed in each of the categories. But guidance provided to medical examiners did not end there. On 3 May 1917, the Adjutant General of the Canadian Militia, had sent Canada's Military Districts a memorandum with detailed directions on how to classify men with a variety of different impairments – including varicose veins, heart conditions, hernias, and flat feet – according to the *Categories in Canada* alphanumeric scale. It also indicated acceptable corrective measures, including the use of both corrective devices and operations, for some of the impairments. For example, the following directives were given regarding hernias:

Inguinal hernia – No man may be accepted for overseas service abroad in classes "A" or "B," who is ruptured in any degree or form.

Femoral hernia – Cases for femoral hernia occurring after enlistment should undergo operation or be classed in "E" for discharge from the service.

Ventral hernia (post-operative) – If a definite protrusion exists, these cases should not be classed higher that "C" (III).

In the case of hernia which have been recently operated upon, if the soldier states there is pain in the region of the operation, but no objective signs are present, the case should be classed in "D."

Where, in addition to pain, there is swelling or atrophy of the testicle, or other signs of pressure, the case should not be classed higher than "C" (III).

When a soldier is fitted with a truss, an entry of the fact should be made in his Medical History Sheet in the space reserved for defects not sufficient to warrant rejection.[63]

Such directives were intended not only to guide medical examiners in classifying recruits and enlisted men in their districts but also to ensure uniform treatment and classification of men by further removing the examiners' interpretative leeway with regard to their physical suitability for combat. The alphanumeric codes soon appeared on recruits' attestation papers (see Figure 1).

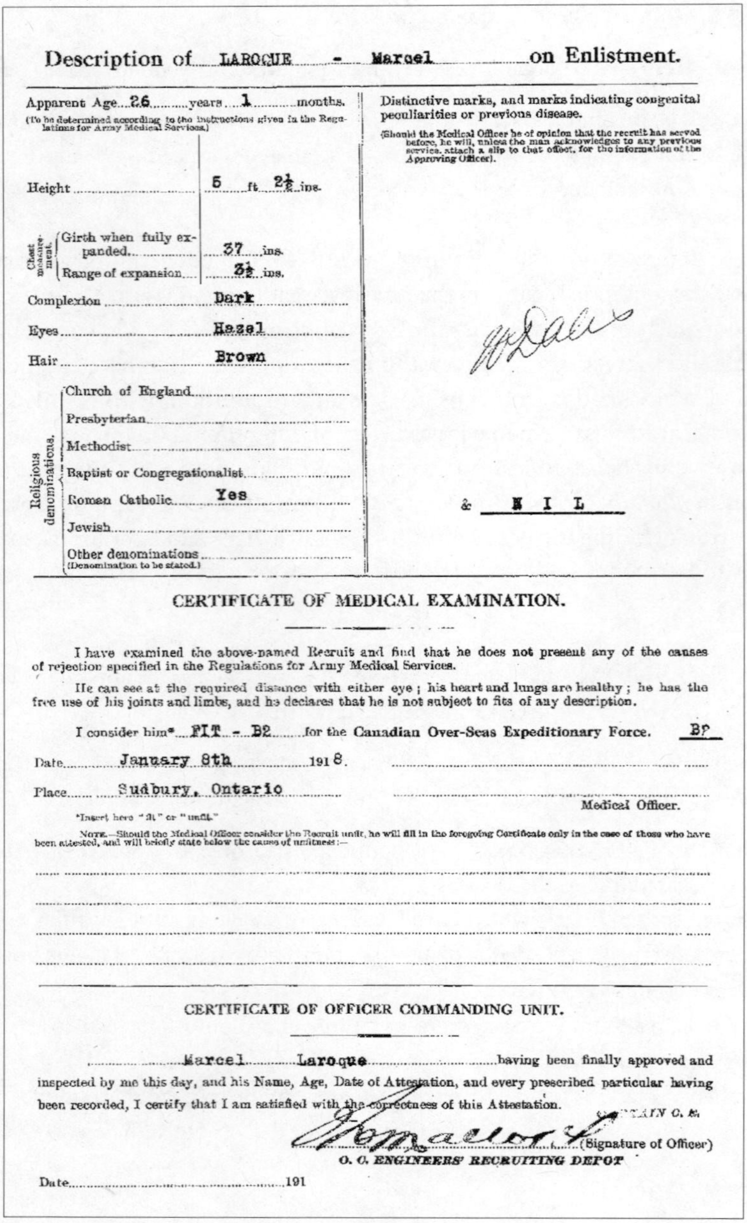

Description of __LAROQUE__ - __Marcel__ on Enlistment.

Apparent Age __26__ years __1__ months.
(To be determined according to the instructions given in the Regulations for Army Medical Service.)

Distinctive marks, and marks indicating congenital peculiarities or previous disease.
(Should the Medical Officer be of opinion that the recruit has served before, he will, unless the man acknowledges to any previous service, attach a slip to that effect, for the information of the Approving Officer).

Height __5__ ft __2½__ ins.

Chest measurement.
Girth when fully expanded __37__ ins.
Range of expansion __2½__ ins.

Complexion __Dark__

Eyes __Hazel__

Hair __Brown__

Religious denominations.
Church of England ....
Presbyterian ....
Methodist ....
Baptist or Congregationalist ....
Roman Catholic __Yes__
Jewish ....
Other denominations ....
(Denomination to be stated.)

& __N I L__

CERTIFICATE OF MEDICAL EXAMINATION.

I have examined the above-named Recruit and find that he does not present any of the causes of rejection specified in the Regulations for Army Medical Services.

He can see at the required distance with either eye ; his heart and lungs are healthy ; he has the free use of his joints and limbs, and he declares that he is not subject to fits of any description.

I consider him* __FIT - B2__ for the Canadian Over-Seas Expeditionary Force. __B?__

Date __January 8th__ 191 8.

Place __Sudbury, Ontario__

Medical Officer.

*Insert here "fit" or "unfit."

NOTE.—Should the Medical Officer consider the Recruit unfit, he will fill in the foregoing Certificate only in the case of those who have been attested, and will briefly state below the cause of unfitness :—

CERTIFICATE OF OFFICER COMMANDING UNIT.

__Marcel__ __Laroque__ having been finally approved and inspected by me this day, and his Name, Age, Date of Attestation, and every prescribed particular having been recorded, I certify that I am satisfied with the correctness of this Attestation.

CAPTAIN O. &.

(Signature of Officer)

O. C. ENGINEERS' RECRUITING DEPOT

Date __191__

FIGURE 1 The attestation paper of Marcel Laroque indicating that he had been graded as B2, "able to stand service conditions in the line of communications in France." *Library and Archives Canada/Ministry of the Overseas Military Forces of Canada Fonds/RG 150, Acc. 1992–93/166, Box 5411-57.*

The classification system used in Canada was based on a British system that had been introduced in 1916. There were minor differences between the two systems in the A and C categories, and major differences in the B and D categories. Unlike the British system, which had three classifications in its B and D categories, the Canadian system had only one classification in those categories (B2 and D3, respectively). This change was made to limit the number of unfit men sent overseas by the Canadian forces. Men who would have been classified as B1 (fit for garrison duty abroad) or B3 (fit for sedentary work abroad) under the British system were placed in Canadian C1 and C3 categories, respectively. The British D1 (temporarily unfit, in command depot), D2 (temporarily unfit, in regimental depot), and D3 (in any unit or depot under or awaiting medical or dental treatment) categories were all rolled into the Canadian D3 category.[64]

The 1916 British classification system had itself evolved from earlier systems. The first of those systems had been introduced along with centralized medical boards in March 1915 as a means of ensuring uniformity in standards of selection among reinforcement drafts. Initially these medical boards, which consisted of two or three members of the Royal Army Medical Corps, were to place groups in four categories: A, fit for service at home or abroad; B, temporarily unfit for service abroad; C, fit for service at home only; and D, unfit for service at home or abroad. The system was reformed that December after it became evident that it was not producing the desired uniformity. Classification of men became far more detailed, with five categories and four subcategories of fitness: 1, Fit for general service; 2, fit for field service at home; 3(a), fit for garrison service abroad; 3(b), fit for garrison service at home; 4(a), fit for labour, such as roadmaking, entrenching, and other works; 4(b), fit for sedentary work only, such as clerical work; 5, unfit for any military service. This system was superseded in 1916 by the alphanumeric classification system that would be modified for Canada in May 1917.[65]

While the Canadian military authorities used a modified version of the British alphanumeric system in Canada, the Overseas Military Forces of Canada retained the use of the British system. Besides the fact that the latter was under the command of the Imperial military authorities, it used such classifications in a different way from the Canadian forces within Canada. The Overseas Military Forces authorities' concern was twofold: that only those fit for overseas service were shipped to Europe, and also that as many men as possible were made fit for the trenches (Category A1) as quickly as possible. Officers were told that all men arriving in drafts from Canada were either Category A2 (men who had not been overseas previously and who would be fit for A1 once trained) or Category A4 (men under the age of nineteen who would be fit for A1 or A2 once they turned nineteen), or temporarily unfit due to illness or dental problems, in which case they were to be classified as D3 (awaiting medical or dental treatment and would join their original category once treated).[66] In other words, officers were to make sure the new troops got the training and medical attention they needed so they would be ready to serve at the front.

Besides ensuring the newly arrived troops' rapid preparation for the front, the Overseas Military Forces of Canada also used the classification system to categorize the fitness of soldiers leaving hospitals after being wounded or otherwise incapacitated. Officers were provided with instruction on how men leaving hospitals should be categorized, and also – if they were not to be discharged as unfit for further service – where they should be stationed once they had received their alphanumeric designation: the frontlines, lines of communication, or support positions in England or Canada. As will be further discussed in Chapter 2, the Canadian military's employment of these classification systems was part of an attempt to ensure that the Canadian Expeditionary Force's manpower reserves were utilized effectively.[67]

In November 1917, Overseas Military Forces of Canada altered its system of classification for Canadian troops serving in Europe. Ultimately titled *Classification of Men by Categories in the British Isles,* the revised system abolished the distinction between Categories B and C, and in doing so promoted men categorized as C1, C2, and C3 to the corresponding subdivisions in Category B. This move, it was stated, was designed to simplify the administration of Overseas Military Forces personnel.[68] In particular, it acknowledged the fact that Category C men (fit for service at home only) did not, by their very classification, meet the requirements of the Overseas Military Forces. It can also be argued that the incorporation of Category C into Category B was a means of disguising the fact that a large number of men serving overseas should not have been there, according to the military's own standards. Although there was some discussion about adopting the *Classification of Men by Categories in the British Isles* in Canada, the idea was eventually rejected.

The rejection of the categories used to classify Canadian troops in the British Isles for use in Canada turned primarily on a question of utility. In a 24 November 1917 memorandum discussing its proposed implementation in Canada, Colonel J.L. Potter, Acting Deputy Director General Medical Services,[69] noted two advantages of retaining the *Classification of Men by Categories in Canada*: (1) civilian and military medical examiners in Canada were familiar with the system; and (2) if it became necessary under the Military Service Act, 1917 to call up men lower than Category A, only those fit for service abroad in units under Category B, and not lower categories, would need to present themselves. This would, Potter stated, save considerable expense and time as medical boards would not have to re-examine men who had already been classified as unfit for overseas service.[70] Potter also noted that adoption of the categories used in the British Isles in Canada would significantly increase the work of medical boards if it became necessary to call up men lower than Category A: because the *Categories in Britain*'s Category B combined the *Categories in Canada*'s B and C categories, if the former's Category B men were to be called up in Canada, a "very great number" of them would be found unfit for overseas service.[71]

Determining whether a recruit was fit for the trenches was thus both an empirical and interpretative process. Many of the minimum physical standards gave medical officers little interpretative leeway. At least on paper, the medical examination wore the mantle of science. A supposedly impartial examiner followed strict methodological guidelines in order to judge an individual's fitness for service in relation to fixed, measurable standards.[72]

Other areas of inquiry gave the medical officer considerable discretion, however. Judgments on whether a recruit met the minimum standards of intelligence, was likely to make an efficient soldier, or had the right moral fibre to be a soldier were often founded on a medical officer's subjective opinion rather than strict objective analysis. Nor was such subjectivity limited to character judgments. For example, determining whether a man with bad teeth was robust enough to serve in spite of his dental deficiencies was a subjective exercise where medical officers had considerable interpretative leeway. Much the same can be said of the requirement that medical officers estimate a recruit's age based on his physical characteristics.

Such subjective decision making would not have been problematic if, in the majority of cases at least, medical officers' decisions to accept or reject individual recruits were regularly sustained during later examinations by their peers and superiors. If successive medical officers had regularly come to the same conclusion when making subjective judgments about a recruit's fitness or unfitness to serve, then the subjective process would have been, for all intents and purposes, an objective one – that is, even in cases where detailed guidelines or exact requirements did not exist, there would have been a fixed, if unwritten, understanding of what characteristics made an individual fit to fight. As we shall see in Chapter 3, however, this was not the case. Large numbers of unfit men were regularly culled from the ranks during medical examinations in Canada and Britain after having been passed by their initial examiners – in many cases due to characteristics that had called for the initial medical officers' subjective judgment.

Admittedly, other factors, including political interference and an inadequate examination infrastructure, also led to unfit men being judged fit to serve. However, the fact that medical officers' interpretative flexibility was increasingly curtailed as the war continued highlights the military authorities' growing concern over allowing them to make subjective judgments about recruits' fitness to serve.

To be sure, not all avenues for subjective judgment were closed off in the later years of the war. Deciding whether a recruit was sufficiently intelligent to serve remained entirely in the hands of the examining medical officer. Like the British *Instructions for the Physical Examination of Recruits* of 1914 on which they were based, the Canadian *Physical Standards and Instructions for the Medical Examination of Recruits for the Canadian Expeditionary Force and for the Active Militia of Canada* of 1917 and 1918 demanded only that recruits be of "sufficient intelligence," without actually providing any indication of what constituted sufficient intelligence. Nor did the increasingly detailed regulations straitjacket those medical officers who, for whatever reason, were determined to pass an individual as fit for service. Nonetheless, by the end of the conflict the Canadian military's definition of military fitness, at least when it came to physical characteristics, was considerably more regimented than in the summer of 1914. It was also significantly more complex. By 1918, Canadian medical officers were no longer using a simple dichotomous classification system where men were labelled as either fit or unfit to serve, but rather a graduated scale that contained either ten (*Classification of Men by Categories in Canada*) or nine (*Classification of Men by Categories in Britain*) levels of military fitness ranging from men deemed fit to fight in the trenches to those deemed unfit to don the khaki.

The evolution of the medical examination and the development of the classification systems are important not only because they delineated the concept of military fitness but also because they reflected the change in how the Canadian military viewed the concept over the course of the Great War. The manpower shortages experienced by the Canadian Expeditionary Force led military authorities to progressively reduce the standards of military fitness for frontline combat personnel, and to focus on utilizing the force's manpower resources as efficiently as possible. As a result, many men rejected at Valcartier in 1914 were later deemed fit for the trenches. Perhaps most importantly, being deemed unfit for the trenches did not necessarily mean that one was also considered unfit to serve.

2

No Longer Cause for Rejection

FEW OF THE PHYSICAL and medical standards set by the Canadian authorities at the start of the Great War survived the conflict unscathed. The two most obvious trends were the lowering of minimum physical standards required for service in the infantry, and the concurrent development of different, often even lower, physical standards for support units. At the core, this evolution was driven by manpower shortages. Faced with the constant need to replenish combat battalions that were hemorrhaging men at an alarming rate, while simultaneously trying to meet its government's increasingly extravagant manpower commitments, the Canadian military was forced to cast its nets ever wider in search of men to fill its ranks. Redefining the Canadian Expeditionary Force's standards of military fitness was a means to this end: as the minimum physical standards required of recruits dropped, the pool of men eligible for service grew. For example, it was estimated in early 1916 that if the minimum height requirement for infantry was reduced from 5 feet, 2 inches to 5 feet, approximately 17,000 more men could be recruited for the 2nd Division alone.[1] While such an estimate was probably overly optimistic, not least because it assumed that all of these men would want to serve, it did point to the fact that the Canadian Expeditionary Force's own physical requirements made up one of its main obstacles in attempting to fill its ranks.[2]

Ultimately, however, these measures did not eliminate the need to pursue conscription in order to meet the force's manpower requirements. A passive means of opening up manpower resources, they were still dependent on the willingness of men to serve. Changes in physical standards opened the door but did not push men through it. This was important because a significant number of eligible Canadian men of military age (eighteen to forty-five years) had little or no enthusiasm for the war. Many French Canadians, recent non-British immigrants, farmers, and some religious communities all exhibited, at the very least, a marked unwillingness to enlist. Even among those segments of the population that supported the war, enlistment relied on men's individual consciences and circumstances. Given these realities, the size of Canada's pre-conscription contribution to the Allied war effort – more than half a million men – reflected an astounding level of commitment from a polity with a population of just over 7 million. Even such commitment had its limits, however, and recruiting fell steadily from late 1915 onward, despite the lowering of medical standards.[3]

In August 1914, the Canadian government committed to sending a single division of 25,000 men to defend the Empire.[4] This commitment increased before the First Contingent even sailed. With recruiting exceeding all requirements and an enthusiastic Sam Hughes unwilling to turn away any man deemed fit to serve, the First Contingent sailed for England on 3 October 1914, approximately 31,000 strong.[5] Authorized a mere four days after the departure of the First Contingent, the Second Contingent added another 20,000 men to the Canadian Expeditionary Force. By the end of 1914, the force had enlisted 56,585 men, and the number kept growing, exceeding 100,000 by the time the Second Contingent was dispatched to England in April 1915.[6] The Dominion government increased Canada's commitment to 150,000 men in June and 250,000 in November. On January 1, 1916, Prime Minister Sir Robert Borden announced that Canadian Expeditionary Force would be increased to half a million men.[7]

Keen to demonstrate both Canada's loyalty to the Empire and her nascent power,[8] the Dominion government placed considerable pressure on military authorities with its promise to field 250,000 men – let alone 500,000 – in uniform. Although half a million men – one-sixteenth of Canada's population in 1914 – were accepted for service before the imposition of conscription in late 1917, many of them were needed to reinforce the units Canada had already committed to the fight.[9] Such needs were not insignificant. Referencing British statistics, Major-General Willoughby Gwatkin, Canada's Chief of the General Staff at the start of the war, warned his civilian masters that a division would require 15,000 to 20,000 men a year to replace losses incurred through battlefield casualties, sickness, accidents, desertion, and the like. Gwatkin estimated that the largest force Canada might comfortably support – especially if the war was a long one – was three divisions. Canada would ultimately place four divisions in the field.[10] Requiring approximately 75,000 reinforcements a year (around 6,250 men a month), Canada faced considerable difficulty keeping these formations at fighting strength from the autumn of 1916 onward.[11] In January 1918, two years after Borden's promise of a half-million-man army, the Canadian Expeditionary Force in France was 140,000 strong. Since the start of the war it had suffered approximately 150,000 casualties, 41 percent of them (61,000) by the end of 1916.[12]

Although the main motivation for reconsidering the physical and medical requirements came to be the incessant demand for men, the first moves to modify the standards occurred even before the force had experienced serious combat losses or indeed a manpower crisis.[13] By this time, however, the realities of the war in which Canada was embroiled had already become readily apparent.[14]

In late 1914, Canadian military authorities took steps to eliminate the possession of dentures or teeth of questionable value as a reason to reject men for service in the Expeditionary Force.[15] Militia Order 162 of 29 March 1915 authorized the temporary appointment of dental surgeons to the Second Contingent to ensure that its members' teeth were in proper condition before they embarked for England. The order also directed that dental surgeons be attached to the overseas forces.[16] Less than a month later, on 26 April, the Canadian Army Dental Corps was established.[17]

By mid-1915, medical examiners and recruiting officers were informed that defective teeth, "so long as they did not seriously impair the man's general physical condition," were no longer grounds for rejection. The possession of dentures, partial or full, were likewise no longer considered a disqualifying characteristic. Rather, men identified as requiring dental work were to be flagged "for the attention of the Dental Corps" on their recruiting documents and sent for treatment as soon as possible after their arrival in training camp. Thus, men rejected due to their teeth in 1914 were now not only considered fit but also provided with free dental care.[18] One should not overstate the level of this care, however. Twenty-two-year-old Bill Michaud's initial examination for the 21st Canadian Infantry Battalion found him fit except for one bad tooth. The offending tooth was removed by an apprentice dentist without the benefit of anesthetic as Michaud sat on a kitchen chair in front of a sink. In Michaud's words, the procedure hurt "one hell of a lot."[19] Likewise, well-known Nova Scotia journalist and essayist Will R. Bird also experienced painkiller-free pliers therapy to ensure his fitness for the trenches.[20]

Disease of the gums remained a potential reason for rejection, with medical officers being directed to take care "that there is no disease of the gums, which might render a man unfit," albeit without any instructions as to which diseases of the gums might cause a man to be unfit. The medical officers were left to their own devices in deciding when a man's decayed dental assets seriously impaired his health.[21]

No reason was given for the military's change in policy regarding recruits' teeth. However, it would be reasonable to believe that it was at least partially motivated by the vast numbers of otherwise fit men that the military was obliged to turn away because of their teeth. The Canadian Expeditionary Force was not yet facing a manpower crisis, but turning away so many volunteers must have been cause for concern. In this sense, the force's dental requirements were a reaction not only to the realities of the battlefield but also to the realities of the dental health of many Canadians. In an age when many Canadians had less than pearly white teeth, if they still had their teeth at all, the military had to adapt its dental standards if it wanted to secure needed manpower. However, it could not simply accept men with rotten teeth or no teeth at all. A man who could not eat military rations was of no use as a soldier. Thus, the military was obliged to repair its would-be warriors before placing them in the field.

More changes followed. In July 1915, less than three months after the 1st Canadian Division suffered horrific casualties in the Second Battle of Ypres,[22] the military authorities lowered the Expeditionary Force's minimum height requirements and adjusted its chest measurement standards. Infantrymen were now required to be 5 feet, 2 inches instead of 5 feet, 3 inches, while the minimum height for artillerymen dropped 3 inches, to 5 feet, 4 inches. The minimum chest measurement for recruits between eighteen and thirty years of age went down half an inch to 33 inches, while recruits between thirty and forty-five years of age were required to have at least a 34-inch expanded chest.[23] The alterations in chest measurements reflected prewar British standards and reflected the belief that men did not reach their full bulk until approximately thirty years of age. These chest measurement requirements remained unchanged for the rest of the war.[24]

The same cannot be said of other physical requirements, however. In late 1915 and again in early 1916, the Canadian military authorized the formation of two infantry battalions for undersized men in Canada. Called bantam battalions, the 143rd (British Columbia) Overseas Battalion and the 216th (Toronto) Canadian Infantry Battalion were modelled after similar units in the United Kingdom. After an initial suggestion of 4 feet, 10 inches, the minimum height requirement for these units was set at 5 feet, 1.5 inches, while a recruit's expanded chest had to reach at least 30 inches. To prevent boys – whose physical immaturity barred them from meeting the height and chest requirements of "normal units" – from enlisting, the minimum age was raised to twenty-two years.[25] Evidence suggests that these regulations were not strictly enforced. Lieutenant-Colonel Frank Lindsay Burton, the commander of the 216th Battalion – unofficially, and much to the chagrin of the military authorities, known as Burton's Bantam Battalion – had to be reminded at least once to ensure that his recruits met the minimum standards mandated for his unit.[26] By 1917, an infantryman would need to only be 5 feet tall, while support battalions such as the Canadian Army Medical Corps, the Canadian Army Service Corps, and the Canadian Army Dental Corps accepted those who stood 4 feet, 11 inches.[27]

In November 1915, Canadian visual acuity standards were also lowered. Recruits would now be considered fit if they had a visual acuity of 20/60 in each eye, or 20/20 in their right eye and no less than 20/80 in the left eye. Glasses were still not allowed.[28] In August 1916, the requirements were relaxed further.

Recruits would be accepted as fit if they had 20/80 vision in each eye without glasses, or 20/80 vision in the right eye and no less than 20/200 vision in the left eye. The Adjutant General's letter announcing this change in standards concluded: "Those rejected under the old standard for defective vision should be encouraged to present themselves for re-examination and possible enlistment under these reduced standards."[29]

When the physical standards for recruits were published in 1917, visual acuity requirements were specified in four standards. Men who met standards I to III were considered fit for combat, while those who met the fourth standard were considered fit to serve in support units. More importantly, while the base standard of the test was the acuity of a recruit's vision without glasses, the regulations not only stated that a recruit should be provided with glasses if they would improve his vision but also had a category for men with glasses. Standard III stated that if a man had 20/80 vision in one eye without glasses, and his right eye could be brought up to 20/40 with glasses, he was to be considered fit for service.[30]

As with the earlier provision of dentures and dental care, by allowing recruits to use glasses to reach the minimum standards of visual acuity, and by supplying spectacles to men who needed them, the military was tacitly acknowledging that in order to meet its manpower requirements, it would need to repair some of those who volunteered for service.

Such thinking extended to flat feet and related conditions that had previously led to rejection or discharge on the grounds of military unfitness. In May 1917, medical officers were informed that some forms of flat feet were curable either with hospital treatment or through the provision of corrective boots. Indeed, they were told that in some cases treatment could bring an afflicted individual up to Category A fitness, while many more could be raised to Category B2.[31] It is difficult to gauge how this directive, which was aimed at enlisted men – both soldiers still in basic training in Canada (i.e., those who had not yet undergone their final examination before being shipped to Europe) and those serving in the trenches – influenced medical examinations at the recruitment level. The 1917 and 1918 editions of the *Physical Standards and Instructions for the Medical Examination of Recruits for the Canadian Expeditionary Force and for the Active Militia of Canada* still directed medical examiners to ensure that a recruit had "well formed" feet and toes and to look for "extreme flatness of feet" when conducting the preliminary examination.[32] Nonetheless, given that both the diagnosis and debility resulting from this condition were strongly debated,[33] and given that the military authorities allowed corrective measures, it is reasonable to think that at least some medical officers passed men they would have rejected in 1914.

While the military accepted that it would need to repair some recruits to ensure that they reached the minimum requirements of service, such acceptance had its limits, especially when it came to surgery. Medical officers were repeatedly told that they were not to pass men suffering from hernias, varicocele, or varicose veins with the idea that such impairments would be corrected by surgery after enlistment. The reasoning was simple. The provision of dental care, including dentures, and glasses to troops involved relatively non-invasive corrective measures with both high rates of success and almost instant results. Surgery was quite different. Operations were not always successful, and could exacerbate the condition or, on rare occasions, even prove fatal. For example, both Alfred Mepham and Arthur Royal's varicose veins got worse, not better, after the men underwent operations intended to correct their impairments.[34] Even if the operation was a success, the recruit would still be unfit for active service for an extended period as he convalesced. The projected returns were not worth the expense.[35]

Just as the military authorities were not prepared to repair all sorts of impairments in order to fill the ranks of the Canadian Expeditionary Force, they were unwilling to allow all standards to decline. In the same year that the minimum height for infantry was lowered to 5 feet, the standards for artillerymen went up. Gunners in garrison, heavy, and siege artillery once again had to be 5 feet, 7 inches, while gunners in horse and field artillery had to be at least 5 feet, 6 inches.[36] In addition, men enlisting in the siege and heavy artillery had to be physically strong and capable of lifting heavy weights[37] – with some shells weighing hundreds of pounds, the heavy artillery was no place for weaklings. Even so, artillery standards were nowhere near as exacting as those of the nascent Royal Flying Corps, whose minimum physical standards for potential recruits far exceeded those found in any other branch of the military. Besides all the ordinary physical standards for recruits, potential pilots had to meet a number of higher standards with regard to vision, hearing, and cardiorespiratory fitness, and they could not be over twenty-five years of age.[38] There were no exceptions, not even the traditional ones for commissioned men. On 20 October 1916, Major-General W.E. Hodgins, Acting Adjutant General of the Canadian Militia, pointedly stated in a letter about the standards of physical fitness required of candidates for the Royal Flying Corps that "none of the relaxations allowed in the case of candidates for commissions in other branches of the service will be permitted in the case of candidates for commission in the Royal Flying Corps."[39]

Although potential pilots had to meet higher physical standards than those volunteering for any other branch of the service, the men who kept their planes airworthy did not. In fact, the physical standards for airplane mechanics were not as high as those for common infantrymen. This was due to the nature of their job, explained Lieutenant-Colonel E.C. Hoare, Officer Commanding (OC)

Imperial Royal Flying Corps Canada: "Air mechanics were not required to make long route marches or undergo severe physical stress and for this reason many minor physical disabilities which would prevent a man from being fit for the infantry would not be sufficient to cause them to be rejected for the Royal Flying Corps." In other words, men deemed unfit for the trenches might still be fit to serve as airplane mechanics.[40] However, a recruit had to have the skills needed to be an air mechanic and his "physical disabilities [would not] prevent him [from] working at this trade."[41]

Nor was airplane mechanic the only position within the Canadian Expeditionary Force that could be filled by men whose physical attributes fell below those required of the common infantryman. When the force lowered its visual acuity standards in late 1915, the new regulation listed the services open to men who failed to meet the minimum requirements for combat soldiers:

If he [the recruit] can read D=20 at twenty feet with left eye, without glasses and not less than D=120 with the right eye, at the same distance, without glasses, he will be considered "fit" for the Canadian Army Service Corps, the Canadian Army Medical Corps, the Canadian Ordnance Corps, or for forestry battalions, or for position as driver in the Canadian Artillery or Canadian Engineers.[42]

When vision standards were again reduced in August 1916, these requirements were also lowered. Men with no less than 20/80 vision in their left eye and 20/200 vision in their right eye were now considered fit to serve in support units.[43]

These support units also accepted men up to the age of forty-eight, provided they had the required skills. In late January 1917, the standards were lowered even more. Not only men standing 4 feet, 11 inches were considered acceptable, but also men deaf in one ear and men with limited eyesight, including those blind in one eye. Men who were missing fingers and toes were also acceptable, as long as those who had lost toes retained their great toes and those with missing fingers were still capable of manual labour. Men with moderately flat feet were also acceptable.[44] In 1918, these standards were further redefined for forestry battalions and railway construction battalions.

In the case of forestry battalions, men had to have, first and foremost, "bush and mill experience" as a general hand, a log maker, an axe man, or a teamster. They also had to be "able to perform a full day's work of 10 hours." Certain individuals were listed for automatic rejection: those subject to rheumatism and those accustomed only to indoor work.[45]

There were similar requirements for men interested in joining railway construction battalions. Men below Category A could be accepted provided they were "specially qualified" and could work a ten-hour day. No men over forty-three years were to be accepted. Because of the heavy labour involved in railway construction, recruits had to be of "as large frame and strong physique as possible." Underlining the heavy physical demands placed on members of railway construction battalions, and the trying conditions under which they often operated, the regulations noted that even some men in Category A lacked the physical development and constitution to serve in these units. Equally high standards were set for a recruit's vision. No one was to be accepted if his visual acuity fell below that required of frontline troops, and moderate flat feet were acceptable only if a recruit could march five miles. All in all, these regulations required men in railway construction battalions to be practically as fit as those in combat battalions.[46]

Home defence forces were also allowed to recruit men who did not meet the physical standards laid down for an infantryman. Indeed, they were encouraged to recruit such men so that fit men within their ranks could be sent to the trenches. Men rejected for combat service due to an impairment might be accepted into one of these units as long as it did not prevent them from carrying out their duties and those duties were not likely to aggravate the impairment. Furthermore, the impairment could not be epilepsy, insanity, or tuberculosis.[47] The use of men with minor impairments that barred them from frontline service was taken a step further in July 1916. Battalion commanders were informed that "members of the Canadian Expeditionary Force of good character who suffer[ed] from minor disabilities, [were] not to be discharged." Rather, they were to be placed in special companies and employed as military police, guards, and clerks. Battalions were also allowed to enlist suitable candidates directly into such companies, which would form the basis of "a [CEF] special services battalion."[48]

Such changes were an official recognition of what had been occurring in England since the arrival of the First Contingent in late 1914. Rather than shipping all men found to be unfit for combat back to Canada for discharge, the Overseas Military Forces of Canada had put them to work in support positions; indeed, by 1916 some 50 percent of men on base duty in England had never been to the Front.[49] Defending permanent base depot men against charges of cowardice, Peter F. Pirie of the 21st Canadian Infantry Battalion noted that "some of the depot men were of low physical category and would not be sent out on active service in any case."[50]

Pirie's observations certainly applied to fifty-three-year-old William Henry Butler. Passed as fit to serve in Cobourg, Ontario, in December 1914, he was deemed unfit for the trenches soon after arrival in England and was placed on permanent base duty. It is not hard to understand why. Besides being overage, Butler suffered from a heart condition, arteriosclerosis, poor vision, poor hearing, and fainting spells, which should have caused him to be rejected as unfit in Canada.[51] Likewise, thirty-one-year-old Arthur Morris, who was suffering from the debilitating aftereffects of a twice-fractured left thigh, was placed on base duty between his frequent visits to hospital.[52] Some men's impairments made them unsuitable even for base duty, however. For example, a depressed fracture in the skull of Michael Ross, a shoemaker from British Columbia, caused him to suffer from incessant, periodically debilitating headaches, and Frederick Jackson's gastritis made him "no good as a soldier or even as a light duty man."[53]

The assignment of "unfit" men to support positions and the subsequent development of support units whose physical requirements were different from those of the infantry reflect the military authorities' realization that such individuals, although not necessarily fit to fight, could play an important role in the war effort. This was most clearly seen in the implementation of the *Classification of Men by Categories in Canada* and *Classification of Men by Categories in Britain*. Both classification systems were part of the Canadian military's attempts to offset the increasingly severe manpower shortage by using its manpower resources as efficiently as possible. Indeed, the *Classification of Men by Categories in Canada* noted that in addition to ensuring that unfit men did not proceed overseas, sorting men into categories enabled the military to "utilize available material to the best purpose." It further instructed medical officers to "carefully consider the raising and lowering of men in categories so that the best use may be made of men according to their physical and mental qualifications."[54] This system enabled commanders to place their men where they would best serve the struggle, and made certain that individuals deemed unfit for the trenches were not lost outright to the military.

As the manpower situation grew increasingly dire, the military authorities were greatly concerned that the services of men deemed unfit for the infantry and artillery were being lost to the Canadian Expeditionary Force. Thus, in January 1917, almost half a year before the *Classification of Men by Categories in Canada* was implemented, the office of the Adjutant General of the Canadian Militia informed all Military Districts that recruits found physically unfit for combat should be strongly encouraged to enlist in units with lower physical standards:[55]

Numerous cases have been reported where men have been lost to the service owing to the fact that, although they do not come up to the physical standard required for Artillery or Infantry Units, yet they would be eligible for service with units requiring lower physical qualifications.

If such men offer their services, instead of being turned down, full particulars should be taken in each case, and sent to this office.[56]

Lieutenant-Colonel Robert A. Robertson, the Chief Recruiting Officer for Hamilton, responded to the Assistant Adjutant General for Military District 2 that every man rejected in Hamilton was "urged to join some other branch of the Service, if he is considered fit in the least degree." He went on to note that "I can assure you that it is hard to find a place for the average of the men that are applying now," and promised to send weekly reports of rejections from his depot forthwith.[57] Many others also began providing lists of individuals found unfit for service, and after the *Classification of Men by Categories in Canada* was introduced, such lists also included the men's alphanumeric designations.[58]

Not all of Robertson's colleagues were so accommodating, however. On 22 March 1917, the Militia Council instructed the Military Districts to remind all infantry and artillery recruiting officers that men who did not meet the physical standards required for the infantry or artillery should be attested into units with lower standards. Indicative of the recruiting officers' power as the military's gatekeepers, the instruction was deemed necessary because many officers had simply turned away men who did not meet the requirements of their branch of the service, instead of directing them to units with lower standards.[59] Two days later, another letter provided similar instructions regarding men already enlisted in combat units. Enlisted men found to be below the standards required for combat service in Europe were to be transferred to a forestry or construction depot or unit if they were fit for such service.[60]

At least some individuals who volunteered to serve in the infantry abjectly refused to serve in units with lower physical requirements when they were told that their impairments disqualified them from their chosen area of service. George Godwin's semi-fictional Stephen Craig declined his medical examiner's advice to consider joining the Canadian Army Service Corps in 1914 after he was deemed unfit for the infantry due to a "bum shooting eye."[61] Craig later gained a commission in the 29th Canadian Infantry Battalion – Vancouver's famed Tobin's Tigers. One factor that made men turn their backs on such forms of service was the perception that such units were lesser battalions manned by lesser men. Few men volunteering for combat wanted to serve in a "lesser" position that would, implicitly at least, single them out as inferior specimens of Canadian manhood – such units were the home of the physically unfit, men who were not able to play a manly part in the war. Such beliefs, it should be noted, were at best unfair. The work conducted by forestry, railway, and tunnelling battalions was physically punishing and not necessarily safe. Railway and tunnelling battalions often operated close to the frontlines and were regularly within range of enemy artillery and snipers. Moreover, Canadian tunnellers battled their German counterparts at close quarters well below the surface.[62]

The same was true of the Canadian Army Medical Corps and the Canadian Army Service Corps.

Canadian military authorities also modified fitness requirements to mitigate the loss of experienced troops to wounds or ill-health. While men who suffered devastating wounds such as the loss of a limb or fell victim to chronic illnesses such as TB were discharged, those with less debilitating injuries were increasingly returned to service, even if their injuries resulted in impairments that would have disqualified them as unfit at recruiting stations. For example, in March 1916 the Canadian Expeditionary Force's Director of Medical Services decreed that men who had lost an eye in active service but were otherwise fit should, upon recovery from their injuries, be returned as fit for general service. This rule, it was stressed, did not apply to new recruits.[63] Three months later, the visual acuity requirements were further modified for "men [who] had been issued uniforms and have had the benefit of more or less extended periods of training":

1. A soldier will not be discharged for defective vision unless the defective vision is due to:

    (a) Squint.
    (b) Some morbid condition of the eyes or lids of either eye, liable to aggravation or recurrence.
    (c) Any defect such as cannot be corrected, by the aid of glasses, up to the standard required for recruits on enlistment.

2. Where the defect can be corrected by the aid of glasses, these may be provided, and will be replaced where necessary at the public expense, provided that loss or breakage has not been due to negligence.[64]

Although this further modification was intended to bring already accepted recruits to the required level of visual acuity for combat infantry (which in itself must be seen as a tacit acknowledgment that many troops in the ranks had substandard vision), men retained in this manner were not necessarily returned to the firing line. As indicated by the 1918 *Physical Standards and Instructions for the Medical Examination of Recruits for the Canadian Expeditionary Force and for the Active Militia of Canada*, most soldiers who lost vision in one eye were placed in rear-echelon positions after recovering from their injuries:

Soldiers who have lost one eye but with 20/60 (6/18) or better in the other eye if such loss is due to the removal of the eye or serious injury should be placed in

Category "C" for at least four months from convalescence and might then be transferred to Category "B" and in exceptional cases to Category "A" ...[65]

In this instance, "exceptional cases" referred to men who were considered to have special training. The pendulum also swung in the opposite direction. In October 1917, the Assistant Inspector of Drafts and Dentistry in Etaples informed the Director of Medical Services that few soldiers who had suffered injuries that destroyed an eye or caused it to be enucleated (removed) were sent into forward positions. This was because, he explained, of "the difficulty in keeping the [empty eye] socket in a healthy condition and in procuring glass eyes for such cases in France."[66]

Besides men who had suffered eye injuries, by early 1917 those who had been placed in Categories B or C after being discharged from hospital were retained for service in the Canadian Army Service Corps, other support units, or training positions. Sergeant Edward Baxter was one such individual. At the Somme in September 1916, the thirty-one-year-old suffered a shrapnel wound to the right shoulder that made it impossible for him to carry a pack without considerable pain. Such an impairment – which meant that the Saskatchewan native was unable to carry an infantryman's equipment – made Baxter unfit for frontline service. He was otherwise fit at the time of his discharge from hospital, however, and the medical board placed him in Category B2 (fit for service abroad, but not fit for general service). Baxter was duly transferred to Bramshott Military Camp, where he served as a musketry instructor until the end of the war.[67]

The policy of retaining Category B and C men for service in rear-echelon positions also enabled the Canadian military, in theory at least, to transfer the Category A class men employed in those positions into infantry battalions. The number of such Category A men was not, relatively speaking, insignificant. In April 1917, it was reported that a combined total of 2,132 Category A men were employed at the seven Canadian Army Service Corps depots in England, some of them for over two years.[68] A month earlier, the commanders of Service Corps units had been directed to reduce the number of Category A men in their formations to "the lowest minimum" and provide explanations for any Category A men they considered it necessary to retain.[69] In a May 1917 communiqué to the Service Corps' Director of Supplies and Transport, the Office of the Adjutant General, Overseas Military Forces of Canada, stressed that Category A men were to be sent to fighting units: "The demand for reinforcements for Infantry Units at present in the Field is so great that all men of this category, if available for transfer, should be sent to fighting units and not to non-combatant corps."[70]

Such directions were not accepted without complaint or criticism. The officer in command of more than one Service Corps depot noted that most of the

Category A men in their units possessed specialist skills that were rare in the general population; they feared that if they relinquished such men, they would be unable to replace them. More pointedly, Captain Robert G. Hargreaves, the commanding officer of the Canadian Army Service Corps's Seaford depot, decried the Service Corps as being "load[ed] down with all the lame and the blind," and noted that "a depot cannot be run efficiently with transport drivers or others who spend more days 'sick' in the lines than they do at work." His negative comments about Category B and C men were at least tempered by an acknowledgment that some of them were "all that could be desired."[71]

Hargreaves was equally critical of the transfer of men with specialist skills from Service Corps units in France to sedentary positions in England because their fitness category marked them as unfit for service in a combat zone. Referring to the case of Farrier Staff Sergeant Bowen, who had recently been reassigned as a clerk after being placed in Category B3,[72] Hargreaves lamented the loss of "one of the best Farrier Staff Sergeants in the service" because of "foolishness." He argued that such transfers based on fitness category ignored the fact that Bowen and others like him were quite capable of carrying out their duties without any "detriment whatever to ... [their] ... health" or any negative impact on the efficiency of Service Corps operations. Indeed, the loss of such valuable men as Bowen hindered the corps' successful prosecution of its mission.[73]

Hargreaves blamed the medical boards that were examining Service Corps men, arguing that the medical officers had erroneously conflated the infantry and Service Corps units with regard to the conditions they faced in the field. As a result, men whose physical characteristics made them unsuitable for combat units but did not hinder their successful performance in Service Corps units were being wrongly classified, in Hargreaves's opinion. "Provision should be made," he argued, "to have a board of MOs [medical officers] who are thoroughly conversant with the requirements of our Service ... [so that they may decide] ... whether a man is fit to carry on [in the Canadian Army Service Corps]."[74]

In fact, a number of medical officers, in both Canada and Britain, were taking service requirements into account when examining Service Corps recruits. Examination of these troops with an eye to transferring Category A men to combat units revealed that more than a few men in the corps did not meet the minimum physical requirements for infantry service. Indeed, rather than being Category A men, a significant number were found to be Category B or C.[75] It seems that medical officers had incorrectly classified them as Category A (fit for general service) knowing that, although not fit for service in combat units, they were fit for service in the Service Corps.[76] This problem, which resulted from a misunderstanding of how fitness categories were to be applied with regard to different units, persisted well into 1918.[77]

Linked to the problem of incorrect classification, if not born of it, was the tendency of some frontline medical examiners to ignore the classification system altogether. In October 1917, Captain R.H. Kerr, Senior Medical Officer, Canadian Railway Troops, noted that medical officers at Etaples paid little attention to the physical categories in which a recently arrived draft of railway construction troops had been placed before their arrival in France. Instead, the medical officers relied on their experience and knowledge of the conditions the men would face. As a result, almost 10 percent of the draft were rejected as unfit for service, despite being passed as fit for service as railway troops before they went to France.

Although Canadian classification systems recognized varying levels of fitness, the comments of officers such as Hargreaves and Kerr indicate that they were far from perfect tools for classifying men's ability to serve. Using combat fitness as a foundational category, these systems, when strictly enforced, caused some men to be barred from roles they could successfully fill, despite the lower physical requirements of some support units. Likewise, the privileging of an individual's fitness category rather than his skill set or experience could, as more than one Service Corps officer pointed out, cause support units to lose men who had rare skills. Most importantly, the success of these systems relied on the competence and cooperation of medical officers. Such reliance was generally well founded but was nonetheless an important and unavoidable weakness. Some medical officers misunderstood, misinterpreted, or, indeed, simply ignored the directives related to the classifications systems, as they did those related to medical examinations more generally.

Despite these problems, the introduction of fitness categories did, generally speaking, enable Canadian military authorities to husband their manpower resources in a much more efficient manner. Rather than simply being turned away, men deemed unfit for the front were directed into support positions where their skills, expertise, or simple muscle power could be used to aid the war effort. In turn, this allowed the Canadian military authorities to place Category A men where they were needed most – the frontlines – instead of holding some back in logistical positions. By 1918, Canadian medical officers were no longer using a simple dichotomous classification system that directed them to label men as either fit or unfit to serve. Rather, recruits were placed in positions for which they were deemed suitable based on their physical attributes and specialized skills. Thus, being unfit for the trenches no longer meant that one was unfit to serve.

Thus, the Great War both witnessed and contributed to a recalibration of the concept of military ability and inability on a number of levels. The most obvious recalibration took the form of repeated lowering of the physical standards for frontline service as the conflict continued. Minimum height and visual acuity requirements were reduced, the use of glasses and dentures by recruits was sanctioned, and some forms of flat feet were deemed acceptable. More widely, the development of different physical standards for different positions in the Canadian Expeditionary Force's ranks reflected a recognition of differing levels and classes of ability. The motivations for these changes were varied. Certainly, the almost constant demand for men pushed Canadian military authorities to develop a much more liberal definition of who was fit to serve and to utilize their manpower resources as efficiently as possible, but this was not the only factor. As we shall see in the following chapters, the lifting of the prohibition against enlisted men wearing glasses and the blanket ban on men thought to have flat feet owed as much to the realities of static industrialized warfare and changing medical opinion as to the need for more men.

3
An Imperfect System

ON 14 DECEMBER 1914, the Minister of Militia and Defence Sam Hughes received a letter from the well-known Canadian surgeon Dr. Frederic Starr.[1] The letter began by congratulating Hughes for his "splendid achievement of raising, training and equipping over 30,000 men for the First Contingent" of the Canadian Expeditionary Force. Starr felt the need, however, to pass on to the minister a serving colleague's concerns about the quality of the men whom Canada had sent in defence of the Empire. Far from being the best Canada breed, according to the doctor more than a few in the contingent fell well below the minimum standards required. Starr blamed this sorry state of affairs on the medical examiners in Canada, who he believed were not conducting medical examinations with the necessary rigidity:

> If you have any pull with the Militia authorities do impress on them the necessity of a more rigid examination of recruits. The number of "weeds" that have to be sent home is a crying disgrace to the regimental surgeons. To-day I found two old hernias and an epileptic. Almost everyday I have to advise one or more to be sent home.[2]

These comments were at the head of what quickly became a long and loud chorus deploring the physical state of some of the men disembarking in Britain from Canadian troopships even in 1914.

Such concerns were not groundless. Medical examinations of Canadian battalions arriving in England during the first two years of the war revealed that on average 5 to 15 percent of their men were unfit to serve.[3] Within individual battalions, the numbers of unfit men could occasionally reach seemingly epic proportions. When the 96th Canadian Infantry Battalion disembarked in England in October 1916, 43 percent (330 out of 770) of its enlisted men were found to be unfit. Within the next month, another three infantry battalions – the 131st, 139th, and 172nd – reached Albion's shores with over 30 percent of their men unfit for service.[4]

The majority of these men were found to be unfit because of their age (62 percent, with 38 percent underage and 24 percent overage) and others were rejected due to impairments sustained after enlistment, but it is clear that more than a few men should have failed the initial medical examination.[5] In a February 1916 letter, the Assistant Director Medical Services of Military District 13 told the regimental medical officers in his district that 15 to 20 percent of those who had recently been returned from England as unfit should never have been accepted. The majority of these cases, he stated, suffered from varicose veins, rheumatism, flat feet, and gonorrhea. He noted further that in the last week alone men had been discharged in the district due to "defective vision, gastric ulcers, paralysis, pthisis [tuberculosis], and endocarditis"[6] – all of which had been present at the time of enlistment. Similar figures were reported five months later in a letter from the Director of Recruiting and Organization of the Canadian Expeditionary Force, Colonel Frank A. Reid, to Major-General John Wallace Carson, who was Sam Hughes's special representative in Britain.[7] Carson forwarded the letter to Hughes, noting that "it shows a remarkable state of affairs and apparent carelessness on the part of our medical authorities in Canada ... I think it should be put right at the earliest possible moment."[8]

Except perhaps for paralysis, many of the pre-existing disqualifying conditions referenced by the Assistant Director Medical Services of Military District 13 and by Colonel Reid would probably have required a thorough medical examination in order to be detected, but this was certainly not true of all unfit individuals arriving in England as members of the Canadian Expeditionary Force. Many unfit men suffered from serious pre-enlistment physical and mental impairments that would have been glaringly obvious to even the most casual observer, such as amputated or deformed limbs and heavy limps. Eighteen-year-old Carl McPhee of Halifax, for example, could not "handle a rifle or do bayonet fighting" due to a childhood injury that had caused his left arm to atrophy to the size of that of a nine-year-old boy.[9] Cecil Hamilton, a twenty-four-year-old musician from Winnipeg, was in even worse shape: his right arm had been amputated six inches below the shoulder in 1910 as a result of a railway accident.[10] Nor were visible impairments restricted to the upper limbs. Among his many impairments, which included a purulent discharge from his right ear, Orilla, Ontario, native Melvin Malcolm noticeably dragged his right foot when walking and could neither march nor drill as a result.[11] Likewise, John Carment of the Canadian Army Medical Corps was "unable to walk properly or stand for any length of time" due to atrophied muscles in his right leg.[12]

Many more men had less obvious but equally disqualifying impairments that would have been quite apparent before they embarked for England.[13] Lance Corporal Edward Beech frequently vomited fresh blood and suffered extreme pain after eating (a condition that worsened when he consumed army rations), and had two large, tender scars on his abdomen from an appendectomy and a gastroenterostomy.[14] Quebec City native Alphonse Vachon suffered from continued headaches, insomnia, and periods of mental stupor resulting from a blow to the head he had received in 1911. The injury had left a two-inch-long hole in Vachon's skull, and the skin around the opening was very tender.[15] Henri Bonenfant had Dercum's disease (adiposis dolorosa), and as a result had numerous painful tumours on his forearms, thighs, legs, and abdomen ranging from the size of a pea to the size of a goose egg.[16] He also suffered from a slowly growing brain tumour that was affecting both his mental state and ability to speak.[17] Described as being affected with a "mental stupor," thirty-two-year-old Joseph Malley had never been to school and could neither read nor write. Indeed, his illiteracy was reportedly so bad that he was unable to identify his name when it was written. A badly healed broken wrist that was incapable of lifting ten pounds further marked the Nova Scotian as unfit to serve, but he was accepted anyway.[18]

In more than one instance, individuals met neither age nor medical requirements. Besides being much too young, sixteen-year-old Private Russell Mick also suffered from the aftereffects of infantile paralysis (polio), which had left him "with underdeveloped and weak muscles in the right hip and thigh" and weighing less than eighty pounds (see Figure 2).[19] Also sixteen years of age, Emile Morin was described as being "underdeveloped" and "stupid." Morin's intellectual limitation was not congenital, nor was its cause invisible. The young Canadian had suffered head injuries when he was struck by a train as a child, and his forehead still bore the scars.[20] Seventy-nine-year-old William J. Clements, on the other hand, suffered from arteriosclerosis and was described as being "very deaf" and "barely able to stand erect."[21]

Clements was not the only septuagenarian to make it into the ranks. A member of the first Canadian Pioneer Draft, Harold Emson was discharged as unfit for service in England in 1916 when it was discovered that he was seventy-two years of age. Seventy-one-year-old Torrence Glazier got even further. A veteran of the Fenian Raids, the Northwest Campaign, and the Anglo-Boer War, he served two months in the trenches with the Royal Engineers in 1916 before being discharged as overage – proving that some British medical examiners also made questionable decisions. Before joining the Royal Engineers, Glazier had been discharged from the 92nd Canadian Infantry Battalion in 1915, and had twice unsuccessfully attempted to enlist in the 21st Canadian Infantry Battalion in 1914. Eager to do his part, the plucky geriatric returned to Canada and went on to enlist again before the war was over. The attestation papers of Clements, Emson, and Glazier recorded their ages as forty-four.[22]

Fears over the nature of the medical examinations being conducted in Canada were made worse by reports, often coming from Canadian soldiers, that men were not being correctly examined or that their examiners were simply ignoring

An Imperfect System 53

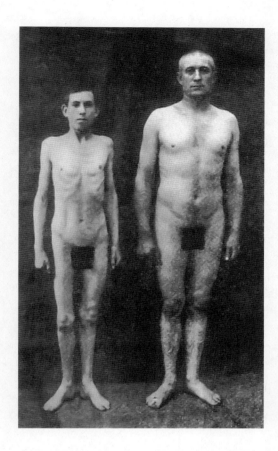

FIGURE 2 Private Russell Mick *(left)*. The man standing next to Mick is 5 feet, 7 inches tall.
Library and Archives Canada/ William Babtie Fonds/R1877-01-E.

obvious impairments. One individual who was returned to Canada from England after it was found that he had a glass eye stated that on noting the impairment, his examining medical officer had simply told him: "You make good on your drills and we will keep you."[23] In another instance, a telegram sent to Militia Headquarters in Ottawa from Military District 4 stated that certain civilian practitioners had been discovered to be passing men in defiance of instructions. "Many men," the telegram continued, "had not even been stripped" during their examination. Other men claimed not to have received eye or foot examinations, or indeed any examination at all. Still others stated that their examiners, recruiters, or commanding officers had openly falsified documents with regard to their age.[24]

These were some of the more dramatic cases. As noted earlier, many of those found to be unfit for reasons other than age were designated as such because of eyesight or other less striking impairments such as endocarditis. None of these cases was unique, however. More than one prospective trench warrior arrived in England with missing or deformed limbs; many others suffered from a variety of other obvious serious physical and mental conditions.[25] Some had even been rejected as unfit by the militaries of other nations. Edward Beech, for example, had been discharged on account of his gastric condition by the British Army in 1915. Missourian Lutie Bealie, who suffered from mental illness, had enlisted in and been discharged from the United States Army three times before being accepted into the Canadian Expeditionary Force in early 1918.[26] No wonder Agar Adamson told his wife in March 1916 that "the medical examinations in Canada are a bit of a farce,"[27] and Lieutenant-Colonel George Cantlie, Officer Commanding 42nd Battalion (The Black Watch of Canada) opined, after receiving a group of reinforcements that included a man missing half of one foot, "that there was either no medical examination of men going overseas or if there is, it is very lax."[28]

Expeditionary Force medical examinations were hindered by a number of interrelated factors: the inexperience and/or professional arrogance of some individuals tasked with conducting examinations; the sheer number of men needing to be examined; recruiting practices; and the willingness of recruits, military authorities, politicians, and medical officers to subvert the medical examination for their own ends. The military authorities did much to combat these problems as the war continued, and, in spite of a myriad of problems, the medical examination process worked better than many believed. This was especially true of the latter years of the war, if for no other reason than the fact that many unfit men were caught at the point of embarkation or upon arrival in England.

In May 1916, Colonel J.L. Potter, Acting Director General Medical Services, observed that in order to be carried out successfully, medical examinations needed to be conducted by specially trained individuals. For much of the war, however, the Canadian military simply lacked enough of these individuals to handle the vast numbers of men that Canada needed in order to meet its battlefield obligations. As a result, it was forced to use inexperienced Canadian Army Medical Corps officers and civilian practitioners, many of them far from being the specially trained individuals mentioned by Potter. In fact, it would appear that some examiners had very little knowledge of the military's medical requirements and the examination.[29]

On 7 November 1914, Dr. George B. Henderson of Creston, British Columbia, wrote to the military authorities in Ottawa requesting a copy of the "regulations regarding medical military examinations of volunteers for active service." He had, he explained, been examining volunteers for the Second Contingent based on second-hand instructions and wanted "a guide to go by or some standard list of physical defects that bar men from service."[30] Henderson may have been an extreme case, but he was not alone. In a 1917 letter to the Assistant Director Medical Services, London Area, Captain R.R. Barker, Senior Medical Officer, Canadian Forestry Corps, highlighted the difficulties and cost of involving inexperienced civilian practitioners in raising the 224th Forestry Battalion in early 1916.[31] As late as September 1916, recruiting officers were being directed to ensure that the practitioners they employed had "received proper instructions" on how to conduct the medical examinations.[32]

Examiners' lack of experience became a common refrain when the military authorities attempted to explain, both during and after the war, why unfit men were passed as fit to serve. To Sam Hughes after the minister had received Starr's letter, Major H.M. Jacques, Assistant Deputy Director General Medical Services, stated that "a few cases as are referred to in Dr. Starr's letter are bound to occur" because "many of the officers who have had to carry out the examination of recruits have not had very much experience" in conducting military medical examinations.[33] Likewise, both the board of inquiry that was convened to examine the Bruce Report and Sir Andrew Macphail in his postwar history of the medical services identified medical examiners' lack of experience as a major causative factor in the passing of unfit men for service.[34]

In some instances, their lack of experience or of understanding of military requirements was obvious. In more than one case, musicians who either had serious physical impairments – including amputated limbs, ulcerated skin, and osteomyelitis (an infection of bone or bone marrow) – or who were well below the Canadian Expeditionary Force's minimum physical requirements (such as twenty-nine-year-old Henry Barnes, who stood 4 feet, 8 inches and weighed ninety pounds) – were passed by medical examiners who, while recognizing their physical inability to serve as combat soldiers, believed them to be fit to serve as bandsmen.[35] Apparently, these medical examiners failed to realize that many bandsmen were used in combat situations as stretcher bearers.[36]

Many medical examiners also had trouble switching their mindset from civilian to military medicine and fully comprehending their role and importance in Canada's war machine. Major J.A. Hislop of the Canadian Army Medical Corps noted in a short paper published after the war in the *Canadian Medical Association Journal* that some doctors had treated medical examinations like insurance examinations. Rather than assessing their subject's suitability to serve, the doctor simply recorded the man's physical condition on entering service. Perhaps of more concern was Hislop's passing acknowledgment that many doctors felt that insurance examinations – and by implication military medical examinations – were both irritating and full of "a lot of silly questions."[37]

Hislop's article identified another problem that had hindered the successful conduct of medical examinations: "a great lack of common language or nomenclature among the profession."[38] Not only were many terms vaguely employed but also many measurements of (dis)ability were based on undefined standards. These problems were equally evident both during and after the war. In December 1917, the Assistant Director Medical Services Canadians, Shorncliffe Area, warned the Senior Medical Officer, 2nd Canadian Reserve Brigade, that a number of descriptions of impairments of recruits – including "eyes" and "chest trouble" – provided in a recent report on the physical fitness of a draft that had recently arrived in England were "very indefinite," and thus of little help to medical authorities when they attempted to identify the health problems suffered by recruits.[39]

The use of indefinite language also had a direct and negative impact on medical examinations. For example, while Canadian recruiting regulations up to 1917 stated that an individual was to be rejected if he had marked varicocele, they did not define how extensive the condition had to be in order to be considered marked. Such ambiguity caused considerable problems. In a July 1915 letter to the General Officer Commanding Military District 3, the Adjutant General's office noted that several men had been passed as fit despite suffering from varicocele so "aggravated [in] form" that operations were required in order to make the men fit to serve. At the other end of the spectrum, a number of recruits had been pronounced unfit as a result of varicocele that was so "slight" in nature that it had neither hindered them in active and laborious occupations in civil life nor been suspected before they had submitted to the medical examination! As a result of these findings, medical officers were requested to use "great care" when making decisions on the fitness of recruits with varicocele, to ensure that such occurrences were not repeated. It should be noted, however, that although the Adjutant General's office identified the problem, it did not correct it. The letter provided no explicit guidance regarding the line between aggravated and slight forms of varicocele.[40] This difference would not be defined by the authorities until the publication of the 1917 *Physical Standards and Instructions for the Medical Examination of Recruits for the Canadian Expeditionary Force and for the Active Militia of Canada.*

The question of marked varicocele was only one of many subjective judgment categories that plagued medical examinations. There were similar problems with many other potentially disqualifying impairments, including, after early 1915, the closely related condition of varicose veins. After March 1915, medical officers were told that they could pass recruits with varicose veins provided they were not marked.[41] Inevitably, such ambiguous directions led to clashes. In April 1916, for example, Dr. J.A. McDonald of Vancouver partially defended his decision to pass a man who was later rejected on account of "moderate varicose veins of [the] left leg" by noting that varicose veins were not a cause for rejection in and of themselves. McDonald noted that the examiner was "allowed to use his brain to a slight extent and pass a man otherwise fit, if he considers the enlargement of the veins is not sufficient to impair his efficiency or confine him to hospital as the result of over exertion."[42]

Given the number of initially passed recruits who were later found to be unfit on account of age, judging a recruit's age was the most problematic of the subjective categories. Medical examiners were instructed to judge a recruit's age based on his appearance, regardless of his statements. While this requirement was based on a number of logical grounds, the obvious problem with it was that medical examiners were expected to ascertain recruits' ages by simply looking at them. This was no easy task. Although one Department of Militia and Defence memorandum observed that it should be possible to "distinguish between men of 45 and men of 50, 60 or 70 years of age,"[43] estimating the age of recruits closer to the cutoff ages could be much more difficult. "A husky farm boy or a lad who had been working hard labour for years might be in better shape [and look older] than a pasty twenty-year-old bank clerk." [44] For example, Douglas Campbell may have been sixteen years old but, his discharge papers noted, the 5 foot, 9 inch farmer's son "look[ed] older."[45] At the opposite end of the scale, a teetotal, fit forty-seven-year-old might look considerably younger and be in much better physical health than a hard-drinking thirty-eight-year-old coal miner whose body had been subjected to decades of backbreaking work underground and an equally severe pummelling from the bottle. Such realities were certainly recognized by the wider public. In June 1915, Mrs. D.C. Glassford wrote to Sam Hughes asking to have her son, George, discharged from the Canadian Expeditionary Force. George, she told Hughes, was not nineteen years old as he had claimed, but rather fifteen. He was, she acknowledged, "large for his age and would easily be taken for [nineteen]."[46]

The difficulty of correctly judging recruits' ages based on physical characteristics was compounded by the fact that perception of age could differ from individual to individual. An individual who looked twenty-one years old to one person could look considerably younger or older to another person. Similar comments can be made with regard to older individuals. Twenty-four-year-old Harold Baldwin recounted that as he was marching through the streets of an Ontario town on the way to Valcartier, an old woman took him to be a child because he was considerably shorter than his comrades. Neither the regimental medical officer nor the medical officer who examined Baldwin at Valcartier questioned the tanned and muscular farmer about his age. The only concern expressed by the regimental examiner was with regard to Baldwin's height, and even that was uncalled for because he met the minimum height requirement.[47]

The difficulties that medical officers had in estimating recruits' ages are best demonstrated by the following responses provided in January 1917 to some doctors' criticisms of the large number of overage and underage men arriving in England. Major W.H. Reilly, Assistant Director Medical Services of Military District 10, defended himself and his medical officers from criticism over the twenty-six underage and forty-one overage men discovered in the 179th Battalion. He noted that if a man stated he was forty-four years of age and did not look more than that, an examiner had no choice but to accept the statement. Examiners' hands were equally tied, he continued, in the case of boys who stated they were eighteen and appeared to be that age. In some cases, Reilly implied, a recruit's true age would come to light only when he got cold feet after enlisting and drew authorities' attention to his age in order to be discharged.[48] Reilly's comments echoed those written two days earlier by Brigadier-General A.O. Fages, General Officer Commanding Military District 5, who stated that "it will be appreciated that in border-line cases, credence must be given to the word of the recruit, otherwise many a good and useful soldier would be lost to the service." However, he did acknowledge that "no excuse can be offered ... [in those cases where there are] ... large discrepancies between age given and general appearance."[49]

Reilly's defence did not stop at pointing out the difficulties medical examiners faced in assessing some individuals' true ages. He also went on to indicate how miscommunication and misunderstanding also caused some underage boys to be passed as fit for service. He noted that some of these boys had been recruited as buglers and passed as fit for service overseas based on the understanding that the bugle band would travel to Europe with the battalion. Reilly's explanation cannot be completely discounted. A number of boys who arrived in England had indeed been enlisted as buglers. Moreover, similar misunderstandings with regard to regimental bands had caused medical examiners to pass men with serious physical disabilities.[50]

These problems do not offer a complete explanation of why so many underage and overage men made it to England. Many were accepted as fit to serve by recruiting agents, medical officers, and battalion commanders who were well aware of their true ages. Not all underage and overage men lied when asked their ages, but they were accepted nonetheless. Douglas Campbell's attestation paper, for example, shows his birth date as 15 December 1901 and his age as sixteen. Fifteen-year-old Norman Williams was equally honest when he signed up in November 1915.[51] It was also common for overage men who gave their true ages at the time of enlistment to find their examining medical officers deciding that they were in fact ten or fifteen years younger than they thought they were. Leonard Pusey's medical examiner, Captain J.M. Fowler altered Pusey's age from forty-eight years and nine months to forty-four years and nine months (see Figure 3).[52] Although in many cases the stunned recruit would have no say in the matter, in some instances the medical officer would make a recruit complicit in the falsehood by encouraging him – as they often did with underage boys – to run around the block and think about his age before coming back.[53]

Equally problematic was the lack of standardization between Canadian and Imperial regulations with regard to maximum age requirements. While men as old as forty-five were considered fit to serve under Canadian regulations, Imperial regulations set the maximum age for a combat infantryman at forty. Since Canadian troops came under Imperial control when they arrived in England, this meant that many men deemed fit to fight when they were in Canada were reclassified as unfit for the trenches soon after their arrival. Although the Canadian authorities were well aware of this discrepancy and expressed more than a little concern over the burden placed on Canadian resources by the large number of men left stranded in England, Canadian standards were not aligned with those of the Imperial forces.[54] This lack of uniformity did not end with differences in age requirements. Surgeon-General G.C. Jones, Director of Military Services, Canadian Contingent, found himself having to ask the British War Office for rulings in a number of different cases in which Imperial standards clashed with Canadian ones.[55] Indicating just how problematic the differences in standards were with regard to classifying men for service, one of the many recommendations made in the Bruce Report was that "close co-operation between Overseas and Canada be established, with a uniform standard of fitness, based on actual experience at the front."[56]

In some cases medical officers simply ignored minimum medical and physical requirements and passed men who should have been rejected. There were many reasons for this. There is little doubt that some civilian doctors believed that they were better able to assess a man's ability to fight than the military authorities. However, it should be noted that medical officers could also be influenced by the tenor of the times and the fervour of the men who stood before them. The case of Harold Peat is a prime example. Rejected for service on 22 August 1914 because the girth of his expanded chest was an inch less than the minimum required (33.5 inches), Peat confronted Major Farquarhson, the medical officer for the 101st Regiment (Edmonton Fusiliers), at his home the next day:

> "Excuse me, Doctor," I said when he appeared, "but I'm sure you'd pass me if you only knew my circumstances."
>
> "Well?" snapped the major.
>
> "You see, sir, my two brothers have been killed by Germans in Belgium, and my mother and sister are there. I *must* go over to avenge them."

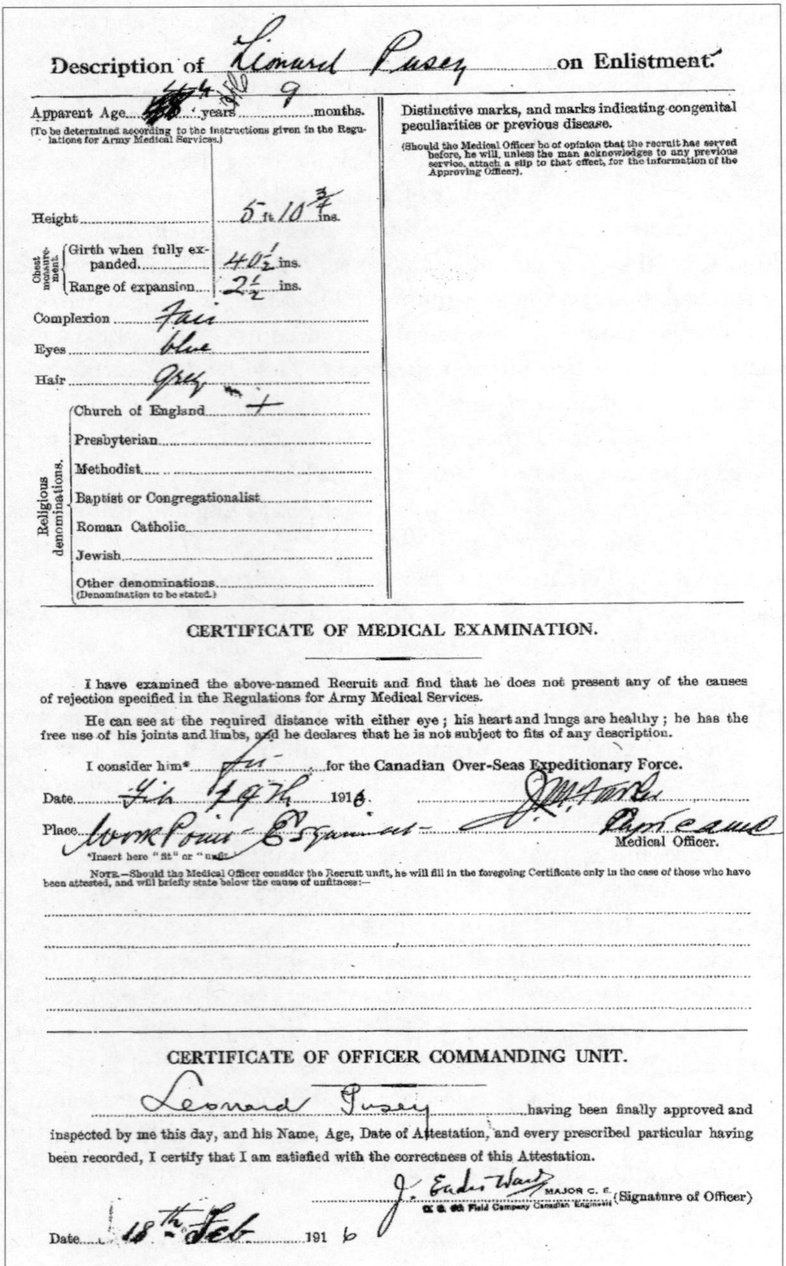

FIGURE 3 Leonard Pusey's attestation paper showing his altered age. *Library and Archives Canada/Ministry of the Overseas Military Forces of Canada Fonds/RG 150, Acc. 1992–93/166, Box 803-25.*

I shivered; I quaked in my shoes. Would the major speak to me in French? I did not then know as much as *Bon jour*. But luck was with me. To my great relief Major Farquarhson replied ... "Report to me this afternoon; I will pass you."[57]

And he did. As did Peat's examiner at Valcartier, who recorded the Albertan's expanded chest measurement as 34 inches. Although the Jamaican-born Peat credited the success of his ruse to his short and slight build as well as his dark complexion and curly hair, which, he contended, enabled him to "pass for a Frenchman, an American, a Belgian; or at a pinch a Jew," it is doubtful that Farquarhson was fooled, especially since the firmly anglophone Peat would have had no trace of a French or Flemish accent and had not made the same claim the day before, when he had first been rejected by the major (he had simply pleaded with Farquarhson to "have a heart").[58]

Peat was not the only individual to find a sympathetic doctor. British-born Harold Baldwin was passed as fit by a medical officer in Saskatoon in August 1914 despite being 2 inches below the 5 foot, 6 inch height required by Saskatchewan's 29th Light Horse Regiment.[59] He countered the medical officer's statement that he was too short by claiming to have served for four years in the 1st Battalion of the British Regular Army's North Staffordshire Regiment. The doctor relented and sent the resolute twenty-four-year-old off to Valcartier with the following words: "Well, you are as fit as any man, but they are sticklers about height. I'll tell you what I'll do. You may leave with the boys for Valcartier and that will bring you two thousand miles nearer to England. *As you are determined to go anyway*, part of your trip will be at the government's expense."[60] Passed as fit to serve at Valcartier, Baldwin went on to serve as a sergeant in the 5th Battalion (Western Cavalry). Eugene Iler was passed as fit, against regulations, after promising medical officer Captain J.S. Carruthers that he would not hold the government accountable for "any trouble arising from hernia or testicles [varicocele?]."[61] The stories of Peat, Baldwin, and Iler all indicate that medical officers would, as David Silbey has noted with regard to recruiting in England, "undercut the minimum requirements necessary for military service, in a conscious and obvious way" to help those men and boys who desired to serve their country.[62]

The self-importance of some civilian medical professionals hindered medical examinations in other ways. Accustomed to charging substantial fees for their services, many civilian doctors strongly resented the government's imposition on 28 February 1916 of a remuneration rate of 50 cents for each man examined beginning on 1 April.[63] A number of them not only strongly protested the imposition of the fee, which was to be paid in addition to the remuneration doctors received from the government for attending troops billeted in their town or village, but also threatened dire consequences as a result.[64] On 19 April, Dr. James R. Bird of Whitewood, Saskatchewan, wrote an ill-tempered letter to the Acting Adjutant General of the Canadian Militia Major-General Hodgins, condemning the government's action. He stated that he had just received the notice of the government's decision earlier in the day, and that he did not feel bound by it when setting his fees for any examinations he had conducted between 1 and 19 April. The fee was "an insult to the profession of which I have been a member for almost thirty years. It is not on par with the wages of a chimney sweep," and Bird could not "conceive of many medical officers in [the Department of Militia and Defence] having such a poor opinion of his fellow members of the medical profession as to put them on par with ... a farm laborer." The medical profession, he concluded, was being most unfairly and unjustly treated by the department. Not content with merely venting his spleen, Bird reinforced his vitriolic attack with a threat: he would continue to examine men, but not to the best of his ability. He would also refuse to accept the "pittance" offered for his services when conducting these examinations.[65]

The firebrand Bird was not the only physician to complain about the fee. In early November 1916, after hearing that he was to be made an examiner on his local medical board, Dr. H.E. Eaglesham of Weyburn, Saskatchewan, wrote to the local military authorities asking to be discharged from the responsibility. He explained that he was "too busy a man to bother with [conducting medical examinations] if there was only 50 c[en]ts an examination"; it was "worth more than that to fill the papers out." Lest he sound overly mercenary or even unpatriotic, he stated his belief that every man should do his bit and "if circumstances were different I would be away to the front now." He believed, however, that the "vast amount of work [he was doing] free for soldiers families" fulfilled his responsibilities to the Dominion.[66]

Forwarding Eaglesham's letter to his superiors in Ottawa, Captain A.S. Gosell, Assistant Director Medical Services of Military District 12, reported that he was "up against this proposition all the time" and that he was enclosing the letter so "you will see the difficulties I am having" getting civilian practitioners to conduct medical examinations. Similarly, in his aforementioned report of January 1917, Brigadier-General Fages informed the Secretary of the Militia Council that many physicians in his district objected "altogether for the fee of $0.50." He indicated that Bird was not the only physician to respond with vindictiveness to the fee offered to him, and went on to state, with evident disgust, that some of the civilian practitioners in his district had been "bold enough to state that any recruit examined by them [would] be given a 50 [cent] examination." Canada's vast geography and many small and isolated communities amplified the impact of such threats. Fages pointed out that given the limited supply of qualified examiners in rural Canada, recruiters were forced to either accept a 50-cent examination or transport recruits to the next nearest depot, which could be well over a hundred miles away. He implied that many of the enlisted men from his district who were found to be unfit in subsequent examinations were victims of such unprofessional behaviour.[67]

It is impossible to ascertain whether civilian practitioners actually carried out their threats to undermine medical examinations. Some were reportedly not following the military authorities' directions for conducting such examinations, but they were not necessarily engaged in deliberate acts of defiance; other factors – such as inexperience or a lack of knowledge – might have played a role. Nonetheless, the military authorities took these threats seriously. Major-General Hodgins replied to the irate Dr. Bird, acknowledging his protest and expressing his regrets that Bird did not "consider the remuneration under the present arrangements sufficient." He directed the doctor to correspond directly with the General Officer Commanding Military District 10 with regard to any other outstanding financial claims he might have.[68] The officer would, Hodgins stated, "be very glad to give your accounts proper consideration."[69]

While Hodgins's reply may have been calm, the authorities were anything but relaxed behind the scenes. Responding to Captain Gosell's letter, Colonel J.L. Potter, Acting Director General Medical Services, stated that he fully appreciated the difficulties Gosell was experiencing and inquired whether a civilian practitioner such as Dr. Eaglesham would accept a lieutenant's pay for his services. However, lest Gosell believe that he was being given carte blanche to retain as many civilian practitioners as he felt necessary, Potter noted that medical officers should be employed full-time only at mobilization centres that processed large numbers of troops: "If only a few recruits have to be examined, pay at so much per diem for the days actually employed will perhaps be more satisfactory." He made no suggestion as to what a reasonable per diem rate might be, but did tell Gosell that the matter was being given further attention.[70] And indeed it was.

The same day that he wrote to the frantic Gosell, Potter wrote to the Assistant Adjutant General, Lieutenant-Colonel C.S. MacInnis, suggesting that "the pay for medical officers to be employed at Mobilization Centres ... should not be at so much per recruit, but by month, regardless of how many recruits are examined." In the case of civilian practitioners, a lieutenant's pay would be sufficient unless there were large numbers of men to be examined, in which case a captain's pay "might be allowed." Potter noted that the current small remuneration would make it difficult "to secure civilian practitioners or Medical Officers who are prepared to give their whole time" to examining recruits.

MacInnis responded sixteen days later. Potter was told that the method of payment depended on the mobilization centre. At large centres, the work should be carried out by regular medical officers, who were to be paid according to their rank. In small centres where the work was not great, examinations were to be paid "on the present basis of so much per recruit." While seemingly logical and economically expedient on paper, such directions missed the point. The very people protesting the fee were small-town doctors. Piecework pay not only insulted them but was also not worth their while.[71]

If physicians' professional pride, lack of experience, and willingness to help eager but unfit volunteers hindered the successful conduct of medical examinations, so did wider wartime realities and the nature of the medical examination itself. Designed for peacetime recruitment and as a means of ensuring that the military gained the best human resources available, the medical examination was a highly complex and time-consuming exercise. Faced with masses of men queuing to defend the Empire, careful examinations were difficult if not impossible.

This was certainly true in Valcartier, where some rejected individuals, such as eighteen-year-old William Dix, used their chaotic surroundings to their advantage. Initially rejected for poor eyesight, Dix simply waited in camp for twenty-two days and tried again.[72] He was passed as fit. It is possible that Dix succeeded the same way as the myopic Alfred Andrews of Qu'appelle, Saskatchewan, who was able to memorize the visual acuity card used to assess recruits' vision and passed his vision test with flying colours. Andrews also evaded discovery of his other disqualifying impairment: a hernia he had sustained while playing football.[73] Cutting corners occurred elsewhere too. In 1915, it was reported that medical examinations at the Toronto Recruiting Depot were conducted in only forty seconds, and such cursory examinations were also common in many other recruiting stations.[74]

There were exceptions, to be sure. Eighteen-year-old Peter Pirie continued with his classes at Albert College in Belleville, Ontario, after enlisting in the 21st Battalion in late 1914 because he was unsure that he would pass the unit's final medical examination and did not want to lose his school year if he was rejected.[75] Kenneth Duggan told his mother in May 1915 that the medical officers examining men for the 5th Canadian Mounted Rifles "were making hay."[76] However, even the most thorough medical examination could be defeated. Recalling his 1917 medical examination for the Black Watch, Danish Victoria Cross awardee Thomas Dinesen stated that "we were examined with the minutest care. Measured from point to point at various angles, examined and probed and commented upon, very much as if we were a number of decrepit old hacks." Nonetheless, the young Dane was able to hide the limited movement he had in his right knee by "stick[ing] my leg very far behind when making a deep genuflexion."[77] While it is impossible to tell whether Dinesen's examiners were aware of his deception and turned a blind eye to it, his insistence on the thoroughness of the examination and his own "mortal terror" of being rejected, along with the fact that a number of men in his group were rejected as unfit, would suggest that his medical examiners were not simply passing all would-be warriors with a wink and a nod.[78]

The problem of unfit recruits became more widespread in late 1915 after the Department of Militia and Defence handed responsibility for recruiting battalions over to individual citizens and communities in an attempt to bolster flagging numbers.[79] As men became harder to find and competition for recruits between battalions grew, recruiters became far more liberal about whom they accepted. As might be expected, this liberalism far exceeded the relaxation of medical standards allowed by the military authorities.

Take, for example, Elvin Wolf of Wetaskiwin, Alberta. Wolf's offer to serve was accepted by Lieutenant John Morrison Peterkin, a recruiting officer for the 151st (Central Alberta) Battalion, on 5 January 1916, even though the nineteen-year-old was missing part of his left hand and was suffering the aftereffects of a compound fracture of the left tibia. Wolf's medical examiner, R.D. Robertson, supported Peterkin's decision. Describing the nineteen-year-old's mangled hand as "strong and pliable," the doctor indicated that it would not hinder him in the profession of soldiering. Importantly, the doctor did not mention Wolf's leg injury, which was readily apparent by all accounts. The medical board that examined Wolf after he joined the battalion in Edmonton was less forgiving. Noting the young man's injuries, it declared him unfit for military service. He was discharged soon after.[80]

Wolf's second enlistment attempt, on 8 April 1916, is even more telling. The young Albertan re-enlisted in Wetaskiwin fifteen days after being declared unfit, and Peterkin – who would have been well aware of who Wolf was and, indeed, that he had been discharged as unfit for military service – once again accepted him. The battalion's commanding officer, Lieutenant-Colonel J.W. Arnott, approved Wolf's enlistment. Arnott, it should be noted, had signed the Albertan's discharge papers following his initial rejection in Edmonton, less than one month earlier, and thus would also have been aware of the young man's medical status. Wolf's second enlistment was also aided by his medical examiner, one H.C. Ruecker, who did not mention Wolf's mutilated hand or injured leg on his attestation paper. There is no evidence that Wolf faced the medical board in Edmonton a second time.[81]

Indeed, Wolf's re-enlistment appears to have been more for Ottawa's benefit than anything else. The Albertan did nothing to hide his identity other than change his name, and even this attempt at concealment was rather unimaginative: all he did was substitute his middle name, Lee, for his first name and then use the first name of one of his brothers, Roy, as a middle name. All other information – address, next of kin, date of birth (which was false), place of birth (Nebraska), and previous military experience (one militia camp) – remained the same.[82] While such changes would not have been enough to fool the officers and men of the 151st Battalion, they would have enabled both Wolf and the battalion to circumvent Ottawa's attempt to prevent the re-enlistment of men deemed medically unfit by keeping records of who had been rejected for service.

Some unscrupulous battalion commanders and recruiting officers took advantage of civilian practitioners' inexperience in conducting military medical examinations. Lieutenant-Colonel John E. de Hertel, Officer Commanding 130th (Lanark and Renfrew) Battalion, was reported to have taken men that his medical officer, Captain E.C. Consitt, refused to pass to "outlying points and got them through there by civilian practitioners who were not familiar with the work."[83] He was not alone: in August 1915, the Assistant Director Medical Services of the 3rd Division noted in a circular letter to the division's recruiting officers that it had come to Ottawa's attention that recruiting officers did not always use authorized medical officers to carry out medical examinations.[84]

Likewise, battalion commanders often chose their own medical examiners, "who were governed by personal direction rather than by established standards," or used the uneven relationship engendered by the chain of command to sway their medical officers' decisions. As a result, more than one commanding officer was able to ensure that men who should have been rejected were passed as fit.[85] For example, Lieutenant-Colonel G.R. Bouchard, Officer Commanding 41st Battalion – himself facing pressure from higher up in the chain of command – directed his medical officer, Captain N. Moring, to pass fifteen-year-old Adore Breton despite his age.[86] In another case, the medical officer of the 197th Battalion told investigators from Military District that he had been coerced by his commanding officer to pass men who in his own judgment "did not come up to the standard" for service. In this instance alone, a commanding officer's heavy hand resulted in over 100 unfit men being passed by a battalion medical officer.[87]

The interference of commanding officers in the medical examinations of recruits was also discussed in the December 1916 issue of the *Canadian Medical Association Journal*. In an editorial titled "The Canadian Medical Services," the editors of the journal noted: "The competitive system of enlistment and the rivalry of recruiting and commanding officers raising regiments in a short space of time [had led many medical officers to] allow themselves to be overruled by the desire of the commanding officers to bring their regiments rapidly up to strength."[88]

If battalion commanders could not rely on their medical officers' good will or bully them into submission, they could simply ignore them. There were numerous instances of commanding officers keeping men in their units despite their being declared unfit to serve during a medical examination or becoming disabled as a result of accident or illness while in Canada.[89] In some cases, the physical impairments of such men were stunning. Thirty-two-year-old Private Jake Kerr of Calgary travelled to England with the 12th Canadian Mounted Rifles despite the fact that a fifty-foot fall had left him with no teeth and one leg 2.5 inches shorter than the other. As though this were not enough, he had also contracted both pneumonia and pleurisy while recovering from his injuries in hospital. Given Kerr's poor medical condition, a report stated, it was "hard to understand why this man was brought to England." Actually, it was not as difficult to understand as the report alleged. A groom in civilian life, Kerr had been employed as a senior officer's batman before his accident and retained the position after his recovery. It appears that at least in the eyes of his master, Kerr was too valuable a servant to be dismissed on account of injuries.[90]

In other instances, commanding officers who were desperate to fill their ranks took men without any medical examination at all.[91] There were many ways of managing this. In some cases, officers ensured that medically questionable men were absent when medical board examinations were carried out; in others, they enlisted men after these examinations had taken place. Indeed, there is evidence that some units added men to their ranks as they travelled to their embarkation points.[92]

The military authorities' efforts to counter such practices (see below) were met with further acts of dishonesty on the part of some battalion commanders. Lieutenant-Colonel W.O. Smyth, Officer Commanding 209th Battalion, certified that all men in his unit had been medically examined and found fit for service before embarkation for Europe. It was later discovered, however, that over a hundred men (approximately 10 percent of the battalion's strength) had been absent when the unit's final pre-embarkation medical inspection was done. Smyth had falsified his documentation in order to bring all his men to Europe.[93]

Not all the blame for missed medical examinations can be laid at the feet of battalion commanders. Others also used their power and influence to get men with disqualifying impairments accepted. The aforementioned Elvin Wolf's initial rejection due to his maimed left hand was overturned by the Minister of Militia and Defence, Edward Kemp, after the intercession of Senator Rufus H. Pope, who wrote regarding the young Albertan's plight and attached a letter from one George B. Campbell criticizing Wolf's rejection and stressing his suitability for service. Campbell, the senator declared, was a "thoroughly reliable man" and was "qualified to express his opinion ... [on Wolf's] ... ability to kill Germans." He trusted that the minister would find an "opportunity to allow him to do so," and Kemp did. Despite the protests of military authorities, the minister directed that the Albertan be allowed to rejoin the 151st Battalion. The Assistant Deputy Director General Medical Services for Alberta, for example, noted that Wolf was unfit according to Canadian recruiting regulations, and that even if he were efficient in Canada, he would probably be rejected by the overseas medical authorities.[94]

Kemp's directive proved irrelevant: Wolf had already re-enlisted in the 151st on 8 April – a mere fifteen days after his rejection and six days after Campbell had put pen to paper on his behalf – and was a member of the 151st Battalion when it sailed for England on the SS *California* on 3 October 1916. However, despite Kemp's instructions and the aid he received from members of the battalion when he enlisted a second time, the Albertan never saw France. As the Assistant Deputy Director General Medical Services for Alberta predicted, Wolf was found to be medically unfit for service by a medical board at Shorncliffe camp on 22 November. Designated a local casualty, he was moved in early December to the Canadian Casualty Assembly Centre at Hastings, where he languished for a month before being shipped back to Canada on 8 January 1917, and was discharged in Quebec City on 4 February.[95]

Besides intentional avoidance, men also escaped medical examination due to Canada's economy and size. In response to criticisms regarding the number of unfit men discovered in the 113th and 151st Battalions, the General Officer Commanding Military District 13 noted that when these two units were called up for deployment overseas, 25 percent of their men were on harvest furlough and had to be recalled by telegram. As many of them worked on farms quite distant from telegraph offices, some reported to their battalions at the last moment while many more had to be picked up at way stations as the battalions headed east. In such circumstances, the General Officer Commanding explained, it was not practical to re-examine all of the men.[96]

In accepting this explanation, Lieutenant-Colonel F. Bell, Assistant Deputy Director General Medical Services, noted in a Department of Militia and Defence memorandum that this problem had been rectified. Bell was referring to a circular letter sent by the Adjutant General's office on 29 December 1916 to the General Officers Commanding Military Districts, who were told that as soon as a unit or reinforcement draft was warned that it would be travelling overseas, no leave was to be granted until all ranks had passed their final medical examination. Any men on leave at the time of the warning were to be recalled immediately so they could be examined with their comrades.[97]

The instructions did not end there. Recognizing that such directives were not always followed, the letter stated that if the examining medical board discovered that there were absentees when conducting the examination, a record of the absentees' names was to be forwarded to the commanding officer of the unit or draft. He, in turn, was to make a nominal roll, in quadruplicate, of these names and include any men who joined the unit subsequent to the final medical inspection. The officer was to forward two copies of the roll, along with the final medical inspection report, to the General Officer Commanding of the unit or draft's Military District, and one copy to the Embarkation Medical Officer at the point of embarkation so that those individuals could be medically examined before proceeding overseas. After using his copy, the Embarkation Medical Officer was to forward it to the headquarters of the district in which the unit embarked, where it would be retained for reference. The final copy was to be retained by the commanding officer of the unit or draft and provided to the overseas authorities when the unit disembarked at its final destination.

Indicative of the continuing problems with unfit men being accepted or maintained in units, medical officers were warned that they were "on no account [to] retain 'misfits' in the service." More directly, in a letter dated 29 December 1916, the Adjutant General's office noted that the "number of 'misfits' arriving in England is still large" and warned both medical officers and commanding officers of units about to travel to England that if this was to continue, the officers responsible would be "held strictly accountable, and if gross neglect is proved, will be liable to dismissal from the service."[98] This warning was just one of many attempts by the military authorities to plug the holes in the leaking dike that was the medical examination. Such attempts took the form of polite reminders about standards, heartfelt pleas noting the present and future economic strain that the acceptance of unfit individuals placed on Canada, open threats of punishment for both the recruits and those who accepted them, and, finally, the introduction of a multi-step examination process. All these initiatives added paperwork to the already paper-clogged military bureaucracy. Moreover, in the face of men who were determined to go to war and medical officers and battalion commanders who wanted to get them there, the measures were not always successful.

On 14 December 1915, one year to the day after Dr. Starr wrote to Sam Hughes expressing his concerns about the Canadian Expeditionary Force's medical examination, the Adjutant General's office sent a circular letter to Canada's Military Districts stressing that "special care is to be taken not only to ensure that men not physically fit are not enlisted, but also that men not medically fit be not retained in service." To ensure that this objective was met, the letter instructed each division to form a medical board of two officers who would inspect all recruits at regular intervals. When an unfit recruit was discovered, the board would inform the divisional or district headquarters, which in turn would send a daily nominal roll of men recommended for discharge to the Secretary of the Militia Council in Ottawa. This roll had to provide the following details about each unfit man: name (in full), rank, unit, nature of disability, name of the medical officer who had passed him at enlistment, and name of the medical officer of his unit. The letter ended by drawing medical officers' attention to the regulations regarding careless examinations. These directions were not always followed, however, and on 26 May 1916 the Adjutant General had to remind the Military Districts to forward their daily returns of men recommended for discharge to headquarters in Ottawa.[99]

Even when the returns of rejected men were well kept, they often failed to prevent men from re-enlisting. Many rejected individuals refused to accept the first and subsequent rejections and presented themselves several times in hopes of being accepted. To increase their chances, many not only travelled to different recruiting stations but also employed pseudonyms in each subsequent attempt. On 18 March 1916, the Toronto *Globe* reported that a man who had been rejected at eight different depots was still expressing "a keen desire to get to the front some how." This man's enthusiasm paled, however, in comparison with the persistence of twenty-three-year-old bushman George Stanley Atkins. Suffering from injury-induced kyphosis (curvature of the spine), Atkins, by his account, attempted to enlist almost 200 times, crossing most of Western Canada in the process, before finally being accepted by the 1st Tunnelling Company on 12 November 1915.[100]

The numbers of repeaters knocking at a recruiting station's door could be significant. At least 25 percent (309 out of 1,234) of the men rejected by the 169th Canadian Battalion in 1916 had been rejected elsewhere previously.[101] Not all repeaters had been turned away by medical examiners at recruiting stations. Some had been accepted for service but later discharged due to physical or medical unfitness; others had been wounded in combat and discharged on account of their injuries; and many were unfit men who had been erroneously accepted for service and later discharged due to their impairments. The under-age polio victim Russell Mick is a prime example of the last: after being discharged as unfit and sent back to Canada in late 1916, the Ontario native re-enlisted in February 1917 and served until 1920. The determination of some unfit repeaters to get back into khaki verged on bloody-mindedness. The records of the Canadian Expeditionary Force contain numerous examples of men declared unfit in England who re-enlisted three or more times. Thomas Fitzpatrick and Frank Stribball, for example, both enlisted four times, and there were many others like them.[102]

More than one repeater made it back to Europe, some with astounding speed. Arthur Lloyd of the 36th Battalion was declared unfit to serve on 11 February 1916 and returned to Canada. He had re-enlisted by 1 March, however, and was in England again two months later with a reinforcement draft. Ironically, he was sent back to his old battalion. When quizzed by his astonished officers, Lloyd replied that nearly all those who had been sent back to Canada on the advice of medical boards in England had successfully re-enlisted.[103]

Besides the difficulty of combatting the tactics used by men who attempted to re-enlist, the sheer size of the lists of rejected men meant that recruiters could not effectively utilize them. In March 1916, a Department of Militia and Defence memorandum to the Judge Advocate General of the Canadian Militia noted that "the numbers [of rejected men] are so large that it is impossible for the Recruiting Officer to go through them before accepting a recruit." A further problem, one not noted by the memorandum, was that not all recruiting officers, especially those in Canada's rural areas, had access to them.[104] The memorandum noted that the only question concerning military experience currently asked of recruits on attestation papers was question number 10 – "Have you ever served in any military force? (if so state the particulars of former service)" – and suggested that, before enlistment, men should be asked certain questions regarding whether they had previously enlisted or attempted to enlist. The officer conducting the interview should draw the interviewee's attention to the existence of a penalty for providing a false answer to such questions. The memorandum also asked whether an Order in Council would have to be passed under the War Measures Act to provide for such a penalty, or "whether the point is already sufficiently covered?"[105]

On 20 March, Major-General H. Smith, the Judge Advocate General, responded to the memorandum. He did not believe that question 10 covered the point sufficiently because a "question might be raised as to what is really meant by 'served' ... a man might be attested to-day and not be really set at service before his deficiencies are discovered." He believed, however, that due to active service conditions, such cases were better judged by civilian rather than military tribunals, and he attached a draft proposal for an Order in Council.[106] The draft legislation made failure to disclose previous service when enlisting in either the Canadian Expeditionary Force or the Active Militia an offence under the Criminal Code. On summary conviction under provision 15 of the code, guilty parties would be sentenced to a maximum of six months' imprisonment, with or without hard labour. Importantly, once accused of the offence

– which necessitated the production of an attestation paper or service roll purportedly signed by the accused and attested by a justice of the peace or a military officer – the onus was on the accused to prove his innocence (i.e., that he had not lied about his previous service), and not on his accusers to prove guilt.[107]

The legislation was passed by the Governor in Council on 8 May 1917. It kept the penalty and evidentiary requirements suggested by Smith, but rather than focusing on men who failed to disclose former service in the Canadian forces, it broadened the scope of the offence to cover all false statements made by an individual on an attestation paper when being examined or attested for service. As Smith had wished, the power to try such offences was given to the civilian authorities.[108]

This period also saw a change in the character of attestation papers. Besides asking whether recruits had ever served in a military force, the attestation paper now asked four other questions:

13. Have you ever been discharged from any Branch of His Majesty's Forces as medically unfit?
14. If so, what was the nature of the disability?
15. Have you ever offered to serve in any Branch of His Majesty's Forces and been rejected?
16. If so, what was the reason?

Furthermore, the following statement was printed at the bottom of the document: "N.B. – ATTENTION IS DRAWN TO THE FACT THAT ANY PERSON MAKING A FALSE ANSWER TO ANY OF THE ABOVE QUESTIONS IS LIABLE TO A PENALTY."

On 23 February 1916, a circular lettergram from the Militia Council reiterated that "full and sufficient inspections" must be made by medical examiners in order to "prevent [the] possibility of men being included [in the CEF] who are not medically fit, or up to the standard required for active service."[109] This was quickly followed by a circular letter on 4 April stressing the need for "most careful examination of the lungs when recruits are being passed as fit for overseas service." There were good grounds, the letter explained, to suspect that a number of men had pulmonary tuberculosis at the time they enlisted. Underlining Ottawa's concern over this issue, a further letter sent to all Military Districts on 26 April stressed the need for "a very careful examination" of potential recruits' lungs at the time of enlistment.[110]

On 29 April, the Adjutant General informed all Military Districts that when troops had been warned of their impending deployment overseas, the Assistant Director Medical Services of the district was to immediately arrange for a careful medical examination of all ranks at the latest possible date before embarkation. Once the examination was completed, the Assistant Director Medical Services was to forward a certificate to the local district headquarters to this effect. The Adjutant General ended by calling attention to paragraphs 857, 859, and 860 of the *King's Regulations and Orders for the Canadian Militia, 1915.*[111]

On 10 June, another circular letter directed medical officers to ensure that none of the men about to proceed overseas suffered from venereal disease. Those who did were "to be sent to the nearest Military Hospital for treatment." Further demarcating the lines of responsibility, the letter also stated that commanding officers of units or drafts were responsible for ensuring that a medical officer had performed a thorough physical examination of all personnel in the unit or draft, and that there were no cases of venereal disease in their command when it travelled overseas.[112]

The issue of medical inspections before embarkation was addressed yet again on 13 July, when another letter from the Adjutant General's office informed the Military Districts that in the months of April and May there had been approximately 287 cases of infectious diseases (measles, rubella, mumps, and diphtheria) among troops preparing to proceed to England. "Every effort," the letter said, was "to be made to prevent the recurrence of this situation." General Officers Commanding Military Districts, camp commandants, and medical officers were to ensure that the noncommissioned ranks under orders to proceed overseas were medically examined as close to the date of embarkation as possible, paying special attention to detecting, preventing, and isolating infectious diseases to stop their further spread. Once again, the order insisted on a paper trail, placing responsibility for ensuring that these examinations took place squarely at the feet of the officers in charge of the drafts and units. Once the examinations were completed, they were to forward a certificate to that effect to either the General Officer Commanding of the Military District or to their camp commandant.[113]

If the Adjutant General's letters of 29 April, 10 June, and 13 July outlined who was responsible for ensuring that unfit men did not board troopships, a letter from the same office dated 31 May upped the ante more generally with regard to unfit men being passed as fit for service. A copy of a letter sent to Ottawa by Major-General Sam Steele, General Officer Commanding Canadians, Shorncliffe, England, listing a number of men found unfit in units arriving from Canada, was attached, and the Adjutant General stated: "It is to be impressed upon all Medical Examiners of Recruits in each District, that the careless examination of Recruits results in much waste of public funds and causes great inconvenience to the various Units in which the men have enlisted." He then requested that the General Officer Commanding of each

Military District obtain, where possible, an explanation of why the men recorded in Steele's list were considered fit to serve by the medical officers who had passed them.[114]

Spurred by the continuing reports from Shorncliffe about the number of unfit men arriving in England, Ottawa moved to further regulate the medical examination of troops.[115] On 26 August, the Adjutant General sent a long letter to the Military Districts. Titled "Medical Inspection of Troops and Reports to be Rendered Regarding the Same," it was basically a distillation of previous instructions, and stressed that "very special and immediate attention" had to be given to the frequent and regular physical and medical inspection of soldiers as "these [examinations] are quite as important as the medical examination of recruits."

As soon as possible after men were mobilized, they were to be given a thorough medical examination by their unit's medical officer. There were three objectives: (1) to discover "any physical or mental defects, disease or disabilities that may have been overlooked" during the recruit's examination at the time of enlistment; (2) to detect any disease the soldier may have become infected with since enlistment; and (3) to determine whether the soldier was within the minimum and maximum age limits. The report of this examination, including a nominal roll of any unfit men, was to be provided by the examining medical officer to the Assistant Director Medical Services of the district or camp, who would then take the "necessary measures." After this preliminary examination, men were to undergo a weekly examination to discover and control venereal, contagious, or parasitic diseases. They were to be stripped for these examinations. Weekly reports regarding the outcomes were to be sent by the examining medical officer to the Assistant Director Medical Services, who in turn would submit monthly reports to the General Officer Commanding of the Military Districts for transmission to the Militia Council.

Echoing the letters of 29 April, 10 June, and 13 July, the instructions stated that all ranks were to be subjected to a "careful medical inspection" as close as possible to their date of embarkation for overseas. Arrangements for this were to be made by the Assistant Director Medical Services of the district or camp where the men were stationed, but the commanding officer was responsible for ensuring that "every opportunity [was] given for the ... medical inspection" to take place. The commanding officer was to prepare a certificate in triplicate stating that the medical examination had taken place. He was to retain one copy, which was to be surrendered to the overseas authorities upon his unit's arrival in the United Kingdom; the Militia Council and the commanding officer's Military District headquarters were to get one copy each. Indicating that Ottawa's previous requests for documentation had not been carried out as closely as they should have been, the Adjutant General's letter closed by saying that "the strictest attention must be paid" to its instructions in order to avoid "the serious situation [i.e., the high number of unfit recruits arriving in England] reported by the overseas authorities."[116]

On 12 September, commissioned and noncomissioned officers engaged in recruiting were advised in a circular letter written by the Adjutant General that they needed to take much more care when selecting and accepting recruits, particularly those who were outside the age limits. The letter specifically stated that they were not to approach such individuals, and that if such men sought to enlist by giving false ages, the recruiters were to bring to their attention the seriousness of giving or swearing a false oath on an attestation paper.[117]

This document further developed the multi-step examination process that saw potential recruits examined several times before finally being accepted into the ranks. Under this system, local medical examiners – who were either officers in the Canadian Army Medical Corps or properly appointed and trained civilian practitioners – made only preliminary medical examinations of recruits. Recruits who were passed as fit were sent to the nearest mobilization centre to be examined by a medical examination board made up of three members and an eye and ear specialist. If the recruit passed this examination, he was sent to the headquarters of the overseas unit that recruited him. No equipment or clothing was provided until he reported to the unit. If a man was rejected at this second examination, a certificate to this effect was prepared by the board and signed by both the recruit and the president of the board. The document recommended that such certificates be photographed and sent to other mobilization centres to prevent rejected men from trying to enlist elsewhere.[118] Medical boards were also required to compile weekly returns of men rejected as unfit and forward copies to the General Officer Commanding of their Military Districts, the district records officer, and all other mobilization centres. This requirement was for general information purposes and was another means of preventing previously rejected men from enlisting at another centre.

Despite being designed as a safety net for less-than-efficient local examiners, medical boards were not considered infallible. Thus, as soon as a medical board passed a recruit, he reported to his unit and underwent a detailed medical examination by the unit's medical officer. If the medical officer disagreed with the findings of the medical board – if believed the recruit to be unfit – he had to "immediately report to the OC [Officer Commanding] the unit requesting a re-consideration of the case before any additional expense to the public [was] incurred."[119]

A memorandum sent by the Acting Director General Medical Services to all medical officers and civilian practitioners on 3 October 1916 indicates that

Ottawa's repeated instructions still fell on deaf ears. The memorandum noted the serious responsibility that examiners assumed when they passed men as fit for overseas service. It also stressed that it was "essential that no other than medical considerations" should influence medical examiners in making their decisions about a man's fitness or unfitness for service.[120] Echoing medical examination documentation, the memorandum stated that men were either fit or unfit in accordance with Canadian Expeditionary Force regulations. No special employment, other than those laid down in the regulations, was permitted to modify a man's designation.

Indicating that Ottawa recognized the problems that unrestricted private recruiting had caused, especially when coupled with the decline in numbers of willing recruits, the missive noted that anxiety to obtain recruits may have influenced medical examiners to relax standards, and warned that this would eventually produce serious (and, by implication, negative) results. It appealed to the medical examiners' professional pride, noting that their appraisals of men's fitness for combat were accepted as an expression of their professional opinion and as such were taken in good faith by the Department of Militia and Defence. It concluded by noting that "the expenditure of the public funds necessary for the training and maintenance of a soldier of the Expeditionary Force" was based upon these expressions of opinion.[121]

Such costs were not insignificant. A detail report produced by Captain S. Ferguson, a member of Shorncliffe's headquarters staff, on 12 July 1916 estimated that by the time a private had completed his eight months of training in England and was ready for the front, he had cost the Canadian government approximately $1,500. Moreover, the soldier would cost a further $1,000 for each year he was in the Canadian Expeditionary Force.[122] As might be expected, the estimated cost of the training and upkeep of commissioned and noncommissioned officers was "considerably more."[123]

Besides the direct costs of equipping, training, clothing, transporting, feeding, paying, and administering soldiers, there were indirect costs. The same report that calculated the costs of training troops also noted that "these men who are worthless to the service [unfit men incorrectly accepted for service] may have been taken away from useful civilian employment which in their absence is possibly being done by physically fit men." This observation not only reflected the military's fears that the enlistment of fit men was being thwarted by the acceptance of unfit volunteers but also implicitly acknowledged that the military had different levels of fitness from civilian society. An individual unfit for the front could still play a useful role in Canada.[124]

The report also noted the long-term costs to Canada of accepting unfit men. It noted that many unfit men passed as fit to serve and then later declared unfit would be eligible for a pension because they could claim that their disability had been caused by military service, despite the fact that it predated their enlistment. Since the pension board could use only the information provided by such men's files, it would be forced to grant them pensions because their documentation would indicate that they "came into the service fit and [were] now unfit."[125]

Such fears were justified. For example, rejected at Valcartier in September 1914 for being almost blind in his left eye, Percy Dealtry waited in camp for three weeks and then tried again, at which time he was accepted for service. In 1917, he was declared unfit for duty and discharged because of an ankle injury resulting from being run over by a field ambulance. He immediately attempted to augment his disability pension by claiming that the problems with his left eye had been caused by a shrapnel wound he suffered while serving at the front. Exhibiting a healthy dose of skepticism, the doctor who examined Dealtry noted that there was no record of his ever receiving such a wound and that the alleged shrapnel scars around Dealtry's eyes appeared to be exceptionally well healed. And well they should, since Dealtry's attestation papers indicate that they were due to a prewar injury. Ever the optimist and perhaps unaware that the authorities were in possession of his attestation papers, Dealtry attempted to explain the lack of documentation relating to his "debilitating wound" by stating that he had not considered his injury serious enough at the time to warrant reporting it to his commanding officer. Unsurprisingly, Dealtry's claim was ultimately unsuccessful.[126]

Apparently all these exhortations were not enough. On 16 December 1916, an obviously exasperated Militia Headquarters in Ottawa again drew the attention of the Military Districts to the "enormous wastage in men, time and money, due to the negligence on the part of Examining Officers, both at Recruiting Offices and in the Canadian Expeditionary Force units," and stated that "the habit of shoving a man through on the assumption that recruits are badly needed, and that he will probably pass future medical examinations must positively cease." Stressing the seriousness of the issue, this letter ended by directing General Officers Commanding Military Districts to bring the matter to the attention of recruiting officers and unit commanders "as forcibly as possible."[127] In the same period, Ottawa seriously considered fining medical officers the $120 it cost to ship an unfit man back to Canada from Britain. This measure was ultimately rejected because it was believed, with more than a little justification, that medical officers would turn away all individuals for fear of being punished for an innocent mistake.[128]

In the end, such fines were unnecessary. By 1917, things appeared to be improving with regard to the number of unfit men arriving in England with drafts from

Canada. Responding to questions in the House of Commons about the number of unfit men arriving in England, specifically comments made in the Bruce Report, Minister of Militia and Defence Sir Edward Kemp tabled a report that he had recently received from Colonel J.L. Potter, Acting Director General Medical Services in Canada. The report indicated that less than 1 percent of the men who had arrived in England in early 1917 were deemed unfit on disembarkation. As for those found unfit, their impairments were either hard to detect or "did not render them absolutely unfit for some duty in England." As a result, Kemp confidently stated that the myriad of problems Canada had faced with regard to the medical examination of recruits had applied "to the earlier, not the later stages of the war." At first glance, Kemp's claim appeared to have a shallow foundation: the total number of men examined in Potter's report was 1,680, spread over seven units, the largest of which numbered 392 men and the smallest, 25.[129] Other evidence supported it. In late 1916, large numbers of men with disqualifying impairments were discovered during mandated post-enlistment examinations before being shipped to Europe, indicating that the checks put in place in response to problems with unit-level medical examinations were working.[130] Indeed, as the case of the 209th Battalion demonstrates, individual units found it increasingly difficult to pass unfit men without their being discovered in Canada. Thus, Kemp's observation that things had improved as "regulations regarding the examination have been bettered in the light of the experience that had been gained" was fair, as was his view that "it was reasonable to suppose that [many of the problems that occurred in relation to the medical examination of recruits] would not have occurred" if the Canadian government and Canadian medical professionals had had more military experience in 1914.[131]

Also fair was Kemp's warning that statistics relating to the number of men unfit for service at the front disembarking in England needed to be taken with a grain of salt. Although a man might be unfit for the trenches upon arrival in England, he might not always be so. Numerous impairments could be corrected by medical procedures or with corrective equipment. Furthermore, even if a man could not be brought up to Category A standards, this did not mean he was unfit for the military, despite what some critics might have thought. By 1917, the Canadian military had not only recognized but also codified within the *Classification of Men by Categories in Canada,* and later the *Classification of Men by Categories in Britain,* the fact that many support positions could be filled by men not fit for the trenches.

4
Clashing Concepts of Fitness

CONCEPTS OF MASCULINITY, health, and indeed martial value played an important role in the way military fitness was defined both officially and unofficially. Civilian perceptions of health sometimes collided violently with military regulations as they intersected in the bodies of Canadian Expeditionary Force recruits. Civilians were shocked by the military's rejection of men because of what they believed were minor impairments. This shock could quickly turn to anger. As the number of the apparently healthy men rejected for service increased, civilian commentators and rejected men alike began penning highly critical, often derogatory assessments of both the Canadian military's selection criteria and those who conducted the medical examinations. Montreal's *Labour World* wondered acerbically in 1916 how a rejected man's "anatomy" could make him unfit "to be destroyed by a machine gun or shot down by a German sniper? What is the matter? Oh! Nothing except perhaps a crooked toe, or an eye that cannot tell an 'O' from an 'A' at fifty yards, or maybe something less important."[1] In some cases, the rancour persisted well after the war had ended. Will R. Bird pulled no punches in his postwar memoir, *And We Go On*, calling the recruiting officers who had rejected him and "hundreds of [other] big, fit men" in the early years of the war "mosquito-brained."[2]

Some of these critics' greatest supporters could be found among those they condemned. Imbued with a belief that their professional expertise made them far more qualified than the military authorities to judge a man's ability to withstand the rigours of combat, a number of medical examiners both implicitly and explicitly questioned the regulations that they were expected to enforce. Some even circumvented them.

The Canadian military authorities were equally perturbed. Despite what many of their critics believed, not all the medical requirements that debarred so many "aspirant[s] to the V.C." were "old-womanish regulations" devised by officious pen-pushers who delighted in bureaucratic standardization; rather, they were based on serious considerations of perceived military realities. A physical condition that posed little or no impediment to a man on the streets of Vancouver, in the wheatfields of Saskatchewan, or on a Nova Scotia fishing boat could be potentially deadly to him and his comrades on the field of battle. The fact that

80   *Unwanted Warriors*

many doctors and civilians could not, or in many cases would not, see this caused the military authorities considerable trouble. The problems took the form not only of the number of unfit men who proceeded overseas and ended up causing a drain on valuable resources but also, ironically, of repeated criticism from numerous quarters, including both civilian and medical, of the Canadian Army Medical Corps for allowing such men into the service. Indeed, in response to criticism of the medical examination of recruits launched in the House of Commons by Alphonse Verville, Member of Parliament for Maisonneuve,[3] in May 1916, Colonel J.L. Potter, Acting Director General Medical Services, noted:

> The examination of recruits, to be carried out successfully, requires special training, and it can be understood how a good general practitioner might overlook points, which from a military standpoint, are considered as impairing efficiency, but which, in civil life, are not considered to be causative of physical unfitness. Men suffering from disabilities which, apparently, do not impair, in their civil occupations, often have disabilities which, when under the hardships of active service, are very likely to render them invalids.[4]

Clashing concepts of fitness and medical health were not the only factors that caused men who did not meet the military's minimum physical and medical requirements to be accepted into the ranks of the Expeditionary Force. However, the clash between civilian and military constructions of combat fitness provides a useful insight into how the interrelated concepts of disability/ability and fitness/unfitness exist on a sliding scale. Moreover, it indicates that these concepts are based as much on social construction as on material reality. A man could be considered fit by civilian society while at the same time be deemed unfit, and even disabled, by the military. Indeed, many of the defects that caused men to be rejected were noteworthy only from a military standpoint. While a man standing 5 feet, 1 inch in 1914 may have been considered unfit for service by the military, he certainly would not have been considered defective in civilian society. Likewise, although mechanical defects, and indeed amputations, may have rendered a man unfit to be a member of a well-oiled fighting machine, they were not necessarily serious impairments, if at all, in civilian life.[5] Unable to walk properly or stand for any length of time due to atrophied muscles in his right thigh, twenty-four-year-old John Carment of Vernon, British Columbia, was of no use as a soldier but his disability did not prevent him from being a law clerk. Lest one think such comments apply to men in white-collar occupations only, it should be noted that similar observations can be made with regard to those working in highly physical occupations. Thirty-one-year-old Charles Martell, for example, was unfit for the Expeditionary Force because of his atrophied left arm, but he worked in the coal mines of Nova Scotia.[6] In many cases, the situation of men with sensory defects differed little from that of men with mechanical impairments. Limited vision could be corrected with glasses, for example, and not all occupations required an individual to have good hearing. Twenty-seven-year-old Sydney Peterson of Toronto had enjoyed a career as a butcher before enlisting despite the fact that he had been almost completely deaf since he was twelve years old.[7]

One of the bitterest conflicts between civilians and the military authorities over what made a man fit to fight centred on volunteers' mouths. At the start of the war, the Canadian Expeditionary Force's rejection of men with bad teeth came under heavy fire repeatedly from members of the public who could not fathom why the force was turning away "healthy" volunteers. This is understandable. Many such men appeared not to be suffering any ill effects from their gummy condition, other than perhaps cosmetic. More importantly, the lack of a full set of teeth did not prevent scores of men from successfully working in Canada's most physically demanding and dangerous occupations, such as logging, mining, construction, farming, and fishing.

Given such realities, few Canadians could understand how rotten or missing teeth could keep a man from becoming an efficient soldier. Perfect teeth were not, after all, required for marching or digging trenches; nor, most significantly, were they essential to the use of a weapon. One critic sarcastically advised Canadian examiners to remember the words of a Scotsman rejected for service because his teeth were not up to standard: "Man, I dinna want tae bite the Germans; I'm offerin' tae shoot them."[8] The author was actually paraphrasing a cartoon that appeared in *Punch* magazine on 19 August 1914. In the cartoon, an incredulous volunteer who had just been rejected on account of his teeth tells his medical examiner, "Man, ye're making a gran' mistake. I'm no wanting to bite the Germans, I'm wanting to shoot them."[9] This is not to say that similar sentiments were not expressed by frustrated volunteers at recruiting stations around Canada and the rest of the Empire. Robert Roberts, for example, described in his memoir of growing up in Salford, England, in the early twentieth century the following exchange between his mother and one Mr. Bickham, an Anglo-Boer War veteran: "On 5 August [1914] in our village we saw Mr. Bickham ... returning from an attempt to join up. 'Turned down!' he said disgustedly – 'Bad teeth! They must want blokes to bite the damned Germans!' ... Mr. Bickham went on his way. 'They'll be pulling me in, though,' he called over his shoulder, 'before this lot's done!'"[10] Apocryphal or not, the cartoon reflected civilian anger and disbelief over military dental requirements. Indeed, one historian would later state that it demonstrated that "even the layman could see the injustice and futility" of the Imperial Army's dental requirements.[11]

The barrage of criticism was exacerbated by the military authorities' concomitant rejection of men who had corrected their dental deficiencies with some form of dental appliance. In early-twentieth-century Canada, it was common, especially among the working class and rural populations, for people to have all their teeth, both rotten and healthy, removed and replaced with dentures in early adulthood. This custom was based on a number of factors. In an era when dental and gum disease was prevalent, particularly in poor communities due to poor dental hygiene, it was cheaper for many to have all their teeth extracted and replaced with dentures in one sitting rather than face the constant expense, not to mention pain, of ongoing dental repair work. This was especially true if one lived in an isolated community with no easy access to medical treatment. Besides being a practical economic choice for many Canadians, the practice of having one's teeth replaced with dentures was supported by many medical practitioners. Indeed, both dentists and doctors saw "dental clear-outs" as a useful precaution against diseases of the gastrointestinal canal and arthritis.[12]

Given such circumstances, civilians asked, why would the military reject men because they wore dentures, especially if they improved a man's long-term health prospects? Often expressed in letters to the editors of Canada's major dailies, these questions grew particularly pointed when they referenced individuals whose overall physical health, at least in the eyes of the general public, made them ideal candidates for military service:

> ... a young man in perfect health, with a strong, hardy body after four years of bush work, who enlisted in the third contingent was ... rejected for what seems a childish reason. The military doctor spent very little time with his tape-line on this young fellow, and, indeed could hardly be said to have examined him at all, being so brawny and well developed as not to require serious medical examination. When the test was thought to be over, the doctor asked to see the teeth, and because this prospective aspirant to the V.C. was fortunate enough to be the possessor of a set of particularly good upper false teeth instead of a mouthful of rotten teeth, as had nearly all of his chums who passed the test, he was rejected as physically unfit on that account. Does it not seem contradictory that the medical and dental professions should recommend the substitution of false for rotten teeth, and now when strong men are wanted that they should be turned down for having false teeth at all? ... Before the war is over the military authorities may be glad to quit their old womanish hard-and-fast regulations and be thankful to enlist men with much more serious defects than false teeth.[13]

Such complaints were echoed, albeit with more reserve, in the *Toronto Star* and by medical professionals. Noting that "bad teeth had been the cause of the rejection of many otherwise sound men," the Toronto *Globe* stated that many dentists agreed that the Expeditionary Force's dental regulations were "too severe."[14]

At least some of the medical officers working at Valcartier in August and September 1914 were sympathetic to, if not in agreement with, the military's civilian critics on the question of bad teeth and dentures. Captain Gordon L. Cockburn, for instance, commented on the attestation paper of the dentally challenged Charles Gallinger that the twenty-seven-year-old would be physically fit if he had an upper plate.[15] He made similar observations on the attestation papers of a number of gummy recruits as well.[16] Cockburn was not alone. Echoing his words, one unidentified officer twice noted that thirty-four-year-old Robert Lahiff would be fit if he had dentures for his upper jaw.[17] Other medical officers' comments were more subtle but no less revealing. Noting that E.A. West was "fit except no teeth upper jaw," Lieutenant N.E. Leslie observed that West "claims he has a plate." Likewise, on rejecting Alfred A. Dasey because he had no upper teeth, Lieutenant Ernest Wilson commented that Dasey had a plate but it had been broken and not replaced. The comments of both Leslie and Wilson suggest that if these two volunteers had possessed dentures, the two doctors would have judged their subjects fit to serve.[18]

In contrast, Captain Cockburn did not consider dentures the key to martial fitness for all gummy volunteers who crossed his path: six days after stating that Charles Gallinger would be fit if he had a plate, Cockburn rejected thirty-eight-year-old Charles Elkes as unfit for service due to his bad teeth.[19] Lieutenants Leslie and Wilson also rejected other volunteers with bad teeth and/or dentures without comment about their military potential.[20] Moreover, even in the cases where the medical examiners may have felt that a dentally deficient individual was fit to fight, they did not pass him, indicating that while they were prepared to critique the military's dental regulations, they were not, at least in these cases, prepared to violate them.

Despite the sentiment expressed by the disgruntled volunteer in the *Punch* cartoon, the military authorities were well aware that dentally challenged would-be warriors were proposing to shoot rather than savage Canada's enemies.[21] However, they were expected to consume army rations. Most, if not all, of the rations provided to British Imperial Forces in the field at the start of the twentieth century could be described as tough at best and unyielding at worst. During the Anglo-Boer War, the combination of hard army biscuits (hardtack) and dried slices of ox not only damaged many men's teeth but also caused a significant number of men to be invalided home because they could not masticate army food. Much of the damage was exacerbated by dental neglect and disease – a fact not lost on the first dental surgeon, Dr. Frederick Newland-Pedley, appointed to the British Forces in South Africa – but these army staples were difficult to chew even for men with healthy teeth.[22] Indeed, observing that the struggle between army rations and soldiers' teeth was "uneven," one British field officer only half-jokingly stated that "even with an average set [of teeth], straining on an average biscuit, you never felt quite certain which would be the first to go – your teeth or the biscuit." The officer also claimed that more than 95 percent of the men in his company suffered some form of dental injury as a result of eating army rations.[23] Hardtack was named thus with good reason.

Little had changed by the outbreak of the Great War.[24] Lieutenant Louis Keene, for example, thought that the chief ingredient of hardtack, which he less than appetizingly described as a "kind of dog biscuit," was "cement." Hinting at the public's bewilderment about the military's dental requirements, he commented: "We always wondered why they were so particular about a man's teeth in the army. Now I know." Keene's analysis was echoed by Sergeant Ernest G. Black, who compared eating the number four variety of hardtack with "gnawing on an old bone." Full of strings of gristle, globs of fat, and patches of skin, bully beef – the major source of protein for men in the trenches – was hardly less malleable and even less appetizing.[25] Indeed, Agar Adamson told his wife in a March 1915 letter that the beef he had recently been served "would have ruined the teeth of a bull-terrier and sent him home with stomach trouble."[26]

Although soldiers' diets might have been supplemented on occasion by stew, illicit foraging, food parcels from home, and shopping trips behind the lines,[27] the fact remained that the army was not in the business of meeting the specialist dietary requirements of its rank-and-file troops. Bully beef and hardtack were the order of the day.[28] Faced with such singular culinary delights, a strong set of choppers (backed up by copious amounts of water for soaking the rations in the hope of making them malleable, or perhaps by a hammer for breaking them up) was essential if one were to get the nutrition required to face the many dangers of the Western Front. Indeed, an inability to chew solid food went from being a simple inconvenience that might cause embarrassment at dinner parties to a serious disability with potentially far-reaching consequences. A soldier who was unable to eat the food supplied to him would very quickly cease to function effectively on the battlefield and would face the very real possibility of becoming more susceptible to the myriad of diseases that stalked the trenches – threatening not only his health but also the safety of his comrades and the effective operation of his unit.

That medical officers at Valcartier were guided by consideration of whether recruits would be able to consume army rations is evidenced by a number of comments written on the attestation papers of men rejected because of the state of their teeth. Captain C.R. Graham rejected Charles Powell believing that the twenty-two-year-old's lack of molars would make it impossible for him to eat. He also rejected twenty-four-year-old Robert Skead, who was unable to chew meat and who lacked opposing molars.[29] More generally, the fact that 25 percent of cases where bad teeth were listed as a reason for rejection directly referenced a lack of chewing teeth indicates the central role the ability to efficiently masticate food played in medical officers' decision on whether the state of a recruit's teeth was good enough to allow him to serve.

Unlike in later years, the plethora of recruits at Valcartier in August–September 1914 meant that medical examiners could afford to be picky in deciding whom to accept for service, and men who were technically fit according to military regulations may well have been rejected. In his memoir *And We Go On,* Will R. Bird attributed his rejection based on broken teeth to the Expeditionary Force's need to find "any old excuse" to whittle down the forest of eager recruits that roughly doubled the force's initial requirement at the outbreak of the war.[30] Bird exceeded all of the force's physical requirements, standing 5 feet, 8.75 inches tall, possessing an expanded chest measurement of 36 inches, and weighing a healthy 154 pounds.[31] Moreover, and much more telling, Bird noted that the recruiting officer who rejected him had stated that the battalion could "get enough good men without taking them we've got to repair."[32] Bird would be rejected two more times before finally being accepted in 1916 by the 193rd Canadian Infantry Battalion.[33] Even after being accepted for service and shipped to England, his shattered teeth continued to be noticed. His attempt to join a draft for the 42nd Battalion was initially turned down by a medical officer who did not believe his teeth were up to standard and, for lack of time, refused Bird's request to extract them. Undeterred, Bird found another way into the draft.[34]

Besides concerns that men with dentures would be unable to eat army rations and that dentures did not always work well, there was an underlying concern in some sectors that these oral prostheses might open the door for recruits to give in to innate moral impairments. As Newland-Pedley noted in the *Lancet* in December 1914: "Artificial teeth do not always yield good results and offer too greater chance to the malingerer. In a moment he may pocket his artificial teeth or get rid of them, and then be sent home amongst the dental failures."[35] These fears were echoed four months later by Dr. Sir Thomas Oliver, the honorary colonel of Britain's 20th Battalion (Tyneside Scottish) in an article discussing the physical defects he had encountered while examining men for the battalion. He noted that one drawback of the army's recent decision to provide artificial teeth to men who needed them was that if a man so supplied was "dissatisfied [at the front] or had a grievance he [might] throw his dentures away" and, claiming to be unable to eat his rations, have to be shipped home when his unit could least afford it.[36]

Eyesight, specifically the use of glasses to meet minimum military standards of vision, was also a point of dispute. At the start of the Great War, the Canadian forces' standards of visual acuity were high, requiring volunteers to have almost if not perfect vision. Such requirements caused large numbers of otherwise healthy men to be rejected as unfit for service. Indeed, they led to a number of men being turned away who were probably unaware that they suffered from any form of visual defect and, more importantly, whose fitness for work was never questioned in civilian society. Walter Hancock, for example, was rejected because his visual acuity was 20/30.[37] Even when standards were lowered, many men were still rejected because they were deemed visually impaired. It was reported in April 1916, for example, that of the 7,122 men rejected as unfit for service in Toronto, 2,348 (around 33 percent) had been rejected because of their eyesight.[38]

The blanket rejection of men with "substandard" eyesight was obliquely questioned by some medical officers at Valcartier. Although forced to reject eighteen-year-old William Dix for substandard vision, Captain A.M. Forbes stated that while the young man was "no good for a rifleman," he was "fit for any other branch of service." These words echoed those that Forbes had inscribed on the attestation paper of twenty-two-year-old William Kavanagh only a day before.[39] In some instances, medical officers went so far as to note that a volunteer's level of visual acuity did not interfere with his designated role in the Expeditionary Force. John Hartnell had "defective vision," Captain S.F. McLaren acknowledged, "but is a mechanic in the automobile section." H.E MacDermot noted that although Norman Health was "almost stone blind in his [right] eye ... [he was employed as] ... Capt. Miekles servant & won't be on active service."[40]

The strongest assault on the military's visual acuity regulations came from the United Kingdom in 1916. In an article published in the 6 May 1916 issue of the *Lancet*, Drs. J.V. Paterson and H.M. Traquair, ophthalmic surgeons at Edinburgh's Royal Infirmary, launched a stinging attack on the visual standards required of recruits by the British Army and, by extension, the Canadian forces. The foremost target of their ire was the policy banning the wearing of spectacles by enlisted men on active service, which they believed was unnecessarily limiting the army's pool of recruits. While acknowledging that such a ban had made sense when the British Army operated in foreign countries far from support centres, Paterson and Traquair could not understand why such a policy was being adhered to when "our main army is fighting in allied and adjacent countries."[41] They buttressed their position by noting not only that the use of corrective eyewear was not proscribed in the armies of the "great continental powers" (Germany, Austria, Italy and France) but also that the military's blanket ban on glasses was potentially causing it to fill its ranks with less efficient marksmen than were found in enemy formations:

> As far as shooting is concerned, it is generally agreed that vision of 6/12 [20/40] at least is necessary, and, on the continent it is believed that a soldier with 6/12 vision wearing glasses is more efficient than another with 6/24 [20/80] vision without glasses. Continental authorities have found that on the average soldiers who see best shoot best and that those who wear correcting spectacles shoot better than those who do not.[42]

The two surgeons also questioned the minimum requirements for a recruit's worse eye, noting that they excluded from service a considerable number of men who had defective vision in one eye even though their vision in the other eye might be excellent. Such men, Paterson and Traquair noted, were likely to be more efficient than men who had 20/80 vision in both eyes. They argued that there was an urgent need to rethink the army's visual requirements.

A similar assault, albeit much less public, was launched in Canada in the same month that Paterson and Traquair's article appeared in the *Lancet*. Responding to a request from Acting Director General Medical Services Colonel Potter for his views regarding the relaxation of vision requirements for recruits, Dr. J.C. Connell, dean of medicine at Queen's University (1903–29) and a pioneer in eye, ear, nose, and throat surgery,[43] recommended that "the use of glasses should be permitted to pass the [visual acuity] tests and should then be ordered for constant use." Connell's reasoning was similar to Paterson and Traquair's. He noted that Europe's continental powers allowed their troops to wear glasses, and raised the possibility that the prohibition had the effect of lowering the average visual acuity of Imperial troops compared with the troops of other powers.[44]

Equally problematic was the army's insistence that the recruit's stronger eye had to be his right eye. This meant that otherwise fit men with weak right eyes but strong left eyes were rejected as unfit for frontline positions. The favouring of the right eye over the left eye as a means of determining a man's fitness for frontline service was, it seems, based on concerns for standardization and efficiency. Recruits, no matter what their preferred hand, were trained to fire right-handed, and therefore needed to be able to aim with their right eye.[45] There were several reasons for this. First, standard-issue rifles were right-handed (both the bolt and spent cartridge ejection point were on the right side of the weapon). Firing such weapons left-handed could potentially reduce the soldier's rate of fire and accuracy significantly.[46] Given that the British Army required its troops to be capable of a high rate of aimed fire (fifteen bullets a minute), anything that was likely to prevent a soldier from reaching this rate of fire –

including, rightly or wrongly, handedness – was jettisoned. More generally, but related to this, infantry drill was very specific and uniform. Troops were drilled and trained uniformly as right-handers. Recruits were to adapt to the weapon, not the weapon to the recruits.

Similar questions arose with regard to the military's height requirements. On 4 November 1914, *Punch* published a cartoon depicting a man challenging his rejection due to his size:

"Not big enough! D'yer know 'oo I am? D'yer know foive year ago I was champion light-weight of Wapping?"

"I've no doubt that you're a good man: But, you see, you don't come up to the required measurements, so I'm afraid that's the end of it."

"Oh, all right then. Only, mind yer, if yer go an lose this 'ere war – well, don't blame me – that's all."[47]

Dramatic as *Punch*'s perturbed pugilist's final comments may have been, they did reflect the position of many individuals who wondered why substantial height was considered necessary to make a man a good soldier. Some even went so far as to attempt to physically demonstrate that being short was not an impairment with regard to combat. The idea of "bantam battalions," which were first formed in England, was said to have occurred to Alfred Bigland, Member of Parliament for Birkenhead, after he was told of a group of miners from Durham who had been rejected for service on account of their height. In response, one of the miners, "scoff[ing] at the idea that an inch height precluded him from joining the Army," offered to fight any man in the room. It took considerable time to remove the enraged miner – who had been rejected four or five times previously – from the office.[48]

The furious miner had a point. The advent of rifles, machine guns, and artillery had greatly levelled the playing field in both reach and killing power. Any advantage a taller man may have had over his shorter opponent when the two were armed with swords or battle-axes was lost when they were shooting at each other over the tops of trenches or were on the receiving end of an artillery barrage.

Medical professionals also supported the Durham coal miner's stance. On 9 February 1915, Dr. M.S. Pembrey, a physiology lecturer at London's Guy's Hospital, presented a paper titled "Tall versus Short Men for the Army" to the London sessional meeting of the Royal Sanitary Institute. It sought to answer the question of whether the raising of bantam battalions in England and Wales could be defended on any grounds other than necessity. Pembrey argued that shorter men were actually physiologically *superior* to taller men when it came to modern warfare. Not only did they present a smaller target to snipers but their build, unlike that of large men, "favoured rapidity of action, strength and endurance." Moreover, short men were far more firmly placed upon their feet because they had a lower centre of gravity. Pembrey buttressed his position with reference to the logistical advantages that smaller men offered the military. As they supposedly required less food, clothing, and shelter and needed smaller boots, the army would save on resources. Nor would trenches need to be so deep. In fact, in Pembrey's mind simple anatomical measurements could never serve as an accurate guide of a man's martial worth. The test of a soldier's efficiency was "not his height nor his weight nor his girth but his ability to stand the physical and mental stresses of active service." He also needed to be able to march, to shoot accurately, and to be willing "to subordinate his interests to those of the race."[49]

Some of Pembrey's arguments are open to question. Not only was the claim that short men offered a smaller target snipers dubious at best but the nature of trench warfare meant that snipers had only small targets to engage; it also ignored the fact that snipers' bullets – and aimed small-arms fire in general – accounted for relatively few casualties. Indeed, a soldier's height was of little consequence when it came to the number one killer on the Western Front: artillery.[50] Nevertheless, Pembrey's ideas – for good or ill – were certainly shared by some Canadians. A Toronto *Globe* article about the proposed raising of a bantam battalion in the city noted that the unit's proponents "urged that short sturdy men are better for trench fighting and present a smaller target for the enemy."[51] Likewise, one of the reasons Mrs. Adelaide Yuill of Granum, Alberta, advanced when attempting to have her son, Lionel, discharged from the Canadian Expeditionary Force was his height: standing 6 feet, 2 inches, he would, she feared, be "a target for sharp shooters."[52] Liberal Senator Philippe-Auguste Choquette countered a spiteful comment from a political rival that implied he would be no good as a soldier because of his small stature by observing that he might be a better soldier than his tormentor because "some big men are not as good as the little ones. The big bottles do not always contain the best medicine."[53]

Both Choquette's riposte and Pembrey's studied argument were supported the observations of men serving in the trenches. Private Donald Fraser of the 31st Canadian Infantry Battalion noted in his journal in late 1915 that while in peacetime people drew their conclusions about a man's suitability to be a soldier from his physique, physical size and strength were poor indicators of a man's worth in the trenches. "The best fighter," he stated, "may be summed up in the words 'fearlessness' and 'grit' two qualities that every husky [man] has not got and qualities that sometimes the weakest, the softest and apparently the most effeminate have." Pushing his point home, Fraser observed that on more than one occasion he had seen "big, strong, noisy fellows" become almost completely paralyzed by fear when faced with trying conditions, while "little insignificant runts" stood by "unconcerned and ready to give a good account of themselves."[54] He made a similar observation in early 1916 with regard to one Lieutenant Robertson. Describing Robertson as very effeminate in his mannerisms, Fraser stated that in spite of initial doubts, the men of the battalion "thought the world" of the lieutenant because he "was absolutely fearless." He observed that "this is a war in which blood counts, not bone; nerve is the test and not strength," and followed this story with a similar account of an officer from the 1st Division who, despite looking as though "he had not the strength or grit of a fly," was exceptionally daring and willing to tackle any dangerous work.[55]

It should be noted that Fraser's comments, like those of Pembrey and Choquette, struck at some of the central characteristics that many members of the public and the military believed made a good soldier: a powerful build and a "manly" demeanour. Size did not matter, but "guts" did. When shells began to fly, it was not necessarily the visual paragons of Canadian manhood who proved to be the best soldiers but rather those who seemed to be – at first glance, at least – the antithesis of the masculine ideal.

If the military's size requirements were open to question, so was its prohibition of men with flat feet. A nebulous term that covered a variety of different conditions, "flat foot," as the term suggests, was taken to be characterized by a low longitudinal arch of the foot. Such low (collapsed) arches were deemed to be a visible indicator of damage to the muscles of the foot. This damage was further characterized by pain when pressure was put on the foot, and, as a result, hindered walking long distances. In a period when the major form of transportation for most soldiers remained their own two feet, such an impairment was an immediate reason for rejection.

A number of medical authorities criticized the practice of using the size of the arch of the foot to diagnose muscle damage, and therefore to reject an individual as unfit. They pointed out that not all cases of a low arch indicated weakened or damaged foot muscles but rather the development of muscle tissue. In fact, more than one observer noted that flat feet were common among labourers and lumberman in Canada. This "flatness" would not, critics argued, impinge on such men's ability to be good soldiers. Alphonse Verville, for example, condemned the rejection of a number of lumbermen due to their flat feet by stating that he would "like to find the doctor who rejected ... [these men] ... who is man enough to walk all day with these woodsmen. This class of men can stand more hardship than any others in the country."[56] Some doctors agreed with him. As Major W.H. Reilly, Assistant Director Medical Services of Military

District 10, noted in a letter to the Assistant Adjutant General in charge of Administration of the military district in early 1917: "There is a variety of opinion among surgeons in reference to Flat Feet. More experienced surgeons and particularly orthopaedic specialists are of the opinion that the man with Flat Feet is quite fit for service."[57] In light of such criticisms the military moved, as they had with other conditions, to provide medical officers with a clear definition of flat feet. Medical examiners were warned that the height of a man's foot arch was no guide.[58] It was also acknowledged that "strains of the longitudinal arches of the foot" and related conditions, such as hallux rigidus and hallux valgus, could either be corrected or elevated, thereby making an individual fit for some forms of military service.[59]

Conceptual differences regarding what characteristics made a man fit to fight caused some medical examiners to pass men as fit to serve despite the fact that they possessed an impairment that should have disqualified them from entering the ranks. This is evinced by the case of hockey great Frank McGee, who was accepted for service in the 21st Canadian Infantry Battalion in 1914 despite being blind in his left eye, an impairment that should have caused him to be declared unfit. An oft-quoted story states that McGee employed a ruse to hide his blindness from his medical examiner, but such was not the case. The senior officers of the 21st Battalion were well aware of his impairment, as was the Canadian hockey public more generally. Such a ruse would have been not only ineffective but also pointless. Rather, McGee was accepted for service in the battalion, and, more importantly, passed as fit for service by his examining medical officer, a Lieutenant Crawford, for two reasons: (1) his undeniable sporting prowess, and (2) his reputation as an unforgiving rink warrior in a period when hockey was known as an exceptionally brutal, and at times deadly, sport. Simply put, in the eyes of his medical examiner, McGee's dominance of the blood-spattered rink trumped his impairment. Indeed, at a time when many Canadians believed that hockey made the male population ready for war, it marked him as prime fighting stock. McGee was killed at the Somme in September 1916.[60]

Perceptions of who was fit to don the khaki were influenced by more than just military regulations and battlefield realities. Civilian and medical professionals' constructions of health and masculinity – which often questioned, if not directly opposed, military authorities' constructions of military fitness – also played a role in dictating not only who was labelled fit to serve but also the evolution of military regulations. This is important because it highlights the shifting foundations on which the concept of military ability was based. Couched in, and built on, social values as much as biological conditions, the concept was at best an insecure and contested formulation. As the case of Frank McGee indicates, in some instances social constructions actually trumped somatic realities when it came to labelling (or, in McGee's case, not labelling) an individual as unfit. McGee did not look or act unfit to fight – ergo, in the eyes of the public, he was not unfit. His disqualifying visual impairment was simply not part of the equation. The tendency of the public to judge an individual's military fitness in this manner, based on visual indicators, caused many rejected volunteers to suffer considerable ill treatment because they did not appear, in the eyes of the public, to be disabled and therefore unfit to serve. Indeed, far from being visibly identifiable, most rejected volunteers were not visibly different from men who were being accepted for service.

5
Not Visibly Different
Describing the Rejected

*In them days, it was rather annoying to go out at all because the men in
uniform, when you would walk down the street, they'd come and tap you on
the shoulder and say, "why ain't you in the army?" And I used to have difficulty
even when I told them I had bad ears because I'd had Scarlet fever. "Go on, try
again." I used to say what the hell's the use of trying after they turned me down?
I tried often enough. But, oh Jesus, they used to pressure the life out of you.
It was hell.*

– Martin Colby, Toronto[1]

The lack of visible difference between many rejected men and those deemed
fit to fight meant that the former faced continual harassment on the streets of
Canada's towns and cities at the hands of zealous recruiters, both official and
unofficial, who sought to bolster the ranks of the Canadian Expeditionary Force.
Moreover, as Martin Colby's comments indicate, many rejected men's legitimate explanations of why they were not wearing the khaki were often dismissed
out of hand. At best, such men were thought not to have tried hard enough to
enlist, a belief that was supported by reports that lauded men who, after being
rejected on their first attempt, kept presenting themselves at recruiting stations.
In March 1916, for example, the Toronto *Globe* wrote approvingly about a man
who had been rejected at eight different depots but was still expressing "a keen
desire to get to the front some how."[2] Seven months later, a similar story appeared in the *Ottawa Citizen*.[3] At worst, rejected volunteers were seen as cowards
and shirkers who were using a convenient, and perhaps fabricated, excuse in
order to avoid their duty.

That many rejected men were largely indistinguishable from their successful
colleagues is supported by a close examination of the characteristics of 3,050
men turned away at Valcartier in 1914.[4] These men shared similar social and
physical characteristics as those judged fit to fight. This is unsurprising. Those
rejected did, after all, come from the same pool of volunteers as those accepted
for service. Importantly, the vast majority of impairments that caused men to
be rejected were either invisible or were not viewed as disabling by civilian
society. As previously noted, evidence drawn from a variety of different sources

– including government reports, newspaper records, and personal memoirs – suggests that such data can be extrapolated to create a general description of men rejected as unfit for service over the entire period of the war.

Rejectees Martin Colby and Will R. Bird, to name but two examples, attest to the validity of this hypothesis. However, one of the strongest pieces of evidence comes from the development of identifying lapel badges for rejected men. Beginning late in 1915, individual battalions and recruiting leagues began providing rejected volunteers with badges indicating that the wearer had attempted to sign up. This was seen as necessary – at least in those parts of Canada that supported the war – because many rejected men were being harassed on the streets. This harassment was directly linked to the fact that many rejected volunteers were not visibly different from those deemed fit to fight.

So what characterized rejected volunteers in August–September 1914? With regard to faith, Anglicans predominated, making up 44 percent of 2,294 rejected volunteers whose attestation papers recorded religious devotion.[5] Roman Catholics and Presbyterians followed, making up 23 percent and 18 percent, respectively. Methodists came in a poor fourth, at 8 percent.[6] These proportions are generally in accordance with those found in the Canadian Expeditionary Force for the years 1914 to 1918, which were 31 percent Anglican, 23 percent Roman Catholic, 21 percent Presbyterian, and 14 percent Methodists.[7]

Moving from the soul to the body, 386 (21 percent) of the 1,822 men in the "Files of CEF Volunteers Who Were Rejected" whose attestation papers recorded distinctive characteristics were tattooed. The level of tattooing varied from individual to individual, ranging from dots or simple initials on hands and forearms to heavy tattooing on arms, legs, and torso. The tattoos borne by these men offer some indication of their personal histories, social backgrounds, and individual affiliations. Such information permits a much more comprehensive description of at least some of those turned away at Valcartier. W. Hadden and M.H. McLeod's sectarian loyalties were, for example, proclaimed by the Orange Order scars they bore over their hearts.[8] James Scott Simmons expressed his Masonic affiliations with the words "Coronation Lodge" on his left forearm.[9] In what can only been seen as an expression of Canadian identity, four men – Ulysses Adlerard, Samuel Jones, Robert W. Wilson, and Ernest Williams – had maple leaves tattooed on their arms.[10] Another three men had the word "Canada" etched on their bodies.[11] Nor were such patriotic symbols limited to the Dominion of Canada or the countries that made up the United Kingdom. Nine men bore either an American flag and/or eagle on their bodies, while one individual, Antonio Lapierre, had the French tricolour tattooed on his left arm.[12]

Besides proclaiming sectarian and national loyalties, many men who marked their bodies with tattoos were proclaiming their membership in specific and highly masculine groups that were often identified with strenuous physical labour and danger. The tattoos of a number of individuals, for instance, indicated that they had spent at least part of their lives before a mast. The heavily tattooed Stanley Norval commemorated his voyage from Barbados to Nova Scotia by having a ship with the letters "BB to NS" below it on his right arm. Another sixty-five men wore other tattoos traditionally associated with sailors – ships, anchors, and depictions of sailors – on their bodies. Besides demonstrating that a number of rejected volunteers had been seafarers, the tattoos worn by three men also directly identified them as having had prior military experience. Reginald Neor, for instance, wore, one assumes with great pride, the words "Soldier South Africa 1899-1902" on his right forearm. Similarly, fifty-three-year-old Joseph Clamondou bore "Pensioners of Transval [sic] War" on his right forearm.[13] For his part, the aforementioned Stanley Norval had the cap badge of the Royal Canadian Regiment tattooed on his right forearm.

Evidence of prior military service extends beyond rejected volunteers' tattoos. Medical examiners noted on the attestation papers of four rejected men that they had seen prior military service. William Chavis, Lawrence Eaves, and George Jobins had served in the Anglo-Boer War, while one-armed bugler Martin Wilson was listed as a veteran of the 1885 Northwest Campaign.[14] This type of information is useful because the section regarding prior military experience was seldom completed on the attestation papers of men rejected at Valcartier. Further evidence relating to the prior military service of many rejected volunteers can be gleaned from the 350 men found to be unfit for service upon arrival in the United Kingdom in 1916 mentioned in the Babtie Report of December 1916.[15] Thirty-one percent (108 men) were listed as having had some form of military service prior to the Great War.[16] For just under half of the men, such experience had been gained outside the rather questionable martial domain of the prewar Canadian militia. At least 40 had spent time in the British military, and 2 had served in the United States Army, one of them for three years in the Philippines.[17] Another had spent a year in the service of the organization that offered the ultimate challenge for the thrill-seeking remittance man: the French Foreign Legion. A further 5 men who were not listed as having served in regular British units had seen action in the Anglo-Boer War as members of either Canadian units or volunteer units raised in Africa.

An examination of the 350 men rejected in England also provides insight into the employment characteristics of those rejected as unfit to serve since the occupations listed for these men covered Canada's employment spectrum. Professions ranged from those based in the tertiary sector to the primary industries. Of the 296 men whose occupations could be traced, one was a bank manager, another a journalist, and a third a law clerk. Three were musicians.

Figure 4

Age of rejected men (years)

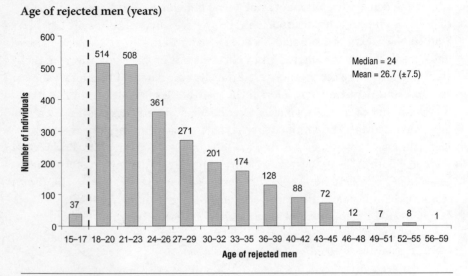

Source: LAC, RG 150, Accession 1992-93/175, "Files of CEF Volunteers Who Were Rejected." One individual, listed as "four years old," an obvious error, has been omitted.

There were also skilled craftsmen mechanics, electricians, and tailors. As one might expect, given the primary-resource focus of the economy of early-twentieth-century Canada, men were also employed in forestry, mining, and agriculture. Just over one-fifth of the total were identified as labourers. Indeed, taking into account the sample size and other factors such as the period, the distribution of occupations, both in variety and representation, were roughly analogous with the civil occupational characteristics of the Canadian Expeditionary Force.[18]

The average age of men rejected for service at Valcartier during this period was 26.7 years, with a median age of 24 years (Figure 4 and Table 1). The majority (96.6 percent) of rejected volunteers fell well within the Expeditionary Force's age limits of 18-45 years (represented by the dotted line on the graph). Of 2,413 men whose age was recorded, only 37 (1.5 percent) were listed as underage and an equally paltry 46 (2 percent) were said to have been over 44 years old. In fact, the average age of these men was within 0.4 years of the average age (26.3 years) recorded for Expeditionary Force members over the entire period of the Great War.[19] Thus, at first glance, it would seem that a majority of rejected volunteers were not geriatrics or juveniles but rather men in the prime of their lives. Admittedly, given that ages were falsified by eager recruits at both ends of the spectrum – often with either the explicit or tacit support of

FIGURE 5

Girth of rejected men's expanded chests (inches)

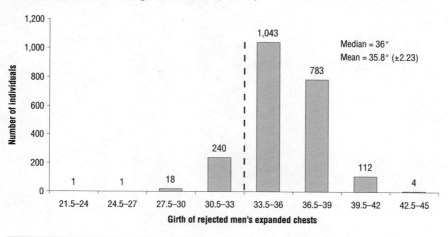

Source: LAC, RG 15, Accession 1992–93/175, "Files of CEF Volunteers Who Were Rejected."

medical examiners and unit commanding officers – one should be cautious about accepting the age statistics for rejected volunteers. It should also be noted, however, that the same caveat can be applied to the age statistics for men passed as fit to serve. Evidence suggests that a significant number of men who claimed to be 44 years of age were well above that mark, while many juveniles successfully – and with relative ease – evaded the minimum age restrictions.[20]

Besides falling comfortably within the Expeditionary Force's age requirements, the majority of rejected volunteers were also well within its minimum physical standards. With an average expanded chest measurement of 35.8 inches (median 36 inches) in girth, most rejected volunteers were comfortably over the requirement that a recruit be able to puff out his chest to at least 33.5 inches. In fact, of the sample of 2,202 individuals whose attestation papers recorded chest size, only 260 men (12 percent) had expanded chest sizes below 33.5 inches. Of these, 130 (50 percent) failed to meet the minimum requirements by an inch or less (see Figure 5 and Table 1). Moreover, the difference between the average chest measurement of men rejected as unfit to serve in 1914 and their successful colleagues (36.6 inches, median 36.5 inches) was less than 1 inch.[21]

Similar observations can be made with regard to the height of rejected volunteers. With an average height of 66.8 inches (5 feet, 7 inches [169.7 centimetres]) (median 67 inches), the majority of these men were well above the 1914 minimum height requirement of 63 inches (5 feet, 3 inches [160 centimetres]) (Figure 6 and Table 1). In fact, of the 2,282 men whose attestation

FIGURE 6

Recorded height of rejected men (inches)

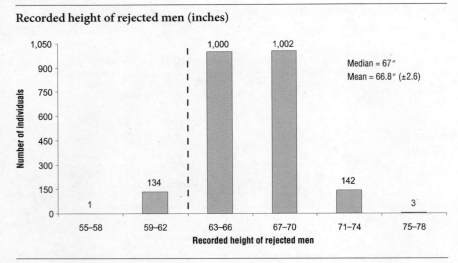

Source: LAC, RG 150, Accession 1992-93/175, "Files of CEF Volunteers Who Were Rejected."

papers recorded a height measurement, only 135 (6 percent) stood below 63 inches. Of these, 85 (63 percent) measured an inch or less under the minimum. The shortest individual in the sample stood at 56 inches (4 feet, 8 inches [142.2 centimetres]), but he was only fifteen years old and thus had not yet reached his full adult height.

If we exclude the 135 men who fell below the minimum height requirements from the calculation of the average height of men rejected as unfit at Valcartier in 1914, the average height rises to 67.1 inches (5 feet, 7 inches [170.4 centimetres]).[22] This places the average height of rejected volunteers on par with that of Canadian-born members of the Expeditionary Force. According to a recent study, the average height of members of the force born in the 1870s and 1880s was 67.4 inches (5 feet, 7 inches [171.2 centimetres]), a figure that declines slightly to 67.2 inches (5 feet, 7 inches [170.7 centimetres]) for those born in the 1890s.[23] No systematic study of the height of British-born members of the Canadian or British Expeditionary Forces has been conducted, but it is likely that the height of the former's British-born recruits was similar to that of their Canadian-born comrades.[24]

The lack of noticeable difference between rejected volunteers and those accepted as fit to serve can be further demonstrated by examining the reasons men were deemed unfit to serve at Valcartier in August-September 1914. Of the 3,050 men examined, 2,534 (83 percent) were rejected because they were

TABLE 1

Summary of the data on height, chest size, and age of men rejected at Valcartier, August–September 1914

	N	N*	Average	Standard deviation
Height (inches)	2,282	768	66.8	2.6
Expanded chest (inches)	2,202	848	35.8	2.2
Age (years)	2,413	637	26.7	7.5

(N = number of responses, N* = missing values)

Note: The files that did not record the required data were excluded from the calculation of averages because their relatively large numbers – ranging from 20.9 and 27.8 percent of the sample, depending on the average being calculated – would have heavily biased the results. The eighteen files held within the sample that were created outside (temporally and/or geographically) of the mobilization of the First Contingent were also excluded from the calculations to ensure that the sample represented volunteers rejected at Valcartier in August–September 1914.

Source: LAC, RG 150, Accession 1992–93/175, "Files of CEF Volunteers Who Were Rejected."

deemed medically unfit. The rest had been discharged for non-medical reasons such as misconduct or family protest, or had records that did not clearly indicate why they had been rejected.[25]

The four most common reasons for rejection were substandard eyesight (24 percent), poor teeth (10 percent), varicose veins (7 percent), and varicocele (6 percent). Hernias (5 percent) and heart problems (5 percent) were also common reasons (Table 2).[26] The two most common reasons for rejection – substandard eyesight and poor teeth – would not have been immediately obvious to the casual observer. Not all men whose eyesight failed to meet the stringent requirements of the Canadian Expeditionary Force in 1914 wore, or needed to wear, glasses. In fact, some of them would have been unaware that they suffered from a visual deficiency.[27] Likewise, until he opened his mouth, the dental deficits of a man rejected due to bad or missing teeth would have been invisible to those around him, especially in the case of individuals who wore a well-fitted pair of dentures.

Of the other four reasons for rejection, three – varicose veins, varicocele, and hernias – would have been hidden to all but the most intimate of observers by a man's clothing, while heart problems would have been, for all intents and purposes, invisible. Advertising one's affliction with these medical conditions did not always help. As with bad teeth and substandard eyesight, some did not consider either varicose veins or hernias, at least when only slight or supported with the appropriate medical equipment, to be valid reasons for keeping a man from serving his country. Furthermore, echoing the comments about eyesight

TABLE 2

Reasons for rejection

	Number	Percentage
Vision	879	24.4
Teeth	354	9.8
Varicose veins	235	6.5
Varicocele	215	6
Medically unfit, reason not specified	197	5.5
Protest	183	5.1
Hernia	166	4.6
Heart condition	161	4.5
Chest	156	4.3
Illegible, unclear, or not recorded	104	2.9
Undesirable	96	2.7
Flat feet	87	2.4
Sexually transmitted disease	80	2.2
Height	75	2.1
Undersize	70	1.9
Hemorrhoids	54	1.5
General foot problem	49	1.4
Appearance	45	1.2
Underage	42	1.2
Request	40	1.1
Injury	39	1.1
Overage	28	(Less than
Lungs	23	1 percent
Deformity	16	of total)
Hearing	16	
Skin condition	16	
Hydrocele	13	
Amputation	12	
Rheumatism	12	
Tuberculosis	11	
Mental competency	9	
Leg problem, not elsewhere categorized	8	
Thyroid	8	
Urethritis	8	
Does not want to go	7	
Post-operative pain/recent operation	7	
Arm problem, not elsewhere categorized	6	
Commanding officer's recommendation	5	

▶

◄ TABLE 2

Reason for rejection	Number	Percentage
Duty complete	5	Less than
Refused oath	5	1 percent
Arthritis	4	of total)
Back problems	4	
Enlarged testicle/s	4	
Genital problem, not elsewhere categorized	4	
Cancer	3	
Does not read/speak English	3	
Pain	3	
Physically unfit	3	
Recent appendicitis	3	
Undescended testicle	3	
Anemia	2	
Blackouts/convulsions	2	
Gall stones	2	
Kidney problems	2	
Over plus (surplus to unit requirements)	2	
Sinus problems	2	
Chest lesions	1	
Chronic ulcers	1	
Clinical history bad	1	
General debility	1	
Inflamed lymph node	1	
Inflamed vaccination scar	1	
Malaria	1	
Not approved	1	
Ostesitis	1	
Paralysis, facial	1	
Poorly nourished	1	
Recovering from measles	1	
Refused examination	1	
Refused for family reasons	1	
Typhoid phlebitis	1	
Underweight	1	
Total (all responses)	3,604	100

Note: There are more reasons for rejection than rejected men (3,604 versus 3,050) because a number of men were rejected on multiple grounds (usually multiple impairments). Record keepers recorded and counted every reason for rejection because it was not possible to divine which impairment on a rejected volunteer's attestation paper had been the most important factor in his rejection for service.

mentioned earlier, a 1915 report on men with disabilities who were examined by a medical board at Canadian Headquarters in Shorncliffe, England, noted that some men were actually unaware that they had varicose veins.[28] In the case of largely, if not totally, invisible circulatory conditions, a man's claims to be physically unfit for service were not always believed. For example, twenty-three-year-old Herrick Duggan, whose four attempts to join the Princess Patricia's Canadian Light Infantry in August 1914 had been thwarted by a heart condition, wrote to his mother, Mildred, from London, England, in October 1914 that few people believed he was physically unfit to serve.[29]

Whereas invisible impairments may have been common among those rejected, more obvious impairments were not. Potentially visible physical deformities (congenital and traumatic) occurred only 16 times (0.4 percent) in the records, and amputations were even rarer (12, or 0.3 percent). The most common physical deformity recorded was spinal curvature (5 instances), followed by deformities of the feet and legs (3 each), the knees (2), and the chest, hands, and toes (1). Of the 12 amputations, 8 involved the removal, either wholly or partially, of a single digit, and 1 each the removal of an arm, a hand, a testicle, and the toes on one foot.

While such impairments might have been readily visible to the trained eye of medical officers examining naked recruits at Valcartier, they would not necessarily have been immediately obvious to the casual observer on the streets of Canada's towns and cities. The men described as having malformed hands and feet could easily have hidden their deformities within shoes or a coat pocket, and a heavy or voluminous coat could disguise all but the most serious spinal deformities. Similar observations might be made regarding the twelve cases of amputation recorded. Like varicocele, hernia, and varicose veins, testicular amputation would not have been obvious when the man was clothed, and missing digits would have been all but invisible to the casual observer, especially from a distance. Only two cases of amputation – of a hand and of an arm – might have been readily apparent to the casual observer, and even then they could have been disguised with the use of prosthetics. The apparently obvious impairment of paralysis requires some consideration. Depending on both the body part affected and the extent of the paralysis, some individuals might have been able to hide their impairment from public view, especially if they had structured their life in such a way as to conceal their disability or else adapted to life with the impairment to such an extent that they were no longer noticeably disabled by it.[30]

Even if an individual's physical condition were noticeable, civilians might not have considered it an impairment or a disability. Men with glasses functioned successfully in numerous roles in civilian society and would not have been considered disabled. Indeed, some men who wore glasses were crack shots. Mark A. Wolff, who was rejected at Valcartier due to his eyesight, had the statement "a good shot with glasses" recorded on his attestation paper.[31] Likewise, in a period when dental hygiene often left much to be desired, rotten and bad teeth were unlikely to have been considered physically disabling. Few of those who worked alongside Will R. Bird in the backbreaking labour of Western Canada's wheat harvests would have thought him disabled even though his teeth had been smashed. Moreover, as indicated above, even more serious physical conditions might be ignored if a person was able to adapt. For example, Charles Schroder was still working on the railroads nineteen years after maiming his left hand in a train wreck, and it is doubtful that many of his colleagues considered him disabled.[32]

The invisibility of many of the impairments for which men were rejected is further evinced by the claims of disability made by men unwilling to experience the trenches and equally unwilling to face denigration for not enlisting, who often claimed to suffer from some form of invisible impairment that made them unable to serve.[33] Such acts of dishonesty, combined with the public denigration to which legitimately rejected volunteers were subjected, caused rejected men, their supporters, and the military authorities to attempt to mitigate such shoddy treatment. In April 1916, the Toronto Recruiting Depot began issuing rejected recruits with a document certifying that the recruit had "applied, been examined and rejected for service" so they could defend themselves if challenged on the streets of the Queen City. This certificate, which was signed by a recruiting officer and included the date of the rejected volunteer's medical examination, was accompanied by a small lapel button marked with the letters "A.R." (Applied, Rejected) (Figure 7).[34] In an effort to combat counterfeiting and misuse, both the button and certificate had an individual serial number that was registered at the recruiting depot. These numbers, the public was informed, could not be duplicated. The public was also warned that "any attempt to procure one dishonestly or wear one if 'fit' will bring the law down upon the individual," although what such legal repercussions would entail was not spelled out.[35] As befitted their exclusive character, "A.R." buttons were publicized as a mark of distinction by recruiting officials, who stressed that those who wore the button deserved respect. In fact, in a statement accompanying the release of the first batch of buttons, Captain R.J. Christie, the Toronto Recruiting Depot's commander, stated that wearing the button was "just as honourable as wearing khaki."[36]

Similar actions were taken in other parts of the country. In Ottawa, the 207th Battalion issued cards to men rejected for enlistment and also proposed to provide them with badges in the future so as to "save them from the annoyance

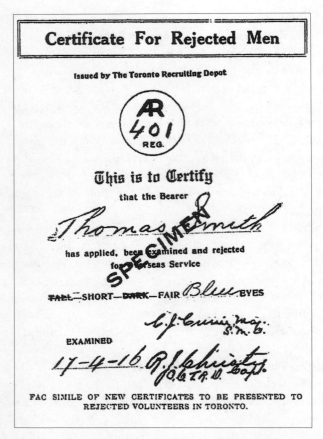

FIGURE 7 Sample of the certificate issued to rejected volunteers by the Toronto Recruiting Depot. Toronto *Globe*, 24 April 1916.

of explaining to recruiting officers why they are not wearing khaki."[37] Likewise, badges marked with "T.R." (Tried, Rejected) over crossed flags were provided to men turned away as unfit by the capital city's artillery units. Like the "A.R." buttons, "T.R." buttons were registered, although with the city rather than with a recruiting depot. Moreover, the onus for registering the button was on the rejected man rather than the unit that had rejected him.[38] Further west, the Citizen's Recruiting League of Winnipeg decided in March 1916 to provide men who had been rejected as physically unfit with a badge inscribed with "Excused" that they could wear "if it pleases them to do so."[39]

In addition to deflecting accusations of cowardice, these buttons had other possible benefits. For example, in late 1915 William M. Wilson of Toronto noted in a letter to the *Toronto Star* that "A.R." buttons would enable recruiters "to tell at a glance whose services had already been offered." Thus, they would not only spare rejected men "much annoyance and public humiliation" by stopping recruiters from approaching them but also distinguish "those who are possibly evading their duty to themselves, their King, and country." In other words, even as "A.R." buttons would shield those who had offered their services and been "honourably acquitted," they could help recruiters identify those who had not attempted to enlist.[40] Likewise, having rejected men register their "T.R." buttons at Ottawa City Hall rather than having the information held at a recruiting station enabled any citizen of the city to find out who was and was not entitled to wear them.[41] Indicating how closely these badges were often tied with recruiting, at the same meeting that Winnipeg's Citizen's Recruiting League announced the creation of the "Excused" badge, it also announced the creation of a new weapon for the city's patriotic female population to use in the ongoing war against slackers and shirkers: a badge that demanded, "Why are you not in Khaki?"[42] It would appear that the league no longer deemed talcum powder–charged feather dusters and bags of white feathers effective enough to shame men into signing up.[43]

Some questioned the buttons' necessity, however. In November 1915, a full six months before the first batch of "A.R." buttons was released in Toronto, a correspondent flatly told *Star* readers that he believed the proposal to give rejected volunteers buttons was defective. Few of these men, he argued, would agree to wear something that advertised their "alleged infirmities," mainly because many did not believe themselves to be unfit. Providing a rejected man with a certificate or card so that he could "produce it *if he cared to do so*" (emphasis added) was, in the writer's opinion, a much more sensible path for the government to take.[44] This opinion is of interest not only for showing that some sections of the Canadian public were critical of the idea of buttons for rejected men but also because of the writer's assumptions. His comment that many rejected men did not agree with their being labelled as physically unfit and his reference to "alleged infirmities" indicates the considerable disconnect between civilian and military concepts of physical fitness and highlights the fact that wearing such buttons could be seen as ignominious.

Although designed as positive identification, the buttons could also be marks of shame. For example, an advertisement placed in the *Globe* by the Mutual Life Assurance Company of Canada in 1917 (Figure 8) extolled the virtues of its life insurance package and warned readers not to put off applying for life insurance lest they suffer the bitter disappointment of rejection like men deemed unfit for service. Central to the advertisement were the following comments about "A.R." badges: "Thousands of men, eager to take their manly part in the Great War, have been bitterly disappointed. Their only consolation is the modest little button that tells their fellow men they *tried* to do their duty. The emblem bears the initials, 'A.R.,' which means – 'Applied – Rejected.'"[45]

The message was clear: these "modest little button[s]" signified inability and weakness. The men who wore them had failed not only in their attempt to do their duty but also to take a "manly part in the Great War." In presenting rejected volunteers with these buttons, which they were advised to wear at all times, the Canadian government branded them as inferior specimens of Canadian manhood. Such branding, especially in light of the Mutual Life advertisements, must have weighed heavily on the psyches of many men. It was a constant physical reminder not only of their rejection for service but also of their perceived physical and masculine inadequacies. The button signalled these inadequacies for all to see. Just as a khaki uniform and campaign medals signified a returning soldier's physical prowess, bravery, and masculinity to his community, the "A.R." button advertised a rejected volunteer's physical and, indeed, masculine failings.[46] Still, some men were willing to be so branded if it meant avoiding the muddy hell of the Western Front. As early as 31 May 1916, approximately a month after the first batch of "A.R." buttons had been delivered to the military authorities, the *Globe* reported that lost or stolen buttons were being worn by men who were not entitled to them, in order to avoid public pressure to enlist.[47]

The sea of buttons, pins, and badges proclaiming exemption in the first two years of the war led to, as Robbie Johnson has noted, "confusion and uncertainty as to whether a badge was genuine and opened the way for counterfeiting badges to avoid service."[48] More than likely, it also led to a situation where the badges of many legitimately rejected men were looked upon with skepticism by both recruiters and the general public.

Partly because of growing fears that local exemption buttons were being abused by shirkers, and partly because returned veterans and soldiers, now in civilian clothes, demanded some form of identification to protect them from the humiliation and hurt caused by "over-age busybodies [and] recruiters ... [asking them] ... why they are not in the army," the Dominion government created an official Canadian Expeditionary Force service badge through Order in Council P.C. 1944 on 16 August 1916.[49] This legislation defined three categories of individuals who were entitled to wear the badge: men who had been honourably discharged from service; men who had volunteered for service but had been rejected as medically unfit; and men whose offer to serve had been declined because their services were considered more valuable to the war effort in their current occupations.

P.C. 1944 also spelled out the rules for issuing the badges and the penalties for their misuse. Only a military officer authorized by the Governor General in

FIGURE 8   Mutual Life Assurance Company advertisement featuring the "A.R." badge. Toronto *Globe*, 8 June 1917.

Council could issue a badge to a qualified individual. Like the "A.R." badges issued in Toronto, each badge was to be inscribed with an individual serial number and have an accompanying card. Signed by the issuing officer, the card was to contain the particulars of the man to whom it was issued, as well as the reasons he had been issued the badge. The individual had to carry the card at all times when wearing the badge, and to produce it if a military officer or police constable demanded to see it. Failure to produce the card for verification would result in the individual's particulars being taken so that both the police and the military might investigate whether the individual was entitled to wear the badge. Badge owners were required to immediately report loss of the badge to the issuing officer. The penalties for misuse were considerable. Providing a badge to someone who was not entitled to one or wearing a badge without authorization carried a fine not exceeding $100 or imprisonment for no more than thirty days.[50] Importantly for the men considered unfit to don khaki, P.C. 1944 also stipulated the following: "In no case will a badge be issued to persons who have been rejected on account of temporary disability, or who are obviously unfit for service in, and have not served with, the Expeditionary Forces; for example, men who are totally blind, crippled, paralytic etc."[51]

With this provision, which was to be included in all succeeding wartime legislation relating to the issue of war badges, the Dominion government implicitly acknowledged that the badges were intended to shield those who looked fit to serve from any suggestion that they had shirked their obligations to King and country. The *obviously* unfit – those with visible impairments that were recognized as disabling by the general population – did not need a badge identifying them as incapable of shouldering a rifle in defence of home and hearth because their appearance itself indicated this. On the other hand, those who were not visibly different from their khaki-clad brethren needed the protection afforded by the badge. This short, forty-five-word proviso underlines the fact that the perceptions of martial ability, and of disability more generally, shared by the vast majority of Canadians were founded on visual indicators, as well as the fact that the military authorities rejected as unfit to serve many men who were not instantly recognizable as such by civilians and recruiting officers.

Although it signalled the government's intention to create a standard Dominion-wide "war badge," P.C. 1944 did little else. It was not until six months later, in February 1917, that Order in Council P.C. 275 established the design of the War Service Badges,[52] and also redefined the classes of men entitled to them. Instead of the three broad classes outlined in P.C. 1944, P.C. 275 created four distinct categories of service: A through D. Class A was to be awarded to honourably discharged men who had served in the Canadian Expeditionary Force and seen actual combat, or, in the case of officers, had served more than six months. Class B was for honourably discharged men who had served in the force but had not seen combat, or, in the case of officers, had served for six months or less. Class C was for men whose offers of service had been rejected because they were medically unfit. Class D was reserved for individuals who had volunteered to serve overseas but were refused because their services were considered more valuable in their current occupations.

P.C. 275 followed the lead of P.C. 1944 regarding the administration and issue of the badges, but provided greater detail on the documentary evidence required of claimants. All applicants for the Class C badge, for example, had to have a medical certificate proving that they had been declared unfit to serve. P.C. 275 also retained P.C. 1944's methods for protecting the integrity of the badge. All badges were to have unique serial numbers and an accompanying certificate that was to be carried at all times. To quell the confusion caused by a surfeit of localized exemption badges and to stop potential counterfeiters, the legislation prohibited the manufacturing, selling, purchasing, or wearing of non-government-issued badges that purported to show that a person fell within one of the four classes of honourably discharged or exempt men. The penalties for those found guilty of misusing the badges were increased to a fine of no more than $500 or a term of imprisonment not exceeding six months (from $100 or thirty days, respectively).[53] These sanctions, which remained unchanged in all succeeding legislation, were embossed on the back of each badge.[54] They were also enforced. On 1 September 1918, Emile Bergeon of Montreal, who, it was stated, had never been examined for service, was found guilty of falsely wearing a war badge by a magistrate in North Bay, Ontario. Perhaps wanting to make an example of Bergeon, the magistrate handed down the most severe penalty possible: either a fine of $500 plus costs, or six months' imprisonment.[55]

The definitions outlined by P.C. 275 did not last long. In May 1917, Order in Council P.C. 1296 further redefined the classes of badges. From this time onward, all men who had served in Europe, whether in combat or not, were entitled to the Class A badge, while Class B was to be awarded to men who had served in either Canada or Bermuda. While Classes C and D remained the same, a greater burden was placed on men applying for Class C to prove that they were unfit for service. Rather than being required to produce only his discharge papers and a medical certificate of disability, the applicant was obliged to produce "a medical certificate obtained at the time of application, duly signed by a Medical Board, or Medical Officer, authorized by an Officer Commanding a Military District." In effect, this stipulation, which became part of all succeeding legislation, required the applicant to face a new military medical examination even if his initial rejection had occurred only days earlier.

P.C. 1296's other major addition to war badge legislation was the expansion of judicial protection to include the "For Service at the Front" badge awarded by the Canadian Patriotic Fund to returned soldiers, although the government did not take over the distribution or administration of these badges. P.C. 1296 had an even shorter lifespan than its predecessor. In August, it was replaced by Order in Council P.C. 2199, which incorporated the "For Service at the Front" badge into the government-administered War Badge scheme.[56] This badge became the new Class A badge while the existing war badges were unceremoniously bumped down one level on the alphabetic ladder. The old Class D badge, which had been provided to men employed in industries deemed essential to the war effort, was dropped altogether,[57] apparently because of the imminent introduction of the Military Service Act. The act created a certificate and a badge (the Military Service Act Exempt Badge) for men exempted from service due to their work in an essential industry, which superseded the original Class D badge.[58]

P.C. 2199 also extended judicial sanctions to individuals who wore "badges so nearly resembling [government-issued war service badges] as to be calculated to deceive, of any Badge purporting to show that the wearer comes within any of the four classes ... or any Badge purporting to show the wearer is on War Service, or in any way exempt from Military Service."[59]

Although the design and categories of Canadian war service badges were finalized by P.C. 2199, it was not until late October that eligible men were advised to start applying for their badges. The badges were first exhibited to the Canadian press on 26 December and allocation began at the start of 1918.[60]

The Class D badge, now the insignia of the medically unfit, did not see out the war. It was cancelled on 22 May 1918 by Order in Council P.C. 1242. The explanation given in the legislation is telling. Men who had been issued the Class D badge were still called up for examination under the Military Service Act despite having already submitted to a second military medical examination when they applied for the badge. On a number of occasions, these men had been found fit to serve. In light of this, the government deemed it "inadvisable" to continue issuing the Class D badge.[61] Inadvisable indeed, since the fact that men who had been recognized as unfit by the military authorities could later be found fit to serve not only cast further doubt on the competency of military medical examinations but also implied that the military was having difficulty filling the Canadian Expeditionary Force's thinning ranks. The impact of such an implication should not be underestimated. Canadian newspapers repeatedly cited the Central Powers', and particularly Germany's, lowering of physical standards for combat troops as evidence that the Allies were winning the war.[62] By accepting into its ranks men who had earlier been categorized as unfit for service, the military authorities appeared to be intimating that Canada was at the end of its tether.

The government's decision may also have been influenced by the Class D badge's apparent unpopularity. Not long after applications for the badge became available, the *Globe* reported that there was "by no means an overwhelming rush by men entitled to the Class D Badges to the Toronto Mobilization Centre to fill out their applications."[63] The truth of the matter is difficult to ascertain since neither the number of Class D badges issued nor the number of applications is known. Indeed, the *Globe* article contained no figures to back up its claims, nor did it discuss how many men were applying for the other classes of badge. The apparent lack of enthusiasm for the Class D badge may have

Not Visibly Different 111

been due to fear on the part of those eligible for it of being passed as fit to serve during the medical examination required as part of the application.[64]

This is not to say, however, that all those declared unfit to serve declined the protection that the badges were meant to offer. As noted above, many rejected men and their supporters demanded these emblems of honour as a shield against the harassment that many of the men faced on a daily basis. Despite the possibility of negative reactions to the buttons on the part of rejected volunteers noted in the *Star*, and the lack of enthusiasm for Class D buttons on the streets of Toronto reported by the *Globe*, at least some rejected men embraced the insignia. Many agreed with the Toronto Recruiting Depot's Captain Christie and saw them as marks of honour. A number of rejected men referred to the badge issued by the federal government as a veteran's pin despite the fact that they had not actually served in a combat zone or outside of Canada. Soon after the government announced that it would be issuing the service badges, men rejected at Valcartier wrote the Department of Militia and Defence to request them. John W. Johnson of Belleville, Ontario, for example, penned "just a few lines" to the "Military Department" in December 1917 to find out "if I can get my Veteran Pin." To prove that he was eligible, Johnston not only provided information regarding his battalion (2nd), company (E), company commander (Lieutenant Stewart), and reason for rejection ("I had the rheumatism ... [and a] ... running sore on my leg") but also offered to supply a photograph "of some boy and myself that was taken at Valcartier," if the officials "cared to see it."[65] It is not known whether officials took Johnston up on his offer or gave him his pin since no return correspondence is contained in his file. It is quite likely that they did, however, as evidence indicates that the military authorities were fulfilling such requests well after the end of the war.

Those requests from men who had been rejected at Valcartier continued into the 1950s. Sixty-five-year-old Charles Garner of Winnipeg wrote the Department of Veterans Affairs in February 1951 asking for a replacement badge. Discharged as unfit in Valcartier in 1914 after three months of service, Garner wanted the badge because "more often ... [than not] ... a service Button goes a long way [to helping senior men get employment]." The department readily obliged.[66] Three months later, Montreal senior Roy T. Coates made a similar request. Claiming to have accidentally burnt his discharge papers while destroying rubbish, the sixty-eight-year-old Coates said he wanted some proof that he had been honourably discharged so he could join the Canadian Legion. Coates laid the blame for his discharge squarely at the feet of his wife, Cora. He told departmental officials that "we [his battalion] were on the point of embarkation when the wife snagged me." The mother of three young children with a fourth on the way, a very ill Cora, whose letters of complaint were supported by equally powerful letters from her mother, had refused to provide her consent for Roy to serve overseas. Coates, like Garner before him, had his request granted.[67]

As these cases indicate, being declared medically unfit for service had the potential to negatively affect men in less obvious ways long after shot and shell had ceased to fly over the battlefields of the Great War. Without his button, Garner feared he would not find odd jobs post-retirement, while Coates's social circle was limited because he could not prove that he had served. These kinds of stories indicate that volunteers who had been rejected for service on medical grounds were casualties of the Great War too. Although they did not experience shelling, poison gas, and machine gun fire, some of them did suffer both short- and long-term detrimental effects as a result of being declared unfit to serve.

6
Uncounted Casualties
The Costs of Rejection

ON THE EVENING OF 17 September 1914, eighteen-year-old Daniel Lane was found lying in a park in Welland, Ontario, his body wracked with violent convulsions caused by strychnine poisoning. A search of the young man's pockets uncovered a note in which he explained that he had taken the deadly toxin because he had failed the Canadian Expeditionary Force's medical examination.[1] Just over a year later, twenty-eight-year-old Joseph Coley of Thorold, Ontario, took his own life by drinking carbolic acid, in part because "the fear of being rejected by the military doctors [due to a recently acquired disability] preyed upon his mind."[2] In March 1917, twenty-four-year-old George Baker of Toronto hanged himself in his sister's cellar after suffering the blows of his brother's death in combat and his own rejection for service.[3] Later that year, another young man stopped attending church after being declared unfit to join the ranks of the Expeditionary Force. He could not, it was said, stand the accusing looks of a congregation that, unlike the military, believed him fit to don the khaki.[4]

These tragic stories indicate the heavy impact that rejection for service could have on Canadian men.[5] Wracked with guilt, their feelings of self-worth and masculinity in tatters, and often denounced and vilified by their communities, which identified them as shirkers, some men chose to end their lives or cut themselves off from society. The psychological, social, and economic wounds could be severe and long-lasting. The ramifications of rejection for service as unfit – like the physical and psychological wounds many Canadians sustained on the battlefields of Europe – could and did negatively affect men long after the end of the war. In effect, many rejected volunteers, whether they chose death at their own hands or carried the scars of their rejection, became uncounted casualties of the Great War. Not all were prepared to accept their fate supinely, however, and they formed their own pressure group, the Honourably Rejected Volunteers of Canada Association. The association not only guarded the rights of rejected volunteers but also pressed for the rewards and recognition they believed they deserved from their communities and the Canadian government.

"I DID NOT," Alfred Andrews of Qu'Appelle, Saskatchewan, recalled, "think very seriously of [the call for men after war was declared on 4 August 1914], till a conference was held in the office ... it was pointed out that as I was Canadian born and had no ties, it was my duty to enlist." Andrews countered by noting that he had a disqualifying impairment – a hernia – but his valid excuse was not good enough for many. "People kept asking me to enlist ... until I couldn't stand it any longer and on August 27, 1914, I made up my mind to enlist." The next day he joined the Fort Garry Horse.[6]

In many parts of Canada, considerable pressure was exerted on men to enlist in the Canadian Expeditionary Force. This pressure took many different forms, ranging from appeals to a man's patriotism, personal honour, and masculinity to acts of public shaming, ostracism, and, violence.[7] Although far from uniformly distributed throughout the country and criticized by some sectors of the populace, this pressure was significant.[8] In April 1916, Chief Justice T.G. Mathers of Manitoba told Prime Minister Robert Borden that "no man who joins the ranks today does so voluntarily. He does so because he can no longer resist the pressure of public opinion."[9] Likewise, Military Cross winner Armine Norris stated that he had enlisted because "I hadn't the nerve to stay at home."[10]

The weight of public pressure to enlist fell heavily and repeatedly on the shoulders of men rejected for service. Driven by their own beliefs and/or public opinion, they had volunteered to serve, often on more than one occasion, only to be turned away. Many, especially those with physical or sensory impairments that were invisible or incomprehensible to the vast majority of civilians (see Chapter 5) were wrongly condemned as shirkers, victims of the dark side of their communities' pro-enlistment sentiment.

The label of shirker carried implications of moral defect, ranging from simple cowardice to outright treason. For example, R.W. Leonard, president of the Coniagas Group of Companies, described shirkers as "friend[s] of Germany" in a flyer he sent to his employees encouraging them to enlist.[11] Shirkers were also often portrayed as wretched specimens of manhood, physically unfit, and effeminate. The shirker depicted on the recruiting poster for the 142nd Battalion (Figure 9) is, for instance, a "striking image of ... 'failed' masculinity."[12] Confronted with a uniform, his face is a mask of terror. His fear is further evidenced by his stance, as, with his shoulders hunched defensively, he "wrings his hands in dread." His body, especially his legs and ankles, are thin, looking more feminine than masculine. The negative effect is reinforced by the arrangement of the shirker's legs in a stance reminiscent of a half-curtsey or implying an attempt to keep from urinating out of fear.

Such thinking was also reflected in literature. For example, in the poem "Missis Moriarty's Boy," influential Anglo-Canadian author and poet Robert W. Service

FIGURE 9   DO IT NOW! Enlist in the 142nd Battalion recruitment campaign. *Library and Archives Canada/National Archives poster collection/ e010697047.*

examines the feelings of a mother whose son, Dinnis, is not in the armed forces. The unidentified woman compares herself to one Missis Moriarty, whose only child, Patsy Boy, has recently been "kilt in the wearful wahr." Patsy is described in glowing terms: his hair was curly and bright, his heart wonderful and tender; he was of "proper height" and shone with pride as he went away to war.[13]

Dinnis is the antithesis of Patsy Boy, bursting into his mother's home blind drunk after "drinkin' his pay" just as Missis Moriarty finishes describing her son. As his mother puts her drunken, cursing son to bed, she contemplates Missis Moriarty's pride in her deceased soldier son, noting that "there's many a way of breakin' a heart" and that she had yet to decide whether she "would be Missis Moriarty, or Missis Moriarty me?" The answer is as obvious as the contemptuous look Missis Moriarty had given Dinnis before silently slipping away.[14]

As apparent as the answer to Dinnis's mother's question is the poem's message: better to have a son killed while honourably serving his country than suffer the humiliation of having a drunkard son who did not enlist. More broadly, however, the poem also implies certain things about the character flaws of men who were not in uniform. That Dinnis is a drunkard is important, not only because his "ravin' and cursin'" and "stumblin' foot on the stair ... [at] ... about half-past three" make him an unsavoury individual but also because it implies both physical and mental defect.[15] In the late nineteenth and early twentieth centuries, alcohol abuse was considered by many to be a symptom of moral and/or mental defect and, more generally, physical degeneration.[16]

As though being portrayed as a shirker were not bad enough, many rejected men probably also faced their own internal inquisitors. Canadian Herrick Duggan, who was based in London, England, wrote his mother on 13 October 1914 that while he did not really want to go to war due to his "very good job" and good future prospects, he felt he must because he knew he "should never feel comfortable in the future if [he] did not."[17] There is little doubt that Duggan attributed some of that future discomfort to the possibility that many people would have considered him a coward for not serving, but it is equally clear that his own values and beliefs compelled him to serve. Indeed, his stated aversion to serving contrasted starkly with many of his actions. By the time he wrote his mother, he had already attempted to enlist in the Princess Patricia's Canadian Light Infantry four times, only to be rejected each time due to a heart condition. Moreover, after successfully gaining a Second Lieutenant's commission in the Royal Engineers in November 1914,[18] the young Canadian actively encouraged both his mother and younger brother, Kenneth, to become de facto recruiters for the Canadian Expeditionary Force. On 9 November 1914, he pressed his mother to "try and rub into any boys who are hesitating about coming what it means – if we don't get it finished there will be no jobs for anyone to keep, much less get in civil life." Eight days later, he asked Kenneth to "take a message from me to some of the D.U. [Delta Upsilon, Duggan's old fraternity at McGill University] boys whose names I see prominently in the football news that there is a bigger game going on over here that's going to need a lot of spare men. It's far more serious than most of you seem to think."[19] Duggan clearly believed that the young men of Canada, himself included, were obligated to do their bit for King and country.

Failure to meet this obligation would have, Duggan's letter suggests, caused the twenty-four-year-old engineer considerable personal discomfort. Many rejected volunteers wanted to serve, in part at least because they believed in the discourses of masculinity and citizenship employed by recruiters to fill the ranks, and viewed negatively those who had not enlisted as soon as they were able. This was evidenced not only by Duggan's letters to his mother but also by the postwar memoirs of Will R. Bird. Rejected repeatedly in 1914, the Nova Scotian said of his acceptance in 1916: "Why did they not let me go before? Now I had to go with the men who never wanted to join, to be a late-goer and it was a rank injustice."[20] More generally, evidence that many rejected men wanted to serve is provided by the simple fact that more than a few men not only made multiple attempts to enlist but were also willing to undergo corrective surgery to ensure their acceptance. Rejected five times, Emmanuel "Smilie" Gravelle agreed to undergo an operation to correct the hernia that had been the cause of his rejections.[21]

The effects on some men of watching their friends, relations, and colleagues march off to war were soul destroying, especially when coupled with accusing looks from the latter's families. This was evidenced by the aforementioned suicide of George Baker, who took his own life after learning that his brother had died in combat. The impact of feeling that one had let one's friends and family down should not be underestimated. More than a few men enlisted with a group of friends or because their brothers had done so. These bonds were so close that some men refused to enlist if they would be transferred away from their friends or if one of their friends was rejected. Expeditionary Force volunteer and Anglo-Boer war veteran Bill Ravenscroft, for example, refused to enlist after his friend Harold Peat, who had accompanied him to the recruiting station, was rejected on account of his chest.[22]

Despite these problems, however, there is also evidence that rejected volunteers – at least when they were recognized – were highly regarded by sectors of society. An article in the *Toronto Star* stated unequivocally that men who volunteered but were rejected as unfit still had the "moral distinction that belongs to men who do their duty to their country as far as their country will let them," and other newspapers expressed similar sentiments.[23] The Dominion government also recognized rejected volunteers' commitment to the cause. The Wartime Elections Act, 1917, which withdrew the franchise from a number of groups that were deemed to have failed in their obligations to the state – including conscientious objectors and individuals convicted of an offence against the Military Service Act, 1917 (defaulters and those who attempted to impede the enforcement or operation of the act) – explicitly stated that individuals who had not served because they had been deemed medically unfit were not to be disqualified from voting.[24] In this way, the government implicitly recognized that rejected men had not shirked their duty to King and country.

Some individuals even went as far as to place the sacrifice of those rejected as unfit to serve *above* the sacrifices of those who served, as Major H.B. MacConnell's poem "Medically Unfit" demonstrates:

Do not look with scornful eye
On the one who is turned away;
The heart that beats in that sickly frame
May beat with a patriot's love and fire;
Though his physical fires burn dim and low
His fires of spirit may soar.
His sacrifice, then is greater than yours;
He stays and endures, while you go.[25]

In eight short lines, MacConnell acknowledged not only that rejected volunteers were neither shirkers nor cowards but also the trials they faced. His admiration was double-edged, however. In drawing attention to the rejected volunteers' loyalty and patriotism, he also shone a spotlight squarely on their infirmities. The martial ardour and patriotic fire of the medically unfit were housed in "sickly frames" that were powered by "dim and low" burning physical fires. Indeed, MacConnell painted his subjects in the image of the pallid-skin cripples who were, in spite of their soaring spirits, far from Canada's best. Rather, they were the weak, the feeble, and the diseased. It is unclear what exactly MacConnell's medically unfit were enduring – their own personal frustration and shame at their inability to go to war, social ostracism and scorn because they were not in the khaki, their physical impairments, or some combination of these? It is clear, however, that although he believed the medically unfit should not be the objects of scorn, they were to be pitied by those deemed fit to serve at least as much as they were to be respected.

The impact of MacConnell's poem on the public's views of rejected volunteers is unknown, but "Medically Unfit" was not the only work to present such sentiments. E.N. Lewis started a recruiting appeal for the artillery aimed at the young men of Ontario's Huron County by "voicing his sympathy for those who from physical disability or age or other unfortunate circumstances are prohibited from enlisting."[26] Mutual Life Assurance Company of Canada's aforementioned advertisement of 1917 (see Figure 8) also portrayed the medically unfit as piteous. The existence of these advertisements along with MacConnell's poem suggests that this depiction of the unfit volunteer had some traction in the public discourse.

Most rejected volunteers would have been unwilling to accept the mantle Lewis and MacConnell had woven for them since few would have identified themselves with the pathetic creatures described by these men. As we have seen, most men rejected as unfit were far from sickly and decrepit, especially in the eyes of civilians. Not only did many of them believe that they were fit to fight but also, in a period when self-reliance and economic productivity were considered central to a man's character, relatively few men would have accepted being an object of pity, let alone being deemed unfit. To be labelled as such was a direct assault on one's self-worth, honour, and masculinity.

By 1914 the term "unfit" had, thanks to a growing eugenics discourse in the West, acquired a highly pejorative patina. Eugenicists used the word "unfit" in a Darwinian sense to describe those individuals – the mentally ill, the congenitally disabled, and social misfits – whose characteristics were deemed detrimental to the long-term survival of the nation, and as such needed to be weeded out. The threat that the "unfit" posed to the state was not only biological but also economic and moral. Eugenicists argued that the "unfit" were the source of most of the crimes that afflicted Canada and that their care exacted a toll on both family and state resources.[27]

Most damagingly for rejected volunteers, many eugenicists, both before and during the Great War, publicly lamented that war selected the strongest (best) men to be killed while leaving the "weakest" (worst) men to procreate, to the great detriment of the nation. Montrealer Robert Dickie, for example, observed in an article published in the *Queen's Quarterly* in 1913 that

> War takes its tribute from the best a nation can bring. The maimed and infirm, the scrofulous and neurotic, the cowardly and irresolute escape this scourge and make contribution to the life and blood of the nation. It is the best blood of the nation that is lost in war.
>
> When we remember that war has been taking its toll from the best blood of communities since the beginning it becomes evident that it has been a most serious detriment to race-improvement, if it has not actually made for race-degeneration. Generation after generation losing its best blood on the field of battle has only to proceed far enough to mean bankruptcy of the nation, and every step means its impoverishment.

Dickie bolstered his argument by drawing his readers' attention to the "serious historians" who had found that many empires had collapsed because their constant wars had drained them of their best blood. Such comments would hardly have placed rejected volunteers in a positive light.[28]

Eugenics discourse also infused recruiting propaganda. Recruiting posters and declarations stated that Canada would send only the best examples of Canadian manhood to the aid of the Empire. Many implied that those declared unfit would have hindered the march to victory if they had not been left behind.[29] Accounts that described unfit recruits as "weeds" that needed to be ruthlessly pulled from the ranks of Canada's army further underline the negative view that many people had of rejected volunteers.[30]

Such beliefs were also evident in works produced by members of the Canadian Expeditionary Force in France. For example, the satirical *Oh, Canada: A Medley of Stories and Pictures by Members of the Canadian Expeditionary Force,* contained a cartoon that may be read as attack on both the quality of medical examinations given to new recruits and the quality of some of the recruits arriving in France (Figure 10). In the cartoon, a burly moustachioed sergeant-major discusses with a fit-looking lieutenant a newly arrived private standing before them. The private presents quite a contrast to his superiors. Far from a perfect specimen of Canadian manhood, the gangly recruit slouches in an ill-fitting tunic with his arms held at awkward angles and his feet splayed. His head is pushed forward on a thin neck that houses a prominent Adam's apple and carries a face that wears what might charitably be called a dimwitted expression. Indeed, his half-closed eyes, protruding lower lip, weak chin, bulbous jowls, and mat of unkempt hair that stick out at all angles from beneath his cap combine to give the private a face that looks vaguely clownish in character. His less than inspiring appearance causes the exasperated sergeant-major to state, "I dunno wot to do with 'im sir ... the M.O. says 'e ain't defective, an, 'e says 'e comes o' fightin' stock. My God, sir, look at 'im – ain't he a fair champion for the Corkscrew Cuirassiers?"[31]

While the cartoon was obviously drawn for comedic effect, it does indicate what its author believed made a man fit to fight. Indeed, although the private looks bad enough compared with his superiors, he looks even worse when juxtaposed with the images of soldiers on recruiting posters. Straight-backed, square-shouldered, and alert, latter were paragons of muscular virility, the very individuals that Canada and the Empire needed in order to win the war against the voracious Hun. The hunched and brainless "Corkscrew Cuirassier" was the antithesis of such Canadian heroes.

Such statements and images were often reinforced by the alarmist reports prepared by military authorities about the numbers of medically unfit men reaching England as part of the Expeditionary Force (and, in the case of frontline troops, some of the individuals who arrived at the front only to be turned away). Seeking to make the greatest possible impact on their readership, many of these reports, including Colonel Herbert A. Bruce's "Report on the Canadian Army Medical Service" (1916; known as the Bruce Report), used the most disturbing cases as examples of medically unfit men in the ranks of the force. As a result, many of the men portrayed in these reports reflected the wan, weak, and mentally defective individuals whose existence eugenicists argued threatened "national deterioration in health and achievement," rather than the vast majority of men who had been declared medically unfit for less serious reasons, such as poor teeth.[32]

SERGEANT-MAJOR.—I dunno wot to do with 'im, sir. 'E ain't been a casualty, an' the M.O. says 'e ain't a defective, an, 'e says 'e comes o' fightin' stock. My God, sir, look at 'im—ain't 'e a fair champion for the Corkscrew Cuirassiers ?

FIGURE 10   "A Fair Champion for the Corkscrew Cuirassiers." From *Oh, Canada: A Medley of Stories and Pictures by Members of the Canadian Expeditionary Force* (London: Simpkin, 1916).

The link between those rejected for service and Canada's dysgenic *hoi polloi* in the minds of many, as well as the degree of negativity with which these individuals could be described, was evident in a debate held in the Canadian Senate in 1916. On 12 April, Senator Philippe-Auguste Choquette called for a halt to recruiting, claiming, in part, that the quality of men being drawn to the colours left much to be desired.[33] Noting that two units that had recently been recruiting in Toronto had rejection rates of over 50 percent, Choquette drew the Senate's attention to a letter he had recently received from one Robert Hazelton, of Todmordon, Ontario. The sixty-two-year-old Hazelton blamed the high rejection rates in Toronto on immigrants, specifically English immigrants. He claimed that 99 percent of men rejected at Toronto's recruiting depots were Englishmen. However, rather than "descendants of cultured Anglo-Saxons that we Britishers of Canadian birth have heard so much" about, these "diseased, depraved, deformed and ... illiterate" individuals were far from the best speci-mens of English manhood. Coming "from the very worst spots in England," this horde of "degenerate, defective and undesirable immigrants" were, in Hazelton's opinion, likely the sons of "foreign sailors and English 'dock-prostitutes'"; such "beasts" not only were unsuitable for the Canadian military but actually hindered recruiting because no "well bred, educated Canadian" would serve with such "cattle."[34]

A stinging condemnation of the character of some of Toronto's recruits, and indeed recruiting more generally, these words were even more powerful be-cause of their source. Far from being an obscure social radical, Hazelton was a senior, well-respected, and well-known member of the local branch of the Conservative Party, a former member of the Royal North West Mounted Police, and a veteran of the Northwest Campaign. He was also a vocal supporter of recruiting and had three sons serving in the military.[35] Indeed, for Choquette – a French Canadian with a long record of expressing antiwar and anti-recruiting sentiments in the Senate and whose sons were not in the khaki[36] – Hazelton's letter provided an excellent weapon with which to counter claims that his op-position to recruiting was driven by political, personal, and *nationaliste* bias along with self-interest.

Choquette's utilization of Hazelton's claims – which were reported, and criti-cized, as far away as London, England – to support his anti-recruiting stance caused a furor, especially in Ontario.[37] He was accused of treason both inside and outside the Senate, and there were unsuccessful demands for his resigna-tion.[38] In the House of Commons, Acting Minister of Militia and Defence A.E. Kemp stated that Toronto's soldiers had been "foully slandered" and that it was "absolutely false that there is any substantial proportion of men offering themselves for enlistment who are 'diseased, depraved or deformed.'"[39] Hazelton fared even worse. On 15 April, he was dragged from his home by an irate mob that included rejected volunteers, and was severely beaten before being rescued by armed police reinforced by soldiers.[40]

The uproar caused by Hazelton's comments can be attributed in part to Canada's wartime climate and pre-existing ethnic tensions, but the terms with which he described rejected volunteers certainly inflamed the situation.[41] In a period that was increasingly dominated by eugenic ideologies, describing in-dividuals as diseased and depraved was more than a simple slur. The parentage and socio-economic origins that Hazelton ascribed to the men being rejected at Toronto's recruiting stations were fraught with negative eugenic assumptions. Besides being seen as morally defective, prostitutes were considered by many eugenicists to be mentally deficient – in fact, their moral defect was regarded as evidence of their mental deficiency – and many were also believed to be physically defective. Eugenicists generally believed that these dysgenic characteristics were hereditary and would therefore manifest themselves in a prostitute's children.[42]

Coming from the lower classes of society and with a reputation for vice, sailors were widely believed to be the carriers of multiple dysgenic characteristics, ranging from a propensity for alcoholism and criminal acts to physical and mental deficiencies. Even more damaging was Hazelton's labelling of these sailors as foreign, thereby reinforcing his contention that rather than being scions of superior Anglo-Saxon stock, these men's bodies were infused with the blood of "lesser" races.

More generally, Hazelton's letter strongly reflected the eugenic fears of many educated Canadians. An editorial in the *Canadian Journal of Medicine and Surgery* in 1909, for example, declared dramatically that Canada had become Great Britain's "garbage pail." Likewise, J.S. Woodsworth's *Strangers within Our Gates, or Coming Canadians,* published in the same year, expressed strong concerns about the numbers of British immigrants from the undesirable classes entering Canada.[43] In one fell swoop, Hazelton had identified Toronto's rejected volunteers as part of the dysgenic horde that threatened Canada's future.

Proof that Hazelton's letter was informed by these considerations is found in the explanations he provided for his comments a day after he was attacked. He told a reporter from the *Ottawa Evening Journal* that he was not referring to respectable English immigrants in his letter to Choquette, but rather to those who came from England's degenerate underclass who "won't work and ... won't pay their bills ... [and] ... spend all Saturday afternoon and Sunday swilling at the beer keg." These individuals were, he asserted, "a curse to the England they left, and a curse to the Canada they came to."[44] Hazelton's explanation was confirmed by his wife, Anna, and Senator Choquette. Mrs. Hazelton told reporters that while she and her sons condemned her husband's letter, "he [Hazelton] did not mean the people here, but only the people all over Canada whom the Salvation Army brought out."[45] Rather than an attack on the character of either Canada's soldiers or the English race, Hazelton's letter was, Choquette told the Senate, a critique of Canada's immigration policies, nothing more and nothing less. Unfortunately for Hazelton, very few people were able, or perhaps willing, to make such a distinction.[46] Fearing further reprisals, the unfortunate Northwest Campaign veteran and his family were forced to flee their home.[47]

Characterizations of rejected volunteers as dysgenics did not end with the war. Ironically, given the righteous indignation expressed in 1916 over Hazelton's letter, these characterizations actually echoed his concerns. The large numbers of men rejected as medically unfit for service were seen to confirm the fears of racial degeneration that had haunted Canadian eugenicists in the prewar period.

The numbers of unfit men discovered as a result of the mobilization of Canada's manhood came as a shock to those Canadians who had believed that the dominion's hardy, young, and vigorous rural population was superior physically and morally to the degenerate urban populations of Europe (including those of Britain).[48] Moreover, such information directly called into question the concomitant belief held by many of these individuals that Canada was destined to become the future centre and dominant portion of the British Empire.[49] Lamenting the loss of 60,000 of the finest specimens of Canadian manhood – which must be seen as a bitter irony, given that a number of these men had been condemned as unfit in 1914 – in the muck and mire of the Western Front, eugenicists claimed that the large number of men rejected for service on medical grounds was a telling indictment of the nature of Canadian society before the war, and argued for social and governmental reforms.[50] While many, though not all, of these reforms would have positive outcomes for Canadian society in the long term, eugenicists effectively cast rejected men in the role of social, economic, and genetic bugbears. In doing so, they pigeonholed these men within a group of individuals that one Canadian social reformer had colourfully described in 1917 as the "the running wounds of society."[51]

Not all Canadians held these views. There were strong critics of the eugenics movement in Canada who questioned its positions and claims on both scientific and moral grounds. Moreover, eugenics tended to be an ideology of the educated anglophone elite rather than Canadian society as a whole.[52] Likewise, at least some reformers placed the blame for the large numbers of rejected men on Canadian society rather than on the rejected men themselves. The Reverend A.H. Sovereign, for example, told the delegates at the Second Annual Convention of the Child Welfare Association of British Columbia in 1919 that the 41 percent of recruits who were found to be unfit for service were a direct "result of our life before the war."[53]

Perhaps more importantly, a number of men rejected as medically unfit were turned away for reasons that even the most ardent eugenicist would have recognized had little, if anything, to do with their biological worth. Those who had lost limbs due to accident or who were outside the Expeditionary Force's age limits are prime examples of such individuals. It should also be remembered that not everyone necessarily agreed with the military authorities' constructions of both disability and the perfect fighting stock.

Nevertheless, the dysgenic branding was a strong one. No matter if they were portrayed as a threat to the survival of society in and of themselves or as symptoms of a wider social illness that needed correction – rejected men were still seen in a negative light because of the way they were used in eugenicist fear-mongering tactics and because of the groups with which they were linked. Indeed, rejected men became the unwilling "poster boys" of the eugenics movement both in Canada and abroad. Thus, a man classified as unfit for service was tarred with a brush that blackened far more than his masculinity or personal bravery, since his value as a human being was called into question. Disturbing as it may have been, however, the growing eugenics discourse was not the only ghost that haunted rejected volunteers both during and after the war.

On 17 May 1916, Harold Innis enlisted in the Canadian Artillery. The twenty-one-year-old recent graduate of McMaster University told his sister that he had been motivated to enlist by three factors: (1) he believed it was his Christian duty to do so; (2) it was better to enlist and choose the branch of the army in which one wanted to serve than be drafted and placed in the infantry; and (3) he felt that those who did not serve would have no chance of success after the war.[54] Although he suffered physical and psychological wounds as a result of his service,[55] Innis survived the war and went on to become one of Canada's most influential academics.[56]

Innis's observation about the postwar fate of men who did not serve reflected the conventional wisdom that men who failed to join up "would face discrimination and isolation ... during the war and in the years ... [that] ... follow[ed]."[57] Men in Brantford, Ontario, were told in late 1915 that "the day [would] come within five, six, or eight years hence when you will be sorry you didn't grasp the opportunity. With you men who evade the call, in a few years the chickens will come home to roost." Echoing the famous Savile Lumley poster of 1915, in which a young girl asks her pensive father, "Daddy, what did YOU do in the Great War?" (emphasis in original), an advertisement in the *Simcoe Reformer* in December 1915 asked its male readers, "What Will You Say in Future Years when People Ask You, 'Where Did You Serve in the Great War?'" Calling attention to the shame they would feel and hinting at the derision they would face, the mayor of St. Thomas, Ontario, cautioned the young men of his city that they would be taking the back streets of the city if they did not enlist.[58]

It would be foolish to think that such sentiment was shared across Canada, especially in communities that opposed the war. Nevertheless, such warnings contained more than a kernel of truth for young men who lived in Canada's prowar communities. As Jonathan Vance has noted, "the young man who stayed at home ... carried a stigma of failure ... [and] ... suffer[ed] by comparison with those men who had gone to the front and 'gambled with the ultimates.'"[59] Indeed, as Vance demonstrates with reference to a variety of fiction and non-fiction sources, "the shirker remained a significant element [of] postwar discourse ... [that] ... perpetuated the notion that men who failed should ... hang their heads in shame."[60] This stigma was, as has been seen, readily transferred to rejected men who did not have obvious disqualifying impairments.

Questions about their character were not the only obstacles that rejected volunteers had to contend with in the postwar period. Not having served in the military, they found employment opportunities closed to them. The Borden government's Civil Service Act, 1918, for example, instituted, admittedly limited, preferential hiring practices for veterans.[61] In the face of such realities, rejected volunteers did what they could, often grasping at the limited military service they had experienced as a means of ensuring their employment. Gustave Johnson, for example, wrote to Ottawa in April 1935 requesting a copy of his discharge papers after having lost the originals. His motivation was simple; he had been offered a job on the condition that he could prove he had (attempted) to serve.[62] As noted in Chapter 5, rejectee Charles Garner requested a new copy of his discharge papers and a replacement service badge for similar reasons in 1951.

Rejection could mean more than just the potential denial of long-term employment opportunities; it could mean that a man's avenues for socialization with his peers were cut off. Roy Coates stated on his application for a replacement record of service that he required the record so that he could "join the Legion for recreation." Such an admission highlights the fact that, at least for some men, rejection for service could have potentially long-term social consequences. Entering into retirement, the sixty-eight-year-old Coates was still blocked in 1951 from one of the places where those of his age and gender could go for social interaction. This observation can be extrapolated to include the numerous battalion reunions, which ran the gamut from refined dinners to raucous drinking parties, and Remembrance Day activities, both official and unofficial, in which veterans took part.

To be sure, other avenues of social interaction, such as church groups and working men's associations, would have remained open to Coates. Likewise, the total membership of Canada's numerous and often opposed and internally fractious veterans' groups should not be overstated. For a variety of reasons, many Great War veterans did not join these associations, and many others left within a few years of joining.[63] However, being barred from the Royal Canadian Legion and the other veterans' activities would have, at the very least, acted as a constant reminder of a man's failure to serve, especially if most of his friends, neighbours, and colleagues were members. It would place an invisible but nonetheless obvious social barrier between him and those who had donned the khaki.

Rejected volunteers were also excluded from the educational opportunities offered to those who had served. This is especially evident with regard to the so-called Khaki University of Canada, which offered educational training at all levels (basic literacy to postgraduate studies) to soldiers serving in England and France.[64] Formed in early 1917 by the president of the University of Alberta, Henry Marshall Tory, the Khaki University was designed in part to stave off the boredom felt by troops in rear-echelon positions while at the same time enabling serving men to work towards recognized academic qualifications. As such, it acted as tool of morale and discipline even as it prepared men for life after the war by enabling them to develop skills – ranging from motor mechanics to farming – that they would be able to use in civilian professions. Indeed, some soldiers had the Khaki University to thank for their literacy. At a time when education was not always considered a right, and, especially at higher levels, was financially out of reach for many Canadians, the Khaki University offered opportunities that many Canadian men left behind could only dream of.[65]

One should not overstate the advantages enjoyed by returned veterans, however. Two of the most influential works on Canadian veterans' postwar experiences are titled *Winning the Second Battle* and *Unfit for Heroes* for very good reason.[66] Not counting veterans who returned to Canada suffering very real physical and psychological wounds, most if not all those who returned from the horrors of the trenches were permanently scarred by their experiences. The scarring was aggravated by the fact that many of their postwar expectations, and their government's promises, were unfulfilled.

The government jobs provided to veterans tended to be ill paid and menial at best, offered little chance of advancement, and were often far from secure.[67] Land settlement schemes were little better. Designed as a means of opening Canada's undeniable land resources to farming, the land offered to veterans was often isolated, difficult to access, and generally of poor quality. Moreover, many of the veterans granted land had little or no agricultural experience and were, as a result, often destined to fail. A prolonged agricultural depression starting in 1921 presented a further, often insurmountable challenge.[68] The veterans who returned to positions in the private sector also faced difficulties. Many who resumed their prewar jobs found themselves with prewar wages, which were vastly inadequate in the face of massive wartime inflation; they also found themselves in subordinate positions relative to younger men who had not served. Others struggled to re-establish their prewar businesses.[69] Moreover, not all employers gave preferential treatment to veterans when hiring. Indeed, some men found that identifying themselves as veterans, either by word or by wearing their veteran's badge, hindered their chances of finding employment.[70]

Nevertheless, these realities took time to hit home, and regardless of the outcome, veterans were offered opportunities that were denied to those who had not served. Although they may have been fleeting, they were seen as worth pursuing by both veterans and others. The fact that such policies were *demanded* by veterans' groups[71] and, as we shall see, rejected volunteers indicates that they were viewed as advantageous rewards for services rendered. And although many veterans failed, a significant number succeeded. In 1931, 43 percent of those granted farms under the government's land settlement scheme still remained on those farms, and more than a few had actually increased their holdings.[72] Many veterans also reintegrate successfully into society, often with the help of the veterans' preference. And even if some may have believed that their service badges hindered their chances of gaining employment, the cases of Garner and Johnson indicate that this was not always the case, even years after the conflict. Both men believed, or in Johnson's case had been told, that wearing marks of service would aid them in their search for employment. Perhaps the greatest indication of the perceived value of both the veterans' preference and land schemes lies in the fact that the Canadian government pre-emptively instituted similar programs at the end of the Second World War.[73]

The pursuit of these advantages, combined with a desire to not be linked with shirkers, caused rejected volunteers to band together and form their own pressure group in 1918: the Honourably Rejected Volunteers of Canada Association. Structured along the lines of the Great War Veterans Association – to which it claimed to be closely allied but independent from – the association's membership comprised men who had, or were eligible for, Class C and D war service badges. Vowing that it would be "entirely independent of any party politics," the association stated that its aim was to safeguard both "the welfare and ... common rights of all its members."[74] Of central concern, and the driving force behind the association's creation, was the belief that there was "no discrimination [in the public sphere] between C and D men and the common 'slacker' who only has himself to blame." Association members also believed that there was far "too much discrimination between A and B men and C and D men."[75] Given these concerns, it was the association's stated aim to defend its members from "undue and unlimited" discrimination because they had not served in the trenches. In practice, this meant ensuring that its members were not treated as slackers and that they received the recognition and rewards to which they were entitled from the Dominion government, provincial authorities, and the public more generally.

Government, public, and, perhaps most importantly, veterans' responses to the association are difficult to measure in more than general terms. Much the same can be said about its size and influence, in part because there is not much extant information about the association. Indeed, all evidence of its existence comes from correspondence emanating from its British Columbia branch.

Moreover, few references, and again only in British Columbia, were made to the association in the print media, and few comments, either positive or negative, were made about its demands. For example, an article in Victoria's *Daily Colonist* reported on the association's demands for compensation without further comment.[76]

The *Daily Colonist*'s silence is curious given that those demands were significant. Evidence for this comes from letters sent to Prime Minister Sir Robert Borden and British Columbia premier John Oliver by the British Columbia branch on 30 November 1919. The letters called on the provincial and Dominion governments to provide the association's members with "recognition in the matter of public appointments (government and civil service positions) and land settlement scheme and fishing licenses next to men of the Canadian Expeditionary Force." In effect, the association demanded that its members be granted almost the same rights and privileges that were being offered to men who had returned from the trenches.[77]

The members' belief that they were entitled to such privileges was based on a similar discourse that returned veterans used to buttress their claims for postwar recognition. The letter of 30 November 1919 described the Honourably Rejected Volunteers of Canada Association as "a body composed of men [who] voluntarily offered their services to the Empire ... [only to be] ... discharged or rejected as medically unfit for overseas service." Driving the point home, the letter stressed that membership in the association was open only to those men who had attempted to enlist before the introduction of conscription in August 1917.[78] The message was clear: members were not slackers and shirkers who had ignored their obligations to their country. Rather, they were either loyal citizens who had *of their own free will* offered themselves for service only to have that offer rejected by the state, or they were men who had provided some form of service in Canada (having been deemed unfit to serve overseas) and had been honourably discharged due to old age, wounds, or sickness. In addition, and just as important, their offer to serve in the trenches had been *honourably* rejected. Ultimately, the underlining message was simple: unlike slackers and shirkers, "who only had [them]selves to blame," the association's members were not at fault for their lack of service. Instead, they were denied their chance to face the guns by forces beyond their control.

In effect, the association used a discourse of arrested heroism in which the *willingness* to sacrifice oneself was almost as important as the act itself. This kind of discourse enabled rejected volunteers and discharged home service men to accept and justify their reasons for not having fought, on both a personal and public level. Indeed, some rejected volunteers considered themselves to be veterans. Take, for example, the aforementioned John W. Johnson (see Chapter 5). Although rejected as unfit at Valcartier in September 1914, he considered himself a veteran, as evidenced by his request for his "Veteran's Pin."[79] Identifying themselves in this manner enabled rejected men to at once reaffirm their masculinity and honour and concurrently condemn the ill treatment they had received from certain sectors of Canadian society during the war. It also enabled the association to argue that since its members had been willing to fight and die for Canada, they were deserving of recognition and reward. It should be noted that this discourse of arrested heroism is open to question since it ignored those men among the ranks of Canada's rejected volunteers who volunteered knowing (or hoping) that their physical impairments would cause them to be declared unfit to serve.

The Honourably Rejected Volunteers of Canada Association proclaimed its members' loyalty both graphically and verbally. At the centre of its letterhead was the Union Jack, with the letters "H.R.V.C." emblazoned on the horizontal arm of the St. George's Cross. Further driving home the association's claim of allegiance to King and country, the Tudor Crown, the traditional cipher of King George V, rested between the "R" and "V" of the initials inscribed on the flag. At the cost of 50 cents, members were also provided with a lapel badge that not only identified them as belonging to the association but also stressed that the wearer had volunteered to serve his country. Twenty-one millimetres in diameter, the badge was made of bronze. Running horizontally across its middle was a white enamel strip emblazoned with the letters "H.R.V.C." in red enamel. "Volunteered For Active Service 1914–17" was inscribed on the outside edge of the badge. As with the previously mentioned badges provided to rejected volunteers by individual battalions and later by the state, these badges were intended to indicate that the wearer had offered himself for service. By the end of 1919, a representation of this button had replaced the Union Jack on the association's letterhead.

Given the character of the association and the discourses it used to buttress its position, it should come as no surprise that it was vocal in its support of the Great War Veterans Association with regard to most issues. Both associations insisted not only that all defaulters receive the full punishment permitted by the Military Service Act, 1917 but also that they be disenfranchised for life and barred from holding any kind of public office in Canada. Likewise, they called for all enemy aliens who had been interned to be repatriated to their homelands as soon as possible.[80]

The Dominion government greeted the Honourably Rejected Volunteers of Canada Association's letters and demands with little enthusiasm. On 7 December 1918, the British Columbia branch sent a letter to the Prime Minister, the

Minister of Justice, and the Minister of Militia and Defence detailing the resolutions passed by its membership at a meeting four days earlier, which condemned draft evaders and demanded that they not be allowed to escape punishment. The government's response was businesslike. Written by the Minister of Justice's private secretary in the minister's absence, it acknowledged receipt of the association's letter and enclosed a statement made by the Minister of Justice indicating the government's intention to punish those who had evaded their duty. "You will see by it [the statement]," the letter brusquely concluded, "that the government has no intention of allowing defaulters under the Military Service Act, to go unpunished." Sent a week later, the British Columbia branch's second letter to Ottawa met with a similar response.[81]

The association received similar treatment from the British Columbia government, which was willing to promise only "due consideration" with regard to the association's letter of 30 November. When the association, after hearing nothing for four months, pressed the issue in April 1920, Premier Oliver appeared to have lost his patience. A short letter stated bluntly that "the opinion of the Executive Council is that those who saw overseas service should have first preference." Oliver made no mention as to what preference, if any, the members of the association were to have.[82]

Rejected volunteers never faced the hell of trenches, but this did not mean they escaped unscathed from the storm of the Great War. Like those who served, many of those who were turned away by the Canadian Expeditionary Force were wounded, sometimes fatally, by their experiences. Like the wounds suffered by those who served in France, those endured by rejected men took a variety of forms that often continued to affect their victims long after the war had ended. Denied the right to serve, rejected volunteers found themselves accused of cowardice and mistreated in other ways, since they were often identified as shirkers. Severe as such wounds could be, others were potentially even more serious. At a time increasingly dominated by eugenics ideologies, being labelled as unfit carried a stigma of defect and degeneration, an implication that one was a threat to the well-being of one's community, if not one's country. This stigma lasted long after the war ended. Indeed, the growth of the eugenics movement was in part fuelled by the "multitude" of unfits discovered during military medical examinations. Nor was this the only long-term impact, as rejection denied these men many of the official and unofficial opportunities, no matter how limited, that were offered to veterans.

The fact that rejected volunteers felt poorly treated and believed that they deserved better is evidenced by the formation of the Honourably Rejected Volunteers of Canada Association in 1918. Mirroring veterans' associations, it acted to defend rejected men's rights and push for the privileges its members believed they deserved, thereby alleviating the wounds many rejected men had suffered. This is not to say, however, that all of the men suffered as a result of their rejection. Indeed, some had actively sought to be rejected as unfit.

7
Claiming Disability to Avoid Military Service

SOME MEN WERE HAPPY to be rejected for service. Certain men sought the ap-
pellation not only as a means of avoiding the trenches of the Western Front but
also to escape public denigration. Others enlisted as a form of social insurance,
remaining in camp with a battalion until they could find work or the battalion
was about to be shipped overseas, at which time they would attempt to have
themselves declared unfit for service.

Stratagems for being branded as unfit were varied. There is evidence of men
enlisting hoping that the impairments from which they suffered would cause
them to fail the army's stringent medical examination; a few sought to ensure
rejection by helpfully pointing out their aliments to their examiners. Others,
lacking impairments that they believed would cause them to be rejected, fabricated them, aided by the limitations of the medical examination and, in some
cases, by sympathetic medical examiners. Some individuals even resorted to
criminal acts, such as bribing doctors to provide false medical certificates regarding their unfitness for service.

Other reluctant enlistees used the impairments of their family members
– physiological, psychological, or economic – to help them evade the khaki.
Meanwhile, the families of some volunteers also used claims of impairment to
frustrate the attempts of their sons, brothers, husbands, or fathers to enlist. They
did so in two ways: (1) by drawing the attention of the military authorities to
physical and mental infirmities that they argued made their man unfit to serve,
or (2) by arguing that their own disabilities necessitated his remaining home.

The use of such assertions of disability by potential recruits or their families
began as soon as war was declared in August 1914 and continued until the end
of the conflict. Such claims were used even before the realities of trench warfare
had become apparent to Canadians, and, more importantly, before the passage
of the Military Service Act in late 1917. This suggests that they were not just
a reaction to the Canadian government's introduction of compulsory military
service, but instead were tools of resistance against wider public pressures to
serve. Viewed in this context, being labelled or identifying oneself or one's
loved ones as impaired or disabled could be, in some cases at least, a positive
and empowering act.

On 12 August 1914, Robert George Johnston of Stouffville, Ontario, wrote directly to Minister of Militia and Defence Sam Hughes, with whom he was distantly acquainted, for his aid as a friend.[1] The Anglo-Boer War veteran explained that a fit of military enthusiasm had overruled his better judgment and made him offer himself for active service, and that his offer had been accepted. Now that his ardour had cooled and he had come to see his enlistment as foolish, he hoped that Hughes would use his executive authority and have his (Johnston's) name removed from the list of volunteers.

At the crux of this request was Johnston's contention that he was unfit to endure the rigours of combat. He explained to Hughes that while serving in South Africa, he had contracted rheumatism and as a result suffered from both lumbago and kidney problems. These problems required almost constant medical treatment and limited both his physical mobility and endurance, so he would be much more a hindrance than a help to his comrades in arms. Indirectly, Johnston implied that his medical conditions would result in his being permanently confined to a base hospital instead of actually serving on the frontlines. Having established himself as a potential long-term invalid due to his pre-existing medical conditions, he then played his trump card. Appealing to the government's fears of the "great pension evil," he noted that Canada neither wanted nor needed any pensioners. His meaning was clear: if he was not removed from the list of volunteers, his many impairments would soon make him a pensioner. Johnston's pleas worked. In red pencil at the bottom of the veteran's letter can be seen the inscription "O.K., S.H." in Hughes's confident hand.

Those who had no connection to people in the halls of power, no matter how slight, or who balked at the thought of contacting them had other avenues of self-denunciation. The most obvious was the medical examination. In his postwar history of the medical services, Sir Andrew Macphail, professor of the history of medicine at McGill University, noted that men who wanted to evade their duty bared their ailments to medical examiners with "startling frankness."[2] At Valcartier, nineteen-year-old Emile Leblanc told the medical officer that his back was very weak. Twenty-two-year-old J. Bunn claimed to be unable to march or hop because of a recently fractured left clavicle and right tibia. Both men were rejected on the basis of their declarations, although Bunn's examiner did raise some questions about the genuineness of his alleged impairment.[3] Twenty-five-year-old James Varley, a labourer from Wentworth, Ontario, openly admitted that he became "dsyphoric very easily." In a period when such afflictions were seen as a serious character flaw at best or as a marker of mental defect at worst, the power of such a forthright admission should not be underestimated. Both the twenty-five-year-old W.H. Aikenhead and the thirty-four-year-old Cyrille Nadean openly confessed that they did not want to go to war. It is possible that Aikenhead, who was afflicted with varicocele, had enlisted hoping that his distended testicles would lead to rejection, and made this statement mainly to ensure it, but Nadean had no such impairment to bank on. Both men were rejected as unfit, Aikenhead because of his varicocele and Nadean because he did not want to go.[4]

The rejection of Aikenhead and Nadean suggests that medical officers could be Janus-faced when it came to judging recruits' military fitness. Not only might a sympathetic medical examiner pass a substandard recruit, he might also find a way to fail a less-than-willing recruit. The fact that Aikenhead's medical examiner, Captain MacDermot, chose to record his unwillingness to serve along with his impairment raises the question of whether MacDermot used the Prairie native's swollen veins as a convenient excuse to let him escape service. Such a possibility is also suggested by the case of J. Bunn, whose examiner rejected him despite finding no evidence of his alleged injuries. Fear was seen by at least some medical officers at Valcartier as a legitimate reason for declaring an individual unfit for service. Eighteen-year-old Mark Purcell's list of reasons for rejection – including bad teeth and being physically unfit – ended with "has the German scare frightfully." Similarly, thirty-seven-year-old J.M. MacFarland had "afraid to go" recorded as a reason for rejection, along with his substandard eyesight.[5]

The surfeit of men volunteering for service in the heady days of 1914 meant that doctors could afford to make such decisions, but there is evidence that at least some doctors continued to declare unwilling men medically unfit throughout the entire period of the war. The November 1916 *Canadian Medical Association Journal* reported that military authorities in Ontario had begun launching sting operations to catch physicians who were suspected of providing, for a small fee, false certificates of ill-health to soldiers who wished to extend their leave. One doctor had already been caught, according to the report, and was facing investigation by the Ontario Council of Physicians and Surgeons. Three months later, an article in the same journal titled "An Appeal to the Profession" reminded physicians to exercise the greatest care in signing statements concerning the physical condition of individuals for military-related purposes. Specifically, they must not accept statements about an individual's health "without thorough investigation or examination." In addition, doctors who knowingly and willfully provided a soldier with a false medical certificate were defrauding the government and opened themselves to criminal prosecution.[6]

Although the appeal focused on doctors who falsified medical certificates to aid returned soldiers in their pension claims or men who were seeking to extend their leave, its broad warning to association members about exercising the greatest care when issuing military-related medical certificates suggests concern that some doctors were providing fraudulent certificates to men who were trying to avoid military service. It was, after all, only a short step from supplying a certificate that allowed a soldier a few extra days of rest and relaxation to providing one that enabled an individual to claim an impairment that disqualified him from serving.

Evidence of the problem is seen in a May 1917 letter to Minister of Militia and Defence Sir Edward Kemp from J.A. Johnson, the mother of a serving soldier. Requesting Kemp's pardon for "offering a suggestion re medical examination," the Nova Scotia native stated her belief that it was unjust to appoint local doctors to conduct the examinations of boys who were being conscripted. Her reasoning was simple: "local doctors were bound to show favour to local mothers or sisters" of recruits and declare them unfit to serve. She herself knew of "three or four [boys in her home town of Parrsboro] who would have been in France today had it not been that the local examiner had been influenced by mothers." She did not think that her hometown was "an exception to the rule" in this regard.[7]

Meanwhile, a circular letter from the Militia Council dated 21 December 1917 informed the Military Districts of allegations that in "many instances" men had been incorrectly categorized by medical boards, "either by reason of deception practised by the men or otherwise." It stated that in any case that came to the attention of the districts' authorities where it was suggested that a man had been wrongly placed in a category below Class A, this fact was to be "immediately communicated to the Register or Deputy Register of the Districts with a request that he order the man concerned to attend for re-examination by a medical board other than the one by which he was originally examined."[8]

It is difficult to ascertain how widespread the problem was since few doctors and men were likely to admit their involvement, but it should be noted that such practices were not limited to Canada. In England, a number of doctors, including those working as army medical officers – were suspected of, and many were charged with, providing false medical certificates to men who did not want to serve. Some doctors even went so far as to provide clients with "pills or an injection which would affect the action of the heart or cause swelling or contractions of the muscles of the arm." Other stratagems included the uncomfortable practice of injecting sugar cane solution directly into the urethra in order to simulate diabetes, or pouring rancid oil (or other substances such as condensed milk or Vaseline) into a man's ears to mimic an ear infection.[9]

Various avenues were open to men who did not want to risk encountering a doctor who would not provide a diagnosis of ill-health, or who were unable or unwilling to pay a bribe. Before conscription, some who signed up with one of the myriad recruiting sergeants prowling the streets of Canada's towns and cities never reported to a recruiting depot to be enlisted. Instead, to conceal their deceit from family and friends, they would "make spurious expression ... that for some imaginary reason the Recruiting Depot found them unfit for service."[10] Others, as discussed earlier, either obtained unlawfully or counterfeited the identifying buttons issued to legitimately rejected individuals and returned veterans by battalions and the federal government. That these deceptions could take place at all is indicative of the haphazard nature of recruiting and, more importantly, shows that many legitimately rejected men were not visibly different from those fit to serve.

The invisibility of certain disqualifying impairments made them popular with men who were trying to avoid service. For example, many feigned poor eyesight. This was much easier than faking good eyesight because of the basic nature of the military's eye examination, which, as discussed earlier, involved the recitation of letters written on a test board six metres in front of the subject. All a recruit had to do was claim that he could not read the letters, or deliberately misread them. Recruits could also claim that they suffered from night blindness or colour-blindness.

Although the 1918 *Physical Standards and Instructions for the Medical Examination of Recruits for the Canadian Expeditionary Force and for the Active Militia of Canada* would inform medical examiners that "in all doubtful cases [of visual impairment] a definite opinion ... should be obtained by a specialist," there was little the military authorities could do to counter these deceptions.[11] Night blindness and colour-blindness could be tested by specialists, but few military medical examiners had the skills, time, or equipment to conduct the necessary tests. More importantly, as Sir Andrew Macphail noted, even specialists lacked tests that would reveal the true visual acuity of an insincere man.[12]

It is not known how many men attempted to use this means of avoiding service or how many were successful, but Macphail's comments and the directive in the *Physical Standards* indicate the tactic was common enough to catch the attention of the Canadian military authorities, including high-ranking officers in the medical services or otherwise. In 1917, for example, Brigadier-General A.O. Fages, General Officer Commanding Military District 5, noted that defective vision was one defect that could "be very easily simulated." He thought, however, that the ruse could be detected if a suspect were examined by an eye specialist: "My personal experience has been that recruits sent back [from England] for defective vision, have in each case, when brought before the Eye Specialist, and put through a variety of tests, been found to measure up to the standard of vision laid down."[13]

Fages's claim that many recruits who were returned to Canada due to substandard eyesight were frauds echoed that of his Eastern Ontario counterpart,

Brigadier-General Thomas D.R. Hemming, in late 1916. Responding to a query from the Militia Council about a number of men from his Military District who had been found unfit to serve upon arrival in England, he openly questioned the veracity of some of the failed eye examinations and accused two of the men, Privates James Connors and Joseph McIntosh, of faking. According to Hemming, McIntosh's visual acuity had been found to be above standard when he was tested in Canada, so "if his eye sight was defective overseas he must have been faking." The general was even more blunt about nineteen-year-old Connors: "Pte. J. Connors is a fakir [sic]. He has no eye trouble."[14]

To be sure, Hemming's comments need to be seen in light of the fact that he was responding to his superiors' criticism of his district's medical examinations, but the evidence suggests he may have been right in suspecting Connors of deliberately failing his vision test in order to avoid frontline service.[15] According to Hemming, Connors had been returned to Canada once before, after claiming that he was suffering from sciatica, another commonly faked medical problem.[16] Upon arriving home, his back problems had miraculously disappeared, and he had re-enlisted in his local depot's ambulance and passed the eyesight examination "perfectly." When ordered overseas for a second time, his sciatica returned. Bad back or not, he was shipped to England in late October 1916, perhaps because his superiors – as Hemming's report implied – were dubious about his claims. It is not outside the realm of possibility that after his attempt to avoid returning to England was thwarted, Connors fell back on a surefire way of getting out of the firing line. In addition, his service file makes no mention of his alleged poor eyesight or any other prewar impairment that would have made him unfit to serve. Given the amount of time that he spent under the medical spotlight, both as a member of the Canadian Army Medical Corps and as a battlefield casualty, this is telling, to say the least. Upon arriving in England, he served at Shorncliffe Military Hospital before being transferred to the 13th Canadian Field Ambulance in mid-April 1917. Five months later, he was invalided out of the trenches after being wounded by a gas shell, and lost the hearing in his left ear after an operation to combat an ear infection caused by the poison gas. Connors's lungs were also ravaged by the toxic fumes. Once again, despite a detailed medical examination, no mention was made of any eyesight problems.[17]

Although Hemming's suspicions about Connors appear to have been legitimate, his accusation of McIntosh was clearly off the mark. A medical board examination on 28 June 1917 concluded that the thirty-three-year-old had myopia. McIntosh's right eye had a visual acuity of 20/200, while his left was slightly better at 20/120. With glasses, his sight improved to 20/60. The board's findings were supported by tests conducted a year later by specialists at the

Canadian Eye and Ear Hospital in Folkestone, Kent, which found McIntosh's left eye to be as weak as his right.

Faking of poor eyesight to avoid service also drew the attention of satirists. The 11 October 1916 issue of *Punch* carried a cartoon that glaringly outlined the issue for all to see. Called "A Bold Bid for Exemption," it depicted a medical officer almost striking a British conscript in the face with the lid of a garbage can. "What is it?" demands the medical officer. "Two bob or 'alf-a-crown," responds the unwilling recruit. Highlighting the recruit's claim of poor eyesight, visual acuity charts printed with ridiculously large letters lie strewn on the floor between the two men, obviously hurled by the exasperated medical officer.[18]

Some men who were driven by economic necessity to enlist in August–September 1914 had no intention of seeing action. For them, enlistment was a form of social insurance, and claims of disability were a useful tool for escaping the colours once they had served their purpose. On 31 March 1915, the Reverend H.A. Elliot, vicar of Saint John's Anglican Church in Port Hope, Ontario, wrote directly to Prime Minister Borden to draw his attention to the practice of men enlisting and then, just before final acceptance and deployment overseas, attempting to get dismissed from the ranks, either through acts of insubordination or by claiming medical impairment – after drawing two or three months' pay and enjoying free food and shelter as well as public adulation. Once the men were dismissed, they would proceed to a recruiting centre where they were unknown and repeat the process. The vicar claimed to know of men who had been in all three contingents of the Canadian Expeditionary Force and, after being released from their current service, were planning to enlist once again.[19]

Others also attempted to draw the attention of the civilian and military authorities to this type of abuse. Less than a month after Elliot wrote to Borden, Hemming, who was then a colonel, informed the secretary of the Militia Council that he believed many of the men who had enlisted in the winter of 1914-15 had done so in order to find a winter job. As soon as spring arrived, and with it a surge of new jobs, large numbers of men in his division, often with the support of family members, began to "demand their discharge for various unfounded reasons"[20] – often a claim that the soldier in question was unfit to serve, or that a family member suffered from a disability and required his support.

Major F.H. Honeywell, Officer Commanding "A" Squadron, 8th Canadian Mounted Rifles, wrote to the battalion's commanding officer to voice concern over the discharge of a number of men in the squadron on the grounds of family members' illnesses or disabilities. He "had serious doubt of the good faith of these cases" and drew his commander's attention to the case of one Private

W.H. Pearce, who had recently re-enlisted after gaining a discharge six weeks earlier due to his wife's illness. When questioned by Honeywell, Pearce had openly admitted that his wife had not been ill at all, and that the real reason he had sought discharge was his belief that economic conditions had improved sufficiently for him to find work in his civilian profession of carpentry. Upon discovering that no work was available, he returned to the colours. Such acts, Honeywell despaired, were "interfering greatly with discipline in the Squadron."[21]

Private Walter Bryant of the 3rd Canadian Infantry Battalion had also joined the colours for economic reasons. Unlike Pearce, however, he appears to have made his request for discharge due to his wife's illness in good faith. In his letter of request, he took great pains to stress his desire to serve. He wanted to do his duty, and wanted a discharge from overseas service only because he feared what would happen to his wife, whose "health [was] pretty bad," should he leave Canada. Under such circumstances, his service on home defence, he believed, would be much better. As though to underline his unwillingness to leave the colours, Bryant made the surprising but truthful admission that being discharged would be economically disastrous for him: "This [situation] is a bad job for me, as being out of work it [being discharged] only makes the matter harder for me."[22]

The cases of Privates Pearce and Bryant indicate that volunteers could be debarred from service because of a family member's impairment, whether physiological, psychological, or economic. Indeed, Department of Militia and Defence records show that the illness of a family member and/or the possibility of economic hardship for those left behind were accepted as valid reasons for discharging a man from service. John Boyd, for example, was discharged after showing his commanding officer a letter from his wife that appeared to demonstrate that she was ill both physically and emotionally.[23] The aforementioned Robert Johnston bolstered his request for discharge by claiming that his doctor believed that his ill sister would be "incalculabl[y] injur[ed]" by worrying if he were to serve overseas.[24]

Such claims were grounded in constructions of gender roles, many of which implicitly contained disabling language or ideas. In the late nineteenth and early twentieth centuries, women were often considered to be frail and emotional creatures who were incapable of responsible citizenship or of taking care of themselves. The anti-suffragettes in particular embraced this discourse, arguing not only that mental and physical deficiencies meant that women lacked the capacity to use the franchise in a responsible manner but also that the pressures of such responsibilities would cause them to become ill, both physically and mentally. Similarly, those who opposed higher education for women argued that they were physically incapable of withstanding the rigours of academic study and that subjecting women to such strenuous activity presented very real dangers to their mental health.[25] These constructions of women as physically and mentally inferior beings – which were strongly intertwined with traditional gender discourses that portrayed the ideal man as both a provider for and a defender of women and children – were actively repudiated by suffragettes. However, women not only used but embraced such discourses when seeking to have their family members discharged from service. Female correspondents claimed that the absence of the male breadwinner grievously impaired the family's ability to survive both economically and socially. In this view, the family was, for all intents and purposes, disabled without its male head.

A. Birch, for example, wrote to the "Comanding [sic] Officer" of Valcartier Camp demanding that her father be sent home because without him the family was starving, ill-clothed, and unable to pay the rent. In a letter memorable for its direct, defiant, and accusatory tone, she ended by challenging her reader to "put yourself in my place and see what it is like." Evidently he did so, and Ms. Birch's father was released from service ten days after his daughter put pen to paper.[26] Likewise, the illiterate Mrs. John A. Pritchard of Battleford, Saskatch-ewan, appealed to the only authorities she knew – the local detachment of the Royal North West Mounted Police – in order to have her husband returned to her after he joined the Saskatchewan Light Horse without her consent.[27] John had, she explained, left her and their seven children destitute, and she did not know what would become of them if he was not returned soon.

Mrs. Pritchard's case was taken up by the detachment commander, who wrote directly to the Mounted Police commissioner in Regina, stating his belief that Pritchard would "best serve his country" by returning to Battleford and sup-porting his wife and children. The commissioner in turn contacted his superiors in Ottawa, who took up Mrs. Pritchard's case with the Department of Militia and Defence. In the end, all of these interventions proved to be unnecessary, as the forty-five-year-old Pritchard was rejected at Valcartier as medically unfit due to rheumatism, only four days after his wife approached the Royal North West Mounted Police.[28]

Besides sending men home, the Dominion government tried different means of alleviating the economic difficulties of families who had lost their primary breadwinners to the Canadian Expeditionary Force. Soldiers could assign up to four-fifths of their pay to their families, who also received a separation al-lowance of $20 per month from the government.[29] Soldiers' dependents also received additional support from the Canadian Patriotic Fund.[30] Although these measures took time and were not perfect, they helped the government counter claims of economic impairment on the part of a soldier's dependents and eased the fears of potential recruits that volunteering for service would impair their families' ability to survive. In fact, cards provided by the Canadian Patriotic

Fund to recruiters in 1915 for distribution to potential recruits stressed the economic support that a recruit's dependents would receive from the fund.[31]

Economic impairment was not the only gender-based impairment claimed by women who wanted to have their sons, brothers, or husbands discharged from service. On 13 April 1915, Aimee Clements of London, Ontario, requested her husband's discharge on the grounds that she required his protection. She claimed that she was being persecuted by her former landlord, a Joseph Fox of 213 King Street, London. Describing Fox as a "German Jew,"[32] she alleged that he had begun victimizing her and her four young children not long after her husband joined the army. She explained that she had lacked money to pay her rent because her husband was away and she had not received a government allowance, and that, as a result, Fox had "practically turned me out on the street." He had then approached the secretary of the local Patriotic Fund in an unsuccessful attempt to get the money she owed him, $30, drawn from her government allowance. Besides making her feel unsafe, his constant harassment had adversely affected her family's health. "I am so weak and ill after all I have gone through these last few weeks," she declared, "I hardly know how to crawl around." As a result of being forced to move in the rain, her four children were "all so sick with croup." Clements thanked her unidentified reader in advance, sure that he would do his best to get her husband free to protect her and her children from "such a man."[33] Besides rapacious landlords, many of the newly minted Johnny Canucks were also seen as a threat by some women. The wife of a career soldier serving in the Quebec Battery of the Royal Canadian Garrison Artillery, Mrs. H.J. Wood demanded that her husband be returned to her on the grounds that the barracks where she and her five children lived were "full of volinteers [sic] and it is not safe for a woman living here alone."[34]

While some correspondents claimed that they needed their husbands at home for protection, others invoked a woman's need for guidance and control. A.B. Higginson, for example, requested Leo Mills's discharge from Valcartier on the grounds that the young soldier's wife had been keeping bad company since his departure. Higginson was loath to imply that the young woman had done anything wrong, but he was "afraid that unless her husband is here to look after her she will be led astray." Furthermore, the young couple had a crippled child who needed almost constant care. Under such circumstances, it was best that Mills be sent home immediately so that he could "take charge of ... [his wife and] ... his infant and relieve others of the anxiety and trouble."[35]

Conflation of gender-based impairments with material and physical impairments or illness, as evidenced by the letters of Aimee Clements and A.B. Higginson, was common. In many such letters, family members were portrayed as suffering from circumstances that made their position especially precarious.

These circumstances were often used to explain or emphasize the family's economic and social disabilities. For example, Mrs. William Brothers of Montreal requested that her son, William, be discharged in September 1914 because the recent death of her husband had left her alone and without any form of support. She could not manage by herself because she was "completely blind."[36] Likewise, Mrs. Joseph Martin of Toronto requested the discharge of her husband from the Fort Garry Horse because she was crippled. Her left foot having been amputated, and often suffering from pains in her right leg, Mrs. Martin was periodically unable to get around and so could not provide for herself or her young son.[37]

Older parents sought to block their son's enlistment or gain their discharge by claiming physical and economic disability. Private Charles Steele's discharge was requested by his mother because he was his aged parents' only support and his father was extremely ill. "We need him home very badly," Mrs. Steele explained, "his father is not well any time he is troubled with his heart he is liable to drop dead any minute now ... you no [sic] what a mother and father are like in there [sic] old days no one can do as there [sic] own children for them." To prove her good faith, Mrs. Steele offered to get the signatures of two doctors to support her statements about her husband's health. She then changed tactics, concluding her letter with what might be described as an attempt at emotional blackmail: "He is in your hands and you can make us happy or miserable the rest of our days please let him come back home ... I would plead on my knees if I was there but am not able to come." Emotional blackmail or not, Mrs. Steele's pleas worked, and Charles was discharged on 12 September 1914.[38]

In a less emotionally charged letter, the law firm of Gagnon, Sasseville and Gagnon challenged the enlistment of their client Patrice Desgagné's son, Joseph, on a number of grounds, including Desgagné's inability to work. Identifying Joseph as Desgagné's "fils unique," the lawyers described the father as "un homme âgé et peu capable de travailler." They argued that Joseph was a minor and "plus sourd, faible et souffre de maladie de coeur."[39] In a similar case, L.C. Belanger, a lawyer from Sherbrooke, Quebec, wrote directly to Sam Hughes in an attempt to have the minister discharge Joseph Gagnon from service. Joseph, Belanger explained, was "about the only support" his mother had because his father had been "paralysed for some years." Besides being his family's breadwinner, Joseph was also deaf.[40]

The cases of Joseph Desgagné and Joseph Gagnon indicate that some soldiers' families attempted to resist the enlistments of their husbands, sons, brothers, and friends by portraying the men as unfit. They drew the military authorities' attention to potential disabilities that had been missed (or ignored) during medical examinations. In many cases, correspondents would bolster their claims by referencing statements made by their family physicians or including written statements signed by the medical practitioner. These tactics were often accompanied by an implicit or explicit attack on the medical examination that had passed the family member as fit to join the colours.

Samuel E. Harris from Cooksville, Ontario, wrote the Department of Militia and Defence on 22 August 1914, challenging his son Cleveland's recent enlistment in the Governor General's Body Guard on the grounds of the young man's ill health. Cleveland, Harris stated, had a heart condition from which his doctor believed he would never recover. This unnamed condition had occasionally caused his son to faint in the street. Apparently, Cleveland's health problems did not end there: on occasion, the young man had "spells" when he would go for twenty-four to thirty-six hours without eating; he had a deformed toe that "trouble[d] him a great deal when he walk[ed]," and he also suffered from severe bronchitis in the winter. Harris went on to criticize the Toronto doctor who had passed his son as fit to serve, calling him "queer" and stating that he and his neighbours were shocked his son had been considered fit to shoulder a rifle because the boy was "so thin and delicate." In addition, Cleveland's mother was "worrying terribly over him for she is afraid that if he does not get shot he will die from either excitement or exposure." In closing, Harris noted that his son would be more trouble to his battalion than he was worth: "They will have trouble enough without taking sick men out with them for soldiers." Harris's request was successful, and his son was not included in the First Contingent of the Canadian Expeditionary Force.[41]

Nevertheless, although Samuel Harris's claim about his son's being thin was warranted – Cleveland stood 6 feet tall, had a 34.5-inch chest, and weighed 155 pounds – his assertion that his son was delicate and sickly appears unjustified. When Cleveland re-enlisted in 1916, the occupation recorded on his attestation paper was lineman. Definitely not a job for those with frail constitutions, working on electrical wires high above the ground was both highly dangerous and physically demanding.[42] Given these realities, "sinewy and strong" would have been a better description of the twenty-year-old volunteer than "thin and delicate," although it would not have helped Samuel Harris's cause. Furthermore, Cleveland's service file indicates that the attacks his father referred to were somewhat dated and his physical impairments overblown. Although he suffered from bronchitis, the only serious attack he had experienced was in 1910, when he was sixteen years old, and he had been in good health since then. And despite his father's claims that Cleveland's hammer toe caused him trouble when he walked, examining medical officers – who were always concerned about the state of a soldier's feet – stated that the deformity was not disabling. Finally, although they noted that Cleveland's heart was slightly enlarged, his examiners did not believe that it was cause for concern or for rejection.

Claiming Disability to Avoid Military Service 145

These impairments might have been sufficient for Cleveland to be rejected as unfit if he had undergone a medical examination at Valcartier in 1914, but it would seem that the doctors were at least partially correct in their diagnosis.[43] At least in the beginning, being in the service appeared to do the Ontarian some good and he gained twenty-five pounds;[44] in fact, one doctor who examined Cleveland in mid-1919 described him as both well built and well nourished – this after he had lost weight due to illness.[45] Ultimately, it was bacteria rather than exposure, excitement, or wounding that caused Cleveland to be invalided out of the trenches. He was hospitalized in England in October 1917, suffering from a severe case of trench fever from which it took him four months to recover.[46] To make matters worse, during his convalescence in England he contracted gonorrhea, which quickly led to a number of other serious ailments.[47]

It is evident, however, that Cleveland's respiratory condition did cause him some problems. Besides trench fever and venereal disease, doctors suspected that Cleveland had contracted tuberculosis in the trenches. After repeated tests for the disease came back negative, they changed their diagnosis – somewhat unwillingly and which much debate – to bronchitis. This judgment caused a medical board held at Moore Barracks, Shorncliffe, on 14 October 1918 to recommend that he be placed in Category BIII: free from serious organic defects, and able to stand service conditions in the line of communications in France; only suitable for sedentary work. He was sent back to Canada in July 1919.

Other parents also criticized regimental medical officers in their attempts to get a son's enlistment overturned. On 8 September 1914, sailor C.G. McWilliam of Picton, Ontario, wrote to Colonel Victor Williams, Commandant of Valcartier Mobilization Camp, requesting that his son Willie be discharged from service.[48] Not one to mince words, McWilliam bluntly stated that if his son had been examined when he enlisted, he would not have been accepted. "Sickly since a small boy," Willie was unfit to be a soldier. He suffered from bronchitis and weak lungs, a condition that as recently as the summer of 1914 had caused the nineteen-year-old to miss work on grounds of ill health. Like Harris, McWilliam bolstered his claim that his son was not fit for service by referring to the opinion of a medical professional. Willie's physician, Dr. Morley Currie, had advised him "to be very careful of him self and keep from getting wet." McWilliam attempted to add further weight to Currie's words by noting that the doctor was a former Member of Parliament.[49] He closed by acknowledging that the department must have been getting "a lot of appeals to release men," but defended his request by stating that his appeal was not for the release of "a healthy boy."[50] The authorities obviously believed McWilliam, as Willie was declared unfit to serve on the basis of his father's protest on 12 September 1914. There is no evidence that Willie attempted to re-enlist at a later date, unlike Cleveland Harris.[51]

Insurance agent Arthur Blake Clarke of Plantersville, South Carolina, went even further than Harris and McWilliam in his attempts to have his brother, G.W. Clarke, dismissed from service. He claimed not only that his brother was suffering or had recently suffered from a wide variety of physical ailments, including pneumonia, diarrhea, and a defective ankle, but that he was also mentally unstable. He had become "erratic" since falling into delirium while in hospital in Vancouver, British Columbia. Clarke stressed the severity of his brother's physical and mental flaws by stating that even he, as an insurance agent, would not insure him. Finally, he offered to pay all expenses related to having his brother sent to him in South Carolina should he be rejected as unfit. G.W. Clarke was rejected as unfit soon after.[52]

Arthur Clarke's letter indicates that in addition to using claims of undetected or ignored physical impairment as grounds for having their loved ones discharged from service, some family members also alleged that they suffered from intellectual or psychiatric impairments. On 13 August 1914, George J. Lynch of Halifax wrote to Sam Hughes regarding his older brother Thomas's previously written request to the minister for the "privilege to go to the front." He informed Hughes that Thomas had only recently recovered from three years of illness during which time he had suffered from melancholia. As a result, his family, whom George stated he was speaking for, felt that Thomas was not mentally responsible for his actions and wanted the minister to disregard Thomas's request and ensure that he was not permitted to enlist.[53] Hughes did so.

In a long letter addressed to "the Minister of Melisha [sic] at [sic] Ottawa," Thomas W. Hicks of Magnetawan, Ontario, warned the military authorities that his son, Clifford, who, in a "state of excitement," had walked forty miles to Parry Sound one night after dinner to enlist, was "not always sain [sic]" and, as a result, was not "always accountable for his actions." Hicks drew attention to the history of insanity in Clifford's maternal ancestors. Not only had Clifford's maternal uncle gone crazy some fourteen years earlier and disappeared but his maternal grandmother had also been committed to an "asylum for a time." Hicks also took great pains to stress the potential danger that Clifford presented to his comrades and his commanders, stating that Clifford "may take you officers for Germans in the excitement [of battle]." In less dramatic fashion, J.H. Fehrenbach of Berlin (now Kitchener), Ontario, turned to his local Member of Parliament, William G. Weichel, for assistance in getting his son, John, released from service. His son was "not a bright boy, in fact ... dull mentally," he said, and was incapable of appreciating what enlistment really meant and of taking care of himself "in the circumstances that must necessarily follow."[54]

The attempts of Fehrenbach and Hicks to have their sons dismissed from the military were unsuccessful, most likely because their claims were questionable at best. The service records of John Fehrenbach and Clifford Hicks contained no evidence that either man suffered from any kind of psychological or mental impairment. Given that the military actively rejected recruits that were judged "mentally deficient," and the length of time both men served (1915–19 in the case of John, and 1915–17 in the case of Clifford), this was significant.[55] Even taking into account the possibility that such impairments may have been missed by a rushed and overworked medical officer during the men's initial examination, the long period during which both men were under the military authorities' gaze suggests that any "mental deficiency" would ultimately have been discovered. Furthermore, both men underwent more than one medical examination during their time in the Canadian forces. In fact, it was during a later examination in January 1917, more than a year after he had enlisted, that John was found unfit to be a combat soldier because of flat feet and slight varicose veins. Both Clifford and John saw action on the Western Front in the 75th Canadian Infantry Battalion and 256th Railway Construction Battalion, respectively. Although gassed at Passchendaele, John survived the war. Clifford was not as fortunate: he was killed at Vimy Ridge on 9 April 1917.[56]

Others attempting to have their loved ones discharged from the military pointed to socially based impairments, the most obvious of which were related to age. Numerous correspondents claimed that their sons should be returned because they were underage. Most of these youths were under the minimum age required to sign up (eighteen), and their parents therefore had every right to ask for their return without any explanation. Many parents, however, chose to speak of their sons' age as a form of impairment. Mrs. J. Cameron of Orangeville, Ontario, for example, stated that she did not want her eighteen-year-old to be sent overseas because he had "not yet attained the strength of a man to endure hardship,"[57] while Mrs. Annie Dash of Hillesdew, Saskatchewan, believed that her eighteen-year-old son, Oliver, was too young to undergo the terrible ordeal of war.[58] Other correspondents stated that their boy's youth had caused him to be influenced to join. P. Boissel explained her sixteen-year-old brother's decision to enlist by stating that the glare of recruiters and the draw of the uniform may have been too much for him to bear.[59] Mrs. Dash made a similar observation regarding her own son, noting that the "glamour of the khaki seems to take the fancy of a boy before he is old enough to realize the seriousness of the thing."[60] Others used the legal disablement that all minors suffered from, saying that they wished to claim their sons until they were old enough to speak for themselves.[61]

These tactics sometimes ended in controversy. Mrs. Margaret McGrath's attempts to pull her eighteen-year-old son, Michael, from the ranks of the 21st Canadian Infantry Battalion on the grounds that he was under the age of majority and therefore unable to contract to serve the state as a soldier without her consent sparked debate about when a young recruit was able to speak for himself. After the failure of her initial attempts to have Michael discharged, not least because Michael wanted to stay in the battalion, she employed a lawyer, D. O'Connell, to push her demands.[62] When his letter to the General Officer Commanding Military District 3 went unanswered, O'Connell wrote directly to Sam Hughes on 23 December 1914, implicitly threatening the Department of Militia and Defence with a writ of habeas corpus if Michael was not returned home immediately.[63] Both the Judge Advocate General and the Assistant Adjutant General advised Lieutenant-Colonel Charles Winter, Militia Secretary, that based on British common law, enlistment was "a valid contract, although entered into by a person under 21, who by ordinary rule of law ... cannot, as a general rule contract any engagement."[64] Common law dictums did not protect Michael from his mother's wrath, however. Not long after O'Connell wrote the Minister of Militia and Defence, Mrs. McGrath arrived in Kingston and "succeeded in inducing the boy to ask for his discharge," which was duly granted.[65]

Correspondents often took great pains to express their loyalty to King and country. More than a few stressed that they would be happy for their loved ones to serve in another capacity if they could stay at home, or that they would support the enlistment if they were in a better position. A number of men who sought their own discharges made similar statements. Mrs. B.B. Gamble, for example, said that if her son did not suffer from the after-effects of a childhood accident, she would think it was his duty to serve.[66] Her words were echoed by Mrs. Robert Burleigh of Toronto, who declared that her objection to her son William's service was not based on any opposition to his "stand[ing] for his country," but rather because there were "lots of others more fit for it than him." Signifying her willingness for her son to serve if he was able, Burleigh added that she did not mind "him be for home duty."[67] Mrs. B.L. Winegard of Collingwood, Ontario, pleaded with Sam Hughes not to view her as a coward because of her request that he place her two sons on home duty due to her ill health. To protect her sons from accusations that they were hiding behind their mother's skirts, Winegard stated twice that her boys were not only brave but also "true Y.M.C.A. members."[68]

Many others noted that their sons or husbands would better serve his country by working in his chosen profession. The aforementioned Mrs. Dash believed that by helping on the family farm – especially now that his aged father was unable to do the work – Oliver "would be doing his duty to his country, just as much here as there."[69] Mrs. F.B. Campbell of St. John, New Brunswick, insisted that her husband, Fred, be returned due to her ill health, declaring that as a machinist he could do much to help the war effort by making shells.[70]

Some went a step further in their attempts to prove their loyalty to the cause. Mrs. William F. Orr ended her letter by objecting to her husband's service overseas on the grounds that his small children needed his support: "If it were not for the babies I would say nothing, I would even volunteer as a nurse myself."[71] C.M. Richardson of Milk River, Alberta, challenged his son's enlistment but stated that should Canada need more men in the future, he would not only support his son's enlistment but also "serve personally in any capacity you desire."[72] Mrs. Dash made a similar statement with respect to her son, Oliver, stressing that when he was older, she would not object to his serving if he was needed.[73]

Despite doing his utmost to have his name removed from the ledger of volunteers, the aforementioned Robert Johnston also took great pains to stress his loyalty and willingness to do his duty to the best of his ability. Identifying himself as the pay sergeant of the 3rd Dragoons, Johnston wrote Sam Hughes that should the unit be sent overseas, "I will be ready to report for duty with it." This kind of promise was not at odds with Johnston's attempt to avoid becoming a soldier. The position of pay sergeant was based at headquarters and not at the front.

Not all correspondents were as diplomatic in their requests. In a letter to Sam Hughes in the summer of 1916, Adelaide Yuill, a sixty-year-old teacher, demanded that Hughes stop her son Lionel, who had enlisted without her knowledge while studying law at McGill University, from serving at the front. She launched vituperative attacks on a number of different targets, including the principal of McGill University, Sir William Peterson, and Hughes himself. "Principal Peterson's knighthood," she declared dramatically, "will be stained with the blood of the poor youths entrusted to his care ... [h]e gets the honor & glory [by encouraging them to enlist]; they death in the shambles." Yuill then warned the minister that "you men at head of affairs will have heavy accounting to answer if our children are wantonly slaughtered to further your ambition for name." After venting her spleen, she softened her tone. Claiming that she could not eat, sleep, or work due to worrying about her "fine looking" son, she declared that she would go mad if he was not sent home. A widow who had the misfortune of having to bury her eldest son, she called Lionel "the only living thing I have."[74] Hughes was obviously willing to gamble with Yuill's mental health, as Lionel was not discharged. Instead, the law student served two and a half years in Europe, obtaining a lieutenant's commission in the process. Moreover, although suffering shrapnel wounds in the right leg and both feet, Lionel survived the war. German snipers obviously did not find the young man the compelling target that his mother believed him to be.[75]

It is doubtful that Lionel approved of his mother's attempts to have him discharged from the Canadian Expeditionary Force. Although some men worked in concert with their family members to obtain their discharge, others strongly opposed their families' efforts. William Burleigh told his commanding officer that he was "unmarried, of age, and ... there is no one who should protest."[76] C.S. Calhoun took another approach. Instead of arguing his case with his commanding officer, he took it up with his mother and appears to have stated his position rather forcefully. His mother withdraw her protest, stating that he had been "not at all pleased" with her interference.[77] Such acts of resistance – especially if they were violent or threatened the family fabric – might explain why some correspondents asked the military authorities not to inform the recruit about the letter that caused him to be discharged. The mothers of Herbert Polk and Garfield Boiling requested that their sons be kept in the dark about the letters they had written in an attempt to get them declared unfit to serve.[78]

The numerous attempts to get their husbands, brothers, and sons discharged can also be seen as forms of resistance by those who were otherwise powerless to stop them from enlisting. In fact, more than one protest letter stressed that the recruit had enlisted without the writer's consent, a requirement for married men before August 1915, or had forced them to give it. Ethyl Weir of Hamilton told Sam Hughes that she had signed the consent form after her husband, Fred, had placed "considerable pressure" on her to do so. She then presented numerous reasons why Fred should be discharged, including a dying three-week-old baby, her inability to provide for their children, and Fred's own medical defect (a hernia).[79]

There is also little doubt that some men employed claims of disability – their own or someone else's – to avoid serving in the trenches. Although many men were wounded by being labelled as unfit and rejected for service, many others welcomed the possibility of such rejection and even pursued it actively. Being declared unfit enabled a man to avoid the trenches without being condemned as a coward or shirker. In fact, it offered him the chance to take on the mantle of a frustrated hero. A man could, in the end, claim that he had volunteered to serve only to have been denied the opportunity by the military's pedantic rules and measurements or by his family. Roy Coates, for example, placed the blame for his failure to serve squarely on the shoulders of his wife in his 1951 letter to the Department of Veterans Affairs: "We were on the point of embarkation, when my wife snagged me, in those days we were supposed to have a paper signed by wife, I did not have one, I nearly made it [to France]." Coates, it should be noted, gave no explanation for not offering to serve when the consent requirement was lifted in August 1915.[80] Likewise, dependents used claims of impairment and disability – physical, mental, and economic – as a means of preventing a loved one from enlisting while still being able to maintain their loyalty to King and country.

As we have noted, the use of claims of impairment in the different ways we have examined complicates our understanding of how people perceived disability and impairment in early-twentieth-century Canada. Claiming to be or being labelled disabled could be empowering as much as it could be limiting. To be sure, these observations should not be pushed too far. Claiming to be unfit for the trenches did not require one to claim that he was unfit for civilian occupations – an obvious but nevertheless important point. By professing one's inability to fight, a man was not declaring his incapacity to contribute to society, nor was he identifying himself as an economic, moral, or genetic threat. In a society that was increasingly infused with eugenics ideologies and that conflated masculinity and morality with financial independence, the importance of this distinction cannot be overstated. Having said that, by employing discourses that drew on perceptions of disability, weakness, inability, and abnormality, such men and their loved ones were *acting* within, implying the validity of, and thereby supporting Canadian society's wider negative constructions of impairment and disability. As discussed in Chapters 5 and 6, such negative constructions certainly did adversely affect many of the men labelled unfit to fight. Nonetheless, for those who wished to avoid serving, the advantages of being so labelled far outweighed the disadvantages.

Conclusion

I remember respectfully like others before me
All those who fell in the war
And I hear you singing songs of lamentation
But I don't wish to hear them no more
What did you do in the time of the war?
It's a question asked by every one
I stood in a line my screwdriver in hand making aircraft out at Laverton
CHORUS

So don't sing no songs about Waltzing Matilda
Don't tell me I tried
And don't tell me I failed
'cause all I recall is the scorn of the women
And the white feather that I received in the mail
I remember the day I went down to enlist
And they said "Read this chart on the wall"
I remember the tone of the voice of the doctor
As he said to me "That will be all. Thank you very much"
Riding home slowly I sat on the tram not sure if to laugh or to cry
For to train in the camps, sure, a man needs his lamps
And a good soldier he must have good eyes
CHORUS

Well it takes more than bullets to murder and maim
Whether worn down or beaten a death's still a death
And you know sometimes when I think back to the forties
I pray for my very last breath
You know I have nothing against those who fought
But for Christ's sake we do what we can
And there's more than one way you can skin a cat
And there's more than one way you can cripple a man
CHORUS (Twice)

– "Scorn of the Women"[1]

THESE LYRICS FROM the song "Scorn of the Women" by Australian musician Michael Thomas reflect the pain, bitterness, and sneaking relief of an Australian man as he reflects on his rejection for service during the Second World War some years after the conflict. Although both geographically and temporally distant from Canada during the Great War, Thomas's lyrics powerfully encapsulate key issues explored in this book. The angry warning "Don't tell me I tried, and don't tell me I failed" could have come equally from the lips of a Canadian rejected for service at Valcartier in 1914 or those of an Australian rejected for service in Melbourne in 1939. Likewise, the observation that "there's more than one way you can cripple a man" points both to the fact that an individual can be disabled by a system of categorization as much as by physical impairment, and to the social and mental wounds that many men suffered as a result of being rejected as unfit for service. Such wounds were, as the song and this book indicate, especially grievous for men whose impairments were not visible or who had been rejected due to impairments that civilian society did not consider made one unfit to shoulder a rifle.

The postwar recollections of Will R. Bird and Martin Colby concerning their multiple rejections for service certainly reflect these realities. Bird's description of his acceptance in 1916, after numerous early rejections because of his shattered teeth as a "rank injustice," and his concomitant deriding of medical examiners as "mosquito brained," is streaked with a palpable anger. Fuelled by perceived – and real – inconsistencies and irrationalities within the Canadian Expeditionary Force's physical requirements for service, Bird's anger was equally informed by a concern that he would be labelled as an unwilling or cowardly Johnny-come-lately by those who did not know better. He, like most Canadian men of military age, would have been well aware of the bitter consequences of being thus tagged. Colby's account of the "hell" he faced on the streets of Toronto highlights the negative treatment that those labelled – incorrectly in the case of Colby – as shirkers faced on a daily basis. That Colby not only had a legitimate, albeit invisible, medical reason for not being in uniform, and also had repeatedly attempted to enlist only further underlines the deleterious position in which many rejected men found themselves.[2] Montreal native Herrick Duggan's letter to his mother reporting that people he encountered in London, England, "scarcely believed" he was unfit on account of a heart condition, and his fears of what might happen to him if "public sentiment should break loose," further evinces this reality.[3] Even more tellingly, the suicides of Daniel Lane and George Baker bear witness to the fact that rejection for service – especially when combined with a public discourse that ineradicably tied masculinity, patriotism, and even biological worth to military service – could have tragic results.

Although each had his own story, Baker, Bird, Colby, Duggan, and Lane are largely representative of rejected volunteers in Canada during the Great War. Data drawn from Valcartier in August–September 1914 demonstrate that rejected volunteers were similar in age, height, and general physical appearance to other volunteers. A large percentage of the impairments that caused men to be turned away would have been unnoticed by the casual observer: eyesight, bad teeth, and varicose veins. In fact, some rejected men did not consider themselves disabled until they were designated as unfit by a medical officer. Moreover, many of these individuals roundly rejected their medical examiners' verdicts, as evidenced by the significant number of men who tried to enlist repeatedly despite being pronounced unfit, and by the critiques levelled at recruiting requirements. Like Bird and Duggan, some of these men would ultimately see service, either because they found ways to circumvent the medical examination or because changing physical requirements later caused them to be classified as fit to don the khaki.

The experiences of these men highlight the amorphous nature of the concept of military fitness during the Great War. Military authorities, medical professionals, and civilians had different views on what made an individual fit or unfit. These differences could and did lead to clashes. Newspapers from Central Canada abounded with criticisms of the military's "old womanish hard-and-fast [medical] regulations" that were denying "prospective aspirant[s] to the V.C. [Victora Cross]" a chance to serve their country.[4] These criticisms were especially marked when military medical regulations appeared to be in direct opposition to standard civilian medical practice or general perceptions of physical fitness. Many civilians were horrified and angered when powerfully built loggers were turned away due to their teeth. The conflict between civilian and military constructions of disability was not limited only to the broadsheets. It is also evident in some volunteers' medical examinations and was inscribed (literally) on their enlistment papers. Some Canadian medical officers at Valcartier implicitly critiqued the regulations they were charged with enforcing when recording their observations about a volunteer's physical condition on his enlistment papers. They did so by stating that an impairment could be cured by resorting to methods the military had proscribed, or by opining that while a volunteer's impairment may have made him unfit for frontline service, it would not hinder his ability to successfully operate in support positions. Others passed men as fit despite regulations.

The fluidity of the concept of military fitness is further demonstrated by the evolution of physical and medical requirements as the war continued. Compelled to meet ever-increasing manpower requirements, military authorities lowered the minimum physical and medical requirements for entry into the

Expeditionary Force as the war progressed. Furthermore, they moved to create a complex categorization system based on physical and medical indicators that allowed for the most efficient use of the manpower resources available to them.

The development of the categorization system was also a reaction to the problems with military medical examinations. Early in the war, large numbers of men who should have been rejected for service according to the criteria of the time were passed fit. This was due to numerous factors, ranging from the inexperience of medical examiners and recruiting officers to deliberate fraud. There was considerable concern over this, as evidenced by numerous reports, including the infamous Bruce Report. As a result, the Canadian military constantly reinforced and improved the system by which men were judged fit or unfit to serve. As a whole, these corrective acts were successful. There is little doubt that by 1917 the medical examination system was considerably more thorough than in 1914.[5] Men incorrectly passed as fit to serve at the local level were often discovered before being shipped to England, as were commanding officers' attempts to circumvent the system. Problems remained – a fact made clear by the case of Elvin Wolf (see Chapter 3) – but one is forced to agree with Sir Edward's Kemp's 1917 claim that the medical examination process had significantly improved by the later years of the war.

Along with efforts to plug the holes in the medical examination system were efforts to combat the negative treatment of rejected volunteers. Regiments, and later the Dominion government, attempted to supply rejected men with identifying badges to set them apart from those who had not offered themselves for service. At the same time, pronouncements were made that those who had offered themselves for service only to be rejected were to be treated with the same respect and honour as those who wore the khaki. The success and popularity of these badges are difficult to judge. Robbie Johnson, an expert on Canadian war service badges, has noted that their relative rarity today might suggest that they were not valued by their recipients.[6] Certainly, contemporary newspaper evidence would seem to indicate that eligible men did not rush to collect the badge when it was offered, and that others were skeptical of their value and use.

The reason these badges met with an apparently lukewarm response may lie in likelihood that few rejected volunteers probably wanted to wear them. Rejected volunteers such as Will Bird and many others who repeatedly attempted to enlist did not believe they were unfit for service. To accept and wear the badge would have been tantamount to accepting that one was unfit. It would also publicly brand a man as disabled at a time when the label "unfit" carried a considerable amount of negative baggage, primarily stemming from eugenics ideologies, and few men were willing to be thus labelled. That some of these badges became symbols of masculine and physical failure is no better demonstrated than by the 1917 Mutual Life Assurance Company advertisement that negatively depicted the Toronto Recruiting Depot's "A.R." badge and those who wore them. More widely, the declarations that acknowledged the honour of rejected men often carried negative undertones. For all its eulogizing with regard to rejected volunteers' "soaring spirits" and great sacrifices, H.B. MacConnell's poem "Medically Unfit" presented such individuals as weak, broken half-men more deserving of pity than respect.

To make this kind of statement is not to deny that some rejected volunteers sought badges, or to imply that all rejected men attempted to hide from society. Identifying badges were demanded by some rejected volunteers and, one can assume, worn by them with a degree of pride. The fact that some rejected volunteers took pride in their identity as men who had offered themselves for service is evidenced by the founding of the Honourably Rejected Volunteers of Canada Association, which, it should be noted, had its own membership badge. The discourse surrounding this association included pride, honour, and heroism.

The formation of the association further indicates the negative results of rejection for men deemed unfit to serve. Turned away from the ranks, rejected volunteers were denied the very real opportunities – economic, educational, and social – afforded to Great War veterans in the postwar period and at the same time had to endure the implication that they had shirked their duty to King and country. The association countered these accusations by stressing that its membership had volunteered to serve, only to be turned away. It did so by limiting membership to men who had been rejected before the introduction of conscription and by taking on the character of a pseudo veterans' group. Central to the adoption of this identity was its support of the demand of veterans' groups that shirkers be punished. By attacking shirkers, the Honourably Rejected Volunteers of Canada Association differentiated its members from them; its members had answered the call, only to be turned away.

The above observations have important implications for our understanding of the Canadian experience of the Great War. Besides highlighting a group that has long been overlooked in the historiography of the Great War, the study of rejected volunteers and the issues surrounding them offers a new vantage point from which to survey and reconceptualize traditional and current historiographical interests, including but not limited to recruiting and manpower mobilization. An analysis of the military medical examination offers insight into one of the most fundamental facets of the recruiting experience, as it was by passing (or defeating) the medical examination that a recruit became an enlisted man. With regard to manpower mobilization, the Canadian military authorities' re-evaluation of the Expeditionary Force's minimum medical standards and development of graded levels of fitness are important aspects of their attempt to overcome the manpower crisis. These acts not only provided the force with a larger pool of possible recruits but also enabled it to use its manpower resources more effectively by creating divisions of labour based on perceived ability.

The way men reacted to being designated as unfit, and the way rejected volunteers were viewed and depicted, are also important. The myriad of negative connotations that surrounded the label "medically unfit" during the Great War reflects early-twentieth-century Canadian society's wider discomfort with disability and the disabled. In a period when eugenics ideologies were spreading across Canada like wildfire, large numbers of men rejected for service on medical grounds not only appeared to confirm but also fuelled fears of racial degeneration. Such fears challenged the belief that a new, vigorous, and strong race was being forged in Canada. That said, the employment of claims of disability by men and their families to either avoid or reverse enlistment serves as an important reminder that the label could be used as a means of empowerment despite, or perhaps because of, these negative connotations.

> MacMillan [an] old man in his sixties, was [the] first [to be examined].
> "You really want to go, old-timer?" asked the medic.
> "Yes, sir! My heart's set on it."
> The doctor looked him over, standing in the raw [naked], his skinny, veined legs planted on the chill floor.
> "Well," he said, "if that's what you want, you can go ... "
> [Joe Bonar] turned to me.
> "You got good eyes, eh?"
> "I can read the chart from here, if that's what you mean."
> "Good. Then you can read 'em off and whisper 'em in my ear when my turn comes."
> Joe passed with my eyes.[7]

Fred Cederberg's recollection of a slipshod army medical examination could be one of many memories of medical examinations during the Great War. However, the young Ontarian's comments relate to an event that occurred some twenty years *after* the end of the war: the embarkation examination of the Cape Breton Highlanders before they were shipped to Europe in 1941. The examination, which was later summed up by Cederberg's comrade Joe Bonar with the observation that "as long as you were warm an' didn't have VD [venereal disease] you were healthy," indicates that lax medical examinations did not end with the Great War but haunted Canadian military authorities into the Second World War.[8] Indeed, evidence such as that provided by Cederberg's memoirs suggests that the medical examination used by the Canadian military during the latter suffered from many of the same basic mechanical problems and weaknesses as during the former.

This observation raises an important question for future study: what influence did the experience of the First World War have on the military medical examination during the second? This question is compelling because a brief examination of official documents and private memoirs from the latter appears to indicate that the trials and tribulations of the Great War medical examination were both remembered and forgotten by the military authorities in equal measure. This is demonstrated best by the Canadian military's introduction of the PULHEMS medical classification system for recruits in 1943.[9] Designed under the direction of Major-General George Brock Chisholm, Director General Medical Services, PULHEMS graded recruits on a scale of 1 to 5 (1 being the best, 5 being cause for rejection) in seven general categories: physique, upper extremities, lower extremities/locomotion, hearing, eyesight, mental capacity (inherent intelligence and acquired knowledge), and (emotional) stability. Recruits' scores across these seven categories – which provided the acronym for the system – were used by the military authorities to assign them to different units and roles in Canada's armed forces.[10]

PULHEMS was not without problems. Although it benefited from interwar medical advancements in training and technology, the medical examination used to implement PULHEMS was not substantively different in a mechanical sense from examination processes employed by the Canadian military in 1918. Medical examiners were still required to search for many of the same impairments, and often employed the same techniques, or variations thereon, as during the Great War. In fact, much of the detail in the instructions provided to medical examiners discussed how to grade men with certain impairments instead of providing new examination techniques or guidelines for assessing a potential impairment.[11]

As in 1914–18, public and professional bewilderment and criticism of the systems used by the military to evaluate men's fitness for service abounded. Intelligence and psychology tests were particular targets of the public's ire and the satirist's pen. For example, in *Turvey: A Military Picaresque* (1949), Earle Birney uses the misadventures of the bumbling Private Thomas Leadbeater Turvey to mercilessly parody the Second World War Canadian Army's various selection processes, and its administration more generally.[12] The most biting but often missed piece of satirical criticism comes at the end of the work, when Turvey aces the intelligence test given during his discharge examination, scoring 202 out of a possible 218 marks.[13] Far from being a genius – Birney later described his hero as having the "intellectual and soldierly capabilities of a farmyard duck"[14] – Turvey excelled in the test because his incompetence while in uniform had caused him to be subjected to multiple psychological examinations and intelligence tests. Birney hammers home this point by having Turvey score a mere 89 marks – indicating, according to the designers of the test, that he was an illiterate imbecile – in the same test during his enlistment. Adding salt to the wound, Turvey cheerfully admits to a stunned personnel officer at the time of his enlistment that he deliberately got a low score in order to avoid being posted to the Engineers.[15]

Birney was not satisfied with showing how the army's supposedly rigorous "scientific" tests could be defeated by even the most foolish of individuals. Obliquely, he indicated that the test itself was flawed, and, much less obliquely, that some of the testers were less fit – psychologically and physically – for military life than the recruits they were tasked with examining. Asked to find the incorrect picture in a set of four, Turvey correctly finds problems with all of them – primarily because he thinks *too much* about them rather than simply choosing the most obvious error.[16] Lieutenant Smith, the personnel officer who interviews Turvey after his poor showing in the intelligence test, suffers from a variety of neurotic disorders ranging from obsessive-compulsive behaviour to hypochondria to a persecution complex.[17]

While the Second World War medical examination may have suffered many of the same problems as its predecessor, the evolution of PULHEMS is of interest because it appears to indicate a further evolution in the Canadian military's concept of military fitness. Following, and considerably lengthening and widening, the path laid down by the earlier *Classification of Men by Categories in Canada* and *Classification of Men by Categories in Britain* systems, PULHEMS focused on defining a recruit's capacity to work. No longer were medical examiners to focus on simply defining a recruit as fit or unfit for service; they were now to ascertain which of the myriad of jobs in the modern military an individual recruit was best suited for, so that he could be effectively employed. In other words, under PULHUMS the emphasis shifted from identifying an individual's inability or disability to identifying his abilities. Some candidates were still rejected as unfit to serve, of course, but the change in focus warrants examination because it suggests that the Canadian military authorities' understanding – gained during the Great War – that a man did not need to be an Adonis to usefully contribute to the nation's armed forces had evolved. Further research is required to identify the factors behind this evolution. Still, given the ways in which the realities of the Western Front influenced the development of the earlier classification systems, it appears likely that PULHUMS was, at least in part, a response to the demands of mechanized warfare for specialists in a wide variety of fields.

More generally, the sentiments expressed in Michael Thomas's song "Scorn of the Women" also raises the question of whether the experiences of men rejected for service during the Second World War were different from those of their Great War predecessors. This question is all the more pointed because the experience of some conscientious objectors in Canada during the Second World War was markedly different on many levels from that of conscientious objectors during the Great War. Most obvious was Ottawa's willingness – demonstrated by amendments made to National War Service Regulations – to allow conscientious objectors to support the war effort through alternative forms of service. These changes were partly the result of the Dominion government's experience in dealing with the same issue during the Great War. Nor was the gaining of knowledge one-sided. Conscientious objectors in Canada during the Second World War benefited from both the guidance and intercession of their predecessors. Admittedly, this is only half the story. Not all conscientious objectors were looked upon with benevolence or tolerance by the Canadian government during the later war. More importantly, even those recognized by the authorities often drew negative reactions on the streets of Canada during the "Good War."[18] Nevertheless, the differential experiences of Canadian conscientious objectors during the two wars raise the question of whether similar changes were experienced by rejected volunteers, especially given the existence of Honourably Rejected Volunteers of Canada Association, the public debates over rejected volunteers, and the ways in which many individual rejected volunteers portrayed themselves both during and after the war.

It will be equally interesting to explore whether Second World War rejected volunteers viewed themselves differently from how many of those turned away in 1914–18 saw themselves. Personal experience suggests that, at least in some cases, there was little difference. My maternal grandfather was rejected for overseas service in the New Zealand Expeditionary Force during the Second World War due to the effects of a combination of serious injuries suffered on the rugby field and in the workshop. He experienced the same feelings of guilt and emasculation as those experienced by many Canadian rejected volunteers during the Great War. Nevertheless, one would be foolish not to believe that, as Thomas's song suggests, at least some men viewed their rejection with a sneaking sense of relief. Of course, wider questions must also be asked regarding how the experience of the Great War influenced the general public's views of these men during the Second World War, particularly given the much more circumspect approach of many Canadians towards the latter conflict.[19]

In the closing scene of the film *Passchendaele*, David Mann is shown reflecting on Michael Dunne's gravestone at the Dunne family farm. Mann is in uniform, having passed the medical examination with the help of an accommodating doctor. He paid a heavy price for his success. The young soldier contemplates Dunne's memorial from a wheelchair, having lost his left leg during the Battle of Passchendaele. As he silently pays his respects, the shot pans and alters, and Dunne's gravestone becomes one of hundreds of Canadian graves in a military cemetery, enjoining viewers to remember the sacrifices of those who served in the trenches. This poignant scene is a fitting one with which to end this book. As we, like Mann, remember those who suffered and died in trenches, may we also take the time to remember those declared unfit to serve.

Appendices

APPENDIX A
Changes in the Physical Requirements for Canadian Combat Units, 1910–18

Date	Minimum height	Minimum chest	Eyes	Other factors	Notes
Prewar Active Militia (1910)	5'4"	34"			
Prewar Permanent Force (1910)	5'4" – Infantry 5'6" – Garrison Artillery	34"	A recruit was considered fit if he had D = 20 vision in both eyes without glasses, or D = 15 vision in one eye and no less than D = 30 vision in the other eye without glasses.	Use of dentures constitutes grounds for rejection. Recruit must have "good" hearing.	
17 August 1914	5'3" – Infantry 5'7" – Artillery	33.5"			These requirements superseded those in the Regulations for the Canadian Medical Service, 1914 with regard to minimum height and chest expansion, which were the same as those recorded for 1910.

Mid-1915			Men are no longer rejected due to defective teeth but are enlisted and then sent to a camp dental surgeon for treatment. Men with dentures are now considered fit to serve.
21 July 1915	5'2" – Infantry 5'4" – Artillery	33" for 18–30-year olds 34" for 30–45-year olds	
19 November 1915			Men with D = 60 vision with each eye without glasses are considered fit. Men with D = 20 vision in their right eye without glasses, and not less than D = 80 vision in their left eye without glasses, are considered fit.

▼ Appendix A

Date	Minimum height	Minimum chest	Eyes	Other factors	Notes
29 November 1915 (Bantam Battalions)	5′1.5″	30″		Must be at least 22 years old.	The 143rd (BC) Overseas Battalion (Bantams) was authorized on 29 November 1915 and began recruiting on 20 February 1917. The 216th (Toronto) Canadian Infantry Battalion was authorized on 17 February 1916 and began recruiting immediately. Both battalions were broken up for reinforcements after arriving in England.
16 March 1916			Soldiers (not recruits) who lost an eye but are otherwise fit can be returned as fit for service.		

| 16 June 1916 | | Serving soldiers are not to be discharged for defective vision unless the defective vision is due to: a squint; a morbid condition of the eyes or lids of either eye, liable to aggravation or recurrence; or cannot be corrected by the aid of glasses up to the standard required for recruits on enlistment. | |
| PS 1917 (see sources) | 5′ – Infantry
5′4″ – Artillery
5′4″ – Cyclist Corps
5′2″ – Other corps | Men with D = 80 vision or better in both eyes without glasses are considered fit. Men with D = 80 vision in their right eye, and no less than D = 200 vision in their left eye, without glasses, are considered fit. Men with D = 80 vision in one eye without glasses, and whose right eye can be brought up to D = 40 with glasses, are considered fit. | *Hearing*: Men who can hear an ordinary voice at 15′ or better in each ear are considered fit.
Men who can hear an ordinary voice at 21′ or better in one ear but have little or no hearing in the other ear are considered fit. Men with organic diseases of the ear are rejected.
Nasal conditions: Men suffering from severe nasal obstructions are rejected. |

▼ Appendix A

Date	Minimum height	Minimum chest	Eyes	Other factors	Notes
September 1917	Heavy, Garrison, and Siege Artillery 5'7" – Gunners 5'4" – Drivers- Horse and Field Artillery 5'6" – Gunners 5'2" – Drivers				Refer to Appendix C to see how Canadian Expeditionary Force fitness categories were utilized.
PS 1918 (see sources)			Men with $D = 80$ vision or better in both eyes without glasses are considered fit. Men with $D = 80$ vision in their right eye, and no less than $D = 200$ vision in their left eye who can be improved with glasses to shoot, are considered fit.		

Sources:

Canada. Army Medical Corps Instructions: General Orders, Militia Orders and Precis of Headquarters Letters Bearing upon the Administration of the Canadian Army Medical Service Published between August 6th, 1914, and December 31st, 1916. Ottawa: Militia Council, 1917.

–. *Canadian Expeditionary Force Units: Instructions Governing Organisation and Administration.* Ottawa: Government Printing Bureau, 1916.

–. *Militia Orders, 1914.* Ottawa: Department of Militia and Defence, 1914.

–. *Physical Standards and Instructions for the Medical Examination of Recruits for the Canadian Expeditionary Force and for the Active Militia of Canada, 1917.* Ottawa: King's Printer, 1917 (PS 1917).

–. *Physical Standards and Instructions for the Medical Examination of Recruits for the Canadian Expeditionary Force and for the Active Militia.* Ottawa: King's Printer, 1918 (PS 1918).

–. *Regulations for the Canadian Medical Service, 1910.* Ottawa: Government Printer, 1910.

–. *Regulations for the Canadian Medical Service, 1914.* Ottawa: Government Printer, 1915.

–. *The King's Regulations and Orders for the Canadian Militia, 1910.* Ottawa: King's Printer, 1910.

–. *The King's Regulations and Orders for the Canadian Militia, 1917.* Ottawa: King's Printer, 1917.

APPENDIX B
Physical Standards Required of Support Units

Date	Minimum height	Minimum chest	Eyes	Other factors	Notes
19 November 1915: Canadian Army Service Corps (CASC); Canadian Army Medical Corps (CAMC); Canadian Ordnance Corps (COC); forestry battalions; and drivers in the Canadian Artillery or Canadian Engineers			Men with D = 20 vision in their left eye without glasses, and no less than D = 120 vision in their right eye without glasses, are considered fit.		
16 June 1916: Forestry Battalions				Absence of one or two toes on either or both feet, provided it is not the great toe, is no longer a cause for rejection.	Maximum age set at 48 years (3 years above infantry maximum), provided the recruit in question had specialized skill (millwright, saw filer, or the like).

	Height	Vision		Age / Other standards
Early 1917: CAMC; Canadian Army Dental Corps (CADC); Pioneers, Labour, Construction, Forestry, and Railway Battalions	Proportional to height	Men with no less than D = 200 vision in their right eye without glasses, and no less than D = 80 with their left eye without glasses, are considered fit. Men who have lost one eye, or the sight thereof, provided the vision in their remaining eye equals D = 60 and they are passed by an Ophthalmic Medical Officer are considered fit. Men with squints, provided the vision in their fixing eye equals D = 60 and they are passed by an Ophthalmic Medical Officer are considered fit.	*Hearing:* Men who can hear an ordinary voice at 15 feet but have little or no hearing in the other ear are considered fit for CAMC; CADC; Pioneers, Labour, Construction, Forestry, and Railway Battalions. *Flat feet:* A moderate degree of flat feet is considered acceptable. *Hands:* A man who has lost one or two fingers on either hand can be accepted provided an examining medical board considers that the loss of the digits does not incapacitate the individual from active manual labour.	As with 19 November 1915, drivers for the Canadian Artillery or the Canadian Engineers are covered by minimum visual acuity standards. Maximum age for CAMC; CADC; Pioneers, Labour, Construction, Forestry, and Railway Battalions is set at 48 years.
1918: Railway Construction Battalions		Men with D = 80 vision or better in both eyes without glasses are considered fit. Men with D = 80 vision in their right eye, and no less than D = 200 vision in their left eye who can be improved with glasses to shoot, are considered fit.		Maximum age is set at 43. Men from categories lower than Category A provided they are: • Specially qualified • Able to perform a full day's work of 10 hours • Have a physical development that fits them for heavy work

▼ **Appendix B**

Date	Minimum height	Minimum chest	Eyes	Other factors	Notes
1918: Forestry Battalions				Men below Category A are accepted, provided they are specially qualified and able to perform a full days' work of 10 hours.	

Sources:

Canada. *Army Medical Corps Instructions: General Orders, Militia Orders and Precis of Headquarters Letters Bearing upon the Administration of the Canadian Army Medical Service Published between August 6th, 1914, and December 31st, 1916. Ottawa: Militia Council, 1917.*

–. *Canadian Expeditionary Force Units: Instructions Governing Organisation and Administration. Ottawa: Government Printing Bureau, 1916.*

–. *Militia Orders, 1914. Ottawa: Department of Militia and Defence, 1914.*

–. *Physical Standards and Instructions for the Medical Examination of Recruits for the Canadian Expeditionary Force and for the Active Militia of Canada, 1917. Ottawa: King's Printer, 1917 (PS 1917).*

–. *Physical Standards and Instructions for the Medical Examination of Recruits for the Canadian Expeditionary Force and for the Active Militia. Ottawa: King's Printer, 1918 (PS 1918).*

–. *Regulations for the Canadian Medical Service, 1910. Ottawa: Government Printer, 1910.*

–. *Regulations for the Canadian Medical Service, 1914. Ottawa: Government Printer, 1915.*

–. *The King's Regulations and Orders for the Canadian Militia, 1910. Ottawa: King's Printer, 1910.*

–. *The King's Regulations and Orders for the Canadian Militia, 1917. Ottawa: King's Printer, 1917.*

APPENDIX C
Categories Used by Canadian and British Forces to Classify Recruits and Soldiers, 1914–18

BRITISH CLASSIFICATIONS

British Classificatory Categories for Recruits and Soldiers as of March 1915

A. Fit for service home or abroad
B. Temporarily unfit for service abroad
C. Fit for service at home only
D. Unfit for service at home or abroad

British Classificatory Categories for Recruits and Soldiers as of December 1915

1. Fit for general service
2. Fit for field service at home
3.
    (a) Fit for garrison service abroad
    (b) Fit for garrison service at home
4.
    (a) Fit for labour, such as road-making, entrenching, and other works
    (b) Fit for sedentary work only, such as clerical work
5. Unfit for any military service

British Classificatory Categories for Recruits and Soldiers, June 1916

A – Fit for general service
    i. Men actually fit for despatch overseas in all respects, as regards training, physical and mental qualifications
    ii. Recruits who should be A(i) as soon as trained
    iii. Returned Expeditionary Force men who should be fit for A(i) as soon as "hardened"[1]
    iv. Men under 19 years of age who should be fit for A(i) or A(ii) as soon as they are 19 years of age

B – Fit for service abroad (but not fit for general service)
    i. In Garrison or Provisional Units
    ii. In Labour Units or on Command Garrison or Regimental outdoor employment
    iii. On sedentary work as clerks or storemen only

---

1 The term "hardening" referred to the physical reconditioning of men who had recovered from illness or wounds, with the aim of enabling them to return to their reserve battalions. It consisted of marching for the first week without arms for one mile in the morning and afternoon. In the second week, this was increased to a two-mile quick march in the morning and afternoon. In the third week, men marched four miles morning and afternoon under the same conditions. Full duty was resumed in the fourth week. By the fifth week men were considered ready to be drafted back into their reserve units. MacPherson, *History of the Great War,* 123; David W. Love, *A Call to Arms,* 180.

172 Appendices

C – Fit for Service at home only
  i.   In Garrison or Provisional Units
  ii. In Labour Units or on Command Garrison or Regimental outdoor employment
  iii. On sedentary work as clerks, storemen, batmen, cooks, orderlies, sanitary duties, etc.

D – Temporarily unfit for service in categories A, B, or C, but likely to become fit within 6 months and meanwhile either
  i.   In Command Depots[2] (Regular Royal Artillery, Royal Engineers, and Infantry and Territorial Force Infantry)
  ii. In Regimental Depots (Regular Cavalry, Royal Artillery, Royal Engineers, and Infantry only)
  iii. In any unit or depot under or awaiting medical or dental treatment (who on completion of treatment will rejoin their own original category)

E – Unfit for service in categories A, B, or C, and not likely to become fit within 6 months
  Awaiting discharge or reclassification

British Classificatory Categories for Recruits and Soldiers Subsequent to October 1917

A – Fit for general service
  i.   Men actually fit for general service in any theatre of war in all respects, as regards training, physical and mental qualifications
  ii. Recruits who should be A(i) as soon as trained
  iii. Men who have previously served with an Expeditionary Force who should be fit for A (i) as soon as "hardened"
  iv. Men under 19 years of age who should be fit for A(i) or A(ii) as soon as they are 19 years of age

B – Not fit for general service, but fit for service at home (and abroad in the case of men passed fit for service overseas)
  i.   In Field Units (at home only) and in Garrison Units, or on duties of analogous nature
  ii. In Labour Units or Garrison or Regimental outdoor employment
  iii. On sedentary work as clerks, storemen, batmen, cooks, orderlies, on sanitary duties etc., or, if skilled tradesmen, at their trades

D – Temporarily unfit for service in categories A or B, but likely to become fit within six months, and meanwhile either
  i.   In Command Depots
  ii. In Regimental Depots
  iii. In any unit under or awaiting medical or dental treatment (who on completion of treatment will rejoin their own original category)

---

2 Command depots were usually associated with one or more military camps. They were intended to provide concentration areas for soldiers who had been discharged from the hospital but were not yet ready to rejoin their units. When sent to a command depot, a soldier was subjected to "hardening" and would also receive any required remedial treatments for his illness or wound. Love, *A Call to Arms*, 103.

E – Unfit for service in categories A or B, and not likely to become fit within six
months
Awaiting discharge, reclassification, or invaliding home from abroad

As well as the categories listed above, the following categories were employed by the
British Expeditionary Force in Flanders and France:

Class TB (Temporary Base): Temporarily unfit for general service

Class PB (Permanent Base): Unfit for general service at the Front, but fit for service
on the lines of communication and in army corps areas and capable of being
regarded Class A

Class PU (Permanently Unfit): Those in Class PB who are never likely to become
Class A, but employed in the same way as Class PB

*Classificatory Categories for Officers and Other Ranks Serving in France
Subsequent to 15 December 1917* (CCO)

A – Fit for general service

B – Not fit for general service but liable to be reclassified as "A"
  i.   Fit for Garrison Units, Divisional Employment Companies, Area
       Employment (Garrison Guard) Companies, Labour Companies em-
       ployed at the Front, NCOs as permanent staff of Reinforcement Camps
       and Convalescent Depots. Men for employment in lieu of RAMC [Royal
       Army Medical Corps]. Nursing or General Duty orderlies and stretcher
       bearers in L. of C. [lines of communication]
  ii. Fit for Labour Corps Units employed in lines of communication or other
       duties of an analogous nature
  iii. On sedentary work as clerks, storemen, batmen, cooks, orderlies other
       than RAMC, sanitary duties, or, if skilled tradesmen, at their trades

E – Unfit for service in France or at home
The classifications TB, PB, and PU were discontinued by this document.[3]

British Ministry of National Service Classifications (November 1917 – November 1918)

Grade I: Those who attain the full normal standard of health and strength and
are capable of enduring physical exertion suitable to their age. Such men must
not suffer from progressive organic disease, nor have any serious disability or
deformity. Minor defects which can be remedied or adequately compensated
by artificial means will not be regarded as disqualifications.
[Comparable to Category A of CCO]

Grade II: Those who for various causes, such as subject to partial disabilities, do
not reach the standard grade I. They must not suffer from progressive organic
disease. They must have fair hearing and vision; be of moderate muscular
development, and be able to undergo a considerable degree of physical exertion
of a nature not involving severe strain.
[Comparable to Categories Bi and Ci of CCO]

---

3   Minor changes were made to this classification system on 17 November 1918.

Grade III: Those who present marked physical disabilities or such evidence of past disease that they are not considered fit to undergo the degree of physical exertion required for the higher grades. Examples of men suitable for this grade are those with badly deformed toes, severe flat foot, and some cases of hernia and varicose veins ... The Third grade will also include those who are fit only for clerical and other sedentary occupations, such as tailoring or bootmaking.
[Comparable to Categories Bii, Cii, Biii, and Ciii of CCO]

Grade IV: All those who are totally or permanently unfit for any form of Military Service.
[Comparable to Category E]

Note: Although recruits were handed over to the military authorities bearing the grades assigned to them by the Ministry of National Service, the military would place these recruits into its own categories and then post them to units accordingly.

CANADIAN CLASSIFICATIONS

After 15 May 1917, the degree of fitness of all warrant officers, noncommissioned officers, enlisted men, and recruits in the Canadian Expeditionary Force were classified by army medical boards according to five categories (A–E), the majority of which contained a number of subdivisions. The aim of this categorization system was to prevent unfit men from proceeding overseas as well as to enable the military to utilize its manpower resources "to the best purpose." To aid in this endeavour, a nominal roll of men on the strength of a unit was to be made and kept up to date in the orderly room of every overseas unit and company or depot in which Canadian Expeditionary Force men were serving. The five categories were defined as follows:

A. Fit for general service[4]
   1. Men actually fit for dispatch overseas, both as regards training in Canada and physical and mental qualifications
   2. Recruits who should be fit for A.1 as soon as trained
   3. Returned overseas Canadian Expeditionary Force men who are not quite fit for A.1
   4. Men under 19 years who should be fit for A.1 when 19

B. Fit for service abroad (but not fit for general service)
   1. Not applicable
   2. In CAMC [Canadian Army Medical Corps], CADC [Canadian Army Dental Corps], Forestry, Pioneer, Labour, and Construction Units, and Sections Skilled Railway Employees
   3. Not applicable to men proceeding from Canada

C. Fit for service in Canada only
   1. In special service company
   2. Special service companies and CAMC
   3. On sedentary work as clerks, storemen, batmen, orderlies – sanitary duties, etc.

---

4 The subdivisions within Category A were to be used only in Canada. All men overseas or proceeding overseas in this category were simply classified as A men.

D. Temporarily unfit
1. Not applicable
2. Not applicable
3. In any unit under, or awaiting medical, including dental, treatment, who, on completion, will rejoin their original category[5]

E. Unfit for service in categories A, B, or C
Awaiting discharge or reclassification

To ensure that medical boards correctly classified the men, they were provided the following guidelines:

A. Men already serving, recruits when trained or returned CEF men when their physical condition warrants it; able to march, see to shoot, hear well and absolutely well able to stand active service conditions

B. Men already serving, recruits when trained or returned Canadian Expeditionary Force men when their physical condition warrants it; free from serious organic defects, able to stand service conditions in the line of communications in France
B.1. Able to march at least 5 miles, see to shoot with glasses, and hear well
B.2. Able to walk to and from work at least five miles, see and hear sufficiently for ordinary purposes and fulfilling conditions laid down in special instructions
B.3. Only suitable for sedentary work

C. Free from serious organic disease, able to stand service conditions in Canada
C.1. Able to march at least 5 miles, see to shoot with glasses, and hear well
C.2. Able to walk to and from work, a distance not exceeding 5 miles
C.3. Only suitable for sedentary work

After 3 November 1917, the categories used to classify the degree of fitness of all warrant officers, noncommissioned officers, and enlisted men in the Canadian Forces serving in Europe were altered by abolishing the distinction between Categories B and C. On this date, all soldiers serving in Europe who were categorized as C(1), C(2), and C(3) were promoted to the corresponding subdivision of Category B. Likewise, all existing instructions referencing Category C were to be read as referring to Category B, and any instructions that differentiated between Categories B and C were cancelled, so far as they referred to Category C.

As a result, soldiers' degrees of fitness were defined as categories:

A. Fit for general service
1. Men actually fit for general service overseas in all respects, as regards training and physical and mental qualifications
2. Men who have not been overseas who should be fit for A(1) as soon as trained
3. Overseas casualties on discharge from hospital on Command Depots who should be fit for A(i) as soon as hardening and training is completed in Reserve Units

---

5   Men in quarantine remained in their original categories and were not placed in D3.

4. Men under 19 years of age who should be fit for A(1) or A(2) as soon as they are 19 years of age[6]

B. Not fit for general service, but fit for service overseas or in British Isles under the following conditions:
   1. In Railway and Forestry Units and upon work of a similar character
   2. In Forestry, Labour, CASC [Canadian Army Service Corps], CAMC (Base Units), Veterinary Units, and on garrison or regimental outdoor employment
   3. On sedentary work, in the British Isles only, as clerks, storemen, batmen, cooks, orderlies, on sanitary duties, etc., or, if skilled tradesmen, at their trades

D. Temporarily unfit for service in categories A or B, but likely to become fit within six months, and meanwhile either:
   1. In Command Depots
   3. In any unit under or awaiting medical or dental treatment who on completion of treatment will rejoin their own original category.[7]

The following standards were laid down as a guide for placing men in the various categories:

A. Able to march, see to shoot, hear well, and stand active conditions

B. Free from serious organic disease, and, in addition, if classified under:
   B.1. Able to march at least 5 miles, see to shoot with glasses, and hear well
   B.2. Able to walk to and from work a distance not exceeding 5 miles, and see and hear sufficiently for normal purposes
   B.3. Only suitable for sedentary work, or on such duties as storemen, batmen, cooks, orderlies, sanitary duties, etc.; also, if skilled tradesmen, fit to work at their trades

Sources:
Library and Archives Canada, Records of the Department of National Defence, vol. 1836, file GAQ 9-25, "Copies of Correspondence Etc. Bearing on the Physical Standards of Recruits for CEF, European War," General Routine Orders by Field-Marshal Sir Douglas Haig, 15 December 1917 and 17 November 1918.
Library and Archives Canada, Records of the Department of National Defence, vol. 4616, file HQ 54-21-4-35, "Classification of Men by Categories," Routine Orders by Lieut.-Gen. Sir R.E.V. Turner, 2 November 1917.
Library and Archives Canada, Records of the Department of National Defence, vol. 6536, file HQ 649-1-79, "Treatment Generally of C.E.F. Soldiers Found Medically Unfit (1917–19)," Adjutant-General, Canadian Militia, 3 May 1917.
Love, David W. *A Call to Arms: The Organization and Administration of Canada's Military in World War One.* Winnipeg: Bunker to Bunker Books, 1999.
MacPherson, W.G. *History of the Great War: Medical Services General History*, vol. 1. London: King's Printer, 1921.
Messanger, Charles. *Call-to-Arms: The British Army 1914–18.* London: Cassell, 2005.

---

6 Medical officers were directed to classify men under nineteen years of age who were not physically or medically fit for Category A in either Category B or E, according to their fitness. The lower age limit for trumpeters, drummers, or pipers was eighteen.
7 Category D3 was a temporary category. Men were placed in this category if they were undergoing medical or dental treatment. When the treatment was completed, they automatically rejoined their original category until reclassified (up or down) by their unit medical officer or a medical board.

Appendix D
Evolution of Canadian War Service Badges, 1916–19

Order in Council	Date	Class	Eligibility	Misuse penalties	Notes
P.C. 1944	16 August 1916	A	Men honourably discharged from the Expeditionary Force	A fine not exceeding $100, or imprisonment for a period not exceeding 30 days	
		B	Men who offered themselves for active service in the present war and have been rejected		
		C	Men who desired to or offered to enlist who were refused upon the ground their services are of more value to the state in the employment in which they are engaged than if they should enlist for active service in the naval or military forces		
P.C. 275	27 February 1917	A	Those who have seen active service at the front in the Canadian Expeditionary Force, and who have been honourably discharged, or, if officers, whose services have been honourably dispensed with	A fine not exceeding $500, or imprisonment for a period not exceeding 6 months	

▼ Appendix D

Order in Council	Date	Class	Eligibility	Misuse penalties	Notes
		B	Those not included in Class A who have served in the present war with the Canadian Expeditionary Force, and who have been honourably discharged, or, if officers, whose services have been honourably dispensed with after 6 months' service, or after less than 6 months' service, provided, in the latter case, that the discharge is for disability due to military service		
		C	Those not included in Class A or Class B who have served in the present war with the Canadian Expeditionary Force, and who have been honourably discharged, or, if officers, whose services have been honourably dispensed with; and those who have offered themselves for Active Service Overseas, and have been rejected as medically unfit, provided that no badge shall be issued to any person who has been discharged or rejected, or whose services have been dispensed with on account of a temporary disability, or who is obviously unfit for service in the Canadian Expeditionary Force		
		D	Those who offered themselves for Active Service Overseas, and have been refused upon the ground their services are of more value to the State in the employment in which they are engaged than on Active Service Overseas		

| P.C. 2199 | 10 August 1917 | A | Members of the Canadian Expeditionary Force who have seen active service at the front in the present war, and who, in the case of officers, have honourably retired or relinquished their commissions in the Canadian Expeditionary Force, or who have been returned to Canada on duty; or, in the case of non-commissioned officers and men, have been honourably discharged from the Canadian Expeditionary Force, or have been returned to or retained in Canada on duty, provided their claims are duly approved | A fine not exceeding $500, or imprisonment for a period not exceeding 6 months |
| | | B | Members of the Canadian Expeditionary Force who have seen active service in the present war in England or at the front, and who, in the case of officers, have honourably retired or relinquished their commissions in the Canadian Expeditionary Force, or, in the case of noncommissioned officers and men, have been honourably discharged from the Canadian Expeditionary Force on account of old age, wounds, or sickness, such as would render them permanently unfit for further military service, provided their claims are approved | |

Appendix D

Order in Council	Date	Class	Eligibility	Misuse penalties	Notes
		C	Members of the Canadian Expeditionary Force not included in Class A or Class B, who have served in the present war and who, in the case of officers, have honourably retired or relinquished their commissions in the Canadian Expeditionary Forces, or, in the case of noncommissioned officers and men, have been honourably discharged from the Canadian Expeditionary Force on account of old age, wounds, or sickness, such as would render them permanently unfit for further military service, provided their claims are duly approved		
		D	Those who, prior to the date hereof, have offered themselves for active service in the Canadian Expeditionary Force, including members of the Canadian Expeditionary Force excluded from Classes A, B, and C... and have been rejected as, and still are, medically unfit		Class D badges issued under the direction of P.C. 1296 withdrawn

P.C. 1242	22 May 1918	Cancels authorization for the issue of Class D badges created by P.C. 2199
P.C. 2816	15 November 1918	Extends eligibility for Class C badges to men on active service in Canada under arrangements authorized by P.C. 1569 (22 June 1918), but not technically members of the Canadian Expeditionary Force
P.C. 777	12 April 1919	Extends eligibility for war service badges to Canadians who served in the Imperial Forces provided they were resident in Canada on 4 August 1914 and had returned to live in the Dominion

Sources:
Library and Archives Canada, Records of the Privy Council Office, File A-1-a, "Orders in Council," 1917–19.

Canada. Military Service Act (1917).

Johnson, Robbie. *Canadian War Service Badges, 1914–1954.* Surrey: Johnston Books, 1995.

Notes

Introduction

Parts of this introduction first appeared in Nic Clarke, "'You Will Not Be Going to This War': The Rejected Volunteers of the Canadian Expeditionary Force," *First World War Studies* 1, 2 (2010): 161–83.

1 Paul Gross, director, *Passchendaele* (Toronto: Whizbang Films, 2008). I am thankful to Mr. Gross and Whizbang Films for generously providing me with a copy of the *Passchendaele* script.

2 Library and Archives Canada (LAC), Department of National Defence, RG 24, vol. 6600, file HQ 1982-1-83, Department of Militia and Defence memorandums, 26 February 1917 and 27 April 1917, "Number of Recruits Rejected as Medically Unfit." With regard to multiple enlistment attempts, see Hon. A.E. Kemp, 14 April 1916, *Debates of the House of Commons of the Dominion Canada, 6th Session, 12th Parliament,* vol. 3 (Ottawa: King's Printer, 1916), 2879–80.

3 Although exact numbers are impossible to ascertain, Amy Shaw has calculated that there were roughly 26,000 conscientious objectors in Canada during the Great War. Amy Shaw, *Crisis of Conscience: Conscientious Objection in Canada during the First World War* (Vancouver: UBC Press, 2009), 10.

4 LAC, William Babtie Fonds, MG30-E3, H.A. Bruce, "Report on the Canadian Army Medical Service" [hereafter Bruce Report], 94–95.

5 A considerable body of literature explores the negative impact of the Great War on soldiers' families, both in Canada and aboard. See, for example, Desmond Morton, *Fight or Pay: Soldiers' Families in the Great War* (Vancouver: UBC Press, 2004), 201–2, 204, 210; Sandy Callister, *The Face of War: New Zealand's Great War Photography* (Auckland: Auckland University Press, 2008), 103–23; Deborah Cohen, *The War Come Home: Disabled Veterans in Britain and Germany, 1914-1939* (Berkeley: University of California Press, 2001); Jessica Meyer, *Men of War: Masculinity and the First World War in Britain* (London: Palgrave Macmillan, 2009), 97–127; Michael Roper, *The Secret Battle: Emotional Survival in the Great War* (Manchester: Manchester University Press, 2009), 218–20.

6 Shaw, *Crisis of Conscience,* 32–33, 62, 64–65, 89–96, 122–35; Bohdan S. Kordon, *Enemy Aliens, Prisoners of War: Internment in Canada during the Great War* (Montreal and Kingston: McGill-Queen's University Press, 2002); Whitney Lackenbauer, "Soldiers Behaving Badly: CEF Soldier 'Rioting' in Canada during the First World War," in *The Apathetic and the Defiant,* ed. Craig Leslie Mantle, 200-13 (Kingston: Canadian Defence Academy Press, 2007).

7 "Disappointed Lad Attempts Suicide," Toronto *Globe,* 18 September 1914.

8 See, for example, Desmond Morton and J.L. Granatstein, *Marching to Armageddon: Canadians and the Great War, 1914-1919* (Toronto: Lester and Orpen Dennys, 1989), 32; Desmond Morton, *When Your Number's Up: The Canadian Soldier in the First World War* (Toronto: Random House, 1993), 10; Tim Cook, *At the Sharp End: Canadians Fighting the Great War, 1914-1916,* vol. 1. (Toronto: Viking, 2007), 24–26; Angus McLaren, *Our Own Master Race: Eugenics in Canada, 1885-1945* (Toronto: McClelland and Stewart, 1990), 43, 63.

9   See Appendix A, "Changes in the Physical Requirements for Canadian Combat Units, 1910–18," and Appendix B, "Physical Standards Required of Support Units."

10 LAC, RG 24, vol. 1836, file GAQ 9–25, "Copies of Correspondence etc. Bearing on the Physical Standards of Recruits for CEF [Canadian Expeditionary Force], European War" [hereafter CCBPS], Col. Frank A. Read, AG, CEF to the Secretary, Headquarters, Militia and Defence, 30 November 1916; LAC, RG 9, Ser. III-A-1, vol. 90, file 10-12-15, "Troops – General – Unfits – Over-Aged or Under-Aged, Sick and Wounded," AG to Perley, 9 November 1916.

11 Sir Edward Kemp, 31 July 1917, *Debates of the House of Commons of the Dominion of Canada, 7th Session, 12th Parliament*, vol. 3 (Ottawa: King's Printer, 1918), 3967.

12 On this point see Nic Clarke, John Cranfield, and Kris Inwood, "Fighting Fit? Diet, Disease and Disability in the Canadian Expeditionary Force, 1914-1918," *War and Society* 33, 2 (2014): 80–97.

13 For an in-depth discussion of the evolution of Great War historiography, see Jay Winter and Antoine Proust, *The Great War in History: Debates and Controversies* (Cambridge: Cambridge University Press, 2005). For three recent Canadian examples of historians' reorientation to the homefront, see Tim Cook, *Clio's Warriors: Canadian Historians and the Writing of the World Wars* (Vancouver: UBC Press, 2006); Robert Rutherdale, *Hometown Horizons: Local Responses to Canada's Great War* (Vancouver: UBC Press, 2004); and Jonathan Vance, *Death So Noble: Memory, Meaning, and the First World War* (Vancouver: UBC Press, 1997).

14 Cook, *At the Sharp End*; and Tim Cook, *Shock Troops: Canadians Fighting the Great War, 1917-1918*, vol. 2. (Toronto: Viking, 2008).

15 Tim Cook, *No Place to Run: The Canadian Corps and Gas Warfare in the First World War* (Vancouver: UBC Press, 1999).

16 Bill Rawling, *Surviving Trench Warfare: Technology and the Canadian Corps, 1914-1918* (Toronto: University of Toronto Press, 1992).

17 Winter and Proust, *The Great War in History*, 19.

18 See, for example, Will R. Bird, *And We Go On* (Toronto: Hunter-Rose, 1930) [republished and re-edited as *Ghosts Have Warm Hands: A Memoir of the Great War, 1916-1919* (Ottawa: CEF Books, 2002)]; Reginald E. Roy, ed., *The Journal of Private Fraser: Canadian Expeditionary Force, 1914-1918* (Ottawa: CEF Books, 1998); and Norm Christie, ed., *Letters of Agar Adamson, 1914-1919: Lieutenant Colonel, Princess Patricia's Canadian Light Infantry* (Ottawa: CEF Books, 1997).

19 See, for example, Michael Adas, *Machines as the Measure of Men* (Ithaca, NY: Cornell University Press, 1989), 365–80.

20 LAC, Records of the Ministry of the Overseas Military Forces of Canada [hereafter RG 150], Accession 1992–93/175, "Files of CEF Volunteers Who Were Rejected" [hereafter FVR]; LAC, William Babtie Fonds, MG30-E3 [hereafter WBF].

21 For further discussion of this source, see Nic Clarke, "'You Will Not Be Going to This War': The Rejected Volunteers of the Canadian Expeditionary Force," *First World War Studies* 1, 2 (2010): 161–83.

22 The board of inquiry published its findings, titled the "Report of the Board of Inquiry into the Report on the Canadian Army Medical Service by Colonel Herbert A. Bruce and the Interim Report of Surgeon-General G.C. Jones" (Babtie Report), on 28 December 1916. The Babtie Report roundly condemned the large majority of Bruce's findings and recommendations. Unsurprisingly, Bruce and his supporters labelled the Babtie Report a whitewash. Indeed, in 1919 Bruce published *Politics and the Canadian Army Medical Corps: A History of Intrigue, Containing Many Facts Omitted from the Official Record Showing How Efforts at Rehabilitation Were Baulked* (Toronto: Briggs, 1919), in which he

gave his interpretation of the controversy and argued that both he and his report were victims of both political bias and a closing of the ranks by members of the medical profession. In spite of the Babtie Report's criticisms, many of Bruce's recommendations were later implemented. See also Ronald G. Haycock, *Sam Hughes: The Public Career of a Controversial Canadian, 1885-1916* (Waterloo, ON: Wilfrid Laurier University Press, 1986), 313–15; Desmond Morton, *A Peculiar Kind of Politics: Canada's Overseas Ministry in the First World War* (Toronto: University of Toronto Press, 1982), 82, 85, 94–95, 103–5, 193–94; Andrew Macphail, *Official History of the Canadian Forces in the Great War, 1914-19: The Medical Services* (Ottawa: King's Printer, 1925), 159–79, 196–202.

Chapter 1: Grading Blocks of Meat

1 D.H. Lawrence, *Kangaroo* (London: Heinemann, 1974), 257–61. The experiences of Richard Lovat Somers in *Kangaroo*, particularly the chapter titled "Nightmare," are a semi-autobiographical account of Lawrence's own experiences during the Great War. See Paul Delany, *D.H. Lawrence's Nightmare: The Writer and His Circle in the Years of the Great War* (New York: Basic Books, 1978), 236–37, 375–76.

2 Mark Harrison, *The Medical War: British Military Medicine in the First World War* (Oxford: Oxford University Press, 2010), 16–17; Peter Leese, *Shell Shock: Traumatic Neurosis and the British Soldiers of the First World War* (London: Palgrave Macmillan, 2002), 34; Cook, *At the Sharp End*, 203–4.

3 Alfred Andrews, "Diary of Alfred Herbert John Andrews," in *Canadian Letters Project*, http://www.canadianletters.ca; Harold Baldwin, *Holding the Line* (Chicago: A.C. McClurg, 1918), 2–3; Bird, *And We Go On*, 11–14; Thomas Dinesen, *MERRY HELL! A Dane with the Canadians* (London: Jarrolds, 1929), 31–32; Bill Michaud, "Thought of a Rainy Day," *21st Battalion Communiqué*, August 1964, 11–12; Harold Peat, *Private Peat* (Indianapolis: Bobbs-Merrill, 1917), 2–3, 12.

4 Cook, *At the Sharp End*, 24–26; A. Fortescue Duguid, *Official History of the Canadian Forces in the Great War, 1914-1919*, vol. 1 (Ottawa: King's Printer, 1938), 20, 71; Morton and Granatstein, *Marching to Armageddon*, 32; G.W.L. Nicholson, *Official History of the Canadian Army in the First World War: The Canadian Expeditionary Force, 1914-1919* (Ottawa: Queen's Printer, 1962), 24, 352. In the British context, see J.M. Winter, "Military Fitness and Civilian Health in Britain during the First World War," *Journal of Contemporary History* 15, 2 (1980): 211–44; David Silbey, "Bodies and Cultures Collide: Enlistment, the Medical Exam, and the British Working Class, 1914–1916," *Social History of Medicine* 17, 1 (2004): 61–76.

5 James W. St. G. Walker, "Race and Recruitment in World War I: Visible Minorities in the Canadian Expeditionary Force," *Canadian Historical Review* 70, 1 (1989): 1–26; P. Whitney Lackenbauer and Katherine McGowan, "Competing Loyalties in a Complex Community: Enlisting the Six Nations in the Canadian Expeditionary Force, 1914–1917," in *Aboriginal Peoples and the Canadian Military: Historical Perspectives*, ed. P. Whitney Lackenbauer and Craig Leslie Mantle (Kingston: Canadian Defence Academy Press, 2007), 89–115; Adam Crerar, "Ontario and the Great War," in *Canada and the First World War: Essays in Honour of Robert Craig Brown*, ed. David Mackenzie (Toronto: University of Toronto Press, 2005), 248–52; Timothy C. Winegard, *For King and Kanata: Canadian Indians and the First World War* (Winnipeg: University of Manitoba Press, 2012), 41–87.

6 Sidney Allinson, *The Bantams: The Untold Story of World War I* (Oakville, ON: Mosaic Press, 1982), 34–35.

7 Tim Cook, "'He Was Determined to Go': Underage Soldiers in the Canadian Expeditionary Force," *Histoire sociale/Social History* 41, 81 (2008): 49.

Notes to pages 15–18 185

8 "With the Volunteers," *Daily British Whig*, 16 November 1914; "Private Terrence [sic] Glazier," *London Free Press*, 30 May 1916; LAC, Accession 1992–93/166, "Personnel Files" [hereafter PF], box 3580-11, #194971 Glazier, Torrence.

9 See Chapter 3.

10 "Medical Services in Connexion with Recruiting," 12 September 1916, *General Orders, Militia Orders and Precis of Headquarters Letters Bearing Upon the Administration of the Canadian Army Medical Service Published between August 6, 1914 and December 31, 1916* (Ottawa: Militia Council, 1917) [hereafter ACAMS], 174–75.

11 LAC, Records of the Ministry of Militia and Defence [hereafter RG 9], Series III-A-1, vol. 37, file 8-2-10, "Non-Effectives Tubercular, Mental, Under and Over-Age" [hereafter NE], Director Medical Services [hereafter DMS], Canadian Contingents to the Secretary, Headquarters, CEF 18 August 1916.

12 *Regulations for the Canadian Medical Service, 1910* (Ottawa: Government Printer, 1910).

13 Ibid., 35.

14 Ibid., 48.

15 What was considered normal hearing is hard to discern as, unlike visual acuity, no standard for measuring was provided in the regulations. However, an examination of later recruiting standard documents suggests that the ability to hear an ordinary spoken voice at approximately 15–20 feet was considered normal hearing. *Physical Standards and Instructions for the Medical Examination of Recruits for the Canadian Expeditionary Force and for the Active Militia of Canada, 1917* (Ottawa: King's Printer, 1917) [hereafter PS17], 11.

16 In other words, did not have any form of speech impediment.

17 By 1916, when the first printed documentation relating to the medical inspection of recruits prepared during the war was released, this statement had been changed to "the appearance of being an intelligent and sober man and likely to make an efficient soldier for a unit of the Expeditionary Force." *Canadian Expeditionary Force Units: Instructions Governing Organisation and Administration* (Ottawa: Government Printing Bureau, 1916) [hereafter IGOA16], 26.

18 FVR, vol. 6, C.E. Lomand.

19 FVR, vol. 1, F. Bennett; FVR, vol. 8, J. Norris.

20 FVR, vol. 1, J. Boyd; FVR, vol. 7, J. McCeary; Cook, *At the Sharp End*, 48–49.

21 Visual acuity is measured relative to what a person with normal eyesight can see at 20 feet (6 metres). Under this system, which is still the most common clinical measurement of visual function, 20/20 (D = 20) means normal vision, while higher numbers expressed increasingly limited visual acuity. For example, a person with a visual acuity of 20/40 (D = 40) has half the visual acuteness of a person with normal eyesight, as he or she sees at 20 feet the same detail a person with 20/20 vision sees at 40 feet. Likewise, a number below 20 indicates increased visual acuity. Therefore a person with a visual acuity of 20/10 (D = 10) sees at 20 feet what a person with 20/20 vision sees at 10 feet. It should be noted that a number of militaries, including the British, were measuring visual acuity in metres by 1914. Under the metric system, 20/20 becomes 6/6, 20/40 becomes 6/12, and so on. In the following text, all standards have been converted to imperial measurements for ease of comparison.

22 *Regulations for the Canadian Medical Service 1910*, 48.

23 Ibid., 49–50.

24 These instructions were the same as those provided in British medical examination instructions. LAC, Records of the Royal Canadian Mounted Police [hereafter RG 18] A-1, vol. 820, file 679-04, "Medical Examination of Recruits for Admission into the Royal Military College of Canada, for Commissions in the Army, and the Permanent Force."

25 G.B. Henderson to Major Lorne Drum, 11 November 1914, LAC, RG 24, vol. 1310, file HQ 593-3-7, "Medical Inspection of Recruits, 2nd Contingent European War" [hereafter MIRSC-1].

26 *The King's Regulations and Orders for the Canadian Militia, 1910* (Ottawa: King's Printer, 1910), 46. According to these regulations young boys could be recruited as buglers.

27 *Regulations for the Canadian Medical Service 1910*, 50.

28 This document became available only in late March 1915. *Regulations for the Canadian Medical Service 1914* (Ottawa: Government Printer, 1915), 46–48. "Regulations for Canadian Medical Service, 1914," ACAMS, 41.

29 "Mobilization Order – Qualifications for Service," ACAMS, 14.

30 The Toronto *Globe* article published on 15 August 1914 stated that this height requirement was an error and that the intended minimum for gunners was 5 feet, 5 inches. Despite this claim, no official evidence exists to indicate that the minimum height requirements for artillerymen were lowered until August 1915. "Mounted Infantry Likely to Be Sent," Toronto *Globe*, 15 August 1914.

31 John Cranfield and Kris Inwood, "The Great Transformation: A Long-Run Perspective on Physical Well-Being in Canada," *Economics and Human Biology* 5, 2 (2007): 204–28.

32 Data drawn from attestation papers of over 50,000 men who served in the Canadian Expeditionary Force between 1914 and 1918 indicate that the average chest circumference of those individuals who met the 1914 requirements for chest expansion (33 inches) was 36.6 inches (median 36.5 inches). John Cranfield and Kris Inwood, personal correspondence, 28 February 2010. I am thankful to Drs. Cranfield and Inwood for generously sharing these data – which is drawn from their ongoing anthropometric research into the physical well-being of Canadians – with me.

33 *Instructions for the Physical Examination of Recruits* (London: King's Printer, 1914) [hereafter IPER], 1

34 Ibid., 4.

35 S.T. Beggs, *The Selection of the Recruit* (London: Ballière, Tindall and Cox, 1915), 9; Silbey "Bodies and Cultures Collide," 64, 70; D.E. Langley, "Bounden Duty and Service: A Royal Welch Fusilier's Perspective of Eligibility and Liability to Serve in the Great War," *Stand To! Journal of the Western Front Association* 68 (2003): 6–17.

36 IPER, 4.

37 Ibid., 4.

38 FVR, vol. 1, Joseph Blake; FVR, vol. 7, Jules Henri Mercier. Also see FVR, vol. 5, William Harris.

39 One wider exception to these visual acuity requirements existed for the Corps of Army Schoolmasters. A candidate for this corps was to be accepted if his medical examiner considered that his vision, with or without glasses, was good.

40 IPER, 4–5.

41 Recruits were required to record any past military service on their attestation papers. Men who had served were, generally speaking, highly valued by the military authorities because they required less training. In fact, Canada's Militia Order 372 of August 1914 required recruiters to show preference to "men who had previously served, or who had undergone some form of military training" when selecting recruits. While men with prior service were valued, the military authorities were also concerned with detecting deserters and those who had been discharged on medical or disciplinary grounds. IPER, 2; "Mobilization Order – Qualifications for Service," 17 August 1914, ACAMS, 14.

42 Although no reason was provided in the documentation for the difference in treatment between these groups of individuals, it was likely due to the fact that undescended testicles in the inguinal canal and subcutaneous ring can lead to hernias.

43 IPER, 6.
44 Canadian medical examiners and recruiting officers had been directed to accept men with bad teeth and dentures in mid-1915. However, the first mention of the acceptance of men with bad teeth and dentures appeared in published recruiting instructions only in 1916. IGOA16, 26; LAC, RG 24, vol. 1311, file HQ593-3-7, "Medical Inspection of Recruits, 2nd Contingent European War" [hereafter MIRSC-2], "Rules for Inspection of Recruits as to Teeth," 15 March 1916.
45 Beggs, *The Selection of the Recruit*, 22–23.
46 Silbey, "Bodies and Cultures Collide," 66.
47 Desmond Morton and Glenn Wright, *Winning the Second Battle: Canadian Veterans and the Return to Civilian Life, 1915-1930* (Toronto: University of Toronto Press, 1987), 25–26.
48 Katherine McGuaig, *The Weariness, the Fever, and the Fret: The Campaign against Tuberculosis in Canada, 1900–1950* (Montreal and Kingston: McGill-Queen's University Press, 1999), 17, 67; Bill Rawling, *Death Their Enemy: Canadian Medical Practitioners and War* (Quebec: AGMV Marquis, 2001), 113; Dr. Carol Byerly, discussion with author, 6 June 2009.
49 Rawling, *Death Their Enemy*, 113; McGuaig, *The Weariness, the Fever, and the Fret*, 24.
50 George Jasper Wherrett, *The Miracle of the Empty Beds: A History of Tuberculosis in Canada* (Toronto: University of Toronto Press, 1997), 36, 128; McGuaig, *The Weariness, the Fever, and the Fret*, 67, 180.
51 Wherrett, *The Miracle of the Empty Beds*, 36, 133–34.
52 See Chapter 2.
53 IGOA16, 26–27.
54 Turner's appointment as GOC Canadians England in December 1916 was part of the reorganization of the administration of Canadian overseas forces that began with the formation of the Ministry of Overseas Military Forces of Canada on 27 October 1916. The ministry had been created in an attempt to combat the chaotic state of Canadian forces overseas, which was limiting the ability of the Canadian Corps to act effectively in the field, particularly with regard to reinforcements and training. It was Sir Sam Hughes's negative reaction to the formation of this ministry – which was designed in part to limit his influence – that finally caused Sir Robert Borden to force him to resign in November 1916. Macphail, *The Medical Services*, 153; Haycock, *Sam Hughes*, 258–310; Morton, *A Peculiar Kind of Politics*, 64–105 (on Turner's appointment, see 97–98).
55 PS17.
56 Ibid., 1
57 MIRSC-2, Adjutant-General [hereafter AG], Canadian Militia to Officer Commanding [hereafter OC], 3rd Division, 28 July 1915; C.J. Bond, "The Medical Profession and Recruiting," *Lancet* 184, 4760 (November 1914): 1219.
58 *Physical Standards and Instructions for the Medical Examination of Recruits for the Canadian Expeditionary Force and for the Active Militia 1918* (Ottawa: King's Printer, 1918) [hereafter PS18].
59 LAC, RG 24, vol. 6536, file HQ 649-1-79, "Treatment Generally of C.E.F. Soldiers Found Medically Unfit (1917-19)" [hereafter TGCS], AG, Canadian Militia, 3 May 1917. Also see Appendix C, "Categories Used by Canadian and British Forces to Classify Recruits and Soldiers, 1914-18."
60 B1 was not an applicable category for men in the *Classification of Men by Categories in Canada*, and it is thus unclear why general physical characteristics for this category were provided. See text below and Appendix C.
61 B3 was not an applicable category for men proceeding overseas. See text below and Appendix C.

188   *Notes to pages 29–36*

62   TGCS, AG, Canadian Militia, 3 May 1917.
63   Quoted in PS18, 18.
64   See Appendix C for a full description of the British classification system.
65   The British would later add another level of classification when the Ministry of National
      Service took over recruiting in November 1917. National Service medical boards did not
      place recruits in the alphanumeric system introduced in 1916, but rather classified them
      in four numbered grades (I to IV). These grades roughly corresponded to the military's
      administrative categories, and when recruits were handed over to the military, they were
      categorized accordingly. For an excellent summary of the development and evolution of
      the British classification system and the forces motivating its introduction, see W.G.
      MacPherson, *History of the Great War: Medical Services General History,* vol. 1 (London:
      King's Printer, 1921), 119–25. Also see Winter, "Military Fitness and Civilian Health in
      Britain during the First World War," 215–22; Appendix C.
66   An obvious but unstated exception to this assumption was, of course, men sent to Europe
      as members of support battalions.
67   CCBPS, "System of Categorisation Explained," date unknown (DMD received stamp dated
      "Jul 26, 1917").
68   CCBPS, DMD, Routine Order No. 2799, 2 November 1917. For a full description of this
      classification system, see Appendix C.
69   Potter held the position of Acting Director General Medical Services from 1915 until 1917.
      He became Acting Deputy Director Medical Services in the wake of reforms that saw
      Major-General John Taylor Fotheringham recalled from overseas service in April 1917 to
      command the Army Medical Corps in Canada. Macphail, *The Medical Services,* 310, 313.
70   The one exception to this general rule, Potter noted, would be where men were needed
      for service in Canada, in which case Category C men could also be called up.
71   CCBPS, Acting Deputy Director General of Medical Services [hereafter A/DDGMS] to
      Acting Director of Medical Services [hereafter A/DMS], 24 November 1917, "The Proposed
      Change of Categorisation to Follow Changes in England as referred to in Routine Order
      No. 2799 by Lt. Gen R.W. Turner, V.C., K.C.M.G., C.B., D.S.O. Folio 121," and A/DMS to
      Deputy Adjutant General, 28 November 1917, "The Proposed Change of Categorisation
      to Follow Changes in England, Routine Order No. 2799 by Lt. Gen R.W. Turner, V.C.,
      K.C.M.G., C.B., D.S.O., Folio 121."
72   Silbey, "Bodies and Cultures Collide," 61–64.

Chapter 2: No Longer Cause for Rejection

1   "Bantam Battalion Is Latest Proposal," Toronto *Globe,* 1 January 1916.
2   This was well recognized by the military. In September 1914, recruiting authorities in
      England temporarily raised the minimum height requirement for infantry from 5 feet,
      3 inches to 5 feet, 6 inches in order to stem the overwhelming tide of men volunteering
      for service. Silbey, "Bodies and Cultures Collide," 70.
3   Tim Cook, *Warlords: Borden, Mackenzie King, and Canada's World Wars* (Toronto: Allen
      Lane, 2012), 61–63, 70–74; R. Craig Brown and Donald Loveridge, "Unrequited Faith:
      Recruiting the CEF, 1914–18," in *Reappraisals in Canadian History: Post Confederation,*
      2nd ed., ed. C.M. Wallace, R.M. Bray, and A.D. Gilbert (Toronto: Prentice Hall, 1996),
      305–6; Patrice A. Dutil, "Against Isolationism: Napoléon Belcourt, French Canada, and
      'La grande guerre,'" in *Canada and the First World War: Essays in Honour of Robert Craig
      Brown,* ed. David Mackenzie (Toronto: University of Toronto Press, 2005), 96–137; J.L.
      Granatstein and J.M. Hitsman, *Broken Promises: A History of Conscription in Canada*
      (Toronto: Oxford University Press, 1977), 22–35; Desmond Morton, "French Canada and
      War, 1868–1917: The Military Background to the Conscription Crisis 1917," in *War and*

Society in North America, ed. J.L. Granatstein and R.D. Cuff (Toronto: Thomas Nelson and Sons, 1971), 84–103; Haycock, *Sam Hughes,* 198–224; Thomas Socknat, *Witness against War: Pacifism in Canada 1900–1945* (Toronto: University of Toronto Press, 1987), 43–89; C.A. Sharpe, "Enlistment in the Canadian Expeditionary Forces: A Regional Analysis," *Journal of Canadian Studies* 18, 4 (1983): 15–29; Shaw, *Crisis of Conscience,* 10; Thompson, *The Harvests of War,* 132–33.

4 This number consisted of one division, including supporting elements and initial reinforcements, as well as troops surplus to divisional requirements, to wit: one cavalry regiment, two batteries of horse artillery, and one infantry battalion. Cook, *At the Sharp End,* 32; Charles Hanbury-Williams, "Creating the Canadian Army," in *Canada in the Great World War, Memorial Edition: An Authentic Account of the Military History of Canada from the Earliest Days to the Close of the War of the Nations,* vol. 1 (Toronto: United Publishers of Canada, 1919), 54; Nicholson, *Official History,* 18.

5 Hanbury-Williams, "Creating the Canadian Army," 55; Cook, *At the Sharp End,* 53; Nicholson, *Official History,* 29.

6 Morton and Granatstein, *Marching to Armageddon,* 30; Hanbury-Williams, "Creating the Canadian Army," 60.

7 Morton and Granatstein, *Marching to Armageddon,* 30.

8 An indication of the belief in Canada's military power held by some Canadians can been seen in Sam Hughes's 7 October 1914 announcement, made in New York, that Canada "could send enough men to add the finishing touches to Germany without the assistance either from England or France." Hughes made similar comments in London, much to the dismay of his cabinet colleagues, who considered his extravagant promises to be further evidence of his mental instability. It should be noted, however, that the firebrand Hughes was not alone in making such pronouncements. In December 1914, Robert Borden responded in the following manner when asked whether the Canadian Expeditionary Force would ever reach 100,000 men: "If the preservation of our Empire demands twice or thrice that number, we shall ask for them." Quoted in Brown and Loveridge, "Unrequited Faith," 301; Cook, *At the Sharp End,* 77.

9 Morton, *Fight or Pay,* 45.

10 The 21,000-strong 5th Canadian Division, which had begun forming in early 1917, was broken up in England in February 1918 in order to reinforce the Canadian Expeditionary Force after it suffered heavy casualties at Passchendaele. Cook, *Shock Troops,* 262; J.L. Granatstein, "Conscription and the Great War," in *Canada and the First World War: Essays in Honour of Robert Craig Brown,* ed. David Mackenzie (Toronto: University of Toronto Press, 2005), 68.

11 In November 1914, Britain's War Office had advised the Canadian government that reinforcements should be provided at a rate of 25 percent per month. This meant that the First Contingent (later named the 1st Division) required between 3,000 and 4,000 men a month, a reinforcement rate that would double when the 2nd Division reached the field. These calculations, which did not include the 300 men per month required to reinforce the privately raised Princess Patricia's Canadian Light Infantry (PPCLI), were significantly higher than prewar estimates, which placed a division's reinforcement requirements at approximately 1,000 men a month to retain its fighting strength. Morton and Granatstein, *Marching to Armageddon,* 30, 144; Hanbury-Williams, "Creating the Canadian Army," 55, 60; Cook, *At the Sharp End,* 88–89.

12 By the end of the war, approximately 425,000 Canadians had served overseas in the Canadian Expeditionary Force. Of this number, 345,000 served in France. Cook, *At the Sharp End,* 527–29; Cook, *Shock Troops,* 368–69, 611–14.

13 The Canadian Division arrived in France in February 1915 after four months of training in England. Although the division had suffered casualties due to shelling, snipers, sickness,

and accident in February and March, it was not until the infamous Second Battle of Ypres that it experienced significant losses. This statement does not include the PPCLI, which first saw combat in early January 1915 as part of the British 27th Division. Cook, *At the Sharp End*, 88–89, 100–1, 159, 165.

14 By the end of 1914, the French, German, and British armies had suffered 800,000, 750,000, and 95,000 casualties, respectively. Cook, *At the Sharp End*, 66.

15 The Imperial authorities had directed in November 1914 that men were not to be discharged on the grounds of dental problems if such problems could be corrected with treatment. Two months later, in January 1915, the same authorities stated that men with dental deficiencies might be taken on strength if they agreed to treatment. While the first directive was put into place in Canada by early December 1914, it is unclear when the second directive was put into place. However, given that Canadian medical officers were being advised that poor teeth were no longer grounds for rejection as late as July 1915, evidence suggests that the directive took some months to trickle down to medical officers in Canada. "Fix Soldiers' Teeth," *Toronto Star*, 16 December 1914; H.M. Jackson, *The Story of the Royal Canadian Dental Corps* (Ottawa: n.p., 1956), 4; see below.

16 "Canadian Expeditionary Force – Dental Services," Militia Order 162, 1915, ACAMS, 41–42.

17 The Canadian military had employed dentists prior to the Great War, but they had been part of the Medical Corps rather than a distinct unit. "Canadian Expeditionary Force – Establishment Canadian Army Dental Corps," Militia Order 219, 26 April 1915, ACAMS, 46–47; "Canadian Expeditionary Force – Establishment Canadian Army Dental Corps," Militia Order 257, 17 May 1915, ACAMS, 54; CCBPS, "Compiled by Major Gorssline from War Diary of A/DMS 1st Div. and DDMS [Deputy Director Medical Services] CDN Corps"; Jackson, *The Story of the Royal Canadian Dental Corps*, 1–7; Col. (Retired) Peter McQueen, RCDC, private correspondence.

18 MIRSC-2, A/DMS 3rd Division to Medical Officers i/c recruiting, 31 July 1915 and 16 August 1915, A/DMS 2nd Division to ?, date unknown.

19 Michaud, "Thought of a Rainy Day," 11.

20 Bird, *And We Go On*, 14.

21 IGOA16, 26.

22 In the space of a week (22–30 April) the division lost 169 officers and 5,248 other ranks, or roughly one-half of its infantry strength. Nathan M. Greenfield, *Baptism of Fire: The Second Battle of Ypres and the Forging of Canada, April 1915* (Toronto: HarperCollins, 2007), 369; Andrew Iarocci, *Shoestring Soldiers: The 1st Canadian Division at War, 1914–1915* (Toronto: University of Toronto Press, 2008), 180–82, 288–89. Also see Nicholson, *Official History*, 92.

23 "Physical Standards for Recruits C.E.F Alterations," 21 July 1915, ACAMS, 62.

24 One notable exception to this rule was Bantam Battalions. See below.

25 Allinson, *The Bantams*, 176–79, 182–83, 187–89.

26 Ibid., 178–81.

27 CCBPS, AG, Canadian Militia, to Canadian Military Districts, 8 December 1917, "Amendment to Pamphlet Physical Standards and Instructions for the Medical Examination of Recruits"; PS17, 7.

28 "Standard of Vision: Revised Requirements," 19 November 1915, ACAMS, 82.

29 "Vision of Recruits: Revised Standards," 24 August 1916, ACAMS, 164–65.

30 PS17, 9.

31 These directives were quoted in PS18, 22–25.

32 PS17, 3–4; PS18, 3–4.

33 See Chapter 4.

34 WBF, "Appendix to the Proceedings of the Board of Inquiry into the Report on the Canadian Army Medical Service by Colonel Herbert A. Bruce and the Interim Report of Surgeon-General G.C. Jones" [hereafter BRA], M22 and M45, #417318 Royal, Arthur and #175381 Mepham, Alfred.

35 "Recruits: Rejection of Those Suffering from Operable Disabilities: Hernia, Varicocele, Varicose Veins," 9 February 1916, ACAMS, 99; "Physical Examination of Recruits: Operations Subsequent to Enlistment to Render Physically Fit," 16 October 1916, ACAMS, 188; LAC, RG 24, vol. 1312, HQ 593-3-7, "Medical Inspection of Recruits 2nd Contingent European War" [hereafter MIRSC-3], "Physical Examination of Recruits: Operations Subsequent to Enlistment to Render Physically Fit," 16 October 1916.

36 Drivers were to be 5 feet, 4 inches and 5 feet, 2 inches, respectively. CCBPS, AG, Canadian Militia, to Canadian Military Districts, 3 September 1917, "Enlistment Regulations, Standard Height for Artillery."

37 CCBPS, AG, Canadian Militia, to ?, 10 October 1917, "Physical Standards for Siege and Heavy Artillery, CEF."

38 "Medical Examination of Candidates for Commission in the Royal Flying Corps," 9 November 1916, ACAMS, 196-97.

39 LAC, RG 24, vol. 4497, file HQ 55-1-5, "Medical Examination Recruits for Royal Flying Corps" [hereafter MERFC], AG, Canadian Militia to ?, 20 October 1916.

40 MERFC, The Officer Commanding Imperial Royal Flying Corps to A/DMS, MD2, 18 February 1917.

41 MERFC, Officer i/c Recruiting, Imperial Royal Flying Corps to MO i/c Toronto Recruiting Depot, 6 February 1916; and, Officer i/c Recruiting, Royal Flying Corps to Major-General E.W. Wilson, OC MD4, 24 March 1917.

42 "Standard of Vision Revised Requirements," ACAMS, 82.

43 "Vision of Recruits: Revised Standards," ACAMS, 164; PS17, 9.

44 LAC, RG 24, vol. 4616, file 7, AG, Canadian Militia, to the Inspector-General of Western Canada, 22 January 1917; PS17.

45 PS18, 9-10.

46 PS18, 10.

47 "Home Service: Physical Standards," 4 April 1916, ACAMS, 114.

48 "Special Service Companies," 19 July 1916, ACAMS, 148.

49 Bruce Report, 11.

50 Peter F. Pirie, The Stump Ranch (Victoria: Morriss Printing, 1975), 54.

51 BRA, M23, #412346 Butler, W.H.

52 Morris had fractured his thigh in 1894 and again in 1911. As a result, his left leg was 2.5 inches shorter than his right leg, and there was "a marked deformity of shaft of [his left] femur." BRA, M47, #57231 Morris, A.R.

53 BRA, M17 and M40, #2804 Jackson, F., and #180849 Ross, M.

54 TGCS, AG, Canadian Militia, 3 May 1917.

55 "Recruits, Physically Unfit, to Be Transferred Where Possible to Branches of Service with Lowered Physical Standards," 7 November 1916, ACAMS, 195-96.

56 LAC, RG 24, vol. 4310, "Full Particulars of Physical Condition to Be Taken of Men Applying for Enlistment in CEF (1917)," Part 1 [hereafter FPP1], CEF Orders, HQ 1982-1-31, 2 January 1917, and W.E. Hodgins, Assistant Adjutant-General (AAG), Canadian Militia to GOC MD 2, Toronto, 2 January 1917.

57 FPP1, Chief Recruiting Officer, Hamilton to AAG MD2, 26 January 1917.

58 See, for example, FPP1, O.C. Toronto Mobilization Centre to A/DMS MD2, 13 August 1917.

59 Militia Orders, General Instructions, 22 May 1917, IX: "Recruiting Generally."

192   *Notes to pages 44–50*

60   *Militia Orders*, General Instructions, 22 May 1917, XIII: "Recruits Rejected for Infantry to Be Transferred to Forestry or Construction Units."

61   Like D.H. Lawrence's Richard Lovat Somers, Craig was a reflection of Godwin. George Godwin, *Why We Stay Here: Odyssey of a Canadian Infantry Officer in France in World War I* (Victoria: Godwin Books, 2002), 33–34.

62   Peter Barton, Peter Doyle, and John Vandewalle, *Beneath Flanders: The Tunnellers' War 1914-18* (Montreal and Kingston: McGill-Queen's University Press, 2004); Michael Boire, "The Underground War: Military Mining Operations in Support of the Attack on Vimy Ridge, 9 April 1917," *Canadian Military History* 1, 1 (1992): 15–24; C.W. Bird and J.B. Davies, *The Canadian Forestry Corps: Its Inception, Development, and Achievements* (London: HMSO, 1919); Nicholson, *Official History*, 337, 368, 371–72, 485–90, 499–503.

63   Evidence suggests that the decree of the DMS formalized a policy that had been followed by some sections of the Canadian Expeditionary Force since January 1916, if not earlier. LAC, RG 9, Ser. III-B-2, vol. 3461, file 10-1-9, "Recruits, (Standard of)" [hereafter RSO], OC West Cliff Eye and Ear Hospital to DMS, Canadians, 3 July 1916. NE, DMS, Canadians to the Secretary, War Office, 9 March 1916; and the Secretary, War Office to DMS, Canadians, 16 March 1916; LAC, RG 24, vol. 1144, HQ 54-21-51-9, "Physical Requirements of Men Included in Overseas Drafts," 31 July 1916.

64   "Defective Vision, Inspection of Recruits, Supply of Glasses," 16 June 1916, ACAMS, 140.

65   PS18, 15. Also see RSO, AG to DMS, Canadians, 8 May 1918, and DMS, Canadians to AG, 14 May 1918.

66   RSO, Assistant Inspector of Drafts and Dentistry, Canadian Troops, Etaples to DMS, Canadians, 21 October 1917.

67   PF, #105747 Baxter, Edward J.

68   LAC, RG 9, Ser. III-B-1, vol. 3240, file P-17-42, "Catergorisation of Soldiers" [hereafter COS], OC CASC [Canadian Army Service Corps] Shorncliffe Area to Secretary, Headquarters Canadians, 8 March 1918; and D. S. & T. [Director of Supplies and Transport] to Quartermaster-General [QG], 3 April 1917.

69   COS, D.D. S. & T. [Deputy Director of Supplies and Transport] to Major F. Hearne, OC, CASC, Shoreham, 8 March 1917.

70   COS, DAAG [Deputy Assistant Adjutant General] to D. S. & T., 11 May 1917.

71   COS, QG to AG, 17 July 1917, and OC CASC Seaford to D. S. & T., 18 August 1917.

72   The Overseas Military Forces of Canada were still using the British classification systems at this time.

73   COS, OC CASC Seaford to D. S. & T., 18 August 1917.

74   Ibid.

75   COS, Headquarters, OMFC to Capt. Ferguson, OC CASC Bramshott, 31 July 1917 [Circular letter sent to all OC CASC Depots in Britain]; and QG to DMS, 31 July 1917.

76   COS, Major F. Hearne to Director of Personal Services, 14 August 1917.

77   LAC, RG 9, Ser. III-B-2, vol. 3484, file 10-14-1, "Reinforcements from Canada, Physical Condition and standard of," Part 6, AG, OMFC to DMS, 23 July 1918; DMS to AG, OMFC, 25 July 1918; AG, OMFC to DMS, 3 August 1918; and AG, OMFC to DMS, 9 August 1918.

Chapter 3: An Imperfect System

1   Frederic Starr was a surgeon at Toronto General Hospital and a professor of clinical surgery at the University of Toronto. During the Great War, he served both as a major in the Canadian Army Medical Corps (CAMC) and as a consultant surgeon for the Imperial Forces in France. Since 1936, the F.N.G. Starr medal has been the highest award the

Canadian Medical Association can bestow upon one of its members. B. Bérubé, "Dr. F.N.G. Starr – in Memory of the Medical Statesman," *Canadian Medical Association Journal* 127, 5 (1982): 417–21.

2 MIRSC-1, F.N.G Starr to Major-General Sam Hughes, 14 December 1914.

3 Bruce Report, 11.

4 CCBPS, Col. Frank A. Read, AG, CEF to the Secretary, Headquarters, Militia and Defence, 30 November 1916; LAC, RG 9, Ser. III-A-1, vol. 90, file 10-12-15, "Troops – General – Unfits – Over-aged or under-aged, sick and wounded," AG to Perley, 9 November 1916.

5 Likewise, J.R. Goodall, Senior Medical Officer (SMO) of the 1st Canadian Training Brigade, noted in his report on medical fitness of the recently arrived 106th Canadian Infantry Battalion that the majority of flea and scabies cases he discovered were of "recent occurrence." BRA, M41, #448129 Kenny, E., and #117333 Kerr, J.; LAC, RG 24, vol. 1144, "Prevention of Re-enlistment in CEF of Men Previously Enlisted and Discharged as Medically Unfit or Undesirable" [hereafter PRE], Senior Medical Officer, 1st Canadian Training Brigade to A/DMS, Canadian Training Division, 29 July 1916; and Officer Commanding MD No. 11 to the Secretary, Militia Council, 19 April 1917.

6 MIRSC-2, A/DMS, MD13 to Regimental Medical Officer, 16 February 1916.

7 On Carson's role in the CEF, see Morton, *A Peculiar Kind of Politics*, 31–63.

8 Three months later, Reid estimated that on average 100 men in each battalion arriving in England were "unsuitable to proceed overseas." NE, Director of Recruiting & Organisation to MGen. Carson, 5 June 1916; MGen. Carson to MGen. Sir Sam Hughes, 7 June 1916; and Director of Recruiting & Organisation to MGen. Carson, 4 September 1916. Also see PRE, Captain S. Ferguson to General Officer Commanding Canadians, Shorncliffe Camp, 12 July 1916.

9 BRA, M8, #414403 McPhee, C.

10 PF, vol. 3977-11, #440913 Hamilton, Calvin Vivan.

11 Malcolm's partial paralysis was probably the result of a stroke. In 1912 he was said to have suffered from two seizures that were "characterised by dizziness, thickness of speech, loss of power right hand and ... numbness in legs." BRA, M46, #643929 Malcolm, Melvin.

12 BRA, M30, #400408 Carment, J.A.S., PF, vol. 1496–53, #400408 Carment, John.

13 PRE, President of Pensions and Claims Board, C.E.F. to Headquarters, Canadian Training Division, Shorncliffe, Kent, 6 July 1916.

14 A gastroenterostomy is an operation in which the duodenum is short-circuited by joining a loop of small intestine to the lower border of the stomach. In Beech's case, this operation had been performed because he had suffered from perforated duodenal ulcer. BRA, M27, #175079 Beech, E.

15 While a silver plate had been inserted under the skin to cover the seat of the fracture, there is no suggestion that the hole in Vachon's skull had been covered. BRA, M11, #417033 Vachon, A.

16 First identified by American neurologist Francis X. Dercum in 1892, Dercum's disease is a rare progressive disorder of unknown etiology that usually affects postmenopausal women. The condition is characterized by the growth of multiple painful lipomas (fatty deposits) over the body; generalized obesity; asthenia, weakness, and fatigability; and mental disturbances, including emotional instability, depression, epilepsy, confusion, and dementia. Marjan Yousefi et al., "Adiposis Dolorosa," *Medscape Reference*, http://emedicine.medscape.com.

17 BRA, M21, #847566 Bonenfant, H.H.

18 Malley signed his attestation papers with a cross. BRA, M17, #847451 Malley, J.; PF, vol. 5872–30, #847451 Malley, J.

194 *Notes to pages 52–55*

19 Bruce Report, 94; PF, vol. 6153–40, #297454 Mick, R. The photograph in Figure 2, which was published in the Bruce Report, is typical of late-nineteenth and early-to-mid-twentieth-century photographic depictions of the disabled that highlighted their impairments by comparing them with "normal" individuals. Indeed, soon after its introduction in the mid-nineteenth century, photography became an important tool with which medical professionals, and later society as a whole, identified and classified the disabled. Mark Jackson, "Images of Deviance: Visual Representations of Mental Defectives in Early Twentieth-Century Medical Texts," *British Journal for the History of Science* 28 (1995): 319–37; Martin Pernick, *The Black Stork: Eugenics and the Death of "Defective" Babies in American Medicine and Motion Pictures Since 1915* (Oxford: Oxford University Press, 1996); Margaret Taylor, "Disabled in Images and Language," in *Disability on Equal Terms,* ed. John Swain and Sally French (Los Angeles: Sage, 2008), 31–41. Also see Rosemary Garland Thomson, "Seeing the Disabled: Visual Rhetorics of Disability in Popular Photography," in *The New Disability History: American Perspectives,* ed. Paul K. Longmore and Lauri Umansky (New York: New York University Press, 2001), 335-74.

20 BRA, M26, #416146 Morin, E.

21 PRE, President of Pensions and Claims Board, CEF to Headquarters, Canadian Training Division, Shorncliffe, Kent, 6 July 1916 and Office of the A/DMS, Headquarters, Canadian Training Division, Moore Barracks, Shorncliffe, Kent to Headquarters, Canadian Training Division, Shorncliffe, Kent, 3 July 1916; PF, vol. 1792–21, #602397 Clements, William John.

22 "With The Volunteers," *Daily British Whig,* 16 November 1914; "Private Terrence [sic] Glazier," London *Free Press,* 30 May 1916; PF, vol. 2910–38, #490592 Emson, Harold; PF, vol. 3580–11, #194971 Glazier, Torrence.

23 MIRSC-3, A/DMS MD13 to Regimental Medical Officer, 16 February 1916.

24 MIRSC-1, OC MD4 to AG, Militia Headquarters, Ottawa, 17 May 1916; BRA, M25, M27, M28, M37, M46, #501277 Alexander, J., #438834 Kerr, S., #550051 Hamilton, J.H.; BRA, M25, M27, M28, M37, M46, #448196 Picotte, H., #501357 Witham, A; PF, vol. 460–9, #654860 Barr, Walter; PF, vol. 519–41, #805678 Baxter, John; LAC, RG 9, Ser. III-B-2, vol. 3483, file 10-14-1, "Reinforcements from Canada, Physical Condition and Standard of" [hereafter RFCPS], Part 2, Senior Medical Officer, Canadian Forestry Corps to A/DMS Canadians, London Area, 26 January 1917.

25 Of the 350 unfit men listed in the Babtie Report, six were reported to be suffering from the effects of serious head injuries, and in another two instances head injuries were implied. The report also recorded 31 cases of men with some form of deformity (including atrophied limbs) and 25 cases of individuals with mental defects.

26 BRA, M27, #175079 Beech, E.; PF, vol. 533–41, #3107060 Beale, Lutie Terrill.

27 Christe, ed., *The Letters of Agar Adamson,* 162.

28 NE, MGen. J.W. Carson to Surgeon-General G.C. Jones, DMS, 17 August 1916.

29 Col. J.L. Potter, A/DGMS, quoted by Sir Robert Borden, 17 May 1916, *Debates of the House of Commons of the Dominion of Canada, 6th Session, 12th Parliament,* vol. 4 (Ottawa: King's Printer, 1916), 4126–27. Note: Potter's second initial is erroneously recorded as "J." in this document.

30 MIRSC-1, G.B. Henderson to Major Lorne Drum, 11 November 1914.

31 RFCPS, Part 2, Senior Medical Officer, Canadian Forestry Corps to A/DMS Canadians, London Area, 26 January 1917.

32 "Medical Services in Connexion with Recruiting," 12 September 1916, ACAMS, 176; also see MIRSC-3, Memorandum: "Medical Services in Connection with Recruiting," 23 August 1916.

33 MIRSC-2, Major Jacques to Major-General Sam Hughes, 24 December 1914.

34 Macphail, *The Medical Services,* 160–61; Babtie Report.

35 PF, vol. 3977–11, #440913 Hamilton, Calvin Vivan; PF, vol. 447–30, #223395 Barnes, Henry Percival; FVR, vol. 11, Martin Wilson; BRA, M28, #427483 Ashworth, M.W.

36 Morton, *When Your Number's Up*, 34.

37 J.A. Hislop, "Terminology of Military Reports," *Canadian Medical Association Journal* 9, 5 (1919): 427–29.

38 J.A. Hislop, "Terminology of Military Reports," 428.

39 RFCPS, Part 3, A/DMS, Canadians, Shorncliffe Area to SMO, 2nd Canadian Reserve Brigade, 20 December 1917.

40 MIRSC-3, AG to Commanding Officer [hereafter CO], 3rd Division, 28 July 1915.

41 PRE, "Physical Requirement of Men Included in Overseas Drafts," date unknown.

42 MIRSC-3, J.A. Macdonald to F.W. Peters, 5 April 1916.

43 PRE, A/DGMS to AAG, 9 August 1916.

44 Cook, "He Was Determined to Go," 62.

45 Ibid.

46 This was the second time George had attempted to enlist and it would not be the last. Each time the 5 foot, 6 inch teenager would lie about his age, and on one occasion even gave a false surname (McFarlane) and provided the name of a cousin in the United States as his next of kin. PF, vol. 3578–52, #219814, 58123, 670051 Glassford, George Duncan; LAC, RG 24, vol. 823, file HQ54-21-10-1, "Endeavours of Parents and Wives of Officers and Men to Prevent Service in CEF" [hereafter EPW], Part 12, Mrs. D.C. Glassford to Gen. Hughes, 7 June 1915.

47 Baldwin, *Holding the Line*, 2–3, 7–8.

48 PRE, A/DMS MD10 to AAG i/c Administration MD10, 11 January 1917.

49 PRE, GOC MD5 to the Secretary, Militia Council, 9 January 1917.

50 FVR, vol. 8, Joseph Reece; BRA, M12, #187616 Kelly; PF, vol. 5064–27, #187616 Kelly, William; BRA, M12, #187287 McLeod, R.K; PF, vol.7093–38, #187287 McLeod, Robert King; BRA, M14, #116818 Gray, R.F.; RFCPS, Part 2, Capt. D.C. Malcolm to DMS, 15 January 1917.

51 PF, vol. 1428–41, #657797 Campbell, Douglas C.M.B.; PF, vol. 10400–31, #766965 Williams, Norman.

52 BRA, M22 and M27, #501357 Witham, A., and #490500 Pusey, L.

53 NE, Medical Officer i/c of the Medical Board Department of the Director of Recruiting and Organisation to Director of Recruiting and Organisation, 22 August 1916.

54 PRE, A/DGMS to AG, "Physical Standards of Recruits, CEF," 15 December 1916; PRE, Director General Medical Services (DGMS) to A/DMS MD13, "Medically Unfits Found in Infantry Battalions from Canada," 5 January 1917.

55 NE, DMS, Canadian Contingents to the Secretary, Headquarters, CEF, 18 August 1916.

56 Bruce Report, 13

57 Peat, *Private Peat*, 2–3.

58 In his memoir Peat claimed he managed "through some very fine work ... [to] ... escape the examination" at Valcartier, and his attestation paper indicates that he was examined on 4 September 1914. It is possible that someone, perhaps Peat's close friend Bill, stood in the Albertan's place, but without further evidence it is impossible to know. Peat, *Private Peat*, 12.

59 Despite the regimental medical examiner's telling Baldwin he was too short, and Baldwin's repeated statements about how people were shocked he was in uniform, he was, in fact, 1 inch above the minimum height requirements for an infantryman.

60 Baldwin, *Holding the Line*, 2–3, emphasis added.

61 Iler's promise was recorded on his attestation paper and signed by both Iler and Carruthers. PF, vol. 4684–8, #470948 Iler, Eugene Phinas.

196 Notes to pages 61–64

62 Silbey, "Bodies and Cultures Collide," 68.
63 Medical officers not under pay were to be paid at the same rate, provided the total remuneration they received each day did not exceed the total of the daily pay and allowances for their substantive rank. Militia Order No. 87, 28 February 1916.
64 Indeed, the day before the government imposed the medical examination fee, the Militia's paymaster sent a memorandum to all of Canada's Military Districts stressing that "it should be made plain that the allowance of [50 cents] per man for examination of recruits is in addition to the allowance for medical attendance." The remuneration rates for medical attendance were as follows:

Remuneration Rates for Civilian Practitioners Attending CEF Members

Number of men	Rate of pay
0–49	$1 a head per month
50–99	$2 a day
100–149	$3 a day
150+	$4 a day

Although an assured income, these rates of pay were well below what a doctor might expect to charge for his services. For example, in 1915 doctors in Ontario charged between $1 and $5 for a house call, and $1–$2 for vaccinations. C.G. Roland, "An Historical Perspective," in *Alternatives in Health Care: Proceedings of a Symposium and Workshop on Health Service Organisations in Ontario,* ed. William E. Seidelman (Hamilton: McMaster University, 1981), 44. MIRSC-3, Paymaster to 6 Divisions & 3 Districts, 31 March 1916; and, DMD, "Medical Attendance to Troops Billeted in Towns and Villages: Civilian Practitioners," 24 January 1916.
65 MIRSC-3, James R. Bird to MGen. W.E. Hodgins, AAG, 19 April 1916.
66 MIRSC-3, H.E. Eaglesham to A.S. Gossell, 7 November 1916.
67 PRE, GOC MD5 to the Secretary, Militia Council, 9 January 1917.
68 Although Saskatchewan had recently become a Military District in its own right (MD12), Bird's claims related to examinations conducted when the province was part of MD10. Thus, Hogdins directed Bird to contact the GOC MD10, rather than the GOC of the new MD12.
69 MIRSC-3, AG to Dr. James R. Bird, 25 April 1916.
70 MIRSC-3, DGMS to A/DMS MD12, 13 November 1916.
71 It should also be noted that more than a few doctors were unhappy with the CAMC's ranking system and remuneration rates. Indeed, during its 51st Annual Session in June 1916, the Medical Council of Ontario passed a motion suggesting to the Militia Council that doctors serving in the CAMC should have rank and remuneration "more in keeping with services rendered." *Announcement of the College of Physicians and Surgeons of Ontario 1916-1917 / Report of Proceedings of the Ontario Medical Council, June 1916* (Toronto: College of Physicians and Surgeons of Ontario, 1916), 102, 109.
72 Success came at a high price for Dix; he was killed on 24 April 1915 during the Second Battle of Ypres. FVR, vol. 3, William J. Dix; PF, vol. 2534–25, #10981 Dix, William John.
73 The extent of Andrews's eyesight limitations is indicated by his admission that he found his assignment as a quartermaster's clerk "a bit hard on my eyes" because he was not able to use his glasses. Andrews, "Diary of Alfred Herbert John Andrews."
74 Ian Miller, *Glory and Our Grief: Torontonians and the Great War* (Toronto: University of Toronto Press, 2002), 79; Michaud, "Thought of a Rainy Day." Also see Silbey, "Bodies and Cultures Collide," 67.

Notes to pages 64–70 197

75 Pirie, *The Stump Ranch*, 13.
76 LAC, Kenneth Duggan Fonds, MG30-E304, Kenneth Duggan [hereafter KD] to Mildred Duggan [hereafter MSD], 27 May 1915.
77 Dinesen had injured his knee while skiing in Norway. Lest one should think the injury was relatively minor, it should be noted that its effects had caused Dinesen to be declared unfit to serve in the Danish Navy in 1916. Moreover, he would later find that his knee – which he openly admitted "had never really been strong since I hurt it" – gave him some trouble while he was in the trenches. Dinesen, *MERRY HELL*, 31.
78 While Dinesen's examination may have been thorough, both his recruiters and the regiment were willing to bend the rules to ensure his entrance into the ranks. As a Danish citizen and an atheist to boot, Dinesen felt he could not in all honesty swear to serve King George V "faithfully and loyally, so help me God!" After some discussion, and against regulations, the recruiting officers of the Black Watch accepted his word of honour that he would serve the regiment faithfully. Dinesen, *MERRY HELL*, 31–32.
79 Brown, "Unrequited Faith," 305.
80 PF, vol. 10517–10, #624378 Wolf, Elvin Lee.
81 It is likely that Wolf was absent (perhaps deliberately) on harvest furlough when the battalion was warned for overseas and joined the battalion only when it was en route to its embarkation point. If this was so, he would have avoided the battalion's final medical examination. In fact, absence on harvest furlough was one of the explanations later provided by the GOC MD13 of why so many members of the 151st Battalion had not been subjected to a final medical examination. See below. PF, vol. 10519–9, #625347 Wolfe [sic], Lee Roy.
82 PF, vol. 10519–9, #625347 Wolfe [sic], Lee Roy.
83 PRE, GOC MD3 to the Secretary, Militia Council, Ottawa, 6 January 1917.
84 MIRSC-3, A/DMS, 3rd Division to the Recruiting Officers, 3rd Division, 16 August 1915.
85 Macphail, *Medical Services*, 161.
86 At the bottom of Breton's attestation paper LCol. Bouchard wrote: "This man is only 15 years old but is to be sworn in on instructions received from OC 16th Inf[antry] Bde [Brigade] verbally." BRA, M31, #416247 Breton, A.; PF, vol. 1046–7, #416247 Breton, A.
87 LAC, RG 24, vol. 804, file HQ 54-21-8-31, "Training Reports CEF Units MD10," Part 3, GOC MD10 to Secretary, Militia Council, 11 April 1917.
88 "The Canadian Medical Services," *Canadian Medical Association Journal* (December 1916): 1106–8.
89 PRE, GOC MD13 to the Secretary, Militia Council, 27 January 1917; RFCPS, Part 2, Senior Medical Officer, Canadian Forestry Corps to A/DMS Canadians, London Area, 26 January 1917.
90 BRA, M41, #117333 Kerr, J.
91 MIRSC-1, GOC MD11 to the Secretary, Militia Council, 28 September 1916.
92 PRE, GOC MD13 to the Secretary, Militia Council, 27 January 1917.
93 PRE, A/DGMS to AAG (1), 21 October 1916. RFCPS, Part 1, AG to Canadian Headquarters, London, 15 December 1916.
94 MIRSC-3, George B. Campbell to R.H. Pope, 2 April 1916; R.H. Pope to A.E. Kemp, 12 April 1916.
95 PF, vol. 10519–9, #625347 Wolfe [sic], Lee Roy.
96 PRE, GOC MD13 to the Secretary, Militia Council, 27 January 1917.
97 "Final Medical Inspection before Embarkation," 29 December 1916, ACAMS, 213–14.
98 Ibid.
99 "Discharge of Recruits Not Medically Fit," 14 December 1915, ACAMS, 26.

100 Atkins's success was short-lived. Sent to France in February 1916, he was deemed unfit to serve due to his impairment before seeing combat. He was discharged as medically unfit six months later. PF, vol. 283–6, #301178 Atkins, George Stanley. BRA, M27, #501178 Atkins, George Stanley.

101 Hon. A.E. Kemp, 14 April 1916, *Debates of the House of Commons of the Dominion of Canada, 6th Session, 12th Parliament*, vol. 3 (Ottawa: King's Printer, 1916), 2879.

102 BRA, M36 and M51, #510427 Fitzpatrick, T. L., and #175385 Stribball, F.

103 NE, Officer Commanding 36th Battalion to Headquarters 3rd Canadian Training Brigade, 9 May 1916.

104 PRE, AAG(1) to Judge-Advocate-General, 18 March 1916.

105 Ibid.

106 PRE, JAG to AAG(1), 20 March 1916, LAC.

107 Ibid.

108 LAC, Records of the Privy Council Office, File A-1-a, "Orders in Council" [hereafter OiC], vol. 1168, P.C. 1257, 8 May 1917.

109 "Physical Standards – Troops Proceeding Overseas," 23 February 1916, ACAMS, 106.

110 "Recruits: Physical Examination: Pulmonary Tuberculosis," 26 April 1916, ACAMS, 120–21.

111 "Medical Inspection of Troops Warned to Proceed Overseas," 29 April 1916, ACAMS, 122.

112 "Special Inspection for Venereal Disease Prior to Embarkation of Troops for Overseas: Responsibility of Officers Commanding," 10 June 1916, ACAMS, 136.

113 "Infectious Diseases in Troops Proceeding to England: Special Medical Inspection Prior to Embarkation: Responsibility of Officer Commanding," 13 July 1916, ACAMS, 147.

114 "Recruits: Enlistment of the Physically Unfit," 31 May 1916, ACAMS, 133.

115 See, for example, PRE, Captain S. Ferguson to the GOC Canadians, Shorncliffe Camp, 12 July 1916.

116 "Medical Inspection of Troops and Reports to Be Rendered Regarding the Same," 26 August 1916, ACAMS, 166–68.

117 "Medical Services in Connexion with Recruiting," 12 September 1916, ACAMS, 176; also see MIRSC-3, Memorandum: "Medical Services in Connection with Recruiting," 23 August 1916.

118 At least one Military District followed this recommendation. On 16 October 1916, the GOC MD5, citing the order of 12 September, sent a letter to Ottawa requesting permission for a number expenditures, including "the purchase of kodak [cameras] for taking photos of rejected recruits at Mobilization Centres, and finishing copies of the same." MIRSC-3, "Extract from Letter," no date.

119 "Medical Services in Connexion with Recruiting," 12 September 1916, ACAMS, 174–76.

120 "Physical Standards for Recruits: Rejection of Physically Unfit," 3 October 1916, ACAMS, 181.

121 Ibid., 181–82.

122 These were far from insignificant sums. $1,500 in 1916 had the equivalent value of approximately $26,500 in 2014, while $1,000 had an equivalent value of approximately $17,700. *Bank of Canada/Banque du Canada Inflation Calculator*, http://www.bankofcanada.ca.

123 Originally presented to Major-General Sam Steele, General Officer Commanding (GOC) Canadians, Shorncliffe. The report was forward to Ottawa, where it was received on 31 July. PRE, Captain S. Ferguson to the GOC Canadians, Shorncliffe Camp, 12 July 1916.

124 Ibid.; LAC, RG 24, vol. 1066, file HQ 54-21-34-27, "Inquiry of House of Commons (Mr. MacDonald) Re. Number of Unfit Men Taken to England and the Cost to the Country by Reason of Their Enlistment, Also Report of Nos. 7 and 8 Hospitals in France Carried

under Canadian Auspices"; Mr. Oliver, 31 July 1917, *Debates of the House of Commons of the Dominion of Canada, 7th Session, 12th Parliament,* vol. 4 (Ottawa: King's Printer, 1917), 3980–81.

125 Ibid.

126 FVR, vol. 3, Percy R. Dealtry; PF, vol. 2388–39, #10967 Dealtry, Percival R. There is some confusion in Dealtry's personnel files as to when he was finally accepted for service. The attestation papers used are of 1915 vintage; however, as in many cases, the "5" in 1915 has been written over with a "4." This can be explained by the military's recopying of attestation papers. His service file indicates that he served from 1914.

127 "Medically Unfits: Enlistment in Infantry Battalions, CEF," 16 December 1916, ACAMS, 207–8.

128 Macphail, *Medical Services,* 157–58.

129 In his speech, Kemp mistakenly referred to Potter as the Director General Medical Services rather than Acting Director General Medical Services. Mr. MacDonald, 31 July 1917, *Debates of the House of Commons of the Dominion of Canada, 7th Session, 12th Parliament,* vol. 4 (Ottawa: King's Printer, 1917), 3963–67; Sir Edward Kemp, 31 July 1917, *Debates of the House of Commons of the Dominion of Canada, 7th Session, 12th Parliament,* vol. 4 (Ottawa: King's Printer, 1917), 3967–68.

130 LAC, RG 24, vol. 1331, MO i/c Troops, St John, NB to A/DMS 6th Division, 4 December 1916; PRE, AG to GOC MD11, 5 April 1917.

131 Sir Edward Kemp, 31 July 1917, *Debates of the House of Commons of the Dominion of Canada, 7th Session, 12th Parliament,* vol. 4 (Ottawa: King's Printer, 1917), 3967.

Chapter 4: Clashing Concepts of Fitness

1 These comments were even more biting because they appeared in an article discussing the plight of men who had been initially accepted as fit to serve and then declared unfit during their second medical examination after some six months of training. Indeed, the article's author went so far as to ask whether the first medical examination given to recruits was in fact a serious examination. *Labour World,* quoted by Alphonse Verville in the House of Commons, 16 May 1916, *Debates of the House of Commons of the Dominion of Canada, 6th Session, 12th Parliament,* vol. 4 (Ottawa: King's Printer, 1916), 4070–71. Also see "Returning Soldiers Criticize Doctors," Toronto *Globe,* 19 March 1917.

2 Bird, *And We Go On,* 13–14.

3 Alphonse Verville, 16 May 1916, *Debates of the House of Commons of the Dominion of Canada, 6th Session, 12th Parliament,* vol. 4 (Ottawa: King's Printer, 1916), 4069–72.

4 Col. J.L. Potter A/DGMS, quoted by Sir Robert Borden, 17 May 1916, *Debates of the House of Commons of the Dominion of Canada, 6th Session, 12th Parliament,* vol. 4 (Ottawa: King's Printer, 1916), 4126.

5 These observations closely follow those made by Albert Love and Charles Davenport when discussing the nature of the defects found in men drafted for the US Army in 1917–18. Love and Davenport noted that of the over 2 million men rejected as medically unfit by the US Army, a full half of them had been rejected for defects that would not have seriously interfered with a "man performing services of the highest order in civil life." Albert G. Love and Charles B. Davenport, *Defects Found in Drafted Men: Statistical Information Compiled from the Draft Records Showing the Physical Condition of Men Registered and Examined in Pursuance of the Requirements of the Selective-Service Act* (Washington, DC: Government Printing Office, 1920), 30.

6 BRA, M30 and M48, #400408 Carment, J., and #501282 Martell, C.

7 BRA, M10, #192093 Peterson, S.

8 "Notes and Comments," Toronto *Globe,* 10 February 1915.

9 The cartoon reached not only *Punch* readers but also the wider public. On 4 September 1914, it was quoted in an article in the *New York Times. Punch, or the London Charivari* 146 (19 August 1914): 166; "Only the English Get Fun Out of War," *New York Times,* 4 September 1914.

10 While this passage suggests that such comments were made by rejected men, some caution does need to be exercised. Roberts described this event almost sixty years after its occurrence and it is possible that his recollections of the event had been moulded by his exposure to the *Punch* cartoon or references to it. This possibility is reinforced by the fact that the exchange depicted in the cartoon has become part of popular memory of the Great War. It has even been depicted in the cinema. The 1981 Australian film *Gallipoli* features the following exchange between a medical officer and the character Snowy: "Teeth aren't all that good." "Supposed to shoot the enemy, not bite them." Robert Roberts, *The Classic Slum: Salford Life in the First Quarter of the Century* (Manchester: Manchester University Press, 1971), 150; Peter Weir, director, *Gallipoli* (Associated R&R Films, 1981).

11 T.V. Anson, *The New Zealand Dental Services* (Wellington: Historical Publications Branch, 1960), 3. Also see G. Butler, *The Australian Army Medical Services in the War of 1914-1918,* 2nd ed. (Melbourne: Australian War Memorial, 1938), 20–21.

12 *The Practitioner's Encyclopaedia of Medical Treatment* (Oxford: Oxford Medical Publications, 1915), 244–45.

13 "Unfit for Military Service," Toronto *Globe,* 27 January 1915. Besides indicating civilian distain for military dental policies, this letter also seems to indicate that by early 1915 there was a growing recognition, at least in some circles, not only that the war would last for some time but also that Canadian forces might suffer large casualties.

14 "Dental Defects and Recruiting," *Toronto Star,* 8 December 1914; "Volunteers Rally to Empire's Cause," Toronto *Globe,* 11 June 1915.

15 FVR, vol. 4, C. Gallinger.

16 FVR, vol. 5, H. Hewitt; FVR, vol. 6, Thomas Kirk.

17 FVR, vol. 6, R. Lahiff. While the medical officer's signature is illegible, thereby making him impossible to identify, it is not the signature of Captain Cockburn.

18 FVR, vol. 3, A.A. Dasey; FVR, vol. 11, E.A. West.

19 FVR, vol. 3, Charles Elkes.

20 FVR, vol. 1, P. Anderson; FVR, vol. 3, George Dillingham; FVR, vol. 7, Richard Moriarty; FVR, vol. 10, John Steveson; FVR, vol. 11, George Walker.

21 Ironically, the initial reason – dating to the seventeenth century – that led to recruits being required to possess good teeth (incisors, and later incisors and canines) had everything to do with shooting the enemy. Before the development in the nineteenth century of breech-loading rifles that fired self-contained cartridges, a soldier was required to bite off the cap off his powder charge when loading his weapon. Jackson, *The Story of the Royal Canadian Dental Corps,* 1.

22 The first dental surgeon ever appointed to the British Army, Newland-Pedley served in South Africa for less than six months (February to June 1900) before returning to the United Kingdom. Despite his early return from the field, his letters to the *Lancet* detailing his experiences working on men's teeth in less than ideal conditions on the veldt caused the army to assign four dentists to replace him. He later served with the British Expeditionary Force in France, where his experiences would cause him to lobby – against considerable resistance from the medical community – for the formation of a permanent army dental corps. G.H. Sperber and Mary Bisset Lucas, "Dentistry in the Anglo-Boer War (1899-1902)," *Adler Museum Bulletin* 12, 2 (1991): 19–22; G.H. Sperber, correspondence with the author.

23 Sperber and Lucas, "Dentistry in the Anglo-Boer War," 19.
24 For a complete breakdown of the Canadian Expeditionary Force field rations, see Love, *A Call to Arms*, 212.
25 Cook, *At the Sharp End*, 245–47 (quotes 245).
26 Christie, *Letters of Agar Adamson*, 33.
27 Agar Adamson repeatedly requested and received luxury food items from his wife and friends in England. Nor were such food parcels simply limited to officers; the rank and file also received gifts of food from home and soldiers' aid societies. Likewise, men used their hard-earned pay to buy desired food items not provided by the military from local people living near their stations. See, for example, Christie, *Letters of Agar Adamson*, 35–36, 48; Roy, *The Journal of Private Fraser*, 27, 37.
28 For a discussion of the diet of troops in the Canadian Expeditionary Force, see Clarke, Cranfield and Inwood, "Fighting Fit?"
29 FVR, vol. 9, Robert Skead.
30 Bird had his teeth smashed while playing hockey as a youth and had never had the damage corrected. Bird, *And We Go On*, 11.
31 These measurements are drawn from Bird's 1916 attestation paper, when he was twenty-four years old. While there may have been some differences in his weight and perhaps chest girth between 1914 and 1916, they are unlikely to have been significant. PF, vol. 748-27, #901552 Bird, William Richard.
32 Bird, *And We Go On*, 11–12.
33 Bird was rejected for service by 25th Canadian Infantry Battalion in the fall of 1914 at the behest of his brother, Stephen, who was a sergeant in the unit. In 1915 he was rejected by a unit in Western Canada while working as a farmhand in Saskatchewan. Although Bird provided no reason for this rejection, his bad teeth were likely the reason. Bird, *And We Go On*, 11–13; Bird *Ghosts Have Warm Hands*, 4–5, 176–77.
34 Bird, *And We Go On*, 14.
35 F. Newland-Pedley, "Our Army's Teeth," *Lancet* 184, 4764 (19 December 1914): 1430.
36 Thomas Oliver, "Some Physical Defects Met with in the Raising of an Army," *Lancet* 185, 4782 (24 April 1915): 849.
37 FVR, vol. 4, Walter Hancock.
38 Hon. A.E. Kemp, 14 April 1916, *Debates of the House of Commons of the Dominion of Canada, 6th Session, 12th Parliament*, vol. 3 (Ottawa: King's Printer, 1916), 2879.
39 FVR, vol. 3, William J. Dix; FVR, vol. 6, William Kavanagh.
40 FVR, vol. 5, John Hartnell; and FVR, vol. 5, Norman Health. Also see FVR, vol. 5, A.H. Jephson.
41 The use of glasses by enlisted men was proscribed based on logistical as much as medical concerns. Traditionally viewed as a force projection arm, the British Army was organized largely with a view to its use on foreign (and often hostile) soil far from support centres. In such circumstances, repairing soldiers' broken glasses or supplying them with new ones was a difficult, if not impossible, task. Soldiers who broke or lost their glasses while on campaign would quickly become a liability to their unit, especially if their vision was very limited without their corrective lenses. Thus, the use of glasses by enlisted men was banned altogether, unless they were either on home service or garrison duty. Officers, who were not expected to be frontline rifle men, were permitted the use of glasses.
42 J.V. Paterson and H.M. Traquair, "The Visual Standards Used in the Medical Examination of Recruits in the British Army and Continental Armies," *Lancet* 187, 4836 (6 May 1916): 955.
43 R.B. Lynn, "James Cameron Connell: 1863-1947," *Canadian Journal of Surgery* 11 (1988): 336–39.

202 *Notes to pages 87–94*

44 It is likely that Connell had read Paterson and Traquair's treatise, which had been published two weeks before he penned his letter to Potter. RSO, J.C. Connell to Col. Potter, DGMS [sic], Ottawa, 29 May 1916.

45 While musketry regulations provided instructions for teaching a recruit to aim that implied that a recruit could fire either left-handed or right-handed, all instructions pertaining to teaching a recruit to fire a rifle were based on the assumption that the recruit was using the weapon right-handed. Indeed, left shoulder (left-handed) firing was not to be permitted unless rendered necessary, in the opinion of a soldier's company commander, by defective eyesight. *Musketry Regulations Part 1 1909 [Reprinted with Amendments, 1914]* (Calcutta: Superintendent Government Printing, 1918), 88; *Musketry* (London: John Murray, 1915), 48.

46 In my discussions with a number of individuals with military experience, I have encountered conflicting opinions regarding whether or not firing a right-handed bolt-action rifle left handed would dramatically affect rate of fire.

47 *Punch, or the London Charivari* 146 (4 November 1914): 369

48 Stephen McGreal, *The Cheshire Bantams* (Barnsley: Pen and Sword, 2006), 21–22.

49 M.S. Pembrey, "Tall versus Short Men for the Army," *Journal of the Royal Sanitary Institute* 36, 3 (1915): 105–13.

50 T.J. Mitchell and G.M. Smith, *Medical Services: Casualties and Medical Statistics of the Great War* (London: King's Printer, 1931), 40. Note, however, Tim Cook's analysis of these statistics. Cook, *Shock Troops*, 614–17.

51 "Bantam Battalion Is Latest Proposal," Toronto *Globe*, 15 January 1916.

52 LAC, RG 24, vol. 823, EPW, Part 12, Adelaide Yuill to Major General Hughes, 14 June 1916.

53 *Debates of the Senate of Canada, 1916*, 308.

54 Roy, *The Journal of Private Fraser*, 38–39.

55 Ibid., 81

56 Alphonse Verville, 16 May 1916, *Debates of the House of Commons of the Dominion of Canada, 6th Session, 12th Parliament*, vol. 4 (Ottawa: King's Printer, 1916), 4072; [Illegible] to A/DGMS, 24 January 1917, PRE.

57 PRE, A/DMS MD10 to AAG i/c Administration MD10, 11 January 1917.

58 PS18, 22.

59 Ibid., 22–25.

60 Nic Clarke, "'The Greater and Grimmer Game': Sport as an Arbiter of Military Fitness in the British Empire – The Case of 'One-Eyed' Frank McGee," *International Journal of the History of Sport* 28, 3–4 (2011): 604–22.

Chapter 5: Not Visibly Different

Parts of this chapter first appeared in Nic Clarke, "You Will Not Be Going to This War: The Rejected Volunteers of the First Contingent of the Canadian Expeditionary Force," *First World War Studies* 1, 2 (2010): 161–83.

1 Quoted in Daphne Read, ed., *The Great War and Canadian Society: An Oral History* (Toronto: New Hogtown Press, 1978), 103.

2 "Chilling Winds Make Recruiting Spiritless," Toronto *Globe*, 18 March 1916.

3 The would-be warrior's dedication was even more notable because he underwent surgery in order to make himself fit for service. "Can't Keep Him Out of the Fight," *Ottawa Citizen*, 13 October 1916; "Is Determined to Go to War," *Ottawa Citizen*, 13 October 1916.

4 See Introduction for a discussion of this sample.

5 Where appropriate, percentages in text are rounded to the nearest whole number for ease of reading.

Notes to pages 94–96   203

6 The Methodist count includes both men recorded as being Methodists (63) and those listed as Wesleyans (119). The Presbyterian count includes one individual who was recorded as being a member of the "Scottish Church."

7 Morton, *When Your Number's Up*, 270. It should be noted that these numbers were not reflective of the relative strength of the denominations within the Canadian population. The 1911 Census of Canada recorded that the dominant religion (based on numbers of adherents) within the Dominion was Roman Catholic, which accounted for 39.3 percent of the population. Despite making up the vast majority of men serving in the Canadian Expeditionary Force, Anglicans, who made up 14.5 percent of the population, came in fourth after Presbyterians (15 percent) and Methodists (15 percent). This difference can best be explained by the underrepresentation of francophone Canadians, who made up the majority of Canada's Roman Catholic population, and the overrepresentation of English-born or first-generation English Canadians in the force. Further explanations might be found in the fact that in a number of cases, the faith recorded on a man's attestation paper often expressed the enlisting officer's sensibilities, rather than the individual's religious beliefs. Admittedly, such acts did not always favour the Anglican Church. Thomas Dinesen, an avowed atheist, had Presbyterian recorded in his attestation paper's religion column because his recruiters stated that all soldiers must have a religion. Presbyterian was chosen because Dinesen had enlisted in a kilted regiment (Canadian Black Watch). These acts of misrepresentation were not limited to Canada; Gervase Phillips has noted that British recruiting officers encouraged nonconformist Welsh recruits to give their religious denomination as Anglican. *Fifth Census of Canada, 1911: Religions, Origins, Birthplace, Citizenship, Literacy and Infirmities, by Provinces, Districts and Sub-Districts* (Ottawa: King's Printer, 1913), vi–vii; Morton, *When Your Number's Up*, 270; Gervase Phillips, "Dai Bach Y Soldiwr: Welsh Soldiers in the British Army, 1914–1918," *Llafur* 6, 2 (1993): 98–99; Dinesen, *MERRY HELL!*, 31–32.

8 FVR, vol. 4, W. Hadden; FVR, vol. 7, M.H. McLeod.

9 FVR, vol. 9, James Scott Simmons.

10 FVR, vol. 1, Ulysses Adlerard; FVR, vol. 5, Samuel Jones; FVR, vol. 11, Robert W. Wilson; FVR, vol. 11, Ernest Williams.

11 FVR, vol. 2, J. Beech; FVR, vol. 8, H. Ouelette, FVR, vol. 10, Amede Sauve.

12 FVR, vol. 1, Ulysses Adlerard; FVR, vol. 2, James Cook, FVR, vol. 4, Arthur Giles; FVR, vol. 6, Antonio E. Lapierre; FVR, vol. 7, Robert Orkney, FVR, vol. 8, Richard Quinn; FVR, vol. 9, John Robillard; FVR, vol. 9, John Strain; FVR, vol. 11, R. Warne; FVR, vol. 11, Charley Woodman.

13 FVR, vol. 8, Reginald Neor; FVR, vol. 2, Joseph Clamondou. Also see FVR, vol. 10, H. Shaw.

14 FVR, vol. 2, William Chavis; FVR, vol. 3, Lawrence Eaves; FVR, vol. 5, George Jobin; FVR, vol. 11, Martin Wilson. It is likely that Wilson had lost his arm as a result of the serious wound he suffered at the Battle of Fish Creek (1 May 1885), during the Riel Rebellion. See "Report of the Department of Militia and Defence, upon the Suppression of the Rebellion in the North-West Territories and Matters in Connection therewith," *Sessional Papers of the Dominion of Canada*, vol. 5 (Ottawa: MacLean, Roger, 1886), 20.

15 WBF, Babtie Report.

16 This count includes two men who were members of the paramilitary Royal North West Mounted Police.

17 In five cases, the entries describing an individual's military experience were illegible.

18 For a breakdown of the civil occupations of Canadian Expeditionary Force members, 1914–19, see Morton, *Fight or Pay*, 245.

19 Morton, *When Your Number's Up*, 279.

20 Cook, "He Was Determined to Go," 42–74.
21 See Chapter 1, note 32.
22 The median remains 67 inches.
23 Cranfield and Inwood, "The Great Transformation."
24 An examination of a number of anthropometric studies suggests that the average height of British males in their early twenties during the late nineteenth and early twentieth centuries fell somewhere between 66.7 inches and 67.4 inches. Allison, *Bantams*, 55; S.T. Beggs, *The Selection of the Recruit* (London: Ballière, Tindall and Cox, 1915), 9; A.W. Boyne and I. Leitich, "Secular Change in the Height of British Adults," *Nutrition Abstracts and Reviews* 24, 2 (1954): 255–69; Roderick Floud, correspondence with the author, 29 August 2007; Roderick Floud, Kenneth Wachter, and Annabel Gregory, *Height, Health and History: Nutritional Status in the United Kingdom, 1750-1980* (Cambridge: Cambridge University Press, 1990), 154–63; Francis Galton, "Final Report of the Anthropometric Committee," *Report of the British Association for the Advancement of Science* (1883): 253–306.
25 This number encompasses all men, whose files listed one or more medical condition(s) in their reasons for rejection, including height and chest size. Rejection due to age (over or under) on its own was not included. Men struck off strength for both medical and non-medical conditions are included.
26 The fifth most common reason for medical rejection was "Medically Unfit," at 5.5 percent. Given that this is a general description, it is impossible to comment on the visibility of the impairments of the men so classified.
27 This point was made in the 6 May 1916 issue of the *Lancet* by Drs. J.V. Paterson and H.M. Traquair, ophthalmic surgeons at Edinburgh's Royal Infirmary. Paterson and Traquair, "The Visual Standards," 955.
28 A. Primrose, "Disabilities, Including Injuries, Caused by Bullets, Shrapnel, High Explosives, etc., as Illustrated by Cases Examined before a Medical Board at Canadian Headquarters, Shorncliffe, England," *Canadian Medical Association Journal* 5, 10 (October 1915): 856.
29 LAC, Herrick S. Duggan Fonds, MG30-E303 [hereafter HDF], Herrick Duggan [hereafter HD] to MSD, 4 November 1914; Nic Clarke, "'He Was My Best Subaltern': The Life and Death of Lieutenant Herrick S. Duggan, 70th Field Company, Royal Engineers," *Canadian Military History* 17, 2 (2008): 21–32.
30 Kaiser Wilhelm II (1859–1941) and Franklin Delano Roosevelt (1882–1945) are two prime examples of individuals who went to considerable lengths to hide their paralytic impairments. Wilhelm II's left arm was withered because of either his traumatic breech birth (which, by many accounts, he was lucky to survive) or a fall suffered by his mother when she was four months pregnant. Roosevelt was paralyzed from the waist down as a result of either poliomyelitis or Guillain-Barré syndrome. From childhood, Wilhelm practised a number of forms of deception to hide his arm's deformity, including placing his left hand in his pocket or holding gloves in his left hand to make his atrophied limb seem longer. In photographs, which were generally taken from his right side, he would often rest his left hand on a sword hilt or cane. Roosevelt took great pains not to be seen in a wheelchair in public or in photographs. Rather, he taught himself to walk short distances with the aid of iron leg braces and a cane. At public appearances he would stand, surreptitiously supported on one side by an aide or one of his sons. Considerable ink has been expended on both men's impairments. For two of the best analyses, see John C.G. Röhl, *The Young Wilhelm: The Kaiser's Early Life, 1859-1888* (Cambridge: Cambridge University Press, 1998), 1–53; and Hugh G. Gallagher, *FDR's Splendid Deception* (New York: Dodd, 1985). For recent explorations of the causes of both Wilhelm II's and Roosevelt's impairments, see Around S. Goldman et al., "What Was the Cause of Franklin Delano Roosevelt's Paralytic Illness?"

Journal of Medical Biography 11 (2003): 232–40; and Venu Jain et al., "Kaiser Wilhelm Syndrome: Obstetric Trauma or Placental Insult in a Historic Case Mimicking Erb's Palsy," *Medical Hypotheses* 65, 1 (2005): 185–91.

31 FVR, vol. 11, Mark A. Wolff.

32 BRA, M35, #437696 Schroder, C.

33 See Chapter 7.

34 Facing similar problems, the British government introduced armbands for rejected volunteers in the same year. The United States Navy also issued badges to rejected volunteers after the United States entered the war in 1917. "Certificate for Rejected Men," Toronto *Globe*, 24 April 1916; Nicoletta F. Gullace, *"The Blood of Our Sons": Men, Women, and the Renegotiation of British Citizenship during the Great War* (New York: Palgrave Macmillan, 2002), 105; "Unfit Volunteers Get Badges of Honor," *New York Times*, 15 April 1917.

35 The United States Navy was also concerned that the badges it issued to rejected volunteers might be duplicated or transferred. However, rather than threatening legal action, the navy appealed to the rejected volunteers' personal honour and pride. The letter given to each man with his badge, which in itself was an attempt to stop either the counterfeiting or transfer of the badges, contained the following warning: "Now, just a word of caution. It would be highly dishonorable for you to permit anyone else to wear this button. It would give him a chance to pretend to do what you have actually done." See "Certificate for Rejected Men"; also see "Put Unfair Burden on Canada's Soldiers," Toronto *Globe*, 29 January 1917, 6.

36 Similar comments were made with regard to the badge issued to rejected volunteers by the United States Navy. Indeed, Lieutenant Commander Taylor, the navy's New York recruiting officer, stated that it was "an honor to have the right to [wear the button] ... wear it and be proud of it." See "Certificate for Rejected Men"; "Unfit Volunteers Get badge of Honor."

37 "Badges for the Rejected," *Ottawa Evening Citizen*, 26 March 1916; Robbie Johnson, *Canadian War Service Badges, 1914-1954* (Surrey: Johnson Books, 1995), 77.

38 "Buttons for the Rejected," *Ottawa Evening Citizen*, 1 March 1916.

39 "Winnipeggers Are to Sport Button on Which Is the Magic Word 'Excused,'" *Vancouver Sun*, 29 March 1916.

40 "Button or Badge for Rejected Ones," *Toronto Star*, 11 December 1915.

41 Johnson, *Canadian War Service Badges*, 77.

42 "Winnipeggers Are to Sport Button on Which Is the Magic Word 'Excused.'"

43 The aforementioned badges issued to rejected volunteers by the United States Navy were intended to serve a similar purpose. The *New York Times* article announcing the issue of badges reported that the inscription on the badge was "worded as to convey a direct challenge to slackers and others who had ... [not volunteered]." And challenge it did; the inscription read: "I have volunteered for the navy. Have you?" Furthermore, the letter given to each rejected volunteer along with the badge stated that "if as a result of wearing this button and showing this letter, you influence some other man to come forward ... [you have served the navy and your country]." See, "Unfit Volunteers Get Badge of Honor."

44 "Note and Comment," *Toronto Star*, 1 November 1915.

45 "Waited Too Long," Toronto *Globe*, 8 June 1917, emphasis in original.

46 Mutual Life was not the only advertiser to play on the fear of rejection in its advertising. The Toronto YMCA also used this fear in its membership drives, promising that it could help men who had been "rejected for some physical defect" become fit enough to be accepted for military service. "Two Whole Battalions of Toronto Boys Enlist from the Y.M.C.A.," Toronto *Globe*, 19 October 1917.

47 "Impostors Wearing Rejected Buttons," Toronto *Globe*, 31 May 1916.

48 Johnson, *Canadian War Service Badges*, 77.

49 "Wanted a Badge of Honour," *Canadian Military Gazette* 31, 14 (25 July 1916): 11.

50 The potential fine set for the misuse of these badges was far from minor. $100 in 1916 was equivalent in value to $1,800 in 2014. Indeed, the fines reflected a significant portion of the average annual wage of the vast majority of Canadians. In 1917, for example, the average annual wage of a person working in Canada's manufacturing industries was approximately $760 ($11,600 in 2014). *Bank of Canada/Banque du Canada Inflation Calculator;* Noah M. Meltz, "Wages and Working Conditions," in *Historical Statistics of Canada*, ed. F.H. Leacy, http://www.statcan.gc.ca.

51 OiC, vol. 1149, P.C. 1944, 16 August 1916; "Registration System Provided for Canada," Toronto *Globe*, 17 August 1916. For a list of Orders in Council relating to the war badges that include the eligibility requirements for each class, see Appendix D, "Evolution of Canadian War Service Badges 1916-19" [hereafter APD].

52 OiC, vol. 1163, P.C. 275, 27 February 1917; "Government Badges for Discharged Men," Toronto *Globe*, 27 February 1917.

53 $500 in 1917 was equivalent in value to approximately $7,650 in 2014. *Bank of Canada/Banque du Canada Inflation Calculator.*

54 OiC, vol. 1163, P.C. 275, 27 February 1917. For pictures of the different badges, including the warning on the reverse side, see Johnson, *Canadian War Service Badges*, 4–16.

55 "Heavy Fine for Wearing Returned Soldiers' Badge," Toronto *Globe*, 2 September 1918.

56 Also subsumed by this legislation were the "For Service at the Front" badges issued by the St. John Association of Canada. OiC, vol. 1176, P.C. 2199, 10 August 1917; "War Badges Will Be Issued by Government," Toronto *Globe*, 14 September 1917; G.O. 106, "Instructions; Regulations etc. War Service Badges," *Canadian Gazette* 51 (October–December 1917): 1718.

57 This move was later criticized by the Great War Veterans' Association on the grounds that the Class B badge (old Class A) was similar to that issued by the Imperial forces for service at the front. This meant, the GWVA argued, that Canadian veterans of the Imperial forces now residing in Canada were not receiving the recognition they deserved. The Dominion government ultimately rectified this problem with Order in Council P.C. 777 in April 1919, which extended the eligibility for Canadian war service badges to Canadians who had served in the Imperial forces. "War Veterans for Change in Badges," Toronto *Globe*, 1 January 1918, 7; OiC, vol. 1221, P.C. 777, 12 April 1919.

58 Johnson, *Canadian War Service Badges*, 16, 151.

59 OiC, vol. 1176, P.C. 2199, 10 August 1917.

60 "Badges Ready Next Week," *Kingston Daily Standard*, 17 October 1917, 7; "Honourably Discharged Men," Toronto *Globe*, 20 October 1917, 25; "War Badges for Veterans," Toronto *Globe*, 27 December 1917; "200 War Badges Given Out Daily," Toronto *Globe*, 8 February 1918.

61 OiC, vol. 1197, P.C. 1242, 22 May 1918.

62 "War Summary," Toronto *Globe*, 3 March 1915; "War Summary," Toronto *Globe*, 17 July 1916.

63 "D Badges Unpopular," Toronto *Globe*, 17 January 1918.

64 "776 Rejected Men Receive Buttons," Toronto *Globe*, 1 May 1916.

65 FVR, vol. 5, John W. Johnson. Despite Johnson's claims to have been rejected because of rheumatism and an open wound, his records indicate that he was rejected because of his poor dentition.

66 FVR, vol. 4, Charles Garner.

67 FVR, vol. 2, Roy T. Coates.

Chapter 6: Uncounted Casualties

1 An American citizen, Lane was still alive when discovered. Although he was taken to a local hospital, it was reported that there was "little chance of his recovery." "Disappointed Lad Attempts Suicide."

2 Coley also feared that the disability, which was not identified, would make him unemployable. "Dragoon Ends His Life In Despondent Mood," Toronto *Globe*, 18 October 1915.

3 "Rejected Three Times, Then Hangs Himself," *Toronto Star*, 17 March 1917.

4 "War's Effect on Religion," Toronto *Globe*, 20 October 1917.

5 It should be noted that suicides caused by fear of or actual rejection for service were not limited to Canada. Paul Fussell, for example, recounted the case of Arthur Annesley, who was said to have thrown himself under a heavy van at Pimlico, London, in August 1914 because he feared he would be rejected for service. Annesley's story has been repeated in a number of texts, including Niall Ferguson's *The Pity of War*. Such acts were not limited to the Great War. The *New York Times* reported in 1899 that J.N. Waldron had committed suicide in Vancouver, Washington, after failing to pass the United States Army's physical examination during the Spanish-American War. Paul Fussell, *The Great War and Modern Memory*, 25th anniv. ed. (Oxford: Oxford University Press, 2000), 19; Ferguson, *The Pity of War: Explaining World War I* (New York: Basic Books, 1999), 359; "A Barrister's Suicide," London *Times*, 17 November 1914; "Rejected Volunteer Kills Himself," *New York Times*, 19 September 1899.

6 Andrews, "Diary of Alfred Herbert John Andrews."

7 A considerable amount of ink has been expended on the pressures placed on men to enlist in Canada. See, for example, Paul Maroney, "'The Great Adventure': The Context and Ideology of Recruiting in Ontario, 1914–1917," *Canadian Historical Review* 77, 1 (1996): 68–98; Miller, *Our Glory and Our Grief*; Thompson, *The Harvests of War*, 42; Whitney Lackenbauer, "Soldiers Behaving Badly," 204–5; Morton, *When Your Number's Up*, 54–55, 59; Pierre van Paassen, *Days of Our Years* (New York: Hillman-Curl, 1939), 64–65; Jonathan F. Vance, *Death So Noble*, 112–15.

8 French Canadian (and notably Québécois) anti-enlistment sentiment is the most obvious and oft-quoted example of criticism of enlistment pressures, but it is certainly not the only one. A considerable anti-enlistment discourse, especially after the introduction of conscription in 1917, also existed in the Prairie west and rural areas, where farmers objected to losing farm labour to the trenches. Canada was also home to a number of sectarian and religious pacifist groups, the most vocal of which openly condemned the war. In such communities, young men's efforts to enlist were often actively discouraged, if not openly criticized. Béatrice Richard, "Henri Bourassa and Conscription: Traitor or Savior," *Canadian Military Journal* (2006–07): 76; J.L. Granatstein, "Conscription and the Great War," in *Canada and the First World War: Essays in Honour of Robert Craig Brown*, ed. David Mackenzie (Toronto: University of Toronto Press, 2005), 65; Socknat, *Witness against War*, 43–89; Shaw, *Crisis of Conscience*; Thompson, *The Harvests of War*, 132–33.

9 Mathers's comments should not be misread as antiwar; he made them while arguing for the introduction of conscription. See Granatstein and Hitsman, *Broken Promises*, 38.

10 Armine Norris, quoted in Cook, "He Was Determined to Go," 52.

11 R.W. Leonard, "In These Times," Canadian War Museum, George Metcalf Archival Collection [hereafter CWM], Call Number: 58B2 1.11, Accession: 19860131-002.

12 Maroney, "The Great Adventure," 93.

13 Robert Service, "Missis Moriarty's Boy," in *Rhymes of a Red Cross Man* (Toronto: William Briggs, 1916), 169–70.

14 Ibid.

15 Ibid.

208   *Notes to pages 116–19*

16   Angus McLaren, *Our Own Master Race: Eugenics in Canada, 1885-1945* (Toronto: McClelland and Stewart, 1990), 40.

17   HDF, HD to MD, 13 October 1914.

18   Duggan's success came at a very high price. On 21 October 1915, less than a year after receiving his commission, he died of wounds he had suffered while leading an assault on a German trench during the last days of the British Expeditionary Force's failed Loos offensive. Clarke, "He Was My Best Subaltern."

19   Herrick and his brother Kenneth joined the Delta Upsilon Fraternity while studying at McGill University. Herrick became the McGill chapter's president in his senior year and sat on the fraternity's council of alumni after he graduated. He also had the dubious privilege of becoming the first member of the fraternity to be killed in the Great War. HDF, HD to MSD, 9 November 1914, and HD to KD, 11 November 1914; HDF, "Delta U Killed at the Front"; "Deceased Members, McGill," spreadsheet provided by Johan Draper, Delta Upsilon McGill Alumni Executive.

20   Bird, *And We Go On,* 13.

21   "Can't Keep Him Out of the Fight," *Ottawa Citizen,* 13 October 1916; "Is Determined to Go to War," *Ottawa Citizen,* 13 October 1916.

22   Peat, *Private Peat,* 2–3. Also see Baldwin, *Holding the Line,* 2–3; Andrews, "Diary of Alfred Herbert John Andrews"; Robert Service "My Mate," in *Rhymes of a Red Cross Man* (Toronto: William Briggs, 1916), 63–66.

23   "The Men Who Volunteer," *Toronto Star,* 2 July 1915; "Reject Soldiers Home," Toronto *Globe,* 14 September 1914. For the British context, see Nicoletta Gullace, "*The Blood of Our Sons*," 105; Nicoletta Gullace, "White Feathers and Wounded Men: Female Patriotism and the Memory of the Great War," *Journal of British Studies* 36, 2 (1997): 178–84; Adrian Gregory, "Gender, Citizenship and Entitlement," *Journal of British Studies* 43, 3 (2004): 412. A similar discourse can also be found in the United States. For example, the *Press* of Sheboygan, Wisconsin, noted in an article discussing the seventy young men of Sheboygan County who had been rejected for service that "it was nothing to their detriment that they were rejected but to the contrary *The Press* is glad to publish the list of those who volunteered their services that every honor possible may be shown them." Sheboygan *Press,* 17 July 1917.

24   British subjects from enemy countries who had been naturalized after 31 May 1902 also lost the franchise. Wartime Electors Act, 1917, Section 67A; Military Service Act, 1917, Sections 15 and 16.

25   H.B. MacConnell, "Medically Unfit," in *Where Duty Leads* (Toronto: William Briggs, 1916), 55.

26   E.N. Lewis, "To the Young Men of Huron," CWM, Call Number: 58B2 1.11, Accession: 19860131-066.

27   For a useful examination of the eugenics movement in Canada, see McLaren, *Our Own Master Race.*

28   Robert M. Dickie, "War and the Survival of the Fit," *Queen's Quarterly* 20 (1912–13): 201–2. Also see Jacob Henry Landman, *Human Sterilization: The History of the Sexual Sterilization Movement* (New York: Macmillan, 1932), 5; McLaren, *Our Own Master Race,* 43, 63; Seth Koven, "Remembering Dismemberment: Crippled Children, Wounded Soldiers, and the Great War in Great Britain," *American Historical Review* 99, 4 (1994): 1189–91; J.M. Winter, "Britain's 'Lost Generation' of the First World War," *Population Studies* 31, 3 (1977): 449–66.

29   Paul Maroney has further noted that recruiting posters, and recruiting propaganda more generally, also tended to reflect eugenicists' "antimodernist impulse" by privileging pastoral lifestyles and chivalric values over the soft, unhealthy, and immoral nature of modern

life. Maroney, "The Great Adventure," 79, 81; "Send Us the Best Ye Breed," Toronto *Globe*, 7 October 1914; "Efficiency and the Drink Habit," Toronto *Globe*, 4 December 1914; Rutherdale, *Hometown Horizons*, 53–54.

30 Agricultural metaphors, especially with regard to weeds and weeding, were commonly used by eugenicists both before and after the Great War when discussing the removal of people they deemed to be dysgenic from society. MIRSC-2, F.N.G Starr to Major-General Sam Hughes, 14 December 1914; PRE, GOC MD11 to the Secretary, Militia Council, 19 April 1917; G.R. Stevens, *A City Goes to War: A History of the Loyal Edmonton Regiment* (Brampton, ON: Charters, 1964), 17; William J. Robinson, *Practical Eugenics: Four Means of Improving the Human Race* (New York: Critic and Guide, 1912), 14; La Reine Helen Baker, *Race Improvement: A Little Book on a Great Subject* (New York: Dodd, Mead, 1912), 26, 32; McLaren, *Our Own Master Race*, 24.

31 *Oh, Canada: A Medley of Stories and Pictures by Members of the Canadian Expeditionary Force* (London: Simpkin, Marshall, Hamilton, Kent, 1916), 42.

32 Cynthia R. Abeele, "'The Infant Soldier': The Great War and the Medical Campaign for Child Welfare," *Canadian Bulletin of Medical History* 5, 2 (1988): 107.

33 Choquette also argued that there was already a surfeit of enlisted men cooling their heels in Canada who were never going reach Europe before the war ended, and that recruiting was endangering Canada's (and particularly Quebec's) rural communities. When young men "leave the farm and enlist to go to war," he argued "they change their mode of life and habits, so that many, if not all of them will be permanently lost to the farm." *Debates of the Senate of Canada, 1916*, 307–8.

34 Ibid., 309.

35 Hazelton's sons served in the Royal Canadian Horse Artillery, the 48th Infantry Battalion, and the Royal Canadian Dragoons, respectively. "Man Who Wrote to Choquette Veteran of Riel Rebellion," Toronto *Daily Star*, 15 April 1916; *Debates of the Senate of Canada, 1916*, 338.

36 In January 1916, Choquette had roundly condemned both Borden's promise to increase the size of the Canadian Expeditionary Force to half-a-million men, and his moves to extend the term of Canada's 12th Parliament. In doing so, Choquette had questioned the dictum "when Britain was at war, Canada was at war" and stated that he believed that Britain was at least partially responsible for the war in which Canada was currently embroiled. Furthermore, he also declared his deep-seated opposition to the introduction of conscription in Canada. Choquette's position on Canada's military obligations to Britain would have come as no surprise to those who knew him. In 1910, he had posed similar questions about Canada's military responsibilities in debates over the Naval Services Bill. True to his word, Choquette was a vocal critic of the Canadian government's introduction of conscription in 1917. Indeed, his opposition to the Military Service Act, 1917 was so strong that it led more than one senator to accuse him of preaching sedition and being a pro-German agitator. *Debates of the Senate of Canada, 1910* (Ottawa: King's Printer, 1910), 779–80; *Debates of the Senate of Canada, 1916*, 18–25; *Debates of the Senate of Canada, 1917* (Ottawa: King's Printer, 1917), 377–86; 841–59; "New Senators Are Introduced," Toronto *Globe*, 3 August 1917.

37 "Character of the Unfit: Toronto Man Ducked for Attack on Rejected Englishmen," London *Times*, 18 April 1916.

38 "Choquette Should Be Kicked Out of the Senate," *Montreal Daily Star*, 13 April 1916. Ottawa's French-language *Le Droit* would later describe the *Star*'s accusations and demands as "*un access de jingoisme*" (an excess of jingoism/excessive jingoism). "Autour du parlement," *Le Droit*, 15 April 1916. Also see "Can Imprison Choquette," Toronto *Evening Standard*, 17 April 1916.

210   *Notes to pages 122–24*

39   *Debates of the House of Commons of the Dominion of Canada, 6th Session, 12th Parliament,* vol. 3 (Ottawa: King's Printer, 1916), 2879–80; "Chette question occupe la Chambre hier: A propos du discourse du Sénateur Choquette," *L'Acadien,* 18 April 1916; "Vigorous Reply to Senator Choquette's Letter," Toronto *Globe,* 15 April 1916.

40   "Mob Drags Hazelton from His House in Todmordon Stands Him in Coffin and Demands an Apology for Insult to British-Born in Letter Sent to Choquette," *Ottawa Evening Journal,* 17 April 1916; "Crowd Mobs Hazelton for Choquette Letter," Toronto *Globe,* 17 April 1916; "Todmordon's Punishment of Slanders on English-Born," Toronto *Evening Standard,* 17 April 1916; "La populace se fait justice," *La Droit,* 17 April 1916; "Character of the Unfit."

41   As they were read by Choquette in the Senate, francophobes quickly attributed Hazelton's "slanderous remarks" – which many anglophones read as a direct attack on Canada's soldiers, rather than just men rejected for service – to Choquette and francophones more generally. As a result, the letter, and the vitriolic responses to it from some anglophone Canadians, added further grist to the mill of anglophone/francophone antipathy. "Can Imprison Choquette"; "Reply to Choquette's Lies," Toronto *Evening Standard,* 17 April 1916.

42   McLaren, *Our Own Master Race,* 40, 42, 51.

43   Ibid., 46–57; J.S. Woodsworth, *Strangers within Our Gates, or Coming Canadians* (Toronto: Missionary Society of the Methodist Church, 1909), 54–61. Also see Carl Berger, *A Sense of Power: Studies in the Ideas of Canadian Imperialism, 1867–1914* (Toronto: University of Toronto Press, 1970), 181; Nic Clarke, "Sacred Daemons: Exploring British Columbian Society's Perceptions of 'Mentally Deficient' Children, 1870–1930," *BC Studies* 144 (Winter 2004/2005): 61–89. For a discussion of similar views held by eugenicists in the United States, see Edwin Black, *War against the Weak: Eugenics and America's Campaign to Create a Master Race* (New York: Thunder's Mouth Press, 2003), 29–31.

44   "Mob Drags Hazelton from His House."

45   "Crowd Mobs Hazelton for Choquette Letter."

46   *Debates of the Senate of Canada, 1916,* 335–38.

47   Such fears were justified. On Monday, 17 April, a crowd gathered outside Hazelton's home. Although no further acts of violence occurred – probably because the General Officer Commanding Toronto had ordered an armed piquet to be stationed outside the house after the events of 15 April – the crowd remained hostile. One member of the crowd told reporters that "unless he [Hazelton] hides himself somewhere the English of the city will get together and make a real job of it ... We will not have him in this neighbourhood for another day." That evening, a meeting was convened by Amos Allpress, one of the ringleaders of the 15 April attack on Hazelton, with the aim of discussing ways of forcing Hazelton out of Todmordon for good. "Mob Drags Hazelton from His House"; "Must Leave Todmordon," Toronto *Evening Standard,* 18 April 1916.

48   For examples of such thinking, see J.S. Woodsworth, *Strangers within Our Gates;* Charles Foster and William Duthie, eds., *Letters from the Front: Being a Record of the Part Played by Officers of the Bank in the Great War* (Toronto: Southam, 1920), 6. For a wider discussion of such beliefs, see Berger, *A Sense of Power,* and McLaren, *Our Own Master Race,* 47–57.

49   The self-confidence and chauvinism that underlay these assumptions and other assertions of Canadian "rights" or superiority in the same period are often interpreted as evidence of a nascent Canadian nationalism among some sections of the Anglo-Canadian population. This interpretation has been challenged by a number of scholars who contend that it erroneously conflates expressions of patriotism (loyalty to a political state) with expressions of nationalism (loyalty to an ethnic nation). These scholars argue that while many Anglo-Canadians were concerned for the advancement of Canada and Canadian interests,

their national (ethnic) identity remained firmly British. See Douglas Cole, "The Problem of 'Nationalism' and 'Imperialism' in British Settlement Colonies," *Journal of British Studies* 10, 2 (1971): 160–82; Phillip Buckner and R. Douglas Francis, eds., *Rediscovering the British World* (Calgary: University of Calgary Press, 2005); Phillip Buckner and R. Douglas Francis, eds., *Canada and the British World: Culture, Migration and Identity* (Vancouver: UBC Press, 2006); and Phillip Buckner, ed., *Canada and the British Empire* (Toronto: Oxford University Press, 2008).

50 Eugenicists and social reformers in Britain and the United States also used recruiting statistics to support their agendas. Indeed, in the United States eugenicists Charles Davenport and Robert Yerkes's highly influential (and highly biased) studies on men drafted into the US Army became major weapons in the eugenics movement's arsenal. Albert G. Love and Charles B. Davenport, *Defects Found in Drafted Men: Statistical Information Compiled from the Draft Showing the Physical Condition of the Men Registered and Examined in Pursuance of the Requirements of the Selective Service Act* (Washington, DC: Government Printer, 1920); *Announcement of the College of Physicians and Surgeons of Ontario, 1918-1919/Report of Proceedings of Ontario Medical Council, June 1918* (Toronto: College of Physicians and Surgeons of Ontario, 1918), 89; Abeele, "The Infant Soldier"; Black, *War against the Weak*, 80–85; McLaren, *Our Own Master Race*, 58–62; Winter, "Military Fitness," 212; Winter, "Lost Generation," 449.

51 "[Bertha Winn] Discusses the Problem of Mental Defectives," Victoria *Daily Colonist*, 21 March 1917.

52 McLaren, *Our Own Master Race*, 150–54; Clarke, "Sacred Daemons," 61–89.

53 Quoted in Veronica Strong-Boag, *The Parliament of Women: The National Council of Women of Canada, 1893-1929* (Ottawa: National Museums of Canada, 1976), 345.

54 Innis chose to serve in the artillery because he believed that it was safer than the infantry. He was wrong. Trained as an artillery spotter, he spent most of his time at the frontlines. Carl Berger, *The Writing of Canadian History: Aspects of English-Canadian Historical Writing since 1900*, 2nd ed. (Toronto: University of Toronto Press, 1986), 86; Alexander John Watson, *Marginal Man: The Dark Vision of Harold Innis* (Toronto: University of Toronto Press, 2006), 70.

55 Innis suffered a severe shrapnel wound to his right thigh at Vimy Ridge on 7 July 1917. He spent eight months in various hospitals in England before returning to Canada in March 1918. He was discharged as "medically unfit [for further military service] due to wounds, although fit for employment in civilian life," two months later. Although he was discharged from medical care in March 1918, his thigh wound took another seven years to heal completely. Innis was also psychologically scarred by his military service. Alexander Watson, his most recent biographer, has argued – citing recurring bouts of anxiety and depression that Innis suffered in the postwar period, and his loss of his strong Baptist faith – that Innis never completely recovered from the psychological traumas he suffered in the trenches. PF, vol. 470221, #339852 Innis, Harold Adam; Watson, *Marginal Man*, 61–117. Also see Donald Creighton, *Harold Adams Innis: Portrait of a Scholar* (Toronto: University of Toronto Press, 1957).

56 For a discussion of Innis's contribution to Canadian scholarship see Berger, *The Writing of Canadian History*, 85–111.

57 Maroney, "The Great Adventure," 96.

58 Quoted in ibid.

59 Vance, *Death So Noble*, 121.

60 Ibid., 113.

61 Canada, Civil Service Act, 1918, Section 39.

62 Johnson enlisted in the 106th Winnipeg Light Infantry in August 1914. He was rejected as medically unfit at Valcartier on 4 September and discharged seventeen days later. No reason for his rejection was provided, although his incomplete attestation paper indicates that his height and chest measurements were well above requirements. FVR, vol. 5, G.E. Johnson.

63 Morton and Wright, *Winning the Second Battle*, 178–201, 215–16.

64 Harold Innis, for example, completed most of the work for his Master of Arts through the Khaki University while convalescing in England after being wounded in July 1917. Watson, *Marginal Man*, 92–93.

65 Tim Cook, "From Destruction to Construction: The Khaki University of Canada, 1917–1919," *Journal of Canadian Studies* 37, 1 (2002): 109–43.

66 Kent Fedorowich, *Unfit for Heroes: Reconstruction and Soldier Settlement in the Empire Between the Wars* (Manchester: Manchester University Press, 1995); Morton and Wright, *Winning the Second Battle*.

67 Gordon H. Josie, "Administration of the Veterans' Preference in the Canadian Civil Service," *Canadian Journal of Economics and Political Science/Revue canadienne d'économique et de science politique* 11, 4 (1945): 608; Morton and Wright, *Winning the Second Battle*, 65, 136–37.

68 Fedorowich, *Unfit for Heroes*, 70–114; Morton and Wright, *Winning the Second Battle*, 102–3, 146, 151–53.

69 Lara Campbell, "'We Who Have Wallowed in the Mud of Flanders': First World War Veterans, Unemployment and the Development of Social Welfare in Canada, 1929–1939," *Journal of the Canadian Historical Association/Revue de la société historique du Canada* 11, 1 (2000): 129–30; Morton and Wright, *Winning the Second Battle*, 117–18, 214 137.

70 Johnson, *Canadian War Service Badges*, 80; Morton and Wright, *Winning the Second Battle*, 117, 214.

71 Morton and Wright, *Winning the Second Battle*, 102–4, 136–37

72 Fedorowich, *Unfit for Heroes*, 105–6.

73 Morton, *Fight or Pay*, 228.

74 There was a $1 entrance fee to the association, after which membership fees were $2 per annum. "Intend Organizing a Branch in Victoria," Victoria *Daily Colonist*, 6 November 1918. The Great War Veterans' Association covered men who had Class A and B badges. See APD for a description of service badges.

75 Ibid.

76 Ibid.

77 LAC, Records of the Department of Justice [hereafter RG 13], Ser. A-2, vol. 244, file 1919-3013, "Honourably Rejected Volunteers of Canada Vancouver – That members be recognised for appointments" [hereafter HRVA], D. Robson, Provincial Secretary, Honourably Rejected Volunteers of Canada to Robert Borden, 30 November 1919; British Columbia Archives, GR-0441, Premier's records 1883–1933, box 206, file 49, "Honourably Rejected Volunteers of Canada" [hereafter BCPR], D. Robson, Provincial Secretary, Honourably Rejected Volunteers of Canada to John Oliver, Premier of British Columbia, 30 November 1919.

78 HRVA, D. Robson, Provincial Secretary, Honourably Rejected Volunteers of Canada to Robert Borden, 30 November 1919.

79 FVR, vol. 5, John W. Johnson.

80 LAC, RG 13, Ser. A-2, vol. 230, file 1918-2787 "Honourably Rejection Volunteers of Canada – Resolutions" [hereafter HRVR], D. Robson, Provincial Secretary, Honourably Rejected Volunteers of Canada, Vancouver to Minister of Justice, 7 December 1918 and 14 December 1918; LAC, RG 13, Ser. A-2, vol. 230, file 1918-2775, Great War Veterans' Association to Sir

Notes to pages 130–38 213

Robert Borden, 13 December 1918; LAC, RG 13, Series A-2, vol. 229, file 2635, Great War Veterans' Association to Arthur Meighen, 13 December 1918.
81 HRVR, Private Secretary, Minister of Justice to D. Robson, Secretary, Honourably Rejected Volunteers of Canada, 13 December 1918 and 21 December 1918.
82 BCPR, Honourably Rejected Volunteers of Canada to John Oliver, Premier of British Columbia, 30 November 1919.

Chapter 7: Claiming Disability to Avoid Military Service
1 Johnston's relationship with Hughes must have been minimal at best. He felt the need not only to remind the minister of who had introduced them (Johnston's cousin) but also to defend his decision to call the minister an acquaintance at all. LAC, RG 24, vol. 820, EPW, Part 1, R.G. Johnston to S. Hughes, 12 August 1914.
2 Macphail, *Medical Services*, 158.
3 FVR, vol. 2, J. Bunn.
4 FVR, vol. 1, W.H. Aikenhead; FVR, vol. 8, Cyrille Nadean.
5 FVR, vol. 7, J.M. McFarland; FVR, vol. 8, Mark Purcell.
6 "Editorial," *Canadian Medical Association Journal* 6, 11 (1916): 1021; "An Appeal to the Profession," *Canadian Medical Association Journal* 7, 2 (1917): 142–43.
7 MIRSC-3, J.A. Johnson to Edward Kemp, 23 May 1917.
8 Cited in *Militia Orders*, General Instructions – Administrative Staff, 31 December 1917, 165: "Re-examination of Men under Military Service Act."
9 MacPherson, *History of the Great War*, 127; J.M. Winter, "Military Fitness," 233–35; "Simulated Diabetes," London *Times*, 11 November 1918. For an example of a medical examiner charged with falsifying medical certificates reported in the press, see "The White City Case," London *Times*, 14 December 1916; "The White City Case," London *Times*, 21 December 1916; "White City Case," London *Times*, 28 December 1916; "The White City Case," London *Times*, 11 January 1917; "The White City Case," London *Times*, 21 February 1917; "White City Recruiting Charges," London *Times*, 22 February 1917; "White City Charges," London *Times*, 24 February 1917; "The White City Case," London *Times*, 27 February 1917; "The White City Case," London *Times*, 28 February 1917; "White City Case," London *Times*, 1 March 1917; "The White City Case," London *Times*, 21 April 1917; "Court of Criminal Appeal: The 'White City' Recruiting Scandal," London *Times*, 24 April 1917; "Court of Criminal Appeal: Recruiting Scandals: Dr. Caley's Conviction Quashed," London *Times*, 24 April 1917. Also see "The Synovitis Case," London *Times*, 9 June 1917; "The Synovitis Case," London *Times*, 30 June 1917; "The Synovitis Case," London *Times*, 6 July 1917. More generally speaking, the fact that some British doctors were involved in such matters, or were believed to be involved in them, is evidenced by two Italian reservists' attempt to blackmail an English doctor, one Gustav Meyer, in 1915 by threatening to tell the British and Italian authorities that he had offered to falsify their medical certificates in exchange for a bribe. "Doctor and Reservist," London *Times*, 8 December 1915.
10 "Force Bogus Recruits to Keep Their Pledges," *Toronto Star*, 26 October 1915.
11 PS18, 15.
12 Macphail, *Medical Services*, 283.
13 PRE, GOC MD 5 to the Secretary, Militia Council, 9 January 1917.
14 MIR2C-3, GOC MD3 to the Secretary, Militia Council, 8 December 1916.
15 Hemming's report also questioned the rejection of other men found unfit for reasons other than poor eyesight. This questioning included a statement indicating his belief that the examinations conducted in England were not up to standard.
16 "Sciatica and Malingering," *Lancet* 187, 4834 (April 1916): 872.

214   *Notes to pages 138–43*

17   Connors recovered sufficiently from his wounds to be returned to active service, and indeed to involve himself in a riot. However, it is clear his lungs were permanently affected by his experience with poison gas. He suffered bouts of pleurisy and pneumonia before succumbing to the Spanish flu in 1919. PF, vol. 1923-43, #536051 Connors, Jas.

18   *Punch, or the London Charivari* 151 (11 October 1916): 271.

19   LAC, RG 24, vol. 856, file HQ 54-21-12-7, "Enlistment of Men in CEF Who Have No Intention of Going to War," Rev. H.A. Elliot to Sir Robert Borden, 31 March 1915.

20   LAC, RG 24, vol. 823, EPW, Part 12, OC 3rd Division to Secretary of the Militia Council, 16 June 1915.

21   LAC, RG 24, vol. 824, EPW, Part. 14, Major F.H. Honeywell to Officer Commanding 8th Canadian Mounted Rifles, 5 July 1915.

22   FVR, vol. 2, Walter Bryant.

23   FVR, vol. 1, J. Boyd.

24   LAC, RG 24, vol. 820, EPW, Part 1, R.G. Johnston to S. Hughes, 12 August 1914.

25   Douglas C. Baynton, "Disability and the Justification of Inequality in American History," in *The New Disability History: American Perspectives,* ed. Paul K. Longmore and Lauri Umansky (New York: New York University Press, 2001), 33, 41–44.

26   FVR, vol. 1, A. Birch.

27   Mrs. Pritchard's letter took the form of a copy of a typed statement that said the original was signed with her mark (X).

28   LAC, RG 24, vol. 821, EPW, Part 4, Mrs. John A. Pritchard to Superintendent West of the RNWMP, 12 September 1914, and related correspondence; FVR, vol. 8, J.A. Pritchard. For further examples, see Desmond Morton, *Fight or Pay,* 30–31.

29   As of 1 April 1915, noncommissioned ranks receiving separation allowance were obliged – barring special circumstances – to assign half their pay to their dependents. Morton, *Fight or Pay,* 30–49, 93.

30   Morton, *Fight or Pay,* 50–132; Herbert Ames, *Our National Benefaction: A Review of the Canadian Patriotic Fund* (Ottawa: n.p., 1915); Philip H. Morris, *The Canadian Patriotic Fund: A Record of Its Activities from 1914 to 1919* (Ottawa: n.p., 1920?).

31   Morton, *Fight or Pay,* 89–90. Susan Pedersen has made similar observations with regard to the provision of separation benefits by the British government. Susan Pedersen, "Gender, Welfare, and Citizenship in Britain during the Great War," *American Historical Review* 95, 4 (1990): 983–1006.

32   Clements repeatedly stressed that Fox was a German, even going so far as stating that "if all Germans are like him, I am sure the world will be well rid of them." In light of his vitriolic denunciations, it should be noted that her identification of Fox's ethnicity was incorrect. The 1911 Census identified him as being an ethnic Russian from Poland. Joseph's wife, Bertha, however, was identified as being ethnically German. Clements was correct in identifying Fox's religion. *1911 Census of Canada Indexing Project,* http://automated genealogy.com/census11.

33   LAC, RG 24, vol. 822, Part 10, Aimee Clements to unidentified correspondent, 13 April 1915.

34   Montrealer Herrick Duggan expressed similar fears to his mother about whether it was safe to send his sister, Margaret, to a private school in Kent, England. FVR, vol. 11, H. Wood; Clarke, "He Was My Best Subaltern," 23.

35   FVR, vol. 7, Leo Mills.

36   FVR, vol. 2, William Brothers.

37   LAC, RG 24, vol. 824, EPW, Part 15, Mrs. Jas. Martin to Secretary of the Militia Council, 21 August 1915.

38 FVR, vol. 10, Charles Steele.

39 LAC, RG 24, vol. 824, EPW, Part 13, Gagnon, Sasseville & Gagnon to M. le Sous-Ministre de Milice, 10 July 1915.

40 LAC, RG 24, vol. 823, EPW, Part 12, L.C. Belanger, K.C. to the Honourable Samuel Hughes, Minister of Militia, 15 May 1915.

41 LAC, RG 24, vol. 820, EPW, Part 1, S.E. Harris to Officer in Charge of Militia Department, 26 August 1914.

42 PF, vol. 4084-13, #775939 Harris, Cleveland O.

43 Twelve (13, if the one instance of an individual with deformed toes is included) men in the sample set had hammer toes recorded as a reason for rejection. All but one of these men, however, suffered from multiple cases of the deformity or also had other unrelated impairments. Enlarged hearts were mentioned in 5 of the 161 cases where heart conditions were recorded as a reason for rejection. As enlarged hearts are often symptomatic of other conditions, it is likely that many of the other 155 men rejected due to heart conditions also had enlarged hearts.

44 Harris was not the only individual to gain weight while serving in the Canadian Expeditionary Force. Nova Scotia author William R. Bird gained sixteen pounds between his enlistment in April 1916 and his demobilization in March 1919. Saskatchewan native Alfred Andrews put on twenty-four pounds from the time of his enlistment in August 1914 to Christmas of the same year. Such physical changes were not confined to Canada. Robert Roberts noted the following in his memoir about life in Salford at the turn of the twentieth century: "In the first few months of hostilities many local recruits returning on their first 'furlough' ... astonished us all. Pounds – sometimes stones – heavier, taller, confident, clean and straight, they were hardly recognisable." If nothing else, the military ensured that its troops were well fed. Bird, *Ghosts Have Warm Hands*, 170; PF, vol. 748-27, #901552 Bird, William Richard. Andrews, "Diary of Alfred Herbert John Andrews"; Roberts, *The Classic Slum*, 152.

45 At the time this comment was made, Harris weighed 132 pounds. PF, vol. 4084-13, #775939 Harris, Cleveland O.

46 Officially known as "pyrexia of unknown origins" (PUO) until its cause was discovered in 1918, trench fever was caused by the bacteria *Bartonella quintana*, which was transmitted to its victims via infected body lice (*Pediculus humanus humanus*). Symptoms included fatigue, fever, eye sensitivity, headaches, high temperatures, nausea, pain in the legs (particularly the shins), and occasionally a maculo-papular pink rash that sometimes lasted for only a few hours. It was also common for the afflicted individual's spleen to be enlarged. Trench fever commonly affected its victims for three to five days, although severe cases, which were characterized by multiple relapses, could last months. Given the prevalence of lice in the trenches and the fact the disease's cause was unknown until 1918, most men suffered from trench fever at least once during their time in the trenches. The estimates provided by Macphail in his history of the Canadian Medical Services is much lower, however. Macphail stated that the Canadian Expeditionary Force suffered from 15,355 cases of fever of unknown origin, 4,987 of which were confirmed as trench fever. See Cook, *At the Sharp End*, 253; Macphail, *Medical Services*, 262–63; A.F. Shipley, *The Minor Horrors of the War*, 2nd ed. (London: Smith and Elder, 1915), 1–29; Geoffrey Miller, "Of Lice and Men: Trench Fever and Trench Life in the AIF," *Medical History of WWI*, http://www.vlib.us/medical.

47 Harris's brush with gonorrhea also led him to suffer from lymphadenitis, epididymitis, and prolatitis. PF, vol. 4084-13, #775939 Harris, Cleveland O.

48 FVR, vol. 7, W. McWilliam.

49 Morley Currie (1869–1944) served as the Liberal Member of Parliament for the Ontario riding of Prince Edward in Canada's 11th Parliament (1909–11). He had previously represented Prince Edward in the Legislative Assembly of Ontario (1902–08). "Currie, Morely" at *Parliament of Canada,* http://www.parl.gc.ca.

50 For other examples of correspondents expressing surprise that the subject of their letter had been passed fit to serve and/or using doctors' letters to support their claims that the individual in question was unfit, see LAC, RG 24, vol. 820, EPW, Part 1, John Fenn to E.G. Porter, 22 August 1914, and Mrs. H.T. Pritchard to Colonel Dunbar, 14 August 1914; and LAC, RG 24, vol. 824, EPW, Part 15, James Scott to General Sam Hughes, 15 August 1915.

51 An examination of attestation papers under both McWilliam and McWilliams (the surname mistakenly attributed to the family in the 1911 census) did not reveal anybody fitting Willie's profile. It is possible, however, that Willie enlisted, as did many men, under an assumed name. *1911 Census of Canada Indexing Project.*

52 FVR, vol. 2, G.W. Clarke.

53 LAC, RG 24, vol. 820, EPW, Part 1, George J. Lynch to Minister of Militia and Defence, 13 August 1914.

54 LAC, RG 24, vol. 825, EPW, Part 18, J.H. Fehrenbach to W.G. Weichel, 8 September 1915; Thomas W. Hicks to the Minister of Militia, 11 October 1915.

55 For examples of individuals rejected as "mentally deficient," "mentally unfit," or "mentally incompetent," see FVR, vol. 8, J. Niell; FVR, vol. 9, Chester Vanderfoal; FVR, vol. 9, Harry Tours; FVR, vol. 11, Joseph Williams.

56 PF, vol. 4323-11, #657185 Hicks, Clifford Mallery; PF, vol. 3026-21, #126080 Fehrenback [sic], John Joseph.

57 FVR, vol. 3, D. Cameron.

58 LAC, RG 24, vol. 824, EPW, Part 15, Mrs. A. Dash to AG, Ottawa, 16 August 1915.

59 FVR, vol. 1, G. Boissel.

60 LAC, RG 24, vol. 824, EPW, Part 15, Mrs. A. Dash to AG, Ottawa, 16 August 1915.

61 FVR, vol. 2, Leonard Bradley.

62 LAC, RG 24, vol. 821, EPW, Part 6, OC 21st Battalion CEF to Mrs. McGrath, 10 November 1916; and OC 21st Battalion CEF to Mrs. McGrath, 16 November 1914.

63 LAC, RG 24, vol. 821, EPW, Part 6, D. O'Connell to Minister of Militia, 23 December 1914.

64 LAC, RG 24, vol. 821, EPW, Part 6, AAG to the Military Secretary, 30 December 1914; and Judge Advocate General to the Military Secretary, 5 January 1915.

65 LAC, RG 24, vol. 821, EPW, Part 6, OC 21st Battalion CEF to LCol. Chas. F. Winter, Militia Secretary, Ottawa, 8 January 1915.

66 FVR, vol. 1, R.B. Anderson.

67 FVR, vol. 2, William Burleigh.

68 FVR, vol. 11, C. Winegard.

69 LAC, RG 24, vol. 824, EPW, Part 15, Mrs. A. Dash to AG, Ottawa, 16 August 1915.

70 LAC, RG 24, vol. 824, EPW, Part 13, Mrs. F.B. Campbell to MGen. W. Gwatkin, 1 July (?) 1915.

71 LAC, RG 24, vol. 824, EPW, Part 13, Mrs. Wm. F. Orr to Sam Hughes, Militia Dept., Ottawa, 20 August 1914.

72 FVR, vol. 10, F.T. Williams.

73 LAC, RG 24, vol. 824, EPW, Part 15, Mrs. A. Dash to AG, Ottawa, 16 August 1915.

74 LAC, RG 24, vol. 823, EPW, Part 12, Adelaide Yuill to Major General Hughes, 14 June 1916.

75 PF, vol. 10673-17, #410916 Yuill, Lionel Henry.

76 FVR, vol. 2, William Burleigh.

77 LAC, RG 24, vol. 820, EPW, Part 1, J. Calhoun to the Minister of Militia, 15 August 1914.

78 LAC, RG 24, vol. 820, EPW, Part 11, Mary Polk to the Military Department, 14 August 1914; and Mrs. Boiling to the Department of Militia, 20 August 1914.
79 FVR, vol. 11, Fred Weir.
80 FVR, vol. 2, Roy Coates.

Conclusion

1 Michael Thomas, "Scorn of the Women," *Scorn of the Women*, WEA Records, 1987.
2 Read, *The Great War and Canadian Society*, 103; Bird, *And We Go On*, 13–14.
3 HDF, HD to MD, 4 November 1914.
4 "Unfit for Military Service," Toronto *Globe*, 27 January 1915.
5 Ilana Bet-El has made the same observation with regard to the medical examination of English recruits. Ilana Bet-El, *Conscripts: Lost Legions of the Great War* (London: Sutton, 1999), 37.
6 Johnson, *Canadian War Service Badges*, 81.
7 Fred Cederberg, *The Long Road Home: The Autobiography of a Canadian Soldier in Italy in World War II* (Toronto: Stoddart, 1984), 20.
8 Ibid., 20.
9 *Physical Standards and Instructions for the Medical Examination of Serving Soldiers and Recruits for the Canadian Army, Active and Reserve 1943* (Ottawa: King's Printer, 1943).
10 Brigadier J.C. Meakins, "The 'PULHEMS' System of Medical Grading," *Canadian Medical Association Journal* 49, 5 (November 1943): 349–54.
11 *Physical Standards and Instructions for the Medical Examination of Serving Soldiers and Recruits for the Canadian Army*.
12 Birney, it should be noted, was in a strong position to make such observations – he had been a personnel selection officer in the Canadian Army during the Second World War. Indeed, some of the episodes in *Turvey* were so close to reality that Birney's publisher feared the possibility of lawsuits. Earle Birney, *The Creative Writer* (Montreal: CBC Publications, 1966), 43.
13 Earle Birney, *Turvey: A Military Picaresque*, rev. ed. (Toronto: McClelland and Stewart, 1976), 285–87.
14 Birney, *The Creative Writer*, 40.
15 Birney, *Turvey*, 5–6.
16 Ibid., 1–2.
17 Ibid., 4–12, 14–15, 284–86.
18 Shaw, *Crisis of Conscience*, 152–55.
19 One should not confuse this circumspection with a lack of commitment to fight. Recruiting stations were inundated with volunteers in September 1939, just as they were in August 1914. Moreover, many Canadians believed that the war was necessary. More broadly, some men experienced pressures to enlist – including aggressive harassment – from some sections of Canadian society during the Second World War. Tim Cook, *The Necessary War: Canadians Fighting the Second World War, 1939-1943*, vol. 1 (Toronto: Allen Lane, 2014), 24–28; Jeffery Keshen, *Saints, Sinners, and Soldiers* (Vancouver: UBC Press, 2004), 12, 22–23. Ian Miller, "Toronto's Response to the Outbreak of War, 1939," *Canadian Military History* 1, 11 (2002): 5–23.

Bibliography

Archival Sources
Archives of Ontario, Toronto, Ontario
British Columbia Archives (BCA), Victoria, British Columbia
 Premier's Records, 1883–1933
Canadian War Museum (CWM), Ottawa, Ontario
 George Metcalf Archival Collection
Library and Archives Canada (LAC), Ottawa, Ontario
 George Herrick Duggan Fonds, MG30-B124
 Herrick Stevenson Duggan Fonds, MG30-E303
 John Taylor Fotheringham Fonds, MG30-E53
 Kenneth L. Duggan Fonds, MG30-E304
 Robert James Manion Fonds, MG27-IIIB7
 William Babtie Fonds, MG30-E3Department of Militia and Defence, RG 9
 Department of National Defence, RG 24
 Ministry of Justice, RG 13
 Ministry of the Overseas Military Forces of Canada, RG 150
 Privy Council Office, RG 2
 Royal Canadian Mounted Police, RG 18
University of Ottawa Library Archives and Special Collections

Newspapers, Magazines, and Journals
21st Battalion Communique
British Medical Journal
Canadian Medical Association Journal
Canadian Military Gazette
Daily British Whig (Kingston, Ontario)
Evening Standard (Toronto)
Globe (Toronto)
Kingston Daily Standard
L'Acadian
Lancet (London)
Le Devoir (Montreal)
Le Droit (Ottawa)
Montreal Star
Montreal Gazette
New York Times
Ottawa Citizen
Ottawa Journal
Punch, or the London Charivari
Toronto Star
Queen's Quarterly

Other Sources

Abbenhuis, Maartje M. *The Art of Staying Neutral: The Netherlands in the First World War, 1914-1918*. Amsterdam: Amsterdam University Press, 2006. http://dx.doi.org/10.5117/9789053568187.

Adami, J.G. *The War Story of the CAMC, 1914-1915*. Toronto: Musson, 1918.

Akers, Dwight. *Drivers Up: The Story of American Harness Racing*. New York: G.P. Putnam's Sons, 1938.

Allinson, Sidney. *The Bantams: The Untold Story of World War One*. Oakville: Mosaic Press, 1982.

Ames, Herbert. *Our National Benefaction: A Review of the Canadian Patriotic Fund*. Ottawa: n.p., 1915.

Anonymous. *Canada in the Great World War, Memorial Edition: An Authentic Account of the Military History of Canada from the Earliest Days to the Close of the War of the Nations*. Vol. 2. Toronto: United Publishers of Canada, 1919.

–. *Oh, Canada: A Medley of Stories and Pictures by Members of the Canadian Expeditionary Force*. London: Simpkin, Marshall, Hamilton, Kent, 1916.

Anson, T.V. *The New Zealand Dental Services*. Wellington: Historical Publications Branch, 1960.

Arnup, Katherine. "'Victims of Vaccination?': Opposition to Compulsory Immunization in Ontario, 1900-1990." *Canadian Bulletin of Medical History* 9 (1992): 159-76.

Atkinson, D., et al., eds. *Forgotten Lives: Exploring the History of Learning Disability*. Kidderminister, UK:BILD Publications, 1997.

Baker, La Reine H., *Race Improvement: A Little Book on a Great Subject*. New York: Dodd, Mead, 1912.

Baldwin, Harold. *Holding the Line*. Chicago: A.C. McClurg, 1918.

Banning, Kendall. *The Military Censorship of Pictures: Photographs That Came under the Ban during the World War, and Why*. United States: Author, 1926.

Barton, Peter, Peter Doyle, and Johan Vandewalle. *Beneath Flanders: The Tunnellers' War, 1914-18*. Montreal and Kingston: McGill-Queens University Press, 2004.

Baynton, Douglas C. "Disability and the Justification of Inequality in American History." In *The New Disability History: American Perspectives*, ed. Paul K. Longmore and Lauri Umansky, 3-57. New York: New York University Press, 2001.

Beckett, I.F.W. *The Great War, 1914-1918*. London: Longman, 2001.

Beggs, S.T. *The Selection of the Recruit*. London: Bailliere, Tindall and Cox, 1915.

Bennett, Y.A., ed. *Kiss the Kids for Dad. Don't Forget to Write: The Wartime Letters of George Timmins, 1916-18*. Vancouver: UBC Press, 2009.

Benton, Sarah. "Women, War and Citizenship." *History Workshop Journal* 58, 1 (2004): 326-34. http://dx.doi.org/10.1093/hwj/58.1.326.

Berger, Carl. *The Writing of Canadian History: Aspects of English-Canadian Historical Writing since 1900*. 2nd ed. Toronto: University of Toronto Press, 1986.

Bérubé, B. "Dr. F.N.G. Starr – in Memory of the Medical Statesman." *Canadian Medical Association Journal* 127, 5 (1982): 417-21.

Bet-El, Ilana. *Conscripts: The Lost Legions of the Great War*. Phoenix Mill, Gloucestershire: Sutton, 1999.

Bibbings, L. "Images of Manliness: The Portrayal of Soldiers and Conscientious Objectors in the Great War." *Social and Legal Studies* 12, 3 (2003): 335-58. http://dx.doi.org/10.1177/09646639030123003.

Bird, C.W., and J.B. Davies. *The Canadian Forestry Corps: Its Inception, Development, and Achievements*. London: HMSO, 1919.

Bird, Will R. *And We Go On.* Toronto: Hunter-Rose, 1930.

–. *Ghosts Have Warm Hands: A Memoir of the Great War.* Ottawa: CEF Books, 2002.

Black, Edwin. *War against the Weak: Eugenics and America's Campaign to Create a Master Race.* New York: Thunder's Mouth Press, 2003.

Bliss, J. "Michael. "The Methodist Church and World War I." *Canadian Historical Review* 49, 3 (September 1968): 213–33. http://dx.doi.org/10.3138/CHR-049-03-01.

Bogacz, Ted. "War Neurosis and Cultural Change in England, 1914–1922: The Work of the War Office Committee of Enquiry into 'Shell-Shock.'" *Journal of Contemporary History* 4, 2 (1989): 227–56.

Boire, Michael. "The Underground War: Military Mining Operations in Support of the Attack on Vimy Ridge, 9 April 1917." *Canadian Military History* 1, 1 (1992): 15–24.

Bond, Brian. *The Unquiet Western Front.* Cambridge: Cambridge University Press, 2002. http://dx.doi.org/10.1017/CBO9780511496158.

Boyne, A.W., and I. Leitich. "Secular Change in the Height of British Adults." *Nutrition Abstracts and Reviews* 24, 2 (1954): 255–69.

Brigham, L., et al., eds. *Crossing Boundaries: Change and Continuity in the History of Learning Disability.* Kidderminister, UK: BILD Publications, 2000.

Brown, R. "Craig and Donald Loveridge. "Unrequited Faith: Recruiting the CEF, 1914–18." In *Reappraisals in Canadian History: Post Confederation,* 2nd ed., ed. C.M. Wallace, R.M. Bray, and A.D. Gilbert, 300–19. Toronto: Prentice Hall, 1996.

Bryder, L. "The First World War: Healthy or Hungry?" *History Workshop Journal* 24, 1 (1987): 141–57. http://dx.doi.org/10.1093/hwj/24.1.141.

Buckner, Phillip, ed. *Canada and the British Empire.* Toronto: Oxford University Press, 2008.

Buckner, Phillip, and R. Douglas Francis, eds. *Rediscovering the British World.* Calgary: University of Calgary Press, 2005.

–. *Canada and the British World: Culture, Migration and Identity.* Vancouver: UBC Press, 2006.

Burke, Joanna. *Dismembering the Male: Men's Bodies, Britain and the Great War.* Chicago: University of Chicago Press, 1996.

Busch, Briton C., ed. *Canada and the Great War: Western Front Association Papers.* Montreal and Kingston: McGill-Queen's University Press, 2003.

Callister, Sandy. *The Face of War: New Zealand's Great War Photography.* Auckland: Auckland University Press, 2008.

Campbell, Lara. "'We Who Have Wallowed in the Mud of Flanders': First World War Veterans, Unemployment and the Development of Social Welfare in Canada, 1929–1939." *Journal of the Canadian Historical Association/Revue de la société historique du Canada* 11, 1 (2000): 125–49.

Campbell, W.E. "A Brief History of the Royal Canadian Service Corps." http://rcasc.org.

Canada. *Army Medical Corps Instructions: General Orders, Militia Orders and Precis of Headquarters Letters Bearing upon the Administration of the Canadian Army Medical Service Published between August 6th, 1914, and December 31st, 1916.* Ottawa: Militia Council, 1917.

–. *Canadian Expeditionary Force Units: Instructions Governing Organisation and Administration.* Ottawa: Government Printing Bureau, 1916.

–. *Civil Service Act, 1918.* Ottawa: King's Printer, 1918.

–. *The King's Regulations and Orders for the Canadian Militia, 1910.* Ottawa: King's Printer, 1910.

–. *The King's Regulations and Orders for the Canadian Militia, 1917.* Ottawa: King's Printer, 1917.

–. *Militia Orders, 1914.* Ottawa: Department of Militia and Defence, 1914.
–. *Militia Orders, 1915.* Ottawa: Department of Militia and Defence, 1915.
–. *Militia Orders, 1916.* Ottawa: Department of Militia and Defence, 1916.
–. *Military Service Act, 1917.* Ottawa: King's Printer, 1917.
–. *Physical Standards and Instructions for the Medical Examination of Recruits for the Canadian Expeditionary Force and for the Active Militia of Canada, 1917.* Ottawa: King's Printer, 1917.
–. *Physical Standards and Instructions for the Medical Examination of Recruits for the Canadian Expeditionary Force and for the Active Militia, 1918.* Ottawa: King's Printer, 1918.
–. *Regulations for the Canadian Medical Service, 1910.* Ottawa: Government Printer, 1910.
–. *Regulations for the Canadian Medical Service, 1914.* Ottawa: Government Printer, 1915.
Caplan, Jane. "'Speaking Scars': The Tattoo in Popular Practice and Medico-Legal Debate in Nineteenth-Century Europe." *History Workshop Journal* 44 (1997): 107–42. http://dx.doi.org/10.1093/hwj/1997.44.107.
Carion, Christian, director. *Joyeux Nöel–Merry Christmas.* Paris: Nord-Ouest Productions, 2005.
Castell Hopkins, J. *The Canadian Annual Review War Series, 1914.* Toronto: Canadian Annual Review Limited, 1918.
–. *The Canadian Annual Review War Series, 1915.* Toronto: Canadian Annual Review Limited, 1918.
–. *The Canadian Annual Review War Series, 1916.* Toronto: Canadian Annual Review Limited, 1918.
–. *The Canadian Annual Review War Series, 1917.* Toronto: Canadian Annual Review Limited, 1918.
Christie, Norm, ed. *The Letters of Agar Adamson 1914 to 1919: Lieutenant Colonel, Princess Patricia's Canadian Light Infantry.* Ottawa: CEF Books, 1997.
Clark, Ann. "Compliance with Infant Smallpox Vaccination Legislation in Nineteenth-Century Rural England: Hollingbourne, 1876-88." *Social History of Medicine* 17, 2 (2004): 175–98. http://dx.doi.org/10.1093/shm/17.2.175.
Clarke, Nic. "'The Greater and Grimmer Game': Sport as an Arbiter of Military Fitness in the British Empire – The Case of 'One-Eyed' Frank McGee." *International Journal of the History of Sport* 28, 3–4 (2011): 604–22. http://dx.doi.org/10.1080/09523367.2011.547320.
–. "'He Was My Best Subaltern': The Life and Death of Lieutenant Herrick S. Duggan, 70th Field Company, Royal Engineers." *Canadian Military History* 17, 2 (2008): 21–32.
–. "'Opening Closed Doors and Breaching High Walls': Some Approaches for Studying Intellectual Disability in Canadian History." *Histoire sociale/Social History* 39, 78 (2007): 467–85.
–. "Sacred Daemons: The Perception and Treatment of Intellectually Disabled Children in British Columbia, 1870-1930." *BC Studies* 144 (Winter 2004/2005): 61–89.
–. "'You Will Not Be Going to This War': The Rejected Volunteers of the First Contingent of the Canadian Expeditionary Force." *First World War Studies* 1, no. 2 (2010): 161–83. http://dx.doi.org/10.1080/19475020.2010.517436.
Clarke, Nic, John Cranfield, and Kris Inwood. "Fighting Fit? Diet, Disease and Disability in the Canadian Expeditionary Force, 1914–1918." *War and Society* 33, 2 (2014): 80–97. http://dx.doi.org/10.1179/0729247314Z.00000000033.
Clyne, Henry Randolph Notman. *Vancouver's 29th: A Chronicle of the 29th in Flanders Field.* Vancouver: Privately printed, 1964.
Cohen, Deborah. *The War Come Home: Disabled Veterans in Britain and Germany, 1914–1939.* Berkeley: University of California Press, 2001.

Cole, Douglas. "The Problem of 'Nationalism' and 'Imperialism' in British Settlement Colonies." *Journal of British Studies* 10, 02 (1971): 160–82. http://dx.doi.org/10.1086/385614.

Cook, Tim. *At the Sharp End: Canadians Fighting the Great War, 1914–1916.* Vol. 1. Toronto: Viking, 2007.

–. *Clio's Warriors: Canadian Historians and the Writing of the World Wars.* Vancouver: UBC Press, 2006.

–. "'He Was Determined to Go': Underage Soldiers in the Canadian Expeditionary Force." *Histoire sociale/Social History* 41, 81 (2008): 42–74.

–. *The Necessary War: Canadians Fighting the Second World War, 1939–1943.* Vol. 1. Toronto: Allen Lane, 2014.

–. *No Place to Run: The Canadian Corps and Gas Warfare in the First World War.* Vancouver: UBC Press, 1999.

–. *Shock Troops: Canadian Fighting the Great War, 1917–1918.* Vol. 2. Toronto: Viking, 2008.

–. *Warlords: Borden, Mackenzie King, and Canada's World Wars.* Toronto: Allen Lane, 2012.

Crammer, J.L. "Extraordinary Deaths of Asylum Inpatients during the 1914–18 War." *Medical History* 36, 4 (1992): 430–41. http://dx.doi.org/10.1017/S0025727300055708.

Cranfield, John, and Kris Inwood. "The Great Transformation: A Long-Run Perspective on Physical Well-Being in Canada." *Economics and Human Biology* 5, 2 (2007): 204–28. http://dx.doi.org/10.1016/j.ehb.2007.02.001.

Creighton, Donald. *Harold Adams Innis: Portrait of a Scholar.* Toronto: University of Toronto Press, 1957.

Davis, L.J. "Crips Strike Back: The Rise of Disability Studies." *American Literary History* 11, 3 (1999): 500–12. http://dx.doi.org/10.1093/alh/11.3.500.

Davis, M. "The Patients' World: British Columbia's Mental Health Facilities, 1910–1935." MA thesis, University of Waterloo, 1989.

Delany, Paul. *D.H. Lawrence's Nightmare: The Writer and His Circle in the Years of the Great War.* New York: Basic Books, 1978.

–. "Dental Inefficiency." *Dental Cosmos: A Monthly Record of Dental Science,* September 1916, 1071–75.

Devivne, Edward, and Lilian Brandt. *Disabled Soldiers and Sailors Pensions and Training.* New York: Oxford University Press, 1919.

Dewsbury, Guy, et al. "The Anti-Social Model of Disability." *Disability and Society* 19, 2 (2004): 145–58. http://dx.doi.org/10.1080/0968759042000181776.

Dickie, Robert M. "War and the Survival of the Fit." *Queen's Quarterly* 20 (1912–13): 194–213.

Dinesen, Thomas. *MERRY HELL! A Dane with the Canadians.* London: Jarrolds, 1929.

Djebabla, Mourad. "'Fight or Farm': Canadian Farmers and the Dilemma of the War Effort in World War One (1914–1918)." *Canadian Military Journal* 13, 2 (2013): 57–67.

Dowbiggen, Ian. *Keeping America Sane: Psychiatry and Eugenics in the United States and Canada, 1880–1940.* Ithaca, NY: Cornell University Press, 1997.

Duguid, A. Fortescue. *Official History of the Canadian Forces in the Great War, 1914–1919.* Vol. 1. Ottawa: King's Printer, 1938.

Durflinger, Serge Marc. *Veterans with A Vision: Canada's War Blinded in Peace and War.* Vancouver: UBC Press, 2010.

Dutil, Patrice A. "Against Isolationism: Napoléon Belcourt, French Canada, and 'La grande guerre.'" In *Canada and the First World War: Essays in Honour of Robert Craig Brown,* ed. David Mackenzie, 96–137. Toronto: University of Toronto Press, 2005.

Edgett, Tom, and David Beatty, eds. *The World War One Diaries and Letters of Louis Stanley Edgett.* Riverview, NB: J.T. Edgett, 2005.

Eksteins, Modris. *Rites of Spring: The Great War and the Birth of the Modern Age.* Toronto: Key Porter, 1989.

Farley, John. *Brock Chisholm, the World Health Organization, and the Cold War.* Vancouver: UBC Press, 2008.

Farrell, Arthur. *Hockey: Canada's Royal Winter Game.* Montreal: J. R. Cornell, 1899.

Fedorowich, Kent. *Unfit For Heroes: Reconstruction And Soldier Settlement in the Empire Between the Wars.* Manchester: Manchester University Press, 1995.

Ferguson, Niall. *The Pity of War: Explaining World War I.* New York: Basic Books, 1999.

Fleming, R.B., ed. *The Wartime Letters of Leslie and Cecil Frost, 1915–1919.* Waterloo, ON: Wilfrid Laurier University Press, 2007.

Floud, Roderick. *An Introduction to Quantitative Methods for Historians.* London: Methuen, 1973.

–. *The People and the British Economy, 1830–1914.* Oxford: Oxford University Press, 1997.

Floud, Roderick, Kenneth Wachter, and Annabel Gregory. *Height, Health and History: Nutritional Status in the United Kingdom.* Cambridge: Cambridge University Press, 1990. http://dx.doi.org/10.1017/CBO9780511983245.

Fraser, Leonard. *Historical Calendar: 21st Infantry Battalion (Eastern Ontario Regiment) Belgium – France – Germany, 1915–1919.* London: Gale and Polden, 1919.

Fussell, Paul. *The Great War and Modern Memory.* Oxford: Oxford University Press, 1975.

Gallagher, Hugh G. *FDR's Splendid Deception.* New York: Dodd, 1985.

Galton, Francis. "Final Report of the Anthropometric Committee." *Report of the British Association for the Advancement of Science* (1883): 253–306.

Gelber, Scott. "A 'Hard-Boiled Order': The Reeducation of Disabled WWI Veterans in New York City." *Journal of Social History* 39, 1 (2005): 161–80. http://dx.doi.org/10.1353/jsh.2005.0101.

Gerber, David A., ed. *Disabled Veterans in History.* Ann Arbor: University of Michigan Press, 2000.

Gleeson, B.J. "Disability Studies: A Historical Materialist View." *Disability and Society* 12, 2 (1997): 179–202. http://dx.doi.org/10.1080/09687599727326.

Godwin, George. *Why Stay We Here? Odyssey of a Canadian Officer in France in World War I.* Victoria: Godwin Books, 2002.

Goldman, Around S., et al. "What Was the Cause of Franklin Delano Roosevelt's Paralytic Illness?" *Journal of Medical Biography* 11 (2003): 232–40.

Granatstein, J.L., and R.D. Cuff, eds. *War and Society in North America.* Toronto: Thomas Nelson and Sons, 1971.

Granatstein, J.L., and J.M. Hitsman. *Broken Promises: A History of Conscription in Canada.* Toronto: Oxford University Press, 1977.

Greenfield, Nathan M. *Baptism of Fire: The Second Battle of Ypres and the Forging of Canada, April 1915.* Toronto: HarperCollins, 2007.

Gregory, Adrian. "Gender, Citizenship and Entitlement." *Journal of British Studies* 43, 03 (2004): 410–15. http://dx.doi.org/10.1086/383603.

Grierson, J.M. *Scarlet into Khaki: The British Army on the Eve of the Boer War.* London: Greenhill Books, 1988 (reprint).

Gross, Paul, director. *Passchendaele.* Toronto: Whizbang Films, 2008.

Gullace, Nicoletta F. *"The Blood of Our Sons": Men, Women, and the Renegotiation of British Citizenship during the Great War.* New York: Palgrave Macmillan, 2002.

–. "Sexual Violence and Family Honor: British Propaganda and International Law during the First World War." *American Historical Review* 102, 3 (1997): 714–47. http://dx.doi.org/10.2307/2171507.

–. "White Feathers and Wounded Men: Female Patriotism and the Memory of the Great War." *Journal of British Studies* 36, 02 (1997): 178–206. http://dx.doi.org/10.1086/386133.

Haycock, Ronald. *Sam Hughes: The Public Career of a Controversial Canadian, 1885–1916.* Waterloo, ON: Wilfrid Laurier University Press, 1986.

Healy, Maureen. *Vienna and the Fall of the Habsburg Empire: Total War and Everyday Life in World War I.* Cambridge: Cambridge University Press, 2004.

Hickel, Walter. "Medicine, Bureaucracy, and Social Welfare: The Politics of Disability Compensation for American Veterans of World War I." In *The New Disability History: American Perspectives,* ed. Paul K. Longmore and Lauri Umansky, 236–67. New York: New York University Press, 2001.

Hirsch, K. "Culture and Disability: The Role of Oral History." *Oral History Review* 22, 1 (1995): 1–28. http://dx.doi.org/10.1093/ohr/22.1.1.

Holt, Tonie, and Valmai Holt. *My Boy Jack: The Search for Kipling's Only Son.* Barnsley, UK: Pen and Sword, 1998.

Horn, Bernd, and Roch Legault, eds. *Loyal Service: Perspectives on French-Canadian Military Leaders.* Kingston, ON: Canadian Defence Academy Press, 2007.

Howe, Glenford. "Military Selection and Civilian Health: Recruiting West Indians for World War I." *Caribbean Quarterly* 44, 3 (1998): 35–49.

Hughes, Colin. *Mametz: Lloyd George's "Welsh Army" at the Battle of the Somme.* Gerrards Cross, UK: Onion Press, 1982.

Hughes, John McKendrick. *The Unwanted: Great War Letters from the Field.* Edmonton: University of Alberta Press, 2005.

Hughes, Michael. "British Methodists and the First World War." *Methodist History* 41, 1 (2000): 316–28.

–. "Development of Methodist Pacifism, 1899–1939." *Proceedings of the Wesley Historical Society* 53, 6 (2002): 203–15.

Iarocci, Andrew. *Shoestring Soldiers: The 1st Canadian Division at War, 1914–1915.* Toronto: University of Toronto Press, 2008.

Isitt, Benjamin. *From Victoria to Vladivostok: Canada's Siberian Expedition, 1917–19.* Vancouver: UBC Press, 2011.

Jackson, H.M. *The Story of the Royal Canadian Dental Corps.* Ottawa: n.p., 1956.

Jackson, M. "Images of Deviance: Visual Representations of Mental Defectives in Early Twentieth-Century Medical Texts." *British Journal for the History of Science* 28, 03 (1995): 319–37. http://dx.doi.org/10.1017/S0007087400033185.

Jain, Venu, Neil J. Sebire, and David G. Talbert. "Kaiser Wilhelm Syndrome: Obstetric Trauma or Placental Insult in a Historic Case Mimicking Erb's Palsy." *Medical Hypotheses* 65, 1 (2005): 185–91. http://dx.doi.org/10.1016/j.mehy.2004.12.027.

Jeunet, Jean-Pierre. *Un long dimanche de fiançailles.* Neuilly-sur-Seine: Warner Independent, 2004.

Johnson, Robbie. *Canadian War Service Badges, 1914–1954.* Surrey, BC: Johnston Books, 1995.

Josie, Gordon H. "Administration of the Veterans' Preference in the Canadian Civil Service." *Canadian Journal of Economics and Political Science/Revue canadienne d'economique et de science politique* 11, 4 (1945): 601–11.

Keshen, Jeffrey. *Propaganda and Censorship during Canada's Great War.* Edmonton: University of Alberta Press, 1996.

–. *Saints, Sinners, and Soldiers.* Vancouver: UBC Press, 2004.

–. "Words as Weapons: Ottawa Newspapers Fight the First World War." In *War and Society in Post-Confederation Canada,* ed. Jeffrey A. Keshen and Serge Marc Durflinger, 78–92. Toronto: Thomas Nelson, 2006.

Keshen, Jeffrey A., and Serge Marc Durflinger, eds. *War and Society in Post-Confederation Canada*. Toronto: Thomson Nelson, 2006.

Kierstead, R.G. "The Canadian Military Medical Experience during the Great War – 1918." MA thesis, Queen's University, 1982.

Kordon, Bohdan S. *Enemy Aliens, Prisoners of War: Internment in Canada during the Great War*. Montreal and Kingston: McGill-Queen's University Press, 2002.

Koven, Seth. "Remembering and Dismemberment: Crippled Children, Wounded Soldiers, and the Great War in Great Britain." *American Historical Review* 99, 4 (1994): 1167–202. http://dx.doi.org/10.2307/2168773.

Kudlick, Catherine. "Disability History: Why We Need Another 'Other.'" *American Historical Review* 108, 3 (2003): 763–93. http://dx.doi.org/10.1086/529597.

Lackenbauer, P. Whitney, and Craig Leslie Mantle, eds. *Aboriginal Peoples and the Canadian Military: Historical Perspectives*. Kingston, ON: Canadian Defence Academy Press, 2007.

Landman, Jacob Henry. *Human Sterilization: The History of the Sexual Sterilization Movement*. New York: Macmillan, 1932.

Langdon-Brown, Sir Walter. *The Practitioner's Encyclopaedia of Medical Treatment*. Oxford: Oxford Medical Publications, 1915.

Langley, D.E. "'Bounden Duty and Service': A Royal Welch Fusilier's Perspective of Eligibility and Liability to Serve in the Great War." *Stand To! Journal of the Western Front Association* 68 (2003): 6–17.

Lawrence, D.H. *Kangaroo*. New York: T. Seltzer, 1923.

Leese, Peter. "Problems Returning Home: The British Psychological Casualties of the Great War." *Historical Journal (Cambridge, England)* 40, 4 (1997): 1055–67. http://dx.doi.org/10.1017/S0018246X97007395.

Longmore, Paul K., and Lauri Umansky, eds. *The New Disability History: American Perspectives*. New York: New York University Press, 2001.

Lorenz, Stacey L., and Geraint B. Osborne. "'Talk about Strenuous Hockey': Violence, Manhood, and the 1907 Ottawa Silver Seven–Montreal Wanderer Rivalry." *Journal of Canadian Studies/Revue d'études canadiennes* 40, 1 (2006): 125–56.

Love, Albert G., and Charles B. Davenport. "Defects Found." In *Drafted Men: Statistical Information Compiled from the Draft Showing the Physical Condition of the Men Registered and Examined in Pursuance of the Requirements of the Selective Service Act*. Washington, DC: Government Printer, 1920.

Love, David W. *A Call to Arms: The Organization and Administration of Canada's Military in World War One*. Winnipeg: Bunker to Bunker Books, 1999.

Lydiatt, W.A. "Lydiatt's Pocket Guide to What's What." In *Canadian Advertising*, 1st ed. Toronto: W.A. Lydiatt, 1914.

MacConnell, H.B. *Where Duty Leads*. Toronto: William Briggs, 1916.

MacDonald, Lyn. *1915: The Death of Innocence*. London: Headline, 1993.

Mackenzie, David, ed. *Canada and the First World War: Essays in Honour of Robert Craig Brown*. Toronto: University of Toronto Press, 2005.

Macleod, Jenny, and Pierre Purseigle, eds. *Uncovered Fields: Perspectives in First World War Studies*. Leiden: Brill, 2004.

Macphail, Andrew. *Official History of the Canadian Forces in the Great War, 1914–19: The Medical Services*. Ottawa: King's Printer, 1925.

MacPherson, W.G. *History of the Great War: Medical Services General History*. Vol. 1. London: King's Printer, 1921.

MacPherson, W.G., et al. *Official History of the War: Medical Services, Diseases of the War*. Vol. 1. London: King's Printer, 1922.

–. *Official History of the War: Medical Services, Diseases of the War.* Vol. 2. London: King's Printer, 1922.

–. *Official History of the War: Medical Services, Surgery of the War.* Vol. 1. London: King's Printer, 1922.

Mantle, Craig Leslie, ed. *The Unwilling and the Reluctant: Theoretical Perspectives on Disobedience in the Military.* Kingston, ON: Canadian Defence Academy Press, 2006.

–. *The Apathetic and the Defiant: Case Studies of Canadian Mutiny and Disobedience, 1812–1919.* Kingston, ON: Canadian Defence Academy Press, 2007.

Maroney, Paul. "'The Great Adventure': The Context and Ideology of Recruiting in Ontario, 1914–1917." *Canadian Historical Review* 77, 1 (1996): 62–98. http://dx.doi.org/10.3138/CHR-077-01-03.

McCartney, John. *The Story of a Great Horse: Cresceus, 2:02.* Indianapolis: Hollenbeck Press, 1902.

McKinley, Michael. *Putting a Roof on Winter: Hockey's Rise from Sport to Spectacle.* Vancouver: Greystone Books, 2000.

McLaren, Angus. *Our Own Master Race: Eugenics in Canada, 1885–1945.* Toronto: McClelland and Stewart, 1990.

McGuaig, Katherine. *The Weariness, the Fever, and the Fret: The Campaign against Tuberculosis in Canada, 1900–1950.* Montreal and Kingston: McGill-Queen's University Press, 1999.

Meltz, Noah. M. "Wages and Working Conditions." In *Historical Statistics of Canada,* ed. F.H. Leacy. http://www.statcan.gc.ca/pub/11-516-x/sectione/4147438-eng.htm.

Messanger, Charles. *Call-to-Arms: The British Army 1914–18.* London: Cassell, 2005.

Meyer, Jessica. *Men of War: Masculinity and the First World War in Britain.* London: Palgrave Macmillan, 2009.

–. "'Not Septimus Now': Wives of Disabled Veterans and the Cultural Memory of the First World War in Britain." *Women's History Review* 13, 1 (2004): 117–38. http://dx.doi.org/10.1080/09612020400200386.

Miller, Ian. *Our Glory and Our Grief: Torontonians and the Great War.* Toronto: University of Toronto Press, 2002.

–. "Toronto's Response to the Outbreak of War, 1939." *Canadian Military History* 1, 11 (2002): 5–23.

Miller, M. Geoffrey. "Of Lice and Men: Trench Fever and Trench Life in the AIF." *Medical History of WWI.* http://www.vlib.us/medical/liceand.htm.

Mitchell, T.J., and G.M. Smith. *Medical Services: Casualties and Medical Statistics of the Great War.* London: King's Printer, 1931.

Morris, Philip. *The Canadian Patriotic Fund: A Record of Its Activities from 1914 to 1919.* Ottawa: n.p., 1920.

Morton, Desmond. *Fight or Pay: Soldiers' Families in the Great War.* Vancouver: UBC Press, 2004.

–. "French Canada and War, 1868–1917: The Military Background to the Conscription Crisis." In *War and Society in North America,* ed. J.L. Granatstein and R.D. Cuff, 84–103. Toronto: Thomas Nelson and Sons, 1971.

–. *Ministers and Generals: Politics and the Canadian Militia.* Toronto: University of Toronto Press, 1970.

–. "'Noblest and Best': Retraining Canada's War Disabled 1915–23." *Journal of Canadian Studies/Revue d'etudes canadiennes* 16, 3 and 4 (1981): 75–85.

–. *A Peculiar Kind of Politics: Canada's Overseas Ministry in the First World War.* Toronto: University of Toronto Press, 1982.

–. *When Your Number's Up: The Canadian Soldier in the First World War*. Toronto: Random House, 1993.

Morton, Desmond, and J.L. Granatstein. *Marching to Armageddon: Canadians and the Great War, 1914–1919*. Toronto: Lester and Orpen Dennys, 1989.

Morton, Desmond, and Glenn Wright. *Winning the Second Battle: Canadian Veterans and the Return to Civilian Life, 1915–1930*. Toronto: University of Toronto Press, 1987.

Mueller, John. "Changing Attitudes towards War: The Impact of the First World War." *British Journal of Political Science* 21, 1 (1991): 1–28. http://dx.doi.org/10.1017/S00071 23400006001.

Murray, W.W. *Five Nines and Whiz Bangs*. Ottawa: Legionary Library, 1937.

Newman, Simon P. "Reading the Bodies of Early American Seafarers." *William and Mary Quarterly* 55, 1 (1998): 59–82. http://dx.doi.org/10.2307/2674323.

Nichol, Stephen J. *Ordinary Heroes: Eastern Ontario's 21st Battalion C.E.F. in the Great War*. Almonte, ON: Self-published, 2008.

Nicholson, G.W.L. *Official History of the Canadian Army in the First World War: Canadian Expeditionary Force, 1914–1919*. Ottawa: Queen's Printer, 1964.

–. *Seventy Years of Service: A History of the Canadian Army Medical Corps*. Ottawa: Borealis Press, 1977.

Nora, Pierre, ed. *Realms of Memory: Rethinking the French Past*. New York: Columbia University Press, 1996.

Norris, Marjorie Barron, ed. *Medicine and Duty: The World War I Memoir of Captain Harold W. McGill, Medical Officer, 31st Battalion C.E.F.* Calgary: University of Calgary Press, 2007.

Pearce, Cyril. *Comrades in Conscience: The Story of an English Community's Opposition to the Great War*. London: Francis Boutle, 2001.

Peat, Harold. *Private Peat*. Indianapolis: Bobbs-Merrill, 1917.

Pedersen, Susan. "Gender, Welfare, and Citizenship in Britain during the Great War." *American Historical Review* 95, 4 (1990): 983–1006. http://dx.doi.org/10.2307/2163475.

Pembrey, M.S. "Tall versus Short Men for the Army." *Journal – Royal Sanitary Institute* 36, 3 (1915): 105–13.

Pernick, M. *The Black Stork: Eugenics and the Death of "Defective" Babies in American Medicine and Motion Pictures since 1915*. Oxford: Oxford University Press, 1996.

–. *Prominent People of the Province of Quebec in Professional, Social and Business Life, 1923–24*. Montreal: Biographical Society of Canada, 192?.

Perry, H.R. *Recycling the Disabled: Army, Medicine and Modernity in WWI Germany*. Manchester: Manchester University Press, 2014.

Phillips, Gervase. "An Army of Giants: Height and Medical Characteristics of Welsh Soldiers, 1914–18." *Archives* 22, 97 (1997): 141–46.

–. "Dai Bach Y Soldiwr: Welsh Soldiers in the British Army, 1914–1918." *Llafur: The Journal of Welsh Labour History* 6, 2 (1993): 94–105.

Pirie, Peter F. *The Stump Ranch*. Victoria: Morriss Publishing, 1975.

Prior, Robin, and Trevor Wilson. "Paul Fussell at War." *War in History* 1, 1 (1994): 63–80. http://dx.doi.org/10.1177/096834459400100105.

Prost, Antoine. *In the Wake of War: Les Anciens Combattants and French Society, 1914–1939*. Trans. Helen MacPhail. Providence: Berg, 1992.

Rawling, Bill. *Death Their Enemy: Canadian Medical Professionals and War*. Quebec: AGMV Marquis, 2001.

–. *Surviving Trench Warfare: Technology and the Canadian Corps, 1914–1918*. Toronto: University of Toronto Press, 1992.

Read, Daphne, ed. *The Great War and Canadian Society: An Oral History*. Toronto: New Hogtown Press, 1978.

Reaume, G. *Remembrances of Patients Past: Patient Life at the Toronto Hospital for the Insane, 1870–1940*. Oxford: Oxford University Press, 2000.

Richard, Béatrice. "Henri Bourassa and Conscription: Traitor or Savior." *Canadian Military Journal* (Winter 2006–07): 75–83.

Roberts, Barbara. "Doctors and Deports: The Role of the Medical Profession in Canadian Deportation, 1900–1920." *Canadian Ethnic Studies* 18, 3 (1986): 17–36.

–. *Whence They Came: Deportation from Canada 1900–1935*. Ottawa: University of Ottawa Press, 1988.

Roberts, Robert. *The Classic Slum: Salford Life in the First Quarter of the Century*. Manchester: Manchester University Press, 1971.

Robinson, William J. *Practical Eugenics: Four Means of Improving the Human Race*. New York: Critic and Guide, 1912.

Röhl, John C.G. *The Young Wilhelm: The Kaiser's Early Life, 1859–1888*. Cambridge: Cambridge University Press, 1998.

Roland, C.G. "An Historical Perspective." In *Alternatives in Health Care: Proceedings of a Symposium and Workshop on Health Service Organizations in Ontario*, ed. William E. Seidelman (Hamilton: McMaster University, 1981).

Roper, Michael. "Between Manliness and Masculinity: The 'War Generation' and the Psychology of Fear in Britain, 1914–1950." *Journal of British Studies* 44, 02 (2005): 343–62. http://dx.doi.org/10.1086/427130.

–. *The Secret Battle: Emotional Survival in the Great War*. Manchester: Manchester University Press, 2009.

Roxborough, Henry. *The Stanley Cup Story*. Toronto: McGraw-Hill, 1964.

Roy, Reginald H., ed. *The Journal of Private Fraser: Canadian Expeditionary Force, 1914–1918*. Ottawa: CEF Books, 1998.

Rutherdale, Robert. *Hometown Horizons: Local Responses to Canada's Great War*. Vancouver: UBC Press, 2004.

Scott, Frederick George. *The Great War as I Saw It*. Toronto: F. D. Goodchild, 1922.

Service, Robert W. *Rhymes of a Red Cross Man*. Toronto: William Briggs, 1916.

Shaw, Amy. *Crisis of Conscience: Conscientious Objection in Canada during the First World War*. Vancouver: UBC Press, 2009.

Sheffield, Gary. *Forgotten Victory: The First World War Myths and Realities*. London: Headline, 2001.

Shipley, A.F. *The Minor Horrors of the War*. London: Smith and Elder, 1915.

Silbey, David. "Bodies and Cultures Collide: Enlistment, the Medical Exam, and the British Working Class, 1914–1916." *Social History of Medicine* 17, 1 (2004): 61–76. http://dx.doi.org/10.1093/shm/17.1.61.

–. *The British Working Class and the Enthusiasm for War, 1914–1916*. London: Frank Cass, 2005.

Smith, Leonard. "Paul Fussell's *The Great War and Modern Memory* Twenty-Five Years Later." *History and Theory* 40, 2 (2001): 241–60. http://dx.doi.org/10.1111/0018-2656.00164.

Socknat, Thomas. *Witness against War: Pacifism in Canada 1900–1945*. Toronto: University of Toronto Press, 1987.

Soloway, Richard. "Counting the Degenerates: The Statistics of Race Deterioration in Edwardian England." *Journal of Contemporary History* 17, 1 (1982): 137–64. http://dx.doi.org/10.1177/002200948201700107.

Sperber, G.H., and Mary Bisset Lucas. "Dentistry in the Anglo-Boer War (1899–1902)." *Adler Museum Bulletin* 12, 2 (1991): 19–22.

Swain, J. and Sally French, eds. *Disability on Equal Terms*. Los Angeles: Sage, 2008.

Thomas, Carol. "How Is Disability Understood? An Examination of Sociological Approaches." *Disability and Society* 19, 6 (2004): 569–83. http://dx.doi.org/10.1080/09 68759042000252506.

Thomson, Mathew. "Community Care and the Control of Mental Defectives in Inter-War Britain." In *The Locus of Care: Families, Communities, Institutions and the Provision of Welfare since Antiquity*, ed. Peregrine Horden and Richard Smith, 198–218. London: Routledge, 1998. http://dx.doi.org/10.4324/9780203428047_chapter_8.

–. *The Problem of Mental Deficiency: Eugenics, Democracy, and Social Policy in Britain c.1870–1959*. Oxford: Clarendon Press, 1998. http://dx.doi.org/10.1093/acprof:oso/9780198206927.001.0001.

Thompson, John Herd. *The Harvests of War: The Prairie West, 1914–1918*. Toronto: McClelland and Stewart, 1978.

Travers, Timothy H.E. "Allies in Conflict: The British and Canadian Official Histories and the Real Story of Second Ypres (1915)." *Journal of Contemporary History* 24, 2 (1989): 301–25. http://dx.doi.org/10.1177/002200948902400206.

Trouillot, Michel-Rolph. *Silencing the Past: Power and the Production of History*. New York: Beacon Press, 1996.

United Kingdom. *Instructions for the Physical Examination of Recruits*. London: King's Printer, 1914.

–. *Musketry (.303 and. 22 Cartridges): Elementary Training, Visual Training, Judging Distance, Fire Discipline, Range Practices, Field Practices*. London: John Murray, 1915.

–. *Musketry (.303 and. 22 Cartridges): Elementary Training, Visual Training, Judging Distance, Fire Discipline, Range Practices, Field Practices*. London: John Murray, 1916.

–. *Musketry Regulations, Part 1, 1909 (Reprinted, with Amendments, 1914)*. London and Calcutta: Government Printer, 1918.

–. *Statistics of the Military Effort of the British Empire during the Great War, 1914–1920*. London: HMSO, 1922.

–. Ministry of National Service. *Report upon the Physical Examination of Men of Military Age by National Service Medical Boards from November 1st, 1917 – October 31st, 1918*. Vol. 1. London: HMSO, 1920.

United States. *Hints for the Inexperienced in Naval or Marine Recruiting, Especially Those Examiners without Experience at Sea*. Washington, DC: Government Printer, 1916.

–. *Second Report of the Provost Marshal General to the Secretary of War on the Operations of the Selective Service System to December 20, 1918*. Washington, DC: Government Printer, 1919.

van Bergen, Leo. *Before My Helpless Sight: Suffering, Dying and Military Medicine on the Western Front, 1914–1918*. Trans. Liz Waters. Farnham, UK: Ashgate, 2009.

van Paassen, Pierre. *Days of Our Years*. New York: Hillman-Curl, 1939.

Vance, Jonathan. *Death So Noble: Memory, Meaning, and the First World War*. Vancouver: UBC Press, 1997.

Walker, James W. St. G. "Race and Recruitment in World War I: Enlistment of Visible Minorities in the Canadian Expeditionary Force." *Canadian Historical Review* 70, 1 (1989): 1–26. http://dx.doi.org/10.3138/CHR-070-01-01.

Walmsley, J. "Normalisation, Emancipatory Research, and Inclusive Research in Learning Disability." *Disability and Society* 16, 2 (2001): 187–205. http://dx.doi.org/10.1080/09687590120035807.

Watson, Alexander John. *Marginal Man: The Dark Vision of Harold Innis.* Toronto: University of Toronto Press, 2006.

Weir, Peter, and David Williamsom, directors. *Gallipoli.* R&R Films, 1981.

Whalen, Robert Weldon. *Bitter Wounds: German Victims of the Great War, 1914–1939.* Ithaca, NY: Cornell University Press, 1984.

Wherrett, George Jasper. *The Miracle of the Empty Beds: A History of Tuberculosis in Canada.* Toronto: University of Toronto Press, 1997.

Wilson, J.J. "Skating to Armageddon: Canada, Hockey and the First World War." *International Journal of the History of Sport* 22, 3 (2005): 315–43. http://dx.doi.org/10. 1080/09523360500048746.

Winegard, Timothy C. *For King and Kanata: Canadian Indians and the First World War.* Winnipeg: University of Manitoba Press, 2012.

Winter, J., and J.-L. Robert, eds. *Capital Cities at War: Paris, London and Berlin, 1914–1919.* Cambridge: Cambridge University Press, 1997. http://dx.doi.org/10.1017/CBO978 0511599613.

Winter, J.M. "Britain's 'Lost Generation' of the First World War." *Population Studies* 31, 3 (1977): 449–66.

–. "Military Fitness and Civilian Health in Britain during the First World War." *Journal of Contemporary History* 15, 2 (1980): 211–22. http://dx.doi.org/10.1177/00220094800 1500201.

–. "Public Health and the Political Economy of War, 1914–1918." *History Workshop Journal* 26, 1 (1988): 163–73. http://dx.doi.org/10.1093/hwj/26.1.163.

–. "Some Aspects of the Demographic Consequences of the First World War in Britain." *Population Studies* 30, 3 (1976): 539–52. http://dx.doi.org/10.1080/00324728.1976.10410 422.

Winter, Jay. *The Great War and the British People.* London: Macmillan, 1985.

–. *Sites of Memory, Sites of Mourning: The Great War in European Cultural History.* Cambridge: Cambridge University Press, 1995.

Winter, Jay, and Antoine Prost. *The Great War in History: Debates and Controversies, 1914 to the Present.* Cambridge: Cambridge University Press, 2005.

Woodsworth, J.S. *Strangers within Our Gates, or Coming Canadians.* Toronto: Missionary Society of the Methodist Church, 1909.

Index

Note: "CEF" = Canadian Expeditionary Force.

1st Canadian Division. *See* Canadian Expeditionary Force (CEF)
1st Tunnelling Company, 70
2nd Canadian Division. See Canadian Expeditionary Force
13th Canadian Field Ambulance, 138
20th Battalion (Tyneside Scottish), British Expeditionary Force, 85
101st Regiment (Edmonton Fusiliers), 59
224th Forestry Battalion, 55

Adamson, Agar, 54, 84
Adlerard, Ulysses, 94
age: average of the CEF (1914–18), 96; average of men rejected at Valcartier, 96–97, 99; falsifying, 53, 58–60, 75; maximum for Royal Flying Corps recruits, 40; maximum for service battalion recruits, 41; methods used to ascertain, 21, 33; minimum for bantam battalion recruits, 38; problems ascertaining, 57–58; regulations regarding, Canada vs Britain, 59; overage recruits, 50, 58–59 (*see also* Clements, William J.; Emson, Harold; Glazier, Torrence); requirements for service (British),1914, 21; requirements for service (Canadian), 1914,18–19; underage recruits, 50, 58–59 (*see also* Boissel, P.; Breton, Adore; Glassford, George; Mick, Russell; Morin, Emile; Raddall, Thomas); as reason for rejection at Valcartier (1914), 100
Aikenhead, A.H., 134–35
amputation, 8, 45, 51, 54, 55, 80, 100, 102, 124. *See also* Martin, Mrs. Joseph
Andrews, Alfred, 64, 114
Anglo-Boer War, 15, 52, 81, 83, 95, 117, 134
Arnott, Lieutenant-Colonel J.W., 65

Babtie, Lieutenant-General William: William Babtie Fonds (LAC), 11–12, 53; Babtie Report (1916), 95
Bachelor, Alexander, 15
badges and buttons
—CEF service badges: creation of, 106; evolution of categories, 108–10, 177–81; penalties for counterfeiting and improper use, 107–8, 109
—for rejected men: as aid for recruiting, 105; cancellation of government approved, 110; counterfeiting, misuse, and theft of, 103, 106, 137; as indication of membership in Honourably Rejected Volunteers of Canada Association, 130; lack of popularity, 110; as mark of honour, 103, 111; as mark of shame, 105–7; as protection for invisibly impaired, 94, 103–4, 108, 111; requests for, 111, 126, 130; shift to government administration of, 106
Baker, George, 113, 117, 153–54
Baldwin, Harold, 57, 61
bands (military), 55, 58
bantam battalions, 38, 88, 89, 164
Barker, Captain R.R., 55
Barnes, Henry, 55
Baxter, Edward, 46
Bealie, Lutie, 54
Beech, Edward, 51, 54
Beggs, Captain S.T., 4–25; *The Selection of the Recruit*, 24
Belangerm L.C., 143
Bell, Lieutenant-Colonel F., 68
Bennett, F., 17
Bigland, Alfred, 88
Birch, A., 141
Bird, James R., 62–63
Bird, Will R., 37, 79, 85, 94, 103, 117, 153–55

Birney, Earle, 158–59; *Turvey: A Military Picaresque*, 158–59
Black, Sergeant Ernest G., 84
Blake, Joseph, 21
blindness. *See under* vision
Boiling, Garfield, 150
Bonar, Joe, 157
Bonenfant, Henri, 52
Borden, Robert, 36, 114, 126, 129, 139
Boissel, P., 147
Bouchard, Lieutenant-Colonel G.R., 66
Boyd, John, 140
Breton, Adore, 66
British Army, 19–21, 54, 86–87, 95
Brothers, William, 143: wife of, 143
Bruce, Colonel Herbert A., 4, 120. *See also* Report on the Canadian Army Medical Service
Bruce Report. *See* Report on the Canadian Army Medical Service
Bryant, Walter, 140
Bunn, J., 134
Burleigh, William, 148, 150
Burleigh, Mrs. Robert, 148
Burton, Lieutenant-Colonel Frank Lindsay, 38
Burton's Bantam Battalion. *See* bantam battalions; Burton, Frank Lindsay
Butler, William Henry, 42

Campbell, Douglas, 57–58
Campbell, George B., 67–68
Campbell, Fred B., 148: wife of, 148
Cameron, Mrs. J., 147
Calhoun, C.S., 150
Canadian Patriotic Fund, 141–42
Canadian Army Dental Corps (CADC), 28, 37–38, 169, 174, 176
Canadian Army Medical Corps (CAMC), 15, 28, 38, 41, 45, 51, 55, 75, 80, 138, 168–69, 174, 176
Canadian Ordnance Corps. *See* support units
Canadian Army Service Corps (CASC), 38, 41, 44–47, 168, 176
Canadian Expeditionary Force: 1st Canadian Division 38, 90; 2nd Canadian Division, 35; casualties, 36; First Contingent, 11, 15, 25, 36, 42, 50, 144;

growth of, 36; reinforcements, 36; Second Contingent, 36–37, 54
Canadian Infantry Battalion: (2nd) 111; (3rd) 140; (5th) 61; (21st) 15, 37, 42, 52, 64, 91, 147; (29th) 44; (31st) 89; (36th) 71; (41st) 66; (42nd) 54, 85; (75th) 147; (92nd) 52; (96th) 50; (113th) 68; (130th) 66; (131st) 50; (139th) 50; (142nd) 114, 115; (143rd) 38; (151st) 65–66, 68; (169th) 70; (172nd) 50; (179th) 58; (193rd) 85; (197th) 66; (207th) 103; (209th) 67, 78; (216th) 38; Princess Patricia's Canadian Light Infantry, 102, 116
Canadian Journal of Medicine and Surgery, 123
Canadian Mounted Rifles: (5th) 64; (8th) 139; (12th) 67
Canadian Medical Association Journal, 55, 66, 135
Cantlie, Lieutenant-Colonel George, 54
Cape Breton Highlanders, 157
Carment, John, 80
Carruthers, Captain J.S., 61
Carson, Major-General John Wallace, 51
categorization of fitness for service, 171–76: alphanumeric system, 28, 31–32, 171–76; and efficient use of manpower, 43, 48, 155; ignored or misunderstood, 48; potential negative impact on unit efficiency, 46–48; shift from simple to complex, 6, 14; specialist skills and experience, 7, 41, 47–48. *See also Classification of Men by Categories in Canada; Classification of Men by Categories in the British Isles*; manpower
Cederberg, Fred, 157–58
Chavis, William, 95
chest girth: average for Canadian men, 19; average of men rejected at Valcartier, 97–99; British minimum requirements, 20–21; Canadian minimum requirements, 17–19, 38, 162 (*see also* Bird, Will R.; Peat, Harold); changes to minimum requirements (Canada), 38, 162; method of measuring, 16, 18, 21; minimum for bantam battalions, 38, 164 (*see also* bantam battalions); minimum for Royal Military College Cadets, 18–19; as reason for rejection at Valcartier, 100

Choquette, Philippe-Auguste, 89–90, 121–23
Civil Service Act (1918), 126
Clamondou, Joseph, 95
Clarke, Arthur Blake 146
Clarke, G.W. 146
Classification of Men by Categories in Canada, 28–29, 32–34, 43–44, 78, 159, 174–75
Classification of Men by Categories in the British Isles, 28, 32–34, 43, 78, 159, 175–76
Clements, Aimee, 142
Clements, William J., 52
Coates, Cora, 111
Coates, Roy T., 111–12, 126, 150
Cockburn, Captain Gordon L., 83
Colby, Martin, 93–94, 153–54
Coley, Joseph, 117
Connell, J.C., 87
Conners, James, 138
conscientious objectors, 4, 117, 160
conscription, 11, 35–36, 129, 136, 156. *See also* Military Service Act (1917)
Consitt, Captain E.C., 66
construction battalions. *See* support units
Cook, Tim, 10
Craig, Stephen. *See* Godwin, George
Crawford, Lieutenant, 91
Currie, Morley, 145
Cyclist Corps, 165

"**Daddy**, What Did YOU Do in the Great War?" (poster), 125
Dash, Annie and Oliver, 147, 149
Dasey, Alfred A., 83
de Hertel, Lieutenant-Colonel John E., 66
deafness. *See* hearing
Department of Militia and Defence, 3, 57, 62, 65, 68, 71, 76, 111, 140
dental care. *See* teeth
dental health. *See* teeth
dentures. *See* teeth
Dercum's disease (adiposis dolorosa), 52
Desgagné, Joseph and Patrice, 143
Dinesen, Thomas, 64
disability and impairment: claim as form of resistance and empowerment, 11, 133, 157; claimed by family members, 11, 136,

139, 143, 151; differing constructions, concepts, and views of, 7, 80, 84, 90–93, 99, 102–3, 108, 124, 154; economic 141–43, 149; faked, 11, 136–39; gendered constructions of, 140–43; invisible, 93, 99, 102–3, 114, 137, 153–54; as means to avoid enlistment or obtain discharge, 133–34, 139; obvious, 51–53, 55, 102, 108, 126; pensions, 25, 77; social construct, 80
Dix, William, 64, 86
Duggan, Herrick, 102, 116–17, 153–54
Duggan, Kenneth, 64, 116

Eaglesham, H.E., 62–63
Eaves, Lawrence, 95
Elkes, Charles, 83
Elliot, Rev. H.A., 139
Emson, Harold, 52
enlistment: competitive system of, 66; as a form of social insurance, 133, 139–40; multiple, 4, 12, 15, 70–72, 75, 139, 153–55 (*see also* Bird, Will R.; Connors, James; Glazier, Torrence; Gravelle, Emmanuel; Mick, Russell; Norris, J.; Pearce, W.H.; Wolf, Elvin); pressures to enlist, 93, 106, 114, 116, 125 (*see also* Duggan, Herrick; "Missis Moriarty's Boy"); pressures against and resistance to, 11, 35,103, 114n8, 140–50, 157. *See also* conscription; recruiting.
eugenics, 5, 119, 131; criticism of, 124; fears caused by war, 119, 123–24; and immigration, 121–23; impact on rejected volunteers, 124–25; and recruiting, 119. See also *Oh, Canada: A Medley of Stories and Pictures*
eyesight. *See* vision.

Fages, Brigadier-General A.O., 5, 58, 62, 137
Fehrenbach, J.H., 146
Fehrenbach, John, 146–47
Ferguson, Captain S., 76
Fitzpatrick, Thomas, 70–71
feet and toes: changing regulations regarding, 39, 42, 49, 169; corrective measures for, 39; debates regarding, 90–91; flat, 22, 29, 51, 90, 147; method of measuring, 22; as reason for rejection

at Valcartier, 100; requirements (general), 20, 22, 39, 41, 168, 174

food. *See* rations

Forbes, Captain A.M., 86

forestry battalions: *See* support units

Fort Garry Horse, 143

Fowler, Captain J.M., 58

Fox, Joseph, 142

Fraser, Donald, 89–90

French Foreign Legion, 95

Gagnon, Joseph, 143

Gallinger, Charles, 83.

Gamble, Mrs. B.B., 148

Garner, Charles, 111–12, 126, 128

gas masks, 27

Glassford, Mrs. D.C., 57

Glassford, George, 57

glasses. *See* vision.

Glazier, Torrance, 15, 52

Godwin, George, 44

gonorrhea. *See* venereal disease

Gosell, Captain A.S., 12, 62–63

Graham, Lieutenant C.R, 22, 84

Gravelle, Emmanuel, 117

Great War Veterans Association, 128

Gross, Paul, 5; *Passchendaele* (film), 3, 5, 9, 161

Gwatkin, Major-General Willoughby, 36

Hadden, W., 94

Hamilton, Cecil, 8, 51

Hargreaves, Captain Robert, 47–48

Hartnell, John, 86

Hazelton, Robert and Anna, 121–23

Health, Norman, 86

hearing, 17, 19, 20, 23–25, 27, 40–41, 100, 158, 162, 165, 169, 173. *See also* Butler, William Henry; Clements, William J.; Colby, Martin; Conners, James; Desgagné, Joseph, 143; Gagnon, Joseph; Peterson, Sydney

height, 21, 27, 35; average for Canadian men, 19, 98; average of men rejected at Valcartier, 97–99, 154; British minimum requirements, 21; changes in requirements (general), 6, 38, 49, 162–66, 169; debates surrounding method of measuring, 16, 18, 21; minimum for

artillery, 8, 18–19, 38, 40, 162–63, 165–66; minimum for bantam battalions, 38, 164; minimum for Cyclist Corps, 165; minimum for infantry 6, 18–19, 38, 40, 162–63, 165 (*see also* Bachelor, Alexander; Baldwin, Harold; Barnes, Henry; "Missis Moriarty's Boy"); minimum for Royal Military College of Canada cadets, 18–19; minimum for service, 88–90 (*see also* Fraser, Donald); minimum for support units, 6, 38, 41, 169

Hemming, Brigadier-General Thomas D.R., 138

Henderson, George B., 18, 54

heart conditions, 23, 29; faking to avoid service, 136; invisible impairment, 99, 102; and rejection at Valcartier, 99–100. *See also* Butler, William Henry; Duggan, Herrick; Steele, Charles

hernia, 17, 20, 40, 50, 99, 174; corrective measures, 29; differing classifications of, 29; invisible impairment, 99, 102; method of testing for, 22; and rejection at Valcartier, 99–100. *See also* Andrews, Alfred; Gravelle, Emmanuel; Iler, Eugene; Weir, Ethyl

Hicks, Clifford, 146–47

Hicks, Thomas W., 146

Higginson, A.B., 142

Hislop, Major J.A., 55

Hoare, Lieutenant-Colonel E.C., 40. *See also* Royal Flying Corps

hockey, 91

Hodgins, Major-General W.E., 40, 62–63

home defence forces, 42

Honeywell, Major F.H., 139–40

Honourably Rejected Volunteers of Canada Association, 160; formation and membership, 113, 128–29; lapel badge, 130; objectives and political activities, 128–31; reaction to, 128, 130–31

Hughes, Sam: appeals for discharge to, 57, 134, 143, 146, 148–50; concerns about unfit troops, 50–51, 55; recruiting, 36

Iler, Eugene, 61

impairment. *See* disability and impairment

Innis, Harold, 125
Instructions for the Physical Examination of Recruits (Great Britain), 19–24, 34
Instructions regarding Physical Qualifications and Medical Inspection of Recruits C.E.F., 26
intelligence: as requirement for service, 17, 19–20, 24–25, 34; tests, 33, 158–59. *See also* Fehrenbach, J.H.; Fehrenbach, John; Malley, Joseph; mental defects; mental illness; Morin, Emile

Jackson, Frederick, 43
Jacques, Major H.M., 55
Jobins, George, 95
Johnson, J.A., 136
Johnson, John W., 111, 130
Johnson, Gustave, 126, 128
Johnson, Robbie, 106, 155
Johnston, Robert George, 134, 140, 149
Jones, G.C., 59
Jones, Samuel, 94

Kangaroo (Lawrence), 13
Kavanagh, William, 86
Keene, Lieutenant Louis, 84
Kemp, Sir Edward, 8, 67–68, 78, 122, 136, 155
Kerr, Jake, 67
Kerr, R.H., 48
Khaki University of Canada, 127
King's Regulations and Orders for the Canadian Militia, 1910, 18
King's Regulations and Orders for the Canadian Militia, 1915, 73

labour battalions. *See* support units
Lahiff, Robert, 83
Lamond, C.E., 17
Lancet, 85–87
Lane, Daniel, 5, 117, 153
Laroque, Marcel, 30
Lawrence, D.H., 13
Leblanc, Emile, 134
Leonard, R.W., 114
Leslie, Lieutenant N.E., 83
Lewis, E.N., 118
Lloyd, Arthur, 71

Lumley, Savile, 125; "Daddy, What Did YOU Do in the Great War?" 125
Lynch, George J., 146
Lynch, Thomas, 146

MacConnell, Major, H.B., 117–18; "Medically Unfit" (poem), 117–18
MacDermot, Captain H.E., 86, 135
MacFarland, J.M., 135
MacInnis, Lieutenant-Colonel C.S., 63
Macphail, Sir Andrew, 55, 134, 137
Mann, David (film character). See *Passchendaele* (film)
Malcolm, Melvin, 51
Malley, Joseph, 52
manpower: efficient use of, 7, 32, 34, 43, 48, 155, 157, 174; and lowering of physical requirements for service, 7, 34–39; shortages, 7, 34–39, 43; specialist skills and experience, 7, 41, 47–48
Martell, Charles, 80
Martin, Mrs. Joseph, 143
masculinity, 95, 114, 151; appeals to by recruiters, 114, 116; and perceptions of military fitness, 79, 90, 91; and service badges, 130, 156; questioned following rejection for service, 4, 106, 113, 119, 125. *See also under* disability and impairment
Mathers, T.G., 114
McCeary, J., 17
McDonald, J.A., 56–57
McGee, Frank, 91–92
McGill University, 116, 134, 149
McGrath, Michael and Margret, 147–48
McIntosh, Joseph, 138–39
McLaren, Captain S.F., 86
McLeod, M.H., 94.
McPhee, Carl, 51
McWilliam, C.G. 145
McWilliam, Willie, 145
medical examinations: attempts to mitigate problems of, 68–78; critiques of, 50, 54; circumvention of, 64, 67, 70; civilian doctors threaten to boycott, 60–63; development of a multistep process for 8, 15–16, 72–73, 75; general problems and limitations, 25, 33, 55–58, 64, 68; improved, 54, 78; interference

in, 66–68; limited by indefinite termin-
ologies, 55–56; not correctly conducted,
52–53; objective and subjective processes, 33–34; overlooked in Great War
studies and soldiers' memoirs, 5, 14;
re-examination of troops before leaving
Canada, 72–75. *See also* categorization
of fitness for service; medical examiners; *individual fitness standards and
guidelines*
medical examiners: as adjudicators, 13;
critiques of, 50; ignore regulations,
59–60, 76, 79, 91; lack of training and
inexperience, 8, 24, 54–55, 66; opinions
overruled or ignored by unit commanders, 66–67; overworked, 25,
147; remuneration for civilian, 60–
64; and rejection of unwilling recruits,
132, 135
"Medically Unfit" (poem), 117–18
mental defects, 74, 116, 134. *See also* intelligence; mental illness
mental illness, 8, 17, 42, 54, 119. *See also*
Clarke, Arthur Blake; Clarke, G.W.;
Hicks, Thomas W.; eugenics; Hicks
Clifford; intelligence; Lynch, George J.;
Lynch, Thomas; mental defect; Varley,
James.
Mepham, Alfred, 40
Mercier, Jules Henri, 22
Michaud, Bill, 37
Mick, Russell, 52–53, 70
militia orders: No. 162 (1915), 37; No. 372
(1914), 19. *See also* Canadian Army
Dental Corps; teeth
Military Hospitals Commission, 25
Military Service Act (1917), 32, 109–10,
117, 130–31, 133. *See also* conscription
Mills, Leo, 142
minorities, 4; ethnic 10, 14–15; and ethnic
tensions, 121–22; First Nations, 15;
French Canadians, 35, 122 (*see also*
Choquette, Philippe-Auguste). *See also*
conscientious objectors
"Missis Moriarty's Boy" (Service), 114–16
Morin, Emile, 52
Moring, Captain N., 66
Morris, Arthur, 43

Nadean, Cyrille, 134–35
Neor, Reginald, 95
New Zealand Expeditionary Force, 160
Newland-Pedley, Frederick, 83, 85
Norris, Armine, 114
Norris, J., 17
North Staffordshire Regiment, 61
Norval, Stanley, 95

O'Connell, D., 148
*Oh, Canada: A Medley of Stories and
Pictures*, 120–21
Oliver, John, 129, 131
Oliver, Honorary Colonel Sir Thomas,
85
Orr, Mrs. William, 149
overage recruits. *See* age
Overseas Military Forces of Canada, 31–
32, 42, 46. *See also* Canadian
Expeditionary Force

paralysis, 102
Passchendaele, Battle of, 9, 147
Passchendaele (film): depiction of Canadian troops, 9; depiction of rejected
volunteers, 3, 5; Mann, David (film
character), 3, 161
Paterson, J.V., 86–87
Pearce, W.H., 139–40
Peat, Harold, 59, 61, 117
Pembrey, M.S., 88–90
pensions, 77
Peterkin, Lieutenant John Morrison, 65
Peterson, Sydney, 81
Peterson, Sir William, 149
physical requirements for service: changes to 36–40, 162–70; civilian critiques
and lack of understanding of, 79, 81–83
86–89, 90–91, 99, 153; higher minimum
standards for some units, 40; lower
minimum standards for some units, 38,
40–42; specialist skills and experience,
7, 41, 47–48. *See also* age; height; manpower; medical examinations; teeth;
vision
*Physical Standards and Instructions for
the Medical Examination of Recruits ...,
1917*, 27, 34, 39, 56

Physical Standards and Instructions for the Medical Examination of Recruits ..., 1918, 27–28, 34, 39, 45, 137
pioneer battalions. *See* support units
Pirie, Peter F., 42, 64
Pritchard, Mrs. John A., 141
Polk, Herbert, 150
Pope, Rufus H., 67–68
Potter, Colonel J.L.: as Acting Deputy Director General Medical Services, 32n69; advocate for medical examiner training, 54, 80; classifying troops, 32–33; medically unfit troops arriving in England, 78; relaxation of vision requirements for recruits, 87 (*see also* vision); remuneration for civilian practitioners examining recruits, 63
Powell, Charles, 84
pthisis. *See* tuberculosis
Punch, 81, 83, 88, 139
Purcell, Mark, 135
PULHEMS, 158–59
Pusey, Leonard, 58, 60
pyrexia of unknown origins (PUO). *See* trench fever

Raddall, Thomas, 15
railway construction battalions. *See* support units
rations, 38, 83–85. *See also* Beech, Edward
Ravenscroft, Bill, 117
Rawling, Bill, 10
recruiting: 5, 7, 137; and ethnic discrimination, 14–15; and negative depictions of rejected men, 118–19; calls for an end to, 121–22; decline in, 36; officers as judges of fitness for service/gatekeepers, 14–15, 44, 75, 85; officers subvert medical examinations, 58, 66, 155; private, 65–66, 76. *See also* badges and buttons; conscription; enlistment
Regulations for the Canadian Medical Service, 1910, 16–19
Regulations for the Canadian Medical Service, 1914, 19
Reid, Colonel Frank A., 51
Reilly, Major W.H., 90–91
rejected volunteers
—demands for recognition and rights, 128

—estimated number, 3
—ill-treatment and negative depictions of: accusations of shirking, cowardice, and treason, 93, 113–14, 116, 126, 131; as effeminate, 106, 114–15; as objects of pity, 118–119; as social, moral, and physical threat to society, 115–16, 119–21, 123–25; as threats to war effort, 119–20, 121–22. *See also* eugenics; rejection; suicide
—positive treatment and depictions of, 103, 117–18
—declared unfit: Canadian soldiers arriving in Britain, 120; cost of accepting unfit men for service, 73, 76–77. *See also* eugenics; Honourably Rejected Volunteers of Canada Association; rejection
rejection: causes self-loathing and self-doubt, 116–17; as a form of wounding, 4–5,113, 131; postwar social and economic impact of, 126–27; rates of, 3, 121; reasons for at Valcartier, 98–102; sought as a means to avoid service, 133–35. *See also* disability and impairment; eugenics; Honourably Rejected Volunteers of Canada Association; rejected volunteers; suicide
religion: faith of those rejected at Valcartier, 94; religious characteristics of the population of Canada, 94n7
Report on the Canadian Army Medical Service (Bruce Report), 4, 12, 55, 59, 78, 120, 155
Richardson, C.M., 149
Roberts, Robert, 81
Robertson, Lieutenant-Colonel Robert A., 44
Robertson, R.D., 65
Roosevelt, Franklin Delano, 102n30
Ross, Michael, 43
Royal Army Medical Corps, 24, 31, 173
Royal, Arthur, 40
Royal Canadian Regiment, 95
Royal North West Mounted Police, 122, 141
Royal Flying Corps: physical requirements for pilots, 40; physical requirements for mechanics, 40–41
Ruecker, H.C., 65

Saskatchewan Light Horse, 61, 141
Scammell, Ernest, 25–26. *See also* tuberculin; tuberculosis; X-ray
"Scorn of the Women" (poem), 152–53, 160
Service, Robert W., 114; "Missis Moriarty's Boy," 114–16
sexually transmitted diseases. *See* venereal disease
shirkers and slackers, 4, 11, 93, 105–6, 113–14, 116, 118, 125–26, 128–29, 131, 150, 153, 156
Shorncliffe Military Hospital, 138
Simmons, James Scott, 94
Skead, Robert, 85
Smith, Major-General H., 71, 148
Smyth, Lieutenant-Colonel W.O., 67
Sovereign, A.H., 124
Starr, Frederic, 50, 69
Steele, Charles, 143
Steele, Major-General Sir Sam, 73–74
Strangers within Our Gates (Woodsworth), 123
stretcher bearers, 55
Stribball, Frank, 71
suicide, 113, 117, 153
support units: employment of men deemed unfit for combat, 28, 41, 44, 174, 176; physical requirements, 41–42, 168–70; specialist skills, 41; negative views of, 44
syphilis. See venereal disease

tattoos, 94–95
teeth: critiques of minimum dental standards, 81–83; dental care, 82, dental health of Canadians, 82; dentures, 82–83, 85; invisible impairment, 99; reason for rejection at Valcartier, 99–100; requirements for service 83–85. *See also* Canadian Army Dental Corps; militia orders 162
The Selection of the Recruit (1915), 24
Thomas, Michael, 153, 160; "Scorn of the Women", 152–53, 160
Toronto Globe, 70, 83, 89, 93, 104, 107
Tory, Henry Marshall, 127
Traquair, H.M., 86–87
trench fever, 145

tubercle bacillus. *See* tuberculosis (TB)
tuberculin, 25–26. *See also* Scammell, Ernest; tuberculosis (TB)
tuberculosis (TB), 20, 25–26, 42, 45, 51, 72, 100. *See also* Scammell, Ernest; tuberculin; X-ray
tunnelling battalions, 44
Turner, R.E.W., 27
Turvey: A Military Picaresque (Birney), 158–59

underage recruits. *See* age
Unfit for Heroes (Fedorwich), 127
United States Army, 95

Vachon, Alphonse, 51–52
Vance, Jonathan, 125
Varley, James, 134
varicocele, 17, 20, 22, 40; aggravated/marked vs slight and problems-defining, 27, 56; invisible impairment, 99, 102; reason for rejection at Valcartier, 99–100. *See also* Aikenhead, W.H.; Iler, Eugene
varicose veins, 17, 20, 22, 29, 40, 51, 174; aggravated/marked versus slight and problems-defining, 56–57; invisible impairment, 99, 102, 154; reason for rejection at Valcartier, 99–100. *See also* Fehrenbach, John
venereal disease, 20, 22, 51, 73, 74, 100, 145, 157
Verville, Alphonse, 80, 90
veterans: postwar advantages, 126–28
Vimy Ridge (battle), 6, 8, 147
vision
—blindness, 41, 45, 47, 108; colour-, 137; feigning, 137; night, 137. *See also* Brothers, Mrs. William; Health, Norman; McGee, Frank
—glasses, 18, 22, 38–39, 86–87, 99, 103. *See also* Wolff, Marke A.
—lost eyes, 45–46, 53, 164
—visual acuity: criticism of minimum standards, 79, 86–87; feigning good, 64, 157; feigning poor, 137–39; invisible impairment, 99; method of measuring,18; reason for rejection (general), 86 (*see also* Butler, William Henry);

reason for rejection at Valcartier, 99–100; requirements for service in British Expeditionary Force, 22, 24, 86; requirements for service in infantry, 18, 38–39, 45, 86–87, 162–66; minimum required for service in support units, 22, 39, 41, 168–69. *Also see* Godwin, George

visual acuity. *See under* vision

Wartime Elections Act (1917), 117
Weichel, William G., 146
weight, 16, 21, 27, 89, 100. *See also* Barnes, Henry; Mick, Russell
Weir, Ethyl, 150
West, E.A., 83
Wilhelm II, 102*n*30
Williams, Ernest, 94
Williams, Norman, 58

Williams, Colonel Victor, 145
Wilson, Lieutenant Ernest, 21, 83
Wilson, Martin, 95
Wilson, Robert W., 94
Winegard, Mrs. B.L., 48
Winning the Second Battle (Morton and Wright), 127
Winter, Lieutenant-Colonel Charles, 148
Wolf, Elvin, 65–68
Wolff, Marke A., 103
Wood, Mrs A.J., 142
Woodsworth, J.S., 123; *Strangers within Our Gates*, 123

X-ray, 26. *See also* tuberculosis (TB)

Ypres, Second Battle of, 58.
Yuill, Adelaide, 89, 149
Yuill, Lionel, 89, 149

STUDIES IN CANADIAN MILITARY HISTORY

John Griffith Armstrong, *The Halifax Explosion and the Royal Canadian Navy: Inquiry and Intrigue*

Andrew Richter, *Avoiding Armageddon: Canadian Military Strategy and Nuclear Weapons, 1950-63*

William Johnston, *A War of Patrols: Canadian Army Operations in Korea*

Julian Gwyn, *Frigates and Foremasts: The North American Squadron in Nova Scotia Waters, 1745-1815*

Jeffrey A. Keshen, *Saints, Sinners, and Soldiers: Canada's Second World War*

Desmond Morton, *Fight or Pay: Soldiers' Families in the Great War*

Douglas E. Delaney, *The Soldiers' General: Bert Hoffmeister at War*

Michael Whitby, ed., *Commanding Canadians: The Second World War Diaries of A.F.C. Layard*

Martin Auger, *Prisoners of the Home Front: German POWs and "Enemy Aliens" in Southern Quebec, 1940-46*

Tim Cook, *Clio's Warriors: Canadian Historians and the Writing of the World Wars*

Serge Marc Durflinger, *Fighting from Home: The Second World War in Verdun, Quebec*

Richard O. Mayne, *Betrayed: Scandal, Politics, and Canadian Naval Leadership*

P. Whitney Lackenbauer, *Battle Grounds: The Canadian Military and Aboriginal Lands*

Cynthia Toman, *An Officer and a Lady: Canadian Military Nursing and the Second World War*

Michael Petrou, *Renegades: Canadians in the Spanish Civil War*

Amy J. Shaw, *Crisis of Conscience: Conscientious Objection in Canada during the First World War*

Serge Marc Durflinger, *Veterans with a Vision: Canada's War Blinded in Peace and War*

James G. Fergusson, *Canada and Ballistic Missile Defence, 1954-2009: Déjà Vu All Over Again*

Benjamin Isitt, *From Victoria to Vladivostok: Canada's Siberian Expedition, 1917-19*

James Wood, *Militia Myths: Ideas of the Canadian Citizen Soldier, 1896-1921*

Timothy Balzer, *The Information Front: The Canadian Army and News Management during the Second World War*

Andrew B. Godefroy, *Defence and Discovery: Canada's Military Space Program, 1945-74*

Douglas E. Delaney, *Corps Commanders: Five British and Canadian Generals at War, 1939-45*

Timothy Wilford, *Canada's Road to the Pacific War: Intelligence, Strategy, and the Far East Crisis*

Randall Wakelam, *Cold War Fighters: Canadian Aircraft Procurement, 1945-54*

Andrew Burtch, *Give Me Shelter: The Failure of Canada's Cold War Civil Defence*

Wendy Cuthbertson, *Labour Goes to War: The CIO and the Construction of a New Social Order, 1939-45*

P. Whitney Lackenbauer, *The Canadian Rangers: A Living History*

Teresa Iacobelli, *Death or Deliverance: Canadian Courts Martial in the Great War*

Graham Broad, *A Small Price to Pay: Consumer Culture on the Canadian Home Front, 1939-45*

Peter Kasurak, *A National Force: The Evolution of Canada's Army, 1950-2000*

Isabel Campbell, *Unlikely Diplomats: The Canadian Brigade in Germany, 1951-64*

Richard M. Reid, *African Canadians in Union Blue: Volunteering for the Cause in the Civil War*

Andrew B. Godefroy, *In Peace Prepared: Innovation and Adaptation in Canada's Cold War Army*

David Zimmerman, *Maritime Command Pacific: The Royal Canadian Navy's West Coast Fleet in the Early Cold War*

STUDIES IN CANADIAN MILITARY HISTORY
is published by UBC Press in association with
the Canadian War Museum.

Printed and bound in Canada by Friesens

Set in Minion and Helvetica Condensed by
Artegraphica Design Co. Ltd.

Copy editor: Francis Chow